MOON

MILAN &
BEYOND

LINDSEY DAVISON

CONTENTS

1 *Aperitivo* in Menaggio

2 Street art in the Isola district

3 The Galleria is always busy with shoppers

4 Punto San Vigilio

5 *Tagliere* are popular *aperitivos*

6 Colorful fishing boats in Bardolino

DISCOVER
MILAN & BEYOND

Only in Milan can you step outside of a 4th-century church to find
a narrow alleyway covered in street art, with all-you-can-eat sushi
restaurants next to *aperitivo* bars, and edgy concept stores next to
stores selling handmade leather goods. If Rome is the Italian city
of history, and Florence is the Italian city
of art, then Milan is the Italian city of
design, diversity, and opportunity. Milan
offers classic Italian culture, from Gothic
churches and Renaissance art to pizzerias, wine bars, and gelato; but it's also
the only city in Italy that blends its historic heritage with modernism and inter-
nationalism in equal measure.

6

The city center is rich with historic
sights, from the Duomo to La Scala, but
the uniqueness of the city lies in the different cultures and communities that
make up the individual neighborhoods
and districts. Between all of them, it's
easy for any visitor to find a little corner
that feels almost like a home away from
home.

Traveling just an hour or two outside of the city gives you access
to some of the most beautiful and charming lakes in the world. The
villages dotting the shores of Lake Como provide old-world charm
and idyllic views. The lush and colorful islands of Lake Maggiore take
you back to another time in Italian history, and the "king of lakes,"
Lake Garda, offers a little bit of everything from mountain views and
sandy beaches to Roman ruins and wine villages. For a bit more tranquility with just as much charm and beauty, head to the smaller lakes
in the region like Lake Molveno, Lake Orta, and Lake Iseo.

Regardless of your interests, you're bound to find something to
suit you here—no other region blends history with modernity and
cosmopolitan glamour with natural beauty in quite the same way.

MY FAVORITE
EXPERIENCES

1 Getting an unparalleled aerial view of Milan and its bustling
piazzas and streets from **the roof of the Duomo** (page 45) or
with a drink in hand at **the Galleria** (page 47).

2 Strolling down the **Navigli canals** in Milan, and popping into the little boutiques and concept stores by up-and-coming designers (page 56).

3 Mingling with locals, sipping on cocktails, and nibbling on finger foods during a lively *aperitivo* hour (page 80).

4 Admiring *The Last Supper,* Leonardo da Vinci's famous mural painting and one of Milan's stand-out sights. Don't forget to reserve your tickets far in advance (page 53).

5 Shopping 'til you drop in Milan: From luxury Italian clothing and shoes on **Via Montenapoleone** (page 68), to edgier, local goods in the **Brera district** (page 68), and more wallet-friendly finds in **Chinatown** (page 69), there's something for every taste and budget.

6 Village-hopping along the idyllic shores of Lake Como, taking a ferry from one charming, postcard-perfect town to another (page 130).

7 Losing yourself in the old-world charm of the **Borromean Islands** of Lake Maggiore, with their colorful and lush Italian gardens and glamorous palazzos (page 193).

<<<

> > >
> >

8 Sipping a glass of Franciacorta wine at one of the wineries along the **Franciacorta wine road** near Lake Iseo (page 320).

9 Discovering the range of **outdoor activities at Lake Garda,** from windsurfing lessons (page 283) to walking through the caves of the Varone waterfalls (page 288) to paragliding off the top of Monte Baldo (page 283).

10 Enjoying a gelato on a shaded bench and people-watching in **Piazza Motta,** the heart of Orta San Giulio, a medieval town on the shores of Lake Orta (page 235).

<<<

11 Canoeing the turquoise waters of **Lake Molveno**, where there are no large motorized boats to disrupt your peace and quiet (page 333).

12 Riding up to the top of a mountain, whether on the **Funicular Monte Brè** (page 212) by Lake Lugano or the **Funivia Molveno-Pradel-Croz dell'Altissimo** (page 332) by Lake Molveno, to take in the glorious panoramic views of the Italian lakes.

>>>

13 Picnicking on the manicured green lawns of **Parco Civico-Ciani** right by the glacial blue waters of Lake Lugano, with the beautiful Swiss Alps as a backdrop (page 211).

EXPLORE
MILAN & BEYOND

THE BEST OF MILAN & LAKE COMO

To get a taste of the city and a lakeside getaway, spend two days in Milan and two days on Lake Como. With this itinerary, only public transportation is needed.

>DAY 1:

Spend your first day in Milan by the city center, where you can visit some of the major sights and soak in the city's bustling atmosphere.

- Start your day off with an espresso and a sweet pastry at a **local café** in the city center.

- Stroll down **Via Montenapoleone,** window-shopping at the flagship stores for some of the most prominent Italian fashion brands such as Prada, Gucci, and Valentino.

- Head to Piazza del Duomo, then spend an hour or two exploring **the roof of the Duomo,** where you can catch unparalleled views of the city from above.

- Grab lunch at one of the many restaurants surrounding the Duomo, such as upscale **Berton** or the traditional **A Santa Lucia.**

Milan's largest public park, Parco Sempione

16

IF YOU HAVE...

- **One day:** Stick to Milan's busy Duomo district, which is full of stunning historic attractions. If you have time, take a short walk to Milan's Sforza Castle, then stroll through Parco Sempione.

- **Two days:** Spend the first day exploring Milan's city center and Duomo district, then take a train to Varenna on Lake Como, Stresa on Lake Maggiore, or Desenzano on Lake Garda.

- **Four days:** Spend two days thoroughly exploring Milan's various neighborhoods, especially the Brera and Navigli districts, then spend a couple of days relaxing on Lake Como or Lake Garda.

- **One week or more:** Give yourself at least three days in Milan, then rent a car and road-trip to a couple of lakes. Lake Maggiore and Lake Orta make a good combination, as do Lake Garda and Lake Iseo.

- Walk off lunch with a leisurely stroll through Milan's largest and most beloved public park, **Parco Sempione.** The **Sforza Castle** stands imposingly at the entrance of the park—go inside to discover some of the city's history.

- In the early evening, indulge in a modern twist on classic Italian recipes or a cocktail (or two), and nibble on some finger foods at a traditional Milanese *aperitivo* hour in a nearby bar, like **Deseo.**

- And if you're still hungry, there's nothing like ending your night with a delicious meal at a neighborhood **pizzeria.**

>DAY 2:

Sample the city's art and design scene on your second day in Milan.

- After breakfasting at your hotel, head to the **Brera Picture Gallery,** the city's most famous Italian picture gallery. You can also take a stroll through Milan's most endearing library, the **Braidense National Library,** which is in the same building.

- Stop into **Pisacco** for lunch, one of the most talked-about restaurants in the city. Sample the city's art and design scene on your second day in Milan.

- Head to **10 Corso Como,** a complex with galleries, shops, a café, and a bookstore—a distillation of Milan's art, design, and cultural scene in one place. Go to the garden and enjoy an espresso with some intricately decorated cookies or up to the rooftop garden for a cocktail.

- Finish your afternoon with some shopping in the local boutiques, concept shops, and vintage stores in the **Ticinese and Navigli districts.**

- Call the canals of **Navigli** home for the evening, barhopping between several places that host lively *aperitivo*, such as **Maya** on the small canal.

WHERE TO GO FROM MILAN

If You Want...	Destination	Why Go	Distance from Milan	Travel Time	How Long To Stay
A quick trip outside Milan	Monza	Tour the royal villa and see fast cars at the late-summer Italian Grand Prix	15 km/9 mi	10-20 minutes by train	half day
Beauty, elegance, and *la dolce vita*	Lake Como	Admire the Alps from a hilly lakeside village, like Bellagio, Como, or Menaggio	50 km/31 mi	To Varenna: 1 hour by train	overnight
				To Lecco: 40 minutes by train	
				To Como: 40-50 minutes by train	
	Lake Iseo	Explore Europe's largest lake island, Monte Isola, with charming fishing villages and winding pathways full of ancient churches	100 km/62 mi	1-1 hour 15 minutes total by train: 35-45 minutes to Brescia, then 30 minutes from Brescia to Iseo by train	one day
	Lake Maggiore	Explore the Borromean Islands, especially the lush gardens of Isola Bella	90 km/56 mi	To Stresa: 55 minutes by freccia; 1.5 hours by regional train	one day

>DAY 3:

Head to **Lake Como,** then village-hop around the lake by ferry.

- Grab an early train from Milan's Central Station to Varenna, then spend your morning exploring **Villa Cipressi,** strolling through the beautiful gardens full of cypress trees.

- Take a boat to Bellagio and enjoy lunch at one of the local eateries in the center of the village, such as **Terrazza Barchetta.**

- Spend two or three hours of your afternoon wandering around charming Bellagio, which is full of **local boutiques,** *gelaterias,* and **lakeside bars** for you to grab a glass of wine and admire the lake as well as the surrounding mountains.

- Take the ferry to the small village of Menaggio on the lake's western shore, and pop into the small **Church of Santa Marta** for a moment of quiet reflection.

- Linger over a dinner of local cuisine at **Osteria Il Pozzo.**

- Call Menaggio home for the evening. For a luxurious night, stay at the **Grand Hotel Menaggio,** which has an on-site wellness center and balconies overlooking the lake. If you're looking for something less expensive, try the family-run **Hotel Garni Corona.**

If You Want...	Destination	Why Go	Distance from Milan	Travel Time	How Long To Stay
A mix of culture and nature	Lugano	Get a taste of Swiss culture with a distinctly Mediterannean twist at this blue glacial lake	80 km/50 mi	1 hour 15 minutes by Eurocity train; 1 hour 10 minutes by Tilo train	overnight
Outdoor adventures	Lake Garda	Enjoy all that the "king of lakes" has to offer, from water sports and amusement parks to panoramic views and hiking atop Monte Baldo	Descenzano (south): 121 km/75 mi — Riva del Garda (north): 170 km/105 mi	Descenzano: 50 minutes to 1 hour 10 minutes by train — Riva del Garda: 2 hours 30 minutes by car	overnight
	Lake Molveno	Relax by the emerald waters of the lake, or head up into the Dolomite mountains for a day of outdoor fun.	250 km/155 mi	3 hours by car	overnight
A Hidden Gem	Lake Orta	Wander the medieval village of Orta San Giulio and the charming colorful lake island, Isola Giulio—without the crowds.	80 km/50 mi	1 hour 15 minutes by car	one day

>DAY 4:

Visit the city of **Como** on Lake Como before heading back to **Milan** for the evening.

- Start your morning by grabbing a quick breakfast at one of the **cafés** in the colorful lakeside square in Menaggio.

- Hop on a ferry to the city of Como, then spend your morning exploring the city center, visiting the historically important **Duomo**, and browsing through **local shops** selling the famous Como silk products.

- Grab lunch in the city center at **Osteria L'Angolo del Silenzio**, serving homemade pastas, fresh lake fish, and more.

- In the afternoon, take the **Brunate Funicular** up to the village of Brunate, for jaw-dropping views of the lake from high above.

- Once you're back down on the lakefront, grab a train back to **Milan's Porta Garibaldi station.** From there, walk through the beautifully designed **Piazza Gae Aulenti** on your way to dinner at one of the restaurants in the **Porta Nuova** neighborhood, such as **Il Solferino.**

BEST OF THE LAKES

If you want to skip Milan altogether and spend your trip hopping around the various lakes, the best and easiest way to do so is to rent a car. This itinerary hits the four largest Italian lakes from west to east, but can easily be done in the opposite direction.

>DAY 1:

On your first day, travel back in time while exploring the **Borromean Islands** on **Lake Maggiore.**

- Hop on a train from Milan's Central Station to **Stresa,** then head straight to the ferry station on the lakefront to purchase a ticket for all three islands.

- Head to **Isola Madre** and spend an hour or two exploring the **Palazzo Borromeo** and the colorful **botanical gardens.**

- Catch a ferry to **Isola dei Pescatori,** and enjoy a leisurely lunch of traditional Northern Italian food.

- Take a brisk stroll around the island, and make sure to pop your head into the historic **Church of San Vittore** before you leave.

- Take a ferry to the third and final island, **Isola Bella,** then walk through the grand **Palazzo Borromeo** and the lush, multi-level **Borromean gardens.**

- End your day by heading back to **Stresa** for the evening for a relaxing drink and dinner overlooking the waters of the lake.

Floating atop Lake Maggiore, Isola Bella's botanical gardens are a lush green getaway surrounded by calming waters.

IF YOU LIKE...

- **Art and design:** Visit *The Last Supper,* the Brera district, and the streets of Isola in Milan. On Lake Lugano, visit the LAC Lugano Arts & Culture.

- **Wine:** Hit one of the dozens of upscale wine bars *(enotecas)* in Milan. Better yet, head to Lake Iseo, and hit the local wine road to immerse yourself in the heart of the Franciacorta wine region.

- **Luxury:** In Milan, visit the flagship stores for all the major luxury brands along Via Montenapoleone, and book a room or suite at Palazzo Parigi or Chateau Monfort. Bask in the baroque glory and lush gardens of the Borromean Islands on Lake Maggiore. Spend a relaxing weekend at the luxurious Villa Cipressi in Varenna or Villa Serbelloni on Lake Garda, or for something a little more low-key with just as much elegance (if not more), stay at Villa Crespi on Lake Orta.

- **Small-town charm:** Go village-hopping in Lake Como, or to escape the crowds, head to the charming medieval village of Orta San Giulio in Lake Orta.

- **Outdoor recreation:** Rent a bike using the public bike-sharing service in Milan, BikeMi, to explore the city on two wheels. Head to Lake Garda for a number of family-friendly activities such as boating, hiking, paragliding, swimming, and more. To enjoy the outdoors without the crowds, head to Lake Molveno.

>DAY 2:

Spend your second day village-hopping around **Lake Como.**

- Drive to **Menaggio** from Stresa (roughly 1 hour and 45 minutes), then spend your morning in this charming lakeside village on Lake Como.

- Ride the **Trombetta Express,** a small trolley that plies western shore of Lake Como, stopping in **Menaggio, Cadenabbia,** and **Tremezzzo** multiple times a day in the high season. Hop on and off as much as you like with a day pass.

- End your day back in **Menaggio** with a meal at **Il Ristorante di Paolo,** then stay the night at one of the many hotels.

>DAY 3:

Head to **Lake Iseo** to see Europe's largest lake island, **Monte Isola.**

- Jumpstart your morning with a two-hour road trip from Menaggio to **Iseo** on Lake Iseo, which you'll call home for the day.

- Take the ferry to **Monte Isola,** and explore the largest lake island in Europe. Starting at the **Church of San Michele** in Peschiera Maraglio, slowly make your way around the footpath on the island's edge.

- Have lunch on the waterfront at **La Foresta.**

- Head back to Iseo, and rent a bike for a ride through the **Franciacorta wine region.** Stop into a winery or two for a tasting and tour.

- Have dinner and spend the night at the intimate **I Due Roccoli.** Book your table and room in advance to make sure you don't miss this spot during the high season.

>DAY 4:

On your fourth day, head to the southern tip of **Lake Garda.**

- Start bright and early with a 45-minute drive to **Desenzano del Garda,** on the southern end of Lake Garda, which has been a popular getaway since the 1st century.

- Head to the waterfront, then grab a boat to **Sirmione** to explore the **Rocca Scaligera** castle and Roman ruins of **Grotte di Catullo.**

- For lunch, head to **La Cambusa** back on Desenzano for a robust *tagliere* plate.

- Spend your afternoon roaming around Desenzano, exploring the ruins of **Villa Romana** and popping into a few local stores for some shopping.

- Head to the **waterfront** and grab a seat and a gelato at one of the handful of *gelaterias* lining the shore.

- Grab dinner at **Molin22,** one of the highest-rated restaurants in Desenzano, serving quality Italian food near the waters of Lake Garda.

>DAY 5:

Spend your last day enjoying the outdoors in the beautiful **Lake Garda** area.

- Kick off your final day with a 1.25-hour drive from Desenzano del Garda up to **Malcesine** on the northeastern end of Lake Garda.

Malcesine's shoreline is always bustling with travelers and locals relaxing near the water.

- Spend your morning on **Monte Baldo,** grabbing the **cable car** to the top and **hiking** or **paragliding** down.

- Head back down to Malcesine for lunch at Michelin-starred **Ristorante Vecchia Malcesine** or another Italian restaurant serving local cuisine.

- Spend your afternoon on the water, either kayaking or trying your hand at windsurfing with **Europa Surf & Sail.**

- In the late afternoon, relax at the **Lido Paina,** a public beach near the center of town, and cool down with a *granita* or gelato.

- Finish a long day with a hearty meal at **Speck & Stube,** creating your own personalized meal full of meats and veggies.

BEFORE YOU GO

WHEN TO GO

To avoid the hordes of tourists, sweltering temperatures, and long lines, visit Milan and the lakes in **April, May, September,** or **October,** when the weather is warm but not miserably hot. The summer season isn't yet in full swing, so you can avoid many of the families traveling with children during summer break.

In the peak of **summer** (June-Aug.), temperatures range 17-29°C (63-85°F). Although the average high temperature may not seem that high, the region is fairly humid and crowded in the summer, so packing yourself into metro cars, trams, and trains along with hundreds of other travelers may not be appealing.

November through mid-March is considered **off season,** as it's quite cold, with temperatures ranging -1°-4°C (30-40°F), and the chances of local shops and restaurants being open are hit or miss in most villages along the major lakes.

If you're a fan of fashion, stop by in September to experience **Vogue's Fashion Night Out** and the **Fall Fashion Week,** a truly authentic and lively experience that is unique to the city. Avoid visiting the area in August, as most Italians escape the heat for long vacations on the beach or in the mountains, so businesses may be closed for weeks at a time and public transportation runs less frequently.

a view of Varenna's waterfront from the ferry to Bellagio

WHAT YOU NEED TO KNOW

- **Currency:** Euro (€)

- **Conversion rate:** €1 = $1.14 or £0.91, but this number fluctuates daily, so do a quick search before you go.

- **Entry requirements:** Valid passport that does not expire for the duration of your trip. No visa is required if you are from the United States, United Kingdom, Canada, Australia, New Zealand, or South Africa unless you plan on staying in the Schengen zone for longer than a 90-day period. Visitors from EU countries only need a valid EU identity card.

- **Emergency numbers: 112:** *carabinieri* (local military police) and emergency police assistance; **116:** A.C.I. (Italian Automobile Club) Roadside Assistance; **118:** medical emergencies and ambulance; **12:** telephone directory

- **Time zone:** (GMT+2), Central European Time (CET)

- **Electrical system:** 220-240 volt system, round 2-pin plugs

- **Opening hours:** Restaurants: 12pm-2:30pm and 7pm-10:30pm; attractions and churches: 10am-6pm; some places closed on Sundays or Mondays

GETTING THERE
BY AIR

Book your air travel as far as possible in advance for the best prices. There are direct flights to Milan from several international cities, including New York, Miami, Atlanta, London, Frankfurt, and almost any other major European city. Most commercial airlines like American Airlines, Emirates, British Airways, Delta, Alitalia, and more fly in and out of the **Malpensa** and **Linate** airports, while the budget airline Easy Jet flies in and out of Malpensa.

BY TRAIN

Milan's **Central Station** has frequent arriving and departing *freccia* (fast) trains from major Italian and European cities, including Paris and Zurich. Tickets should be reserved online 3-6 months in advance to ensure best prices and seat reservation.

Most trains to the lakes are run by either **Trenitalia,** Italy's main train company, or **Trenord,** northern Italy's train company. Tickets for both companies can be purchased on www.trenitalia.com or at most (but not all) train stations throughout the city and at the lakes. Train tickets from France can be purchased from SNCF (www.sncf.com) and tickets from Switzerland can be bought at www.sbb.ch.

There are two types of trains to the lakes: **regional** and *freccia* (fast) trains. Most people opt for regional trains: They are cheaper, there are no assigned seats so there is no cap on tickets sold, and they stop in more places. From Milan, each of the three major lakes are directly accessible by a single train. However, getting from one major lake to the other by train

Passengers travel through the impressive Centrale Railway Station in Milan

is not direct: It involves heading back to Milan first, then catching a train to your next lake.

BY CAR

Milan is also well connected to major highways in Italy, and is a notable stop on the **A4** between Turin and Trieste and the **A9/2** tollway from Basel, as well as other tollways and highways connecting to all major lakes. You will need to obtain an **international driver's license** in order to drive a car in Italy, so be sure to apply for one and obtain it before your arrival. This means that, of course, you will need a valid driver's license from your home country that does not expire during your trip. Most car rental companies require your **passport** and a **credit card**

deposit in order to reserve a car, which you should do in advance using sites such as www.autoeurope.com or www.rentalcars.com.

If you're planning on a longer getaway to the lakes, renting a car is useful. Traveling to the smaller lakes that are farther away like Lake Molveno or Lake Orta, hopping between lakes, or hopping between villages on larger lakes like Lake Garda is much easier to do by car than by train. However, parking can often be difficult, expensive, and limited the villages around the lakes.

BY BUS

Popular European bus lines such as **Megabus** (https://megabus.com) and **Flixbus** (https://global.flixbus.com) offer bus routes directly from hundreds of European cities, including Paris, Zurich, Munich, Lyon, Basel, Venice, Florence, and Rome, to various bus stops in Milan. You can purchase tickets directly on the companies' websites and prices are often as low as €5-20 per trip. The most popular stops in Milan are **Milan Lampugnano** and **Milan Sesto San Giovanni,** both of which have a corresponding metro stop.

Although **FlixBus** (www.flixbus.com) offers trips between Milan and several villages on the lakes, often **traveling by train is quicker,** and train tickets often rival bus prices.

BEFORE YOU GO

GETTING AROUND

In general, you can travel by train to the lakes from Milan in most cases, and for the larger lakes, you can hop between

most sights by ferry, with the exception of Lake Garda, which is so large that it's best to rent a car in order to village-hop.

25

KEY RESERVATIONS

While most attractions and restaurants won't require reservations, planning ahead for a few key spots will avoid putting a damper on your trip:

- **The Last Supper, Milan:** Book tickets as far in advance as possible, as the limited tickets per day usually sell out months ahead of time. If tickets are no longer available for the day you want to go, find a city tour through Viator or another similar travel company that includes it in its itinerary.

- **Roof of the Duomo, Milan:** Purchase these tickets online in advance as well, so you can avoid the long line upon your arrival

- **Restaurant reservations:** While most restaurants in Milan won't require reservations for lunch, do book a table for any fine-dining establishment a few days in advance. On the lakes, dinner reservations are highly recommended, as the best restaurants in each village fill up quickly during high season.

- **Freccia train tickets:** Book these a few months in advance to score discounted prices. During the spring and summer, these tickets generally run out a day or so in advance during peak traveling times, so don't wait too long to buy.

BY CAR

I don't recommend driving around the Milan area, as traffic in the city can get hectic, and there are plenty of good public transit options in the city. Italians also tend to be more offensive drivers rather than defensive drivers, switching lanes without warning and often trying to get ahead rather than waiting patiently in traffic. Parking can often be difficult, expensive, and limited in both Milan and the villages around the lakes.

Most cars here have a **manual transmission,** so if that's not something you're comfortable with, be sure to book your rental car well in advance in order to get one with an automatic transmission. You will also need to an **international driver's license** to drive in Italy, so be sure to get one before you leave if you don't have one already.

BY METRO, TRAM, AND BUS

Within Milan, the public transportation system of metros, trams, and buses will get you nearly everywhere you need to go, making a car unnecessary and inconvenient. At Lake Como, there is a bus that connects smaller villages to a town on the train line and a charming *trenino* that travels up and down a portion of the western side of the lake; otherwise,

Menaggio's shoreline offers private water taxi services to jet travelers all over the lake

BUDGETING

- **Cup of coffee:** €1-2

- **Glass of wine:** €4-8

- **Gelato:** €1.50-4

- *Aperitivo:* €10-20

- **Breakfast:** €3-7

- **Lunch:** €10-20

- **Dinner:** €20-40

- **Pizza:** €5-10

- **Entrance fees for museums or art galleries:** €10

- **Milan public transportation:** €1.50 per trip, €4.50 day pass

- **Train to Lake Como:** €5-12 one-way

- **Train to Lake Garda:** €10-20 one-way

- **Train to Lake Maggiore:** €10-20 one-way

- **Hotel:** €100 per night

The old-style trams are a transportation method unique to Milan

land-based public transit options are nonexistent at the lakes.

BY FERRY
Most lakes are serviced by a public ferry that will take you between the major villages and lake islands. For the three major lakes, Lakes Como, Maggiore, and Garda, **Gestione Navigazione Laghi** (www.navigazionelaghi.it) operates the ferry services to and from a majority of the villages. Lakes Lugano, Orta, and Iseo also have public ferries. Official timetables and prices vary depending on the season, so you should always check the ferry service's website for the most up-to-date timetables and fares.

WHAT TO PACK
The first thing to consider when packing your bag is the weather, of course, as Milan sees all four seasons: winter in late November-March, spring in April-June, summer in July-mid-September, and fall mid-September-November. Pack cold gear in the winter and summer clothes and swimwear in the warmer months, and check the weather before your trip to prepare for rain, as precipitation is not uncommon in Milan and on the surrounding lakes.

An essential item for your trip is comfortable, durable **walking shoes.** Despite Milan being one of the fashion capitals of the world, it's not uncommon to see locals wearing dresses and office attire

27

with comfortable shoes, for public transportation. If you plan on swimming in the lakes or hitting up one of the shoreline beaches, keep in mind that they are rock or pebble beaches, so bringing along a pair of sporty **water shoes** may be a wise idea.

You'll also need to pack **converters and adapters** to accommodate European electrical outlets which take round, 2-pin plugs. For hair straighteners or blow dryers, pay close attention to how many volts are required to turn them on and use them properly. Consider searching for appliances that have the built-in **220-240 volt system** plugs.

Other things to consider, depending on when you're going and your itinerary, are **sunscreen,** necessary **medications** or a **small emergency kit, bug repellent** (mosquitos are common in this region in the summer), and multiple **printed copies of your passport,** other ID cards, and credit cards. (U.S. travelers in particular should to memorize credit card PIN numbers before departure since some transactions in Italy may require it.) During the day, carry printed copies of your passport and IDs, but leave your actual documents

DAILY REMINDERS

- In Milan, shops, restaurants, and sights are generally **closed on Sundays and Mondays** or have abbreviated hours.

- On the lakes, in order to ensure that not all restaurants or bars are closed on the same day, places may change their closing day to Tuesdays or Wednesdays, so be sure to **check the opening hours.**

- On the **first Sunday or Tuesday of every month,** you may find free or discounted admission to several attractions, including the civic museums of Sforza Castle in Milan, so check the website of each sight if you're in town during the first week of the month.

stored safely in a safety deposit box in your hotel. However, if you're traveling to **Lake Lugano,** make sure you grab your actual passport, as you'll be crossing the Italian-Swiss border.

If possible, obtain a few hundred **euros in cash** before your arrival in Milan, as converting at airports or train stations can often be expensive, and you may need cash on hand for transportation or other last-minute costs in case there are problems with your cards upon arrival.

MILAN

Although Milan's rich history is steeped in traditional Italian culture, its modern identity is shaped by international influences, earning it its reputations as Italy's "melting pot city" and "the gateway to the rest of the world." Known as a global fashion capital, and the center of Italy's economic power, Milan is uniquely classic yet modern, eclectic, and design-forward. An ever-changing and resilient metropolis, it has worked hard to differentiate itself from some of Italy's, and the rest of Europe's, most beautiful and historic cities. Although it is constantly

HIGHLIGHTS

✪ **DUOMO DI MILANO:** Italy's largest church, the Duomo sits on its throne in the heart of Milan's city center. While the stunning exterior and interior architecture alone make it worth the visit, a walk on the cathedral's roof, where visitors can view the city skyline and the Alps, is the top attraction (page 45).

✪ **THE GALLERIA:** The world's oldest shopping mall, the Galleria comprises four levels of luxury stores, cafés, restaurants, bars, and a skywalk stretching between the Piazza della Scala and the Piazza del Duomo; visitors can easily spend an entire afternoon strolling through this impressive mall (page 47).

✪ **LA SCALA:** Italy's most famous opera house hosts waves of performing artists and arts enthusiasts every year. Those not attending a show can still visit the theater to admire its grandeur and the museum to learn about its history (page 48).

✪ **VIA MONTENAPOLEONE:** Considered the heart of Milan's fashion district, this is the place to go for upscale shopping. Located in the city center, this narrow street is lined with shops carrying top fashion brands and footwear by famous Italian shoemakers (page 49).

✪ **CASTELLO SFORZESCO:** Just a short walk from the Duomo, this 15th-century castle is now home to various civic museums, with exhibits ranging from art to archaeology (page 51).

✪ **PARCO SEMPIONE:** Milan's largest park, Parco Sempione stretches from Castello Sforzesco to Arco della Pace and offers a refreshing respite from the city's hustle and bustle (page 52).

✪ *THE LAST SUPPER:* Leonardo da Vinci's famous mural *The Last Supper* is one of Milan's standout sights, and the dark, quiet room where it dominates the front wall allows you to appreciate the rich details, if only for the allotted 15 minutes. Visitors should be sure to reserve tickets far in advance to see it (page 53).

✪ **NAVIGLI AND THE CANALS:** Packed with colorful buildings, local artisan boutiques, and creative concept stores, Navigli is a great place to wander during the day, but it really comes to life after dark, with the small canals serving as the perfect backdrop for a night of barhopping (page 56).

✪ **BRERA PICTURE GALLEY:** This famous picture gallery, located in the artsy Brera district, is the city's most famous Italian art gallery. Visit this gallery for an in-depth retrospective of the art and culture of Milan (page 57).

✪ *APERITIVO* HOUR: Sipping cocktails and sampling a smorgasbord of tasty snacks at a local bar is the perfect way to wind down your day in Milan (page 80).

evolving and recreating itself, it remains distinctly Milanese. For travelers wanting to experience classic Italy with a splash of the rest of Europe and the world, Milan is the perfect place to visit.

Unlike other Italian cities, Milan offers a little bit of everything—from ancient piazzas to historic monuments, expansive green spaces to high-end shopping, tranquil respites to a spirited nightlife. It is the home of Italy's largest church, the Duomo di Milano, which sits directly next to the world's oldest shopping mall and commands the city's central piazza. It's from this historic heart that the rest of the city blossoms to life.

Orientation and Planning

Unlike many medium or large cities, Milan isn't built on a grid, but rather in concentric circles that radiate around the Piazza del Duomo. Many of Milan's more popular neighborhoods and districts are northwest of Piazza del Duomo: Castello, Sempione, Brera, and Chinatown. North of the Duomo are Porta Nuova, Porta Venezia, and Isola. South of the Duomo are Porta Ticinese and Navigli, while San Siro lies to the west, Although all of these districts are close in proximity and the borders are blurred, each brings its own personality to the cultural makeup of Milan.

CITY CENTER AND DUOMO DISTRICT

Milan's most historical gems are found in the Duomo district, which is the city's most important area. It all starts in the Piazza del Duomo, the city's heart; here, you'll find the famous Duomo di Milano cathedral and the Galleria. This area also comprises San Babila and Via Montenapoleone. If you have just one day to get the most out of the city, this is the place to go, as it gives you a taste of Milan's best characteristics: design, shopping, history, and elegance.

CASTELLO AND SEMPIONE

The Castello and Sempione neighborhoods sit just west of the city center and are about a 10-minute walk from Piazza del Duomo. Castello, also referred to as the Castle district, is home to Milan's Castello Sforzesco, and in the castle's backyard is Milan's largest public park, Parco Sempione. The park's vast and vivid greenery stretches from the castle to the Arco della Pace. While a stroll through this tranquil park and the castle courtyards is completely free to the public during operating hours, consider visiting the numerous museums and collections available in both areas for a small fee.

TICINESE AND NAVIGLI DISTRICTS

Located to the south of Piazza del Duomo, occupying the edge of the city center and stretching beyond it, are the Porta Ticinese and Navigli districts, much beloved by locals. Here you'll find some of Milan's more eclectic neighborhoods and street culture. In many ways, this is a district of contrasts: Porta Ticinese's Basilica of Sant'Eustorgio and Basilica

Milan

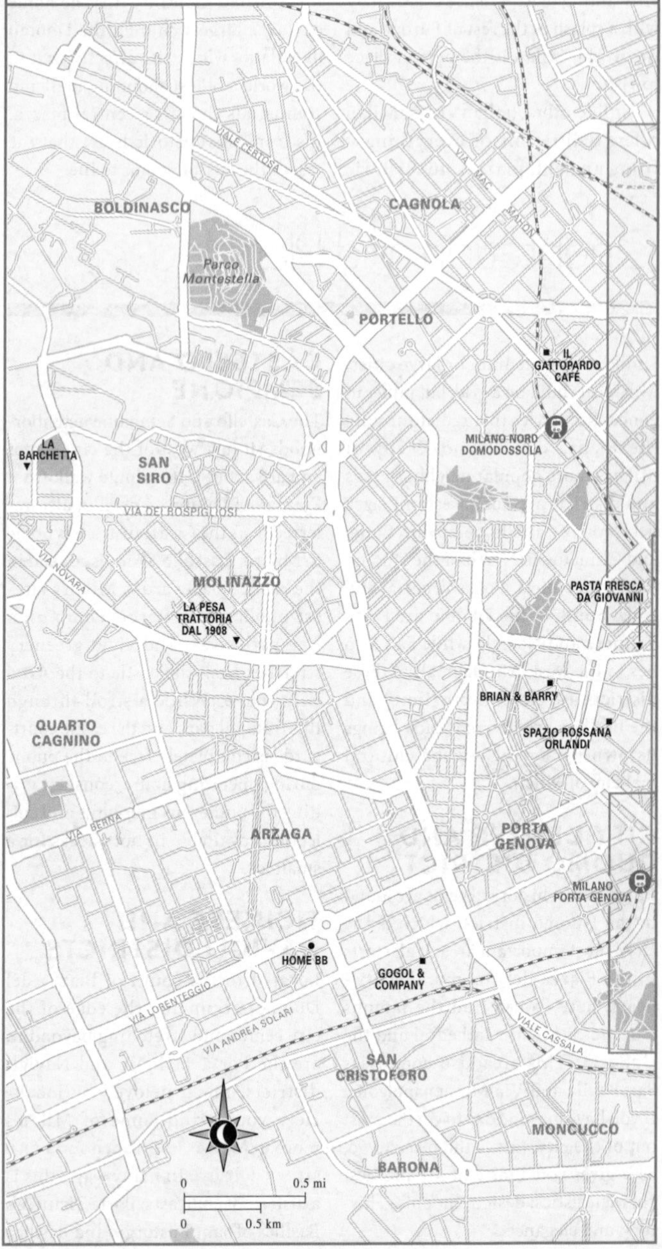
VIALE CERTOSA
VIA MAC MAHON
BOLDINASCO
CAGNOLA
Parco Montestella
PORTELLO
IL GATTOPARDO CAFÉ
MILANO NORD DOMODOSSOLA
LA BARCHETTA
SAN SIRO
VIA DEI ROSPIGLIOSI
VIA NOVARA
MOLINAZZO
LA PESA TRATTORIA DAL 1908
PASTA FRESCA DA GIOVANNI
BRIAN & BARRY
SPAZIO ROSSANA ORLANDI
QUARTO CAGNINO
VIA BERNA
ARZAGA
PORTA GENOVA
MILANO PORTA GENOVA
HOME BB
GOGOL & COMPANY
VIA LORENTEGGIO
VIA ANDREA SOLARI
VIALE CASSALA
SAN CRISTOFORO
MONCUCCO
BARONA
0
0.5 mi
0
0.5 km

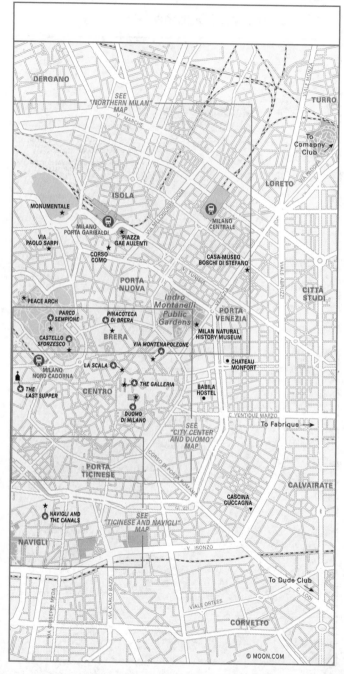

DERGANO

TURRO

SEE "NORTHERN MILAN" MAP

V. MARCHE

To Comapny Club

LORETO

VIALE MONZA

VIA PADOVA

ISOLA

MONUMENTALE

MILANO PORTA GARIBALDI

PIAZZA GAE AULENTI

CORSO COMO

VIA PAOLO SARPI

MILANO CENTRALE

CASA-MUSEO BOSCHI DI STEFANO

CITTÀ STUDI

VIALE ABRUZZI

PORTA NUOVA

Indro Montanelli Public Gardens

PORTA VENEZIA

PEACE ARCH

PARCO SEMPIONE

PINACOTECA DI BRERA

BRERA

VIA MONTENAPOLEONE

MILAN NATURAL HISTORY MUSEUM

CASTELLO SFORZESCO

LA SCALA

CHATEAU MONFORT

MILANO NORD CADORNA

THE LAST SUPPER

CENTRO

THE GALLERIA

BABILA HOSTEL

DUOMO DI MILANO

C. VENTIQUE MARZO

To Fabrique

SEE "CITY CENTER AND DUOMO" MAP

CORSO DI PORTA ROMANA

PORTA TICINESE

CALVAIRATE

CASCINA CUCCAGNA

NAVIGLI AND THE CANALS

SEE "TICINESE AND NAVIGLI" MAP

NAVIGLI

V. ISONZO

To Dude Club

VIA GIUSEPPE MEDA

VIA CARLO BAZZI

VIALE ORTLES

CORVETTO

© MOON.COM

City Center and Duomo

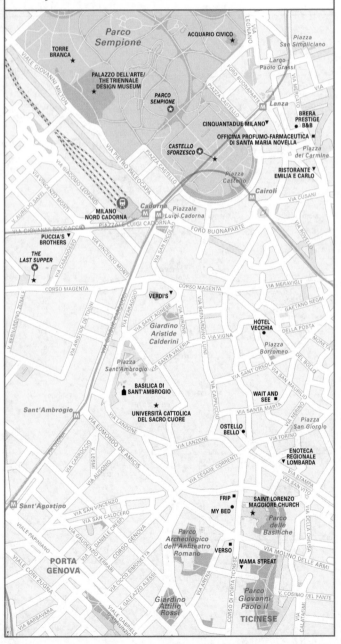

Parco Sempione

ACQUARIO CIVICO ★

TORRE BRANCA ★

VIALE LEGNANO

Piazza San Simpliciano

VIA MERCATO

Largo Paolo Grassi

VIALE GIOVANNI MILTON

PALAZZO DELL'ARTE/ THE TRIENNALE DESIGN MUSEUM ★

PARCO SEMPIONE ✪

FORO BUONAPARTE

PIAZZA CASTELLO

Ⓜ Lanza

BRERA PRESTIGE B&B ■

CINQUANTADUE MILANO ▼

OFFICINA PROFUMO-FARMACEUTICA DI SANTA MARIA NOVELLA ■

Piazza del Carmine

VIA PIETRO PALEOCAPA

PIAZZA CASTELLO

CASTELLO SFORZESCO ✪ ★

Piazza Castello

RISTORANTE ▼ EMILIA E CARLO

Cairoli

VIA CUSANI

VIA GIACOMO LEOPARDI

VIA VINCENZO MONTI

VIA AURELIO SAFFI

🚉

MILANO NORD CADORNA

Ⓜ Cadorna Piazzale Luigi Cadorna

PIAZZALE LUIGI CADORNA

FORO BUONAPARTE

VIA SAN NICAO

VIA ROVELLO

VIA GIOVANNI BOCCACCIO

PUCCIA'S BROTHERS ▼

THE LAST SUPPER ★

VIA CARDUCCIO

VIA VINCENZO MONTI

CORSO MAGENTA

CORSO MAGENTA

VIA MERAVIGLI

V. BERNARDINO ZENALE

VIA ARISTIDE DE TOGNI

VERDI'S ▼

VIA SANT'AGNESE

VIA TERRAGGIO

VIA NIRONE

VIA BERNARDINO LUINI

CORSO MAGENTA

GAETANO NEGRI

HOTEL VECCHIA ●

DELLA POSTA

Giardino Aristide Calderini

VIA VIGNA

MONETA

Piazza Borromeo

VIA SANTA VALERIA

DEL BOLLO

Piazza Sant'Ambrogio

BASILICA DI SANT'AMBROGIO ⛪

VIA SANT'ORSOLA

VIA SAN MAURILIO

VIA CAPPUCCIO

WAIT AND SEE ■

Sant'Ambrogio Ⓜ

UNIVERSITÀ CATTOLICA DEL SACRO CUORE ★

VIA EDMONDO DE AMICIS

VIA LANZONE

VIA SANTA MARTA

VIA NERINO

VIA TORINO

Piazza San Giorgio

OSTELLO BELLO ●

VIA CARROCCIO

V. LESMI

VIA LANZONE

ENOTECA REGIONALE ▼ LOMBARDA

VIA STAMPA

VIA SAN VITO

VIA AUSONIO

VIA CESARE CORRENTI

Sant'Agostino Ⓜ

VIA SAN VINCENZO

VIA SAN CALOCERO

FRIP ■

MY BED ●

SAINT LORENZO MAGGIORE CHURCH ★

Parco delle Basiliche

VIA DELLA CHIESA

VIALE PAPINIANO

VIA GAUDENZIO DANIELE CRESPI

CORSO GENOVA

Parco Archeologico dell'Anfiteatro Romano

VERSO ■

MAMA STREAT ▼

VIA MOLINO DELLE ARMI

VIA COL DI LANA

PORTA GENOVA

VIA CICCO SIMONETTA

CORSO DI PORTA TICINESE

VIA ARENA

V. COSIMO DEL FANTE

VIALE CON ZUGNA

VIA GALEAZZO ALESSI

Giardino Attilio Rossi

Parco Giovanni Paolo II

VIA CALATAFIMI

VIALE BARBAVARA

VIALE GABRIELE D'ANNUNZIO

TICINESE

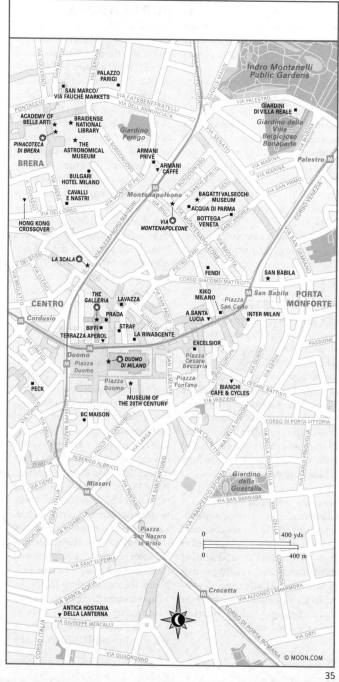

Indro Montanelli Public Gardens

PALAZZO PARIGI

SAN MARCO/VIA FAUCHÉ MARKETS

GIARDINI DI VILLA REALE

Giardino della Villa Belgiojoso Bonaparte

ACADEMY OF BELLE ARTI

BRAIDENSE NATIONAL LIBRARY

Giardino Perego

PINACOTECA DI BRERA

THE ASTRONOMICAL MUSEUM

BRERA

ARMANI PRIVÉ

ARMANI CAFFÈ

Palestro

BULGARI HOTEL MILANO

BAGATTI VALSECCHI MUSEUM

CAVALLI E NASTRI

Montenapoleone

ACQUA DI PARMA

HONG KONG CROSSOVER

VIA MONTENAPOLEONE

BOTTEGA VENETA

LA SCALA

FENDI

SAN BABILA

THE GALLERIA

LAVAZZA

KIKO MILANO

Piazza San Carlo

San Babila

PORTA MONFORTE

CENTRO

PRADA

A SANTA LUCIA

INTER MILAN

Cordusio

BIFFI

STRAF

TERRAZZA APEROL

LA RINASCENTE

EXCELSIOR

Duomo

Piazza Duomo

DUOMO DI MILANO

Piazza Cesare Beccaria

PECK

Piazza Duomo

MUSEUM OF THE 20TH CENTURY

Piazza Fontana

BIANCHI CAFE & CYCLES

BC MAISON

Missori

Giardino della Guastalla

Piazza San Nazaro in Brolo

0   400 yds

0   400 m

Crocetta

ANTICA HOSTARIA DELLA LANTERNA

© MOON.COM

San Lorenzo Maggiore and its medieval city wall contrast sharply against its street culture, street art, and other modern elements. Navigli (a district so named for the canals that are at its heart) is popular for its *aperitivo* venues. To reach Porta Ticinese, which sits between the Navigli and Duomo districts, start near the Colonne di San Lorenzo in the Piazza del Duomo and walk south for about 15 minutes. From Porta Ticinese, walk south for an additional five minutes to reach Navigli. Here, you'll encounter the charming canals that characterize the district. Porta Ticinese and Navigli are the heart of Milan's *aperitivo* culture, and because of their popular nightlife, they tend to attract a younger crowd.

BRERA DISTRICT

The artsy Brera district lies just north of the historic center and east of the Castle district. To get there, take the metro Line M2 (green) to the Moscova or Lanza stops, which are both found in the heart of the district. Brera, known mostly for its shops, galleries, and vibrant nightlife, is also considered the beating heart of Milan's art and design culture. You can enjoy everything from artisan workshops to professional art collections, from elegant dining experiences to relaxing happy hours at outdoor cafés. Brera is chic, sophisticated, and alluring, often compared to the Montmartre neighborhood of Paris. While there are a handful of standout experiences and attractions in Brera, you're likely to pass a wonderful afternoon simply browsing the loads of boutiques and concept stores along the cobblestone streets.

PORTA NUOVA

Named after Milan's neoclassical gate, the once industrial Porta Nuova district is now the main business hub of the city. Here, modern and international design meets traditional Italian architecture. In the late 1990s, after decades of urban decay, a team of real estate developers renovated the area in the vein of London and other post-industrial cities, turning this district into one of the city's finer and more modern areas. Several of Milan's skyscrapers, including Italy's tallest—the Torre Unicredit—and luxury residences are located here. It serves as the middleman between the Brera and Porta Venezia districts and is dominated by Piazza Gae Aulenti. The best way to get to this district is by taking the metro Line M2 (green) or Line M5 (purple) to the Porta Garibaldi stop.

PORTA VENEZIA

Located north of the historic city center, Porta Venezia is roughly a 15-minute walk from Piazza del Duomo. You'll find several metro Line M1 (red) stops in this area, including Palestro, Porta Venezia, Lima, and Loreto. Porta Venezia, which dates back to the 12th century, shares its name with the city gate, situated in the heart of the district. Like most districts in Milan, Porta Venezia lacks official lines or boundaries of demarcation. While the district itself is centuries old, most of its defining neoclassical and art nouveau architecture dates from the 1800s and 1900s, including several important old palaces and gardens. Today, the area is known for the department stores lining Corso Buenos Aires and its large public gardens. The rising influx of new immigrants and the thriving LGBT community

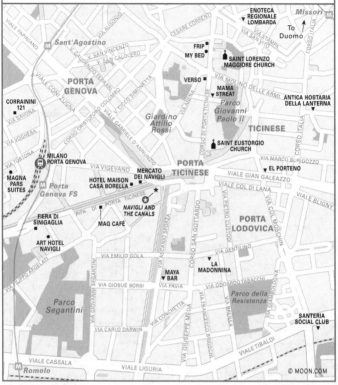

Ticinese and Navigli

VIALE PAPINIANO

M Sant'Agostino

VIA ALSONIO

CESARE CORRENTI

ENOTECA
REGIONALE
LOMBARDA

Missori M

CORSO ITALIA

To
Duomo

VIA SAN VITO

VIA STAMPA

V. SAN VINCENZO

V. SAN CALOCERO

VIALE GIAN GALDINO FERRARI

FRIP
MY BED

VIA MOLINO DELLE ARMI

SAINT LORENZO
MAGGIORE CHURCH

PORTA
GENOVA

VIALE COL DI ZUGNA

VERSO

VIA AREVA

CORRAININI
121

VIA SAVONA

MAMA
STREAT

ANTICA HOSTARIA
DELLA LANTERNA

*Parco
Giovanni
Paolo II*

VIA CRISTOFORO COLOMBO

V. CICCO SIMONETTA

VIA GABRIELE D'ANNUNZIO

CORSO DI PORTA TICINESE

TICINESE

VIA VOGHERA

*Giardino
Attilio
Rossi*

CORSO ITALIA

VIA TORTONA

MILANO
PORTA GENOVA

SAINT EUSTORGIO
CHURCH

VIA MARCO BURIGOZZO

MAGNA
PARS
SUITES

M Porta
Genova FS

VIA VIGEVANO

MERCATO
DEI NAVIGLI

PORTA
TICINESE

EL PORTENO

VIALE GIAN GALEAZZO

HOTEL MAISON
CASA BORELLA

VIALE COL DI LANA

VIALE BLIGNY

FIERA DI
SINIGAGLIA

RIPA DI PORTA TICINESE

NAVIGLI AND
THE CANALS

VIA PIETRO CUSTODI

PORTA
LODOVICA

VIA COL MOSCHIN

MAG CAFÉ

VIA FILIPPO ARGELATI

ART HOTEL
NAVIGLI

VIA EMILIO GOLA

VIA GENTILINO

VIA GIOVANNI SEGANTINI

MAYA
BAR

LA
MADONNINA

CORSO SAN GOTTARDO

VIA GIUSEPPE MEDA

VIA ODOARDO TABACCHI

VIA GIOSUÈ BORSI

VIA PAVIA

*Parco
Segantini*

VIA CONCHETTA

*Parco della
Resistenza*

VIA BAILLA

SANTERIA
SOCIAL CLUB

VIA CARLO DARWIN

CORSO SAN VINCENZO MEDA

VIALE TIBALDI

M Romolo

VIALE CASSALA

VIALE LIGURIA

© MOON.COM

has made this area one of the most diverse in the city.

CHINATOWN

As with most truly international cities, Milan has its very own Chinatown tucked in between the Castello and Porta Nuova districts, just north of Brera. It's about a 25-minute walk from Piazza del Duomo, or you can take the tram 14 from the Cadorna station (on metro Line M1 [red] and Line M2 [green]) to the Via Bramante Via Sarpi stop. Although it's much smaller than those in other major cities (it focuses mainly on just one street), it is the largest Chinatown in Italy. Despite

its namesake, the cobblestone streets and colorful buildings are characteristically Italian. Visitors staying more than a day or two in Milan could devote an hour strolling through the streets of Chinatown.

ISOLA

The district of Isola, which means "island" in Italian, is a residential area that sits north of the Porta Nuova district, stretching north from Milan's Porta Garibaldi station. (A tunnel connects the station to the district.) The neighborhood, though not surrounded by water, is separated from the surrounding districts by railroad

Northern Milan

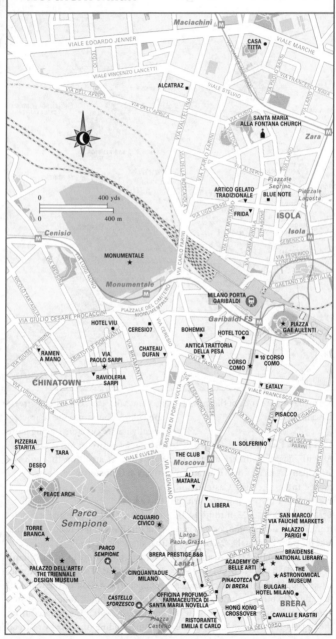

Maciachini

VIALE EDOARDO JENNER

CASA TITTA

VIALE MARCHE

VIALE VINCENZO LANCETTI

ALCATRAZ

VIALE STELVIO

VIA DELL'AFRICA

VIA DELL'APRILA

SANTA MARIA
ALLA FONTANA CHURCH

Zara

Piazzale
Segrino

ARTICO GELATO
TRADIZIONALE

BLUE NOTE

Piazzale
Lagosta

0   400 yds

0   400 m

FRIDA

ISOLA

Cenisio

Isola

MONUMENTALE

Monumentale

MILANO PORTA
GARIBALDI

Garibaldi FS

PIAZZA
GAE AULENTI

PIAZZALE DEL CIMITERO
MONUMENTALE

VIA GIULIO CESARE PROCACCINI

HOTEL VIU

CERESIO7

BOHEMKI

HOTEL TOCQ

CHATEAU
DUFAN

ANTICA TRATTORIA
DELLA PESA

RAMEN
A MANO

VIA
PAOLO SARPI

10 CORSO
COMO

CORSO
COMO

RAVIOLERIA
SARPI

CHINATOWN

VIA GIUSEPPE GIUSTI

EATALY

VIALE FRANCESCO CRISPI

PISACCO

PIZZERIA
STARITA

TARA

IL SOLFERINO

DESEO

THE CLUB

Moscova

PEACE ARCH

AL
MATARAL

Parco
Sempione

LA LIBERA

ACQUARIO
CIVICO

SAN MARCO/
VIA FAUCHE MARKETS

PALAZZO
PARIGI

TORRE
BRANCA

Largo
Paolo Grassi

VIA PONTACCIO

BRAIDENSE
NATIONAL LIBRARY

PARCO
SEMPIONE

BRERA PRESTIGE B&B

Lanza

ACADEMY OF
BELLE ARTI

THE
ASTRONOMICAL
MUSEUM

PALAZZO DELL'ARTE/
THE TRIENNALE/
DESIGN MUSEUM

CINQUANTADUE
MILANO

PINACOTECA
DI BRERA

BULGARI
HOTEL MILANO

CASTELLO
SFORZESCO

OFFICINA PROFUMO-
FARMACEUTICA DI
SANTA MARIA NOVELLA

HONG KONG
CROSSOVER

BRERA

CAVALLI E NASTRI

Piazza
Castello

RISTORANTE
EMILIA E CARLO

VIA DELL'ORSO

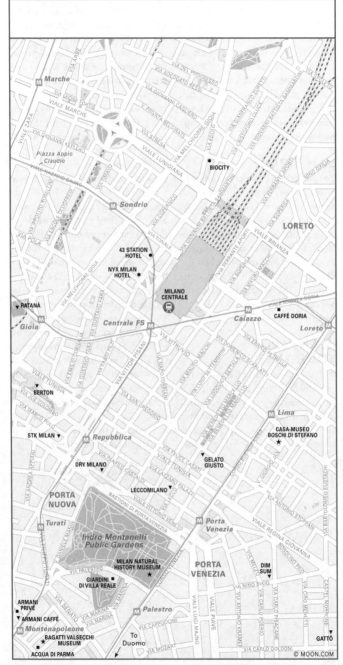

tracks, and is like an urbanized island within the city itself. Unlike Porta Nuova and its skyscrapers, Isola maintains a local, homey feel with its long-standing neighborhood bars, shops, and restaurants. It is one of the most densely populated areas of the city, with an estimated 20,000 local residents—as such, local and community pride run deep here.

SAN SIRO

The San Siro area is not considered a major touristy spot (it is largely residential and located outside of the city center), but if you're a football (that is, soccer) fan wanting to catch a professional A.C. Milan or Inter match, San Siro is ranked one of the best stadiums in Europe. San Siro sits quite west from the historic center, but can be reached via metro: Take Line M5 (purple) to San Siro.

PLANNING YOUR TIME

By European standards, Milan is not considered a large city. While it is Italy's second largest in terms of population density, it doesn't even make the top 10 largest cities in terms of square kilometers. The city's various modes of public transportation are frequent and reliable and serve nearly every street of the city center. Compared to neighborhoods in larger cities such as Paris, London, or Rome, Milan's districts are quite small, making this a walkable city and easily navigable by bus, tram, or metro. In the city center, you rarely need to walk more than 10 minutes before running into a metro, bus, or tram stop.

While you can see several of Milan's top sights and attractions in a day or two, to fully appreciate the city's cultural complexity and unique personality, you'll need at least three days. Plan to explore not only the Duomo district, but the other districts as well. Milan's small, closely situated neighborhoods allow you to make anywhere in the Duomo, Brera, Porta Nuova, or Castello districts your home base. Most major sights are concentrated in these areas, and all are well served by public transportation. In the city center, you'll find plenty of dining and accommodation options that meet the needs of most budgets. For tons of restaurants and bars at your doorstep, stick to Porta Nuova, Porta Ticinese, or Navigli. If you want a more local feel, stick to Navigli or Brera.

Itinerary Ideas

With three days in Milan, you can see a number of the city's top sights, indulge in world-class shopping, and experience the local art scene. With less time, you can stick to one theme or mix and match to get a little bit of everything.

MILAN ON DAY 1

If you're spending just one day in Milan, it's best to focus on the Duomo district to get a little taste of the city's sights and culture.

1 To fuel up for a day of sightseeing, grab a cappuccino or espresso and a pastry at the historic **Armani Caffè,** located directly outside the Montenapoleone metro stop.

2 From there, stroll along **Via Montenapoleone,** Milan's iconic narrow street lined with the flagship stores of Italy's most popular and exclusive brands as well as boutiques of famous Italian designers and shoemakers. Even if you only plan to window shop, stop into a store simply to take in the experience.

3 Once you've reached the end of Via Montenapoleone, you'll find yourself in **Piazza San Babila.** Peek into the small but beloved Church of San Babila for a bit of quiet reflection before heading southwest toward the busier Piazza del Duomo.

4 Upon entering **Piazza del Duomo,** you'll find yourself in the very heart of Milan. Head up to the roof of the **Duomo** for an unparalleled view of the city.

5 Enjoy a late lunch at **A Santa Lucia,** when the crowds have died down a little.

6 Head northeast on Via Orefici or Piazza dei Mercanti toward **Castello Sforzesco.** Inside the castle, you'll find some of Milan's most important pieces of art. Visit the Museum of Rondanini Pietà to see Michelangelo's last sculpture.

7 Then, wander behind the castle to Milan's most beloved park, **Parco Sempione.** Buy a gelato from one of the kiosks and find a shaded bench on which to sit and enjoy some people-watching.

8 Take a leisurely stroll through the park and exit out the **Arco della Pace** back into the bustle of the city. Head to **Deseo** for one of the more robust *aperitivos* in the city, a true Milanese experience.

Milan Itinerary Ideas

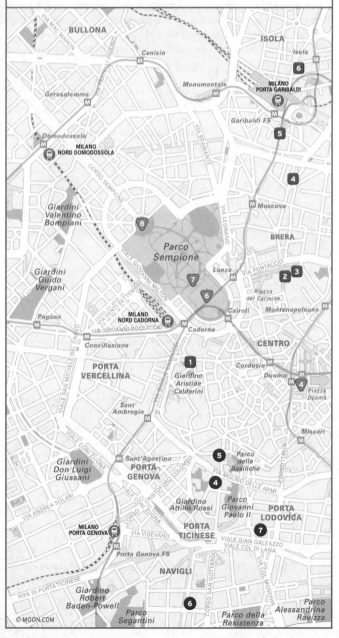

MILAN DAY ONE	MILAN DAY TWO	LIKE A LOCAL
1 Armani Caffè	1 Corso Buenos Aires	1 Verdi's
2 Via Montenapoleone	2 Gattò	2 Brera Picture Gallery
3 Piazza San Babila	3 Corso di Porta Ticinese	3 Braidense National Library
4 Piazza del Duomo	4 Verso	4 Pisacco
5 A Santa Lucia	5 Frip	5 10 Corso Como
6 Castello Sforzesco	6 Maya Bar	6 Isola District
7 Parco Sempione	7 El Porteno	7 Ratanà
8 Arco della Pace		

MILAN ON DAY 2

For your second day in Milan, focus on one of the city's top experiences: shopping.

1 Head straight to **Corso Buenos Aires,** the longest shopping street in Europe. Its more than 300 stores include budget-friendly shops, luxurious boutiques, and everything in between—there's a little something for everyone.

2 Spend the morning strolling in and out of shops, then fuel up at **Gattò** on a lunch of southern Italian food with a Milanese twist.

3 After lunch, head to **Corso di Porta Ticinese** (from Corso Buenos Aires, take metro Line M1 [red] to the Duomo, then take tram 3 south to the Colonne di San Lorenzo), one of the most vibrant and eclectic streets in the city. Along this street, you'll find a mix of vintage and thrift shops, local boutiques, and more.

4 Pop into **Verso** to grab an afternoon espresso and browse through their selection of indie books.

5 Looking for new statement piece to add to your closet? Look no further than **Frip,** an edgy clothing and accessory store frequented by locals.

6 Settle in for *aperitivo* hour at **Maya Bar.** Enjoy your cocktail and finger foods and watch the Navigli district come alive starting around 6pm. This is the place to be for a taste of Milan's heady nightlife.

7 If you haven't filled up on *aperitivo* food, find your way to **El Porteno** for an international flair.

MILAN LIKE A LOCAL

For a taste of authentic Milan, visit the Brera district. Locals will tell you this is the heart of the city's design and fashion culture, with shops, galleries, concept stores, and some of the best nightlife in the city. Brera caters to a range of artistic sensibilities, from quaint artisan shows featuring modern designs to historic art galleries.

1 Grab breakfast at **Verdi's** near the Cadorna metro station for organic pastries and coffee, then take the metro Line M2 (green) to Lanza.

2 Start your morning at the **Pinacoteca di Brera,** the city's most famous Italian picture gallery with works from the 13th through 20th centuries, including those from Raphael and Andrea Mantegna.

3 In the same building, stroll through Milan's most endearing library, the **Biblioteca di Brera.** The library houses more than 895,000 books, as well as a reading room filled with poetry manuscripts from renowned Italian poets.

4 For lunch, grab a bite to eat at **Pisacco,** one of the hottest spots in the city. Its modern ambiance and contemporary Italian food, with untraditional dishes like pasta with black pepper and bay powder, are hard to beat.

5 Once sated, head to **10 Corso Como** for a full design-oriented experience that's only possible in Milan. Wander through the art gallery and bookstore, and have a drink in the garden with locals.

6 After your drink, walk over to the **Isola district** and spend the late afternoon admiring the signature street art adorning its buildings and garage doors.

7 Dine at **Ratanà** for dinner, a renowned Milanese restaurant popular for its tasty dishes, such as the classic veal chop with tuna sauce, made exclusively with high-quality local ingredients. Make sure to book a table in advance.

Sights

Most of Milan's best sights are concentrated in the city center and a few of its surrounding districts. It offers a diverse range of things to see from a wide span of time periods—perhaps more than any other Italian city and arguably as much as other famous cities in Europe.

For historic churches and unparalleled architecture, stick to the city center, where you can find the landmark Duomo di Milano. Here you'll also find a mix of modern museums and luxury shopping experiences. For local gems beloved by the Milanese people, head to the Brera district. For contemporary high-rise skyscrapers and lively piazzas, try Porta Nuova.

While the La Scala, the Galleria, and *The Last Supper* are definitely not to be missed, many of the city's most interesting places to see are not as widely mentioned, and sights such as the Pinacoteca di Brera or the canals of Navigli might just be a couple of Italy's best kept secrets.

CITY CENTER AND DUOMO DISTRICT

TOP EXPERIENCE

✪ DUOMO DI MILANO

Piazza del Duomo; 02/7202-3375; www. duomomilano.it; cathedral 8am-7pm daily, adults €3; rooftop terraces 9am-7pm daily, adults €9 on foot, €13 by elevator, children and students €4.50 on foot, €7 by elevator; Metro M1, M3: Duomo ◆

The Duomo di Milano, built in the Gothic style, is Italy's largest church (some mistakenly believe that title goes to St. Peter's Basilica, which is commonly thought to be in Rome,

the front of the Duomo cathedral

but is actually in the State of Vatican City, a separate country) and the third largest in the world. The Duomo, constructed over a period of nearly six centuries, is the pride and joy of Milan, and its dominating presence seems to breathe life into the rest of the city. Its five broad naves and 40 pillars can be viewed for a fee from the roof, but its grand external and internal architecture can be appreciated for free from the ground. The Duomo is intricately designed and delicately detailed, with several statues and pillars complementing the subtle shades of gray, white, pink, and orange marble. The inside of the church is not so well-lit, but visitors can still see plenty of statues of archbishops and saints, including the notable statue of Saint Bartholomew, with his skin draped over his body. If you plan to visit during Milan's hot summers, you might be tempted to dress as comfortably as possible. However, be prepared not to be granted entrance if your shoulders and knees are exposed.

As the Duomo is the seat of the Archbishop of Milan, Catholic mass services take place multiple times every day; however, visitors can freely access specific areas, such as the pews in the main area of the cathedral, for personal worship. Although several areas of the church can be seen without purchasing a ticket, you will still find a lengthy line of people waiting to get in, especially during high season; expect to see security guards managing the flow and entrance of guests. If you want to see the special parts of the Duomo that require a fee (such as the main part of the cathedral or the visitor's area), or you know you definitely want to experience the rooftop, purchase tickets online in advance to avoid the queues. Combination passes for the cathedral and rooftop are available.

On the roof, follow the marked paths and stairways to view Milan's skyline from all angles, and to experience the Piazza del Duomo from a bird's eye view. While it's cheaper to reach the roof by climbing the 250 steps than by taking the elevator, take the lift if you want a more relaxing experience.

Guided English tours that offer an in-depth history of the cathedral and its importance are available for booking. Tours also include a trip through the **Duomo museum**, which includes tons of information about the building's structure and timeline and is also open for self-guided visits (10am-6pm Thurs.-Tues.).

MUSEUM OF THE 20TH CENTURY (Museo del Novecento)

Piazza del Duomo, 8; 02/8844-4061; www. museodelnovecento.org; 9:30am-7:30pm Tues.-Sun., until 10:30pm Thurs. and Sat., 2:30pm-7:30pm Mon.; adults €10, over 65 €8, ages 12-25 €5, under 12 free; Metro M1, M3: Duomo

Milan's Museo del Novecento is a museum in the Palazzo dell'Arengario that overlooks the Duomo in Piazza del Duomo. The roughly 400 works of 20th-century art on display at the museum are mostly by Italian artists, although some are by such non-Italian greats as Picasso, Andy Warhol, and Roy Lichtenstein.

The largest section of the museum is dedicated to Italian futurism, but smaller sections are dedicated to other movements and themes, including abstractionism, Italy in the 20th century, post-impressionism, landscape, and realism. Due to the plethora of attractions in Milan's city center, this museum is often overlooked, so it's a great place to escape the crowds and noise for a few hours. If you're an art buff, consider this place a must-see, as you won't find a greater and more diverse modern art collection anywhere else in Italy. After browsing the collection, head to the top floor for a drink at the museum's bar, **Giacomo all'Arengario**, to enjoy an unparalleled view of the Piazza del Duomo. Bar access is granted with the price of admission and only available to museum visitors, so grab a spritz and enjoy the bustling square below.

✪ GALLERIA VITTORIO EMANUELE II

Piazza del Duomo; www.turismo.milano. it; open 24 hours daily; free; Metro M1, M3: Duomo

The Galleria Vittorio Emanuele II, often called Il Salotto di Milano (Milan's Drawing Room) by locals, is the world's oldest active shopping mall. Sitting right next to the Duomo cathedral in Piazza del Duomo since its completion in 1877, the landmark is named after Victor Emmanuel II, the first king of the Kingdom of Italy.

The four-story structure consists of two glass-vaulted arcades that meet to form an octagon. It houses some of the city's best shopping and dining options, including luxury and

The Galleria is always busy with shoppers

La Scala opera house

designer stores, restaurants and bars, and a five-star hotel with a world-class skywalk. It's currently home to two Michelin-star chefs (Carlo Cracco at Cracco and Felix Lo Basso at Felix Lo Basso Restaurant) and boasts one of the most famous *aperitivo* spots in the city, **Camparino in Galleria.**

The mall structure is open 24 hours daily, but shops and restaurants within the Galleria have various opening and closing times. The place is almost always buzzing with activity, and people shuffling around the ground floor staring up at the glass ceiling. You'll find mostly tourists here, as most locals tend to shop in Montenapoleone or other areas of the city.

To get the best Galleria experience, take the escalators to explore its different levels. You'll find the higher floors are quieter and less hectic. Beyond the ground floor, you'll also discover some of the mall's hidden gems; if you're a book lover, check out **Bocca.** If you love elegant handmade gloves, check out **Piumelli.**

✪ LA SCALA

Via Filodrammatici 2; 02/88-791; www. teatroallascala.org; box office 10am-6pm Mon.-Sat., 12pm-6pm Sun.; Metro M1, M3: Duomo

Italy's most famous opera house, La Scala (Teatro alla Scala), sits just behind the Galleria and is a stone's throw away from Piazza del Duomo. The theater is also home to **La Scala Theater Ballet, Theater Chorus,** and **Theater Orchestra.** Many of the world's most iconic opera singers have performed at La Scala since its opening in 1778. It is internationally considered one of the leading opera and ballet theaters in the world.

The opera season opens every year on December 7, a public holiday honoring Milan's patron saint, Sant'Ambrogio (St. Ambrose). After a major three-year, €61 million renovation that was completed in 2004, every seat in the opera house now includes a monitor with an electronic libretto system so audiences can follow the opera libretti in both Italian and

English as well as in the original language of the performance.

Travelers can opt to skip a performance and spend time exploring the opera house and its museum (Museo Teatrale alla Scala, 9am-5:30pm daily, €9) instead. Museum exhibits focus on La Scala's history and international importance, and tickets can be purchased directly at the front door. Guided English tours of the theater and museum are also available upon reservation, included in the price of admission.

✪ VIA MONTENAPOLEONE

Via Montenapoleone; www.
viamontenapoleone.org; Metro M3:
Montenapoleone, M1: San Babila

Other than the Galleria, Via Monte Napoleone (Montenapoleone), just a short walk away from Piazza del Duomo, is one of the most well-known places for upscale and luxury shopping in Milan's city center. In 2018, Italian media reported this to be Europe's "most expensive street," and Italians regard it as the most important and iconic street in Milan's fashion district.

Via Montenapoleone

Even if you have no plans to fill your luggage with designer labels during your trip to Milan, consider taking a stroll down Via Montenapoleone for the window-shopping experience alone—it is worth a small chunk of your time. You'll see some of the world's most lavish brands on display: Gucci, Prada, Armani, Dolce & Gabbana, and Fendi. Begin at the Montenapoleone metro station and head southeast toward Piazza San Babila, or viceversa, to wander the street's full length.

While Via Montenapoleone's upscale and extravagant character may appear to invite only patrons of the same ilk, all are welcome, and no one is turned away. Store employees are friendly and inviting and encourage passersby into the shops for inside scoops on what's trending—everyone is a potential sale, so rest assured, they will try their best to ensure you don't leave empty-handed.

BAGATTI VALSECCHI MUSEUM

Via Gesù, 5; 02/7600-6132; https://
museobagattivalsecchi.org; 1pm-5:45pm
Tues.-Sun.; adults €9, students and seniors
€6, children 6-18 €2, children under 6 and
caretakers of disabled visitors free; Metro
M3: Montenapoleone, M1: San Babila; Tram
1: Via Manzoni

Just off of Via Montenapoleone is this family home turned museum with its impressive collection of Italian Renaissance furniture and paintings. Two brothers (Barons Fausto and Giuseppe Bagatti Valsecchi) spent the latter years of the 19th century refurbishing the family mansion and filling it with what is now considered one of the more extraordinary, privately owned design collections in the city.

The heirs of the brothers moved out of the mansion in 1974, and the family opened the private home to the public as a museum in 1994. Walking through this home, one of the first true treasure troves of Milanese design and modernism, you'll come across original paintings from Donatello's students, grand libraries, lavish bedrooms, displays of highly expensive and world-class arms, globes, iron and bronze household items, clothes, jewelry, ceramics, and much more.

Considering that the opening hours of the museum are far shorter than other museums in the city, there is not one single best time of day to go, but you may find less of a crowd during weekday afternoons. Guided tours, for a price of €8, are available in English, Italian, French, and German. Free-of-charge self-guided audio tours are available in English, Italian, French, German, Japanese, Chinese, and Russian, and a smartphone app (for iOS and Android devices) was recently launched for visitors wanting a virtual tour of the mansion.

BASILICA OF SAN BABILA

Corso Monforte, 1; 02/7600-2877; www.santiprofeti.it/basilica-di-san-babila; 8am-12pm, 3:30pm-7pm Mon.-Sat., 4pm-7pm Sun.; free; Metro M1: San Babila

The Basilica of San Babila seems tiny sitting in the shadow of the Duomo, which is just a few hundred meters away, but it is one of the most beloved Catholic churches of the Milanese people. While the original construction of the church is debated, the current construction began in the late 1800s into the early 1900s. Considering that the church is smaller and locally revered, there are no tickets, tours, or admission prices. Simply step inside to enjoy a piece of local culture and a few minutes of quiet from the busy city streets.

The square in which the basilica sits, **Piazza San Babila,** is named after the church itself and has been a historically popular meeting place for the local upper class and many political groups over the past several decades. In the 1970s it was called the *trincea nera* (black trench) of Milan, referring to followers of the Milanese neo-fascism movement during this same time. The square is also the site of the first official skyscraper constructed in the city, the **Snia Viscosa Tower.**

UNIVERSITÀ CATTOLICA DEL SACRO CUORE AND BASILICA DI SANT'AMBROGIO

Piazza Sant'Ambrogio, 15; www.basilicasantambrogio.it; free; Metro M1, M2: Cadorna, M2: Sant'Ambrogio; Bus 94: Sant'Ambrogio

The Basilica di Sant'Ambrogio, named after Milan's patron saint, St. Ambrose, is one of Milan's oldest churches. Its construction was completed in 386 CE and is one of four that St. Ambrose built around the same time as symbols of anti-Arianism, wealth, and power of the pro-Nicene time period in Milan. The site on which the basilica is built is the same site where many martyrs were killed during the Roman Empire.

The current structure was completed in the Romanesque style in the 12th century after centuries of multiple reconstructions. Between the two world wars, Milan's Università Cattolica del Sacro Cuore, locally known as Cattolica, was built around the basilica and expanded throughout the 20th century. Bombings from the Allied forces during World War II heavily damaged the university and

Milan's castle in the heart of the city

the church, but both were completely rebuilt.

Strolling through the basilica and the public courtyards of the university—where you'll see various monuments, grassy courtyards, quiet classrooms, and churches—takes an hour or so. Both are reachable from the Sant'Ambrogio or Cadorna metro stops or from the 94 bus line.

CASTELLO AND SEMPIONE

✪ CASTELLO SFORZESCO

Piazza Castello; www.milanocastello. it; castle: 7am-7:30pm daily, museums: 9am-5:30pm Tues.-Sun.; castle and museums: adults €10, over 65 €8, under 18 free; Metro M1, M2: Cadorna, M1: Cairoli

Castello Sforzesco was built by Francesco Sforza, the fourth Duke of Milan and the founder of the famous Milanese Sforza dynasty. It was first constructed in the 15th century but has since undergone extensive transformations. The castle comprises a number of walls and moats

for defense, towers, courtyards, and the famous Sforza rooms. The building's most recognizable feature is the **Filarete tower,** which has become a symbol of the castle due to its unique architecture and prominent position at the front of the structure.

Despites its size, the castle is a quiet presence in the city center. It faces the Piazza del Duomo just a few blocks away and is often overshadowed by the more globally recognized Duomo and Galleria. The castle square, with its thick brick-and-mortar walls, creates a serene, verdant internal courtyard—an ever-present reminder of historical Milan amidst a backdrop of modernity.

Within the castle are several civic museums and collections, including Pinacoteca del Castello Sforzesco art gallery, the Museum of Ancient Art, the Museum of Musical Instruments, the Archaeological Museum of Milan, the Antique Furniture & Wooden Sculpture Museum, the Egyptian Museum, the Achille Bertarelli

Print Collection, the Applied Arts Collection, the Museum of Rondanini Pietà, and the Trivulziana Library. Each museum is fairly small, consisting of just one or a few rooms, but you'll need at least an afternoon in order to see all of them.

Don't miss seeing the Museum of Rondanini Pietà, named after Michelangelo's famous last sculpture. After much debate about whether to move the sculpture from its original location, the technically unfinished *Rondanini Pietà* finally found its permanent residence in the Arms Courtyard of the castle. Another can't-miss stop at the castle is the Trivulziana Library, which houses Leonardo da Vinci's Codex *Trivulzianus*, a 55-page manuscript he wrote in the effort to improve his literary education.

Paid entrance into the castle also grants you entrance into each museum and collection within the castle, but you can enter the castle and the museums for free every Tuesday after 2pm, for the last hour before closing on Wednesday through Sundays, and all day on the first Sunday of every month.

✪ PARCO SEMPIONE

Piazza Sempione; www.turismo.milano. it; 6:30am-11:30pm daily June-Sept., 6:30am-10pm daily May, 6:30am-9pm daily Oct.-Apr.; free; Metro M1, M2: Cadorna, M1: Cairoli

Sitting between Castello Sforzesco and the Arco della Pace is Parco Sempione, the city's largest park. The park takes up 95 acres of the city's historic center and was originally designed to offer panoramic views between the castle and the arch. Named after Corso Sempione, the English-style park is webbed with leisurely strolls around ponds, sculptures, holly trees, play areas for children, and a handful of food and beverage kiosks.

Palazzo dell'Arte and the Triennale Design Museum

Viale Emilio Alemagna, 6; 02/724-341, www. triennale.org; 10:30am-8:30pm Tues.-Sun.; adults €9, under 14 €3, under 6 free; Metro M1, M2: Cadorna, M1: Cairoli

Located approximately halfway between the castle and the arch on the westward side of the park is the Palazzo dell'Arte, headquarters of the famous Triennale Design Museum. The building was originally constructed in 1935 to showcase international exhibitions of modern design, industrial arts, and architecture. The museum itself, the first in Italy to focus exclusively on design, was founded in 2007 by the Triennale organization; it has since become a globally recognized museum on modern design.

The museum features numerous permanent and temporary installations on architecture, visual arts, audio and video production, and design and fashion, as well as a few interactive exhibits. It also includes a trendy café, Terrazza Triennale (www. osteriaconvista.it; 12pm-1am Tues.-Sun., 6pm-1am Mon.), that serves pizza and bar food in an eclectic, relaxed atmosphere. At the café, you can enjoy traditional Italian dishes with a twist whipped up by a Michelin-star chef on the restaurant's terrace or a quiet, intimate *aperitivo* in the garden. You can eat at the restaurant without visiting the museum, as well.

Arch of Peace (Arco della Pace)

Piazza Sempione; www.turismo.milano.it; free; Metro M5: Domodossola; Tram 1: Arco della Pace

Arco della Pace

Standing as the gate between Corso Sempione and Parco Sempione is the Arco della Pace, one of the most significant neoclassical monuments in the city. Constructed by architect Luigi Cagnola at the request of the city government and Napoleon in the early 1800s, the arch took 30 years to complete. This triumphal marble arch, standing tall with horse-drawn chariots at its crest, was built as a celebration of peace; instead it ended up bearing witness to the victory and losses of war. After being defeated in a Milanese rebellion in 1848, Austrian marshal Josef Radetzky and his army escaped through this gate. After winning the Battle of Magenta in 1859, Napoleon III and Victor Emmanuel II of Italy proudly passed through it. Since the monument is not within the park itself, it can be visited at any time for free.

Branca Tower (Torre Branca)

Viale Luigi Camoens, 2; http://museobranca. it/torre-branca-2; 10:30am-12am Tues.-Thurs., Sat.-Sun., 12pm-12am Fri.; €4; Metro M1: Cadorna; Trams 1, 19: Via Venti Settembre

Built in 1933 during the fascist period in Milan, the panoramic Torre Branca was originally named Torre Littoria, then later renamed Torre del Parco after World War II. It was renamed once again after its 2002 reconstruction by the Branca liquor company. Since 2002, the tower has been open to the public. Visitors can ride the elevator to the top for a pleasant view of the Milanese skyline, the Alps, and a portion of the Po Valley. A visit to the top, which includes stops to the observation deck and back down again, takes approximately seven minutes. The tower is closed to visitors on days of bad weather. Although the views aren't as impressive as what you'll see from the rooftop of the Duomo, a trip up to the tower offers a nice alternative if you want to skip the lines and beat the crowds.

Civic Aquarium (Acquario Civico)

Viale Gadio, 2; www.acquariocivicomilano. eu/cms; 9am-5:30pm Tues.-Sun.; €5; Metro M2: Lanza

Milan's Acquario Civico, which opened in 1906, is one of the oldest of its kind in the world. Follow the paths that take you along a mountain stream into the sea. You'll encounter a handful of marine-themed statues, as well as one of the country's most impressive collection of marine biology publications. Although small, marine lovers will enjoy this local aquarium's unique approach. Free access is granted every day from 4:30pm, every Tuesday from 2pm, and all day on the first Sunday of every month. Due to the architecture of the building, the terrace of the aquarium is not wheelchair accessible.

TOP EXPERIENCE

✪ THE LAST SUPPER

Piazza Santa Maria delle Grazie, 2; 02/9280-0360; www.turismo.milano.it; 8:15am-7pm Tues.-Sun.; adults €10, 18 and under free; Metro M1, M2: Cadorna

the famous *Last Supper* painting

Leonardo da Vinci's 15th-century mural, *The Last Supper,* is one of Milan's most prized possessions. It depicts a scene from the Gospel of John, where Jesus is sitting down to supper with his Twelve Disciples and telling them that one would soon betray him. The mural is on display at **Santa Maria delle Grazie church,** where it is highly protected.

Although a majority of the church was destroyed by Allied bombing during World War II, the painting, protected by heavy sandbags, survived. (Some have claimed that vibrations from the bombings may have caused slight damage.) In the effort to stabilize and maintain the painting's beauty, art conservators over time have worked to restore and preserve the piece, but some restorations may have detracted from the original work. While the room in which the mural is displayed is fairly small, quiet, and dark, the mural itself is nothing less

that astonishing, so put your camera away and spend your 15 minutes taking in every single color and detail, especially the still-vibrant colors of the clothes on Jesus and the disciples.

Booking is absolutely mandatory here, and tickets should be purchased well in advance. Due to the mural's fragility, visitors are only allowed into the viewing room 30 at a time for 15 minutes at a time. Entrance to see the painting is free on the first Sunday of every month, but booking is still required. Tickets can be purchased directly on Vivaticket's official website (https://vivaticket.it), or by calling the call center. (The call center is your best bet if trying to book tickets yourself.) In case tickets are already sold out from Vivaticket for the day you want to visit, don't fear—tour companies and ticket vendors, such as Tiqets or Viator, will sell tickets for a surcharge or in conjunction with city tours directly from their websites.

Although Milan does not suffer from as much overtourism as some other Italian cities, it does have its share of popular attractions. Here are some alternatives if you'd prefer to avoid the crowds and the waiting that are almost inevitable at the blockbuster sights.

- **Views:** The rooftop of the Duomo, though a singularly impressive experience, is almost always full of people. For a less crowded view of the city skyline and Alps, try **Branca Tower** (page 53).

- **Greenery in the city:** Most tourists go to Parco Sempione for open-air pursuits, but for a more local experience, go to **Indro Montanelli Public Gardens,** where you can walk along wide paths or enjoy some time on its benches, as the journalist for whom the park is named was said to do (page 59).

- **Historical church:** The Duomo is Milan's centerpiece, but two basilicas in what is known locally as Basilicas Park, **Basilica San Lorenzo Maggiore** and **Basilica of Sant'Eustorgio,** both trace their beginnings to the 4th century and make for a peaceful visit. The latter contains fragments of the bones of the Three Wise Men (page 55).

- **Hidden gem: Monumental Cemetery of Milan** is the resting place for many of Milan's elite, including poets, politicians, and actors. Though it is under the radar for many tourists, it is a beautiful and illuminating place (page 59).

TICINESE AND NAVIGLI

BASILICA SAN LORENZO MAGGIORE

*Corso di Porta Ticinese, 35; www.
sanlorenzomaggiore.com; 8am-6:30pm
Mon.-Sat., 9am-7pm Sun.; free; Bus 94:
Colonne Di S. Lorenzo*

Basilica San Lorenzo Maggiore is one of the city's oldest churches, first breaking ground in the year 364 and consecrated in 402. The church has undergone several renovations over

ancient Roman Columns of San Lorenzo and Basilica San Lorenzo Maggiore

the centuries, with the last completed in the 18th century. The church is next to Milan's Porta Ticinese and, along with Basilica of Sant'Eustorgio, makes up the city's **Basilicas Park.** Its most notable architectural features are the **Colonne di San Lorenzo** (Columns of San Lorenzo), Roman ruins that were moved to the front of the church in the 4th century. This church tends to fly under the radar, as it sits on the southern end of the city center and in the shadow of the Duomo. It is worth entering though, as it is a rather peaceful experience. Be mindful of the regular mass services that take place on Sundays and throughout the week.

BASILICA OF SANT'EUSTORGIO

*Piazza Sant'Eustorgio, 1; 02/5810-1583;
www.santeustorgio.it; 10am-6pm Tues.-Sun.;
€6; Tram 3: Piazza San Eustorgio*

At the southern cap of Milan's Basilicas Park is the Basilica of

Sant'Eustorgio, a church that broke ground in the 4th century and was an important stop for religious pilgrims on their way to Rome or the Holy Land. The church was said to be the home of the tomb of the Three Wise Men that brought gifts to Jesus upon his birth. Fragments of their bones still remain in the Three Kings altar, marked by a star instead of a cross. You'll find several altars and interesting pieces of art inside this tranquil, historic church. Although not free, the small price for entrance is worth it.

PORTA TICINESE AND CORSO DI PORTA TICINESE

Piazzale XIV Maggio; www.turismo.milano.it; Tram 3, 10: Ventiquattro Maggio

The former city gate of Porta Ticinese —first created by the city's Spanish walls in the 16th century and later rebuilt in the 19th century—dominates Milan's Piazza XXIV Maggio as well as the surrounding neighborhood resting between the Duomo and Navigli districts. Corso di Porta Ticinese, which stretches from the columns of Basilica San Lorenzo to Piazza XXIV Maggio, is one of the city's most eccentric and lively streets. It offers plenty of shopping options as well as a well-balanced mixed of culinary alternatives—from pizzerias to cafés and bars, from sushi, to Italian, and other international cuisines.

TOP EXPERIENCE

✪ NAVIGLI AND THE CANALS

Navigli district; www.turismo.milano.it; Metro M2: Porta Genova; Tram 9, 10: Via Vegevano Viale Gorizio

The Navigli district, which starts from the Marina Darsena next to Porta Ticinese and splits into two canals, is one of the most charming districts of Milan. The area is filled with colorful buildings replete with artisan workshops, local bars, boutiques, creative concept stores, and more. As one of the most popular neighborhoods for *aperitivo* and nightlife, the canals are filled with locals most evenings, especially on the weekends. The two canals, the Naviglio Grande and the Naviglio Pavese, are lined with enough restaurants, bars, galleries, and shops to fill an afternoon. Mercato Dei Navigli, the vintage antique market near Porta Genova that operates on the last Sunday of every month, is one of the largest and most frequented street markets in the city.

Navigli district tends to come to life as the day progresses, although you'll find plenty of locals wandering in and out of bars and cafés in the mornings or grabbing a tram to the office. Around mid-morning, as more shops and restaurants open their doors, you'll see the streets start to get a little more crowded and hear live music start drifting out from the bars. By the time you reach the normal *aperitivo* hour (5pm-7pm), Navigli will be bustling with chattering locals and

the Grand Canal of the Navigli district

tourists mingling on the canals with drinks in hand, making it one of the liveliest and most entertaining night districts in the city.

BRERA DISTRICT

NEW ACADEMY OF FINE ARTS
(Nuova Accademia di Belle Arti)

Via Brera, 28; 02/869-551; www. accademiadibrera.milano.it; Metro M2: Lanza; Bus 61: Piazza San Marco

Brera Academy

The Nuova Accademia di Belle Arti (NABA) is one of the gems of the Brera district. The internationally known art and design academy is also the largest of its kind in Italy and offers university programs in both Italian and English. Most programs are held in the historic and beautiful 12th-century Palazzo Brera. Since its opening in 1776, the academy has attracted artists from the romantic to the modern periods, with NABA officially forming in 1980. Roam the halls of the academy in the palazzo and stop into the Pinacoteca di Brera and the Biblioteca di Brera. Because it is an educational institution, the opening hours follow that of the school year, so there are no official hours of operation or admission fee, but it's worth a quick trip around the halls if you're already visiting the other sights in the building.

❂ Brera Picture Gallery (Pinacoteca di Brera) ✳

Via Brera, 28; 055/713-655; http:// pinacotecabrera.org; 8:30am-7:15pm Tues.-Sun.; adults €10, 18 and under free; Metro M2: Lanza; Bus 61: Piazza San Marco

The Pinacoteca di Brera is the most famous picture gallery in Milan and regarded as one of the most important in Europe. Housing one of the largest historic collections of Italian paintings, you can find several

world-renowned masterpieces, including Raphael's *The Marriage of the Virgin* and a few works by Andrea Mantegna. For travelers that appreciate art, especially European art, this gallery is a must-see. Audio guides in Italian, English, French, Spanish, and German are available for €5 per person. Step behind the picture gallery building and you will find the Brera Astronomical Observatory and the Brera Botanical Gardens, both of which are free to visit.

Braidense National Library (Biblioteca di Brera)

Via Brera, 28; www.braidense.it; 8:30am-6:15pm Mon.-Fri., 9am-1:45pm Sat.; free; Metro M2: Lanza; Bus 61: Piazza San Marco

The Biblioteca di Brera is one of the largest libraries in Italy, containing mostly historical, legal, and scientific collections. Founded in 1770 by Maria Theresa of Austria, the library has been housed in the Palazzo Brera since its beginning. An acting preservation site of historic literary works, it also maintains a collection of all books that have been published in Milan. The library is currently home to more than 895,000 books. Not to be missed here is the small, quiet manuscript reading room (which closes 15 minutes earlier than the library each

MILAN'S CITY GATES

Three different wall systems defended Milan over its history. **Roman walls** were constructed in the heart of the city during the Republican and Imperial eras but no longer remain. The second set of walls were built in the 12th century to defend against the many raids of Frederick I Barbarossa. Traces of these **medieval walls** still remain around Porta Nuova, Porta Ticinese, and Porta Romana.

The last wall system was built in the 16th century when Milan was under Spanish rule. Little of the original structure remains, but most walls have been restructured or rebuilt—consciously maintained as a way to preserve an important piece of Milan's history. These **Spanish walls** included **11 gates**—many of which are now the names of Milan's districts today: Porta Romana, Porta Vittoria, Porta Venezia, Porta Nuova, Porta Garibaldi, Porta Tenaglia, Porta Sempione, Porta Vercellina, Porta Ticinese, Porta Lodovica, and Porta Vigentina.

day) that includes the collections of Italian poet and novelist Alessandro Manzoni. Entry is free and worth it for literature and history lovers.

Brera Astronomical Observatory

Via Brera, 28; 02/7232-0300; www.brera. unimi.it/eng/museo; 10am-6pm Mon.-Fri. Apr.-Oct., 9:30am-4:30pm Mon.-Fri. Nov.-Mar.; free; Metro M3: Montenapoleone

The Brera Astronomical Observatory, built in 1764 by astronomer Ruggero Boscovich, is yet another sight to catch in the Palazzo Brera. It's most known for its ancient collection of scientific instruments, including the Schiaparelli Dome, from which the famous astronomer of the same name studied Mars via telescope. Entrance into the observatory is free, as are the English and Italian audio guides.

PORTA NUOVA
PIAZZA GAE AULENTI

Piazza Gae Aulenti; www.turismo.milano. it; open 24 hours daily; free; Metro M2, M5: Porta Garibaldi

Milan's most contemporary square, Piazza Gae Aulenti, is where you really see a modern Milan on display. Just 100 meters (328 feet) in diameter and 6 meters (19 feet) above street level, the square is home to the Unicredit Tower (Torre UniCredit), Italy's tallest skyscraper. When the weather is warm and sunny, take a walk through the three large jumping fountains in the center of the square, where you'll find several locals and children doing the same thing on hot summer days. Alternatively, stop into the several bars and stores, such as Pandora jewelry store. The easily accessible piazza is directly next to the Porta Garibaldi railway and metro station. Below the square is an extensive food court that caters to a diverse palate, as well as an outpost of the Esselunga supermarket.

CORSO COMO

Corso Como; Metro M2, M5: Porta Garibaldi

Corso Como is one of Milan's most treasured streets for shopping and *aperitivo* hour. The street runs from the Porta Garibaldi Gate in Piazza XXV Aprile, north toward the Porta Garibaldi railway station, and straight into Piazza Gae Aulenti. Along the way, you'll find some of the trendiest boutiques and bars in the city. If you're looking for a typical Milanese evening, try barhopping here, starting with an *aperitivo* and staying out into the early morning hours.

10 Corso Como

10 Corso Como; 02/2900-2674; www.10corsocomo.com; 10:30am-7:30pm daily, until 9pm Wed. and Thurs.; Metro M2, M5: Porta Garibaldi

A must-stop place along Corso Como is this shopping and dining complex that combines art, fashion, food, design, and culture. Here, you can leisurely peruse an art gallery or bookstore, shop for clothes or design items, and grab a drink in the garden afterward. The complex is more than 25 years old, and locals will tell you that it keeps getting better with age. Founded by former Italian *Vogue* editor Carla Sozzani, 10 Corso Como is at once comfortable and cozy, yet chic and fashionable. Stay for a while to sip on an espresso and nibble on a plate of intricately decorated cookies. If you visit on a late afternoon, head up to the rooftop terrace for a cocktail.

MONUMENTAL CEMETERY OF MILAN
(Piazzale Cimitero Monumentale)

Piazzale Cimitero Monumentale; www. turismo.milano.it; Metro M5: Monumentale

Piazzale Cimitero Monumentale (Monumental Cemetery of Milan)

Monumentale, Milan's "open air museum" cemetery

is the city's second-largest cemetery; its numerous extravagant tombs and mausoleums liken it to an open-air museum. Many Italian politicians, actors, novelists, athletes, poets, and musicians are buried here.

Planning of Monumentale began in 1864 and was intended to consolidate a series of smaller cemeteries that were dispersed throughout the city; it officially opened in 1866. A church was originally planned for where the Famedio now stands at the main entrance, with the actual cemetery behind it. However, the church was never built and was instead turned into the main memorial for the Milanese elite buried there. Monumentale is definitely one of Milan's hidden gems, and locals can attest to the its spaciousness and beauty. Be sure to dedicate at least an hour to this place—it will give you a sense of how Italians memorialize their loved ones.

PORTA VENEZIA

INDRO MONTANELLI PUBLIC GARDENS
(Giardini Pubblici Indro Montanelli)

Bastioni di Porta Venezia; www.comune. milano.it; 6:30am-11:30pm daily; free; Metro M3: Turati, M1: Palestro

The Giardini Pubblici Indro Montanelli (formerly Gardens of Porta Venezia) is one of Milan's top public parks and was named after the famous Italian journalist Indro Montanelli, who spent much of his time on the park's benches writing. It hosts the city's planetarium (Civico Planetario Ulrico Hoepli) and the Milan Natural History Museum (Museo Civico di Storia Naturale di Milano). On nice days, visitors can amble along the wide paths to delight in the fountains, geometric flower beds, and butterfly oasis; younger travelers can enjoy the play area. You'll find an overwhelming amount of greenery here. If you want a truly local park experience, this may be your best bet since most tourists opt for the larger and more central Parco Sempione.

Milan Natural History Museum (Museo Civico di Storia Naturale di Milano)

Corso Venezia, 55; www.comune.milano.it; 9am-5:30pm Tues.-Sun.; €5, free on Friday afternoons

Not only is Milan's Natural History Museum (Museo Civico di Storia Naturale di Milano) the city's oldest museum, it's also the only museum in Italy with a real dinosaur skeleton on display. Also on display are several diverse collections: botanical, mineral, zoological, fossils, and more. There is really nothing else similar to this museum in the city, so for history buffs, consider this your place to go. The museum is also quite interactive for children, with plenty of hands-on and colorful exhibits.

CASA-MUSEO BOSCHI DI STEFANO

Via Giorgio Jan, 15; www. fondazioneboschidistefano.it; 10am-6pm Tues.-Sun.; free; Metro M1: Lima

This house turned museum opened to the public in 2003, after Antonio Boschi, who died in 1988, wrote in his will that he wanted his house and art collection to be shared with the Milanese people. Construction of the historic building Via Giorgio Jan, in which the house is located, finished in 1931. Throughout their marriage, Boschi and his wife Marieda Di Stefano collected more than 2,000 pieces of art. After the collection was donated to the city, a specific selection of nearly 300 works was chosen for display in the museum; most works date from the early 20th century through the 1960s. Casa-Museo Boschi di Stefano is yet another one of Milan's hidden treasures. It gives visitors a true insider's perspective of the depth of the city's design roots. Those particularly interested in interior design and the history of design shouldn't miss an opportunity to view this beloved Milanese home.

CHINATOWN
VIA PAOLO SARPI

Via Paolo Sarpi; Trams 12, 14: Via Bramante Via Sarpi

Via Paolo Sarpi, a cobblestone street that runs approximately one kilometer long (0.6 miles), is the backbone of Milan's Chinatown. This narrow pedestrian street is lined with more than 150 silk and leather shops, small boutiques, hair salons, travel agencies, and more.

The Chinatown district in Milan first came to life in the 1920s, when a group from China's Zhejiang region first migrated to the city to work in the silk industry. Chinese immigrants to Milan, specifically to this neighborhood, began growing exponentially in 1980 following a lax in Deng Xiaoping's regime that opened up migration opportunities.

Today, Milan's Chinatown is also the headquarters of Italian-Chinese companies, including the editorial desk of the *Europe China Daily* newspaper. Since the early 1980s, this neighborhood has become Shanghai's twin city—the first pair of twin cities between Italy and China. (Others include Guangzhou with Bari, Florence with Nanjing, and Rome with Beijing.)

Chinatown is known for selling authentic ethnic products and other

A historically residential area, Isola boasts some of the most creative street art in the city—one of its most notable characteristics. Fostering its strong sense of local pride, this soulful artwork can be found on old concrete walls and on the garage shutters of closed shops in the area.

Several street artists have made Isola a home for their signature pieces. One of the most popular artists is **Zibe,** who often creates works depicting Arnold, his friend who committed suicide nearly 20 years ago. You'll see Arnold's face pop up throughout the city, but the biggest Arnold portrait is on the wall just next to **Frida** (Via Antonio Pollaiuolo, 3; 02/680-260; www.fridaisola.it), a local Isola bar. The **underground tunnel** connecting Isola to the Porta Garibaldi station is covered in wall paintings commissioned by a local art school, giving you a sense of the area's vibe.

The district also displays collaborative works that have been financed by local businesses. While other European cities have turned their street art into an interesting tourist draw, Milan's street artists still work almost exclusively in secret, as public opinion is still slow to deem it as worthy as the other historic art in the city.

international items that may not be offered in other areas of the city. While you can find Italian cuisine here, skip it for some of the city's best East Asian dishes, such as ramen, street food (including dumplings and Chinese crepes), and bubble tea. Unlike many other Chinatowns throughout the world, Milan's Chinatown is neither bustling nor crowded. Although the street itself remains rather tranquil and calm, it is never empty.

ISOLA

The Isola district has always been known as a working-class neighborhood populated by factory workers, but the redesign and modernization of neighboring Porta Nuova resulted in the gentrification and renovation of the once very isolated Isola. A walk around the neighborhood still shows evidence of its true artisan and avant-garde roots, with plenty of street art to admire and creative stores to browse. Mingling among remains of old Isola are new office buildings, high-quality art-related businesses, and art deco apartment buildings that have popped up over the past few decades as a result of the rejuvenation of surrounding districts.

SANTA MARIA ALLA FONTANA CHURCH

Piazza Santa Maria alla Fontana 11; www. turismo.milano.it; 11am-3pm and 6pm-12am daily; free; Metro M3, M5: Zara

The Santa Maria alla Fontana Church is considered the most historic and eminent landmark in the Isola district and is often overlooked by tourists. The church was designed by famous Italian Renaissance architect Giovanni Antonio Amadeo during his final years and built in 1507 under the commission of the city's French governor Charles II d'Ambroise. Some of the city's most intricate and distinctive frescos are found in this sanctuary. Themes of healing characterize the chapel art because d'Ambroise claimed to have been healed by a spring on the site where the church was built. During your walk through the sanctuary, be sure to head to the back to admire the marble-framed *Madonna col Bambino (Madonna and Child)* oil painting.

Recreation

As with most cities of Milan's size, visitors arrive with the impression that they're in for a lot of cobblestone and concrete. While that isn't far from the truth, Milan actually boasts more than 80 public gardens and parks, all located within the city center and just outside the city limits. You'll also find several ways to burn some calories while sightseeing—consider exploring the city via a running or biking tour. Milan's bike-sharing system is one of the most widely used and efficient in Europe, and allows you to rent bikes for hours at a time.

PARKS

While Parco Sempione has been and always will be the principal public park in Milan, you'll find several green havens sprinkled throughout the city. Locals flock to these parks on sunny days, pushing strollers on the dirt or concrete paths and letting their children or grandchildren enjoy some time on the playgrounds after school. Italians are a very physically active population, so you'll also find plenty of local runners and cyclists taking advantage of these spaces.

Indro Montanelli Public Gardens (Giardini Pubblici Indro Montanelli)

Bastioni di Porta Venezia; www.comune. milano.it; Metro M3: Turati, M1: Palestro

The Giardini Pubblici Indro Montanelli is one of Milan's top-rated public parks, and it's also home to the city's planetarium (Civico Planetario Ulrico Hoepli) and the Milan Natural History Museum. Being a public garden, you won't find wide areas of open grass here, but you will be treated to manicured lawns, fountains, geometric flower beds, and streams—you'll even meet a swan or two.

Giardini di Villa Reale

Via Palestro, 16; www.comune.milano.it; Metro M3: Turati, M1: Palestro

This unique park is reserved for families with children under the age of 12. Small and peaceful with an open grassy area, tranquil ponds, a charming gazebo, small caves, and a handful of footbridges, it provides a welcome haven for caretakers, where the children can run freely and the adults can relax.

Parco Giovanni Paolo II

Piazza della Vetra; www.comune.milano.it; Bus 94: Via Molino Delle Armi P.za Vetra

To combine nature with some classic Italian architecture, visit Parco Giovanni Paolo II. This park is a local favorite, especially for the younger crowd, as it's situated between the Basilica of Sant'Eustorgio and the Basilica of San Lorenzo near Corso di Porta Ticinese and the Navigli area, a popular vintage shopping and nightlife area. Here, you'll find Roman ruins, well-equipped play zones for children, and plenty of people picnicking or grabbing food from the numerous nearby eateries. This park is also called Parco delle Basiliche (Park of the Basilicas) by locals.

BIKING

Exploring Milan by bike has become increasingly popular over recent years. The good news for bike enthusiasts visiting Milan is that the city is

Naturally, as with any city that has two professional teams in the same division and sport, **A.C. Milan** and **Inter Milan** are fierce rivals. It's been long stated that local Inter fans are from the Milanese middle-class bourgeoisie, while A.C. Milan fans are from the working class. In English, the bi-annual match between the two is called the **Derby di Milano** (Milan Derby), but the name in Italian holds much more significance and history. For Italians, this match is the **Derby della Madonnina** (Derby of the Little Madonna), in honor of the statue of the Virgin Mary on top of the Duomo, one of Milan's most beloved and significant landmarks. To date, the teams have met more than 200 times when counting both official and unofficial matches. While Milan has won the most total matches, Inter actually takes the prize for winning the most official matches. As far as cross-town rivalries go, there is the rare characteristic of the home field advantage being omitted for this one, as both teams call San Siro Stadium home.

virtually completely flat, and traveling by bike has long been a part of Italy's transportation history. Additionally, the city's parks offer multiple biking paths. Be aware, though, that Italian drivers are not known for their disciplined driving and patience; make sure to wear a helmet and stay cognizant of your surroundings when cycling around the city.

For an easy-to-follow bike path, consider cycling around one of the concentric circles encompassing the city center, such as the circle that includes Via Carducci and Via Molino delle Arme.

Line M1 Route

Corso Buenos Aires to Parco Sempione

You can follow metro Line M1 (red) aboveground on two wheels, starting from the bike path on Corso Buenos Aires and making your way down Via Palestro to Piazza San Babila, past Piazza del Duomo, and straight to the castle before reaching Parco Sempione. The whole trip covers about 4 kilometers (2.5 miles) and passes some of the city's top sights.

BikeMi

Duomo, Cadorna, Loreto, Romolo, Garibaldi, and Centrale metro stations; www.bikemi. com

The public bike sharing service, BikeMi, is very popular and reliable for short trips, as bikes can only be rented for up to two hours at a time. The concept is simple: subscribe to BikeMi online or through the app (€4.50 per day, €9 per week), pick up a bike from one of the more than 200 BikeMi stations throughout the city, ride it to your destination, and return the bike to any one of the stations when finished. The first 30 minutes of each traditional bike ride are included (while it's another €0.25 for e-bikes), and each additional half hour costs €0.50. If you don't have Internet access, you can subscribe to the service at one of the ATM points available at Duomo, Cadorna, Loreto, Romolo, Garibaldi, and Centrale metro stations.

Viator Bike Tours

www.viator.com/tours/Milan

Viator offers guided bike tours of the city, with each tour lasting roughly 3.5 hours and costing €35 per person. Visitors can choose from a morning, afternoon, or evening tour, and each tour includes most of Milan's highlights, like the Duomo, the Galleria, La Scala, Brera district, Piazza Gae Aulenti, Castello Sforzesco, and Parco Sempione. While morning tours are offered year-round, afternoon tours are offered May-October, and evening tours June-September. Tours should be booked in advance online.

FOOTBALL

Like most European countries, Italy's primary sport is football—that is, soccer. Milan is home to two of Italy's most successful and followed teams, A.C. Milan (often just called *Milan*) and Inter Milan (often simply referred to as *Inter*). Both clubs are more than 100 years old, and both call the San Siro Stadium their home field. Serie A, Italy's top league in which both clubs have played for the past decades, holds regular season matches from mid-August until the end of May the following year, with each team usually playing a couple matches each week. Tickets can be purchased in advance online or directly at the stadium, which is easily reachable using Milan's purple (M5) metro line.

San Siro Stadium (Stadio Giuseppe Meazza)

Piazzale Angelo Moratti; 02/404-2432; www.sansiro.net; museum: 9:30am-5pm daily, adults €7, 14 and under or 65 and older €5; Metro M5: San Siro

For football fans, San Siro Stadium (officially named Stadio Giuseppe Meazza) is a must see. As the home to both the A.C. Milan and Inter Milan football clubs and a popular location for large concerts, San Siro sees plenty of action throughout the year. With a seating capacity of more than 80,000, it is the largest stadium in Italy and one of the largest in Europe.

Along with a handful of well-known European stadiums, San Siro is a category-four UEFA stadium, meaning that it meets the top-level requirements of specific sizing, capacity, and accommodations to host UEFA championships. While your best bet

people in front of San Siro stadium in Milan

for seeing the stadium is by catching a football match or concert, there is a museum, Museum San Siro, inside about the history of A.C. Milan and Inter open daily.

A.C. Milan

www.acmilan.com

Associazione Calcio Milan (A.C. Milan) is Milan's oldest football team and historically one of the world's wealthiest. Founded in 1899, not only is it the fourth most successful football club in the world in terms of the number of UEFA and FIFA titles won, it is also the most successful to come from Italy on an international scale. The team, which sports black and red uniforms, is often called *I Rossoneri* (The Red and Blacks) or *Il Diavolo* (The Devil) by Italian football fans. While Milan's Inter club is A.C. Milan's top rival, the football club from Genoa also brings a heated rivalry. While you're bound to find A.C. Milan gear anywhere in the city, the official megastore (Milan Store; Galleria San Carlo; 10am-8pm daily) is found in the Galleria.

Inter Milan

www.inter.it

Football Club Internazionale Milano S.p.A. is the official name of Milan's

110-year-old football club, but since that's a mouthful, sports fans refer to the club simply as Inter. Since its debut in 1909, the club has consistently played in Serie A, a rare feat by Italian football standards. Due to the color of their jerseys, many people refer to the squad as i Nerazzurri (The Black and Blues). As with many football clubs, they are also represented by an animal, a grass snake (serpent), called a biscione in Italian. Apart from its rivalry with A.C. Milan, the club also has a heated rivalry, especially in recent years, with the Italian Juventus football club from Turin. Just as with A.C. Milan, you'll find plenty of Inter gear on nearly every corner in the city, but you can find the **official megastore** (Inter Store Milano; Galleria Passarella, 2; 10am-8pam daily) in the city center.

Entertainment and Events

CONCERTS AND LIVE MUSIC
Alcatraz
Via Valtellina, 25; 02/6901-6352; www.alcatrazmilano.it; 11pm-4:30am Fri. and Sat.; €5-8; Metro M3: Maciachini, Tram 2, Buses 70, 82: Via Farini V.le Stelvio

Located close to the Isola and Porta Nuova districts, Alcatraz is arguably Milan's most popular music venue amongst locals, serving as both a concert space and a disco club, with multiple dance floors surrounding the stage. The venue has hosted such big-name acts as Passenger, Harry Styles, Alice Cooper, and other internationally known musicians. On the weekends, the live DJ plays original club mixes, drawing a flood of young locals. The calendar is usually filled with a variety of live musical guests, from mellow, acoustic acts to hip-hop and alternative rock artists.

Arcimboldi Theater (Teatro Arcimboldi)
Via Valtellina, 25; 02/641-142-212; www.alcatrazmilano.it; hours and ticket prices vary by performance; Metro M5: Bicocca; Bus 52: Teatro Arcimboldi

If you're interested in classical music and performing arts, Teatro Arcimboldi in the northern Bicocca area of Milan hosts pianists, symphonies, jazz musicians, ballets, musicals, and more. The theater was originally built as a temporary replacement for La Scala during its three-year renovation. Some of Italy's most beloved classical musicians, such as Ludovico Einaudi, frequently play here, as well as internationally recognized artists such as Elvis Costello. The theater also hosts a number of child-friendly plays and musicals, such as *Beauty and the Beast* and *Madagascar*.

FESTIVALS AND EVENTS
Italians are known for celebrating anything and everything, from seasonal fruits and vegetables to regional patron saints. Milan upholds this celebratory tradition with its semiannual Fashion Week, held every February and September, and annual Design Week, held every April. Every year during these few weeks, thousands of fashion and design enthusiasts, designers, models, hair and makeup

artists, art directors, photographers, and so many more from the industry saturate the city—setting it apart as one of the premier fashion and design cities in the world.

Fashion Week

https://fashionweekonline.com/milan

Milan Fashion Week is one of the "Big Four" of international fashion weeks, with the others being Paris, London, and New York. The event has been held semiannually every **February/ March** and **September/October** since 1958. Obtaining tickets for the big designer runway shows is almost impossible, but that doesn't stop thousands of fashionistas from trying. Many celebrities flock to the city to either participate in the event or simply soak in the fashion culture; during this time of year, the city stays up a little longer and a little later than usual.

Vogue's Fashion Night Out

https://vfno2012.vogue.it

One night each fall, starting just after dinnertime and running well into the early morning hours, locals and fashion enthusiasts from the world over gather into Milan's historic city center for Vogue's Fashion Night Out—the city's official kick-off to **fall fashion week.** Local shops and high-end designer stores on Via Montenapoleone stay open late and offer passing shoppers free wine, cocktails, and finger foods. Bars stay packed through extended business hours. You don't have to be a fashionista to appreciate this dynamic event. It is a not-to-be-missed experience worth fully immersing in—from the great music and high energy emanating from every street corner to the kaleidoscope of local and celebrity attendees all dressed in their finest and looking their most fabulous.

Design Week (Salone del Mobile Milano)

www.salonemilano.it; mid-late Apr.

Milan's Design Week is one of the most important international design events of the year and is often considered to be the "Oscars of Design." Unlike international fashion week, this event brings with it a more local Milanese feel; it is when local designers emerge from their studios and into the streets to showcase their best work, and the true design heart of the city vigorously pumps with life. What began as a local design event has since turned into a global celebration of design, during which the entire Brera district becomes completely abuzz with activity for six days straight. The week is usually scheduled in mid- to late April and includes **Salone del Mobile Rho,** a large furniture fair at Rho Fiera Milano (Strada Statale Sempione, 28), a huge exhibition and fair center on the outskirts of the city, as well as small pop-up shops and street markets throughout the city center.

Feast of St. Ambrose

Most of Italy's cities and villages hold festival days to celebrate their respective patron saints, and Milan is no exception. Every **December 7** the Milanese celebrate their patron saint, Sant'Ambrogio. While most bars and restaurants stay open, all schools and public offices close. After a celebratory mass in the Basilica of Sant'Ambrogio, festivities continue at the annual **Oh Bej! Oh Bej! Christmas market** (the name is in the Milanese dialect and translates to "Oh beautiful! Oh beautiful!"), already in full swing. Revelers feast on local food and drinks and delight in local arts and crafts. Crowds also congregate in Piazza del Duomo to marvel at the **giant Christmas tree** lit each year outside the cathedral. Some fortunate tourists get to participate in this special celebration and experience some of Milan's best historic and local culture.

Ambrosian Carnival
Mid-late Feb.

The carnival celebration, held in all Italian cities and towns, is an important religious and cultural event. Although not as globally known as Venice's Carnival, Milan's Ambrosian Carnival, after the city's patron saint St. Ambrose, takes place each year for 2-3 days in mid- to late February. On the day of Carnival, the city shuts down (with the exception of some bars and restaurants that stay open to accommodate local families). A rainbow of confetti, streamers, and balloons decorate the streets, and families can enjoy the parade of extravagant floats and costumed participants making its way through the streets near Piazza del Duomo. Some local bars and restaurants also host masquerade parties during this week.

Shopping

While most people associate Milan with Gucci, Dolce & Gabbana, Fendi, Prada, and other Italian fashion powerhouses, Milan actually offers thousands of shopping options, all of which are divided into concentrated retail districts. These options meet a variety of budgets and interests—of course, there's designer fashion, but there are also bustling open-air markets, charming vintage shops, antique markets, dedicated cosmetic, skincare, and fragrance boutiques, artisan home décor and custom furniture shops, bookstores, and gourmet shops.

Given that fashion is part of what put Milan on the map, fashion-forward trendsetters are part of the cultural fabric that make Milan distinctly Milan. The locals take their style, and their shopping, quite seriously—as much as shopping is like a sport for them, there is no such thing as running to the grocery store in sweats.

SHOPPING DISTRICTS

Despite names like Gucci and Dolce & Gabbana headlining the shopping scene, Milan is a city that accommodates a variety of budgets and interests. If you're looking to empty a packed wallet on designer fashion, you'll have no trouble doing so in the Galleria or Via Montenapoleone. To shop local, hit the Brera district or Navigli. If you're on a strict budget but still want to have a full shopping experience, the department stores and more than 300 shops along Corso Buenos Aires may suit you best, or you can scavenge around Milan's Chinatown for even more budget-friendly options.

The Galleria
Piazza del Duomo; www.turismo.milano.it;
Metro M1, M3: Duomo

The Galleria houses two of the world's most famous fashion powerhouses: Armani and Louis Vuitton. In contrast, it also houses many of Milan's family-owned boutiques. While it is easy to cash out at the Galleria, you can also

Dolce & Gabbana shop on Via Montenapoleone

avoid spending altogether if you stick to window shopping. Just a stroll to explore the different levels of the Galleria alone is worth the experience.

Via Montenapoleone

Via Montenapoleone; www. viamontenapoleone.org; Metro M3: Montenapoleone, M1: San Babila

Via Montenapoleone, the backbone of the city's Golden Quadrilateral, is home to some of the world's preeminent fashion brands, including La Perla, Louis Vuitton, Ralph Lauren, and Gucci. This area is like the more historical, Italian version of Los Angeles' Rodeo Drive.

Brera District

Brera district, Corso Como; Metro M2: Lanza, M2: Moscova

For local products with a little bit of eccentric, upscale, or Bohemian flair, hit the quieter Brera district, where you'll find some of Milan's best boutiques.

Corso Buenos Aires

Corso Buenos Aires, Porta Venezia District; Metro M1: Porta Venezia or Lima

Corso Buenos Aires is one of the longest shopping streets in the world, where you can find everything from major department stores, to international alternative brands, to enduring, family-run boutiques. This street best accommodates a variety of budgets.

Ticinese and Navigli

Corso di Porta Ticinese and along the canals; Metro M2: Porta Genova

To shop without breaking the bank, head to Corso di Porta Ticinese then south to Navigli, where you'll find vintage stores, local showrooms, thrift shops, and alternative international brands like Herschel, Vans, Diesel, and Carhartt. You'll also find a smattering of local shoe boutiques, record stores, and antique shops.

Chinatown

Via Paolo Sarpi, Chinatown; Trams 2, 4: Piazzale Baiamonti; Tram 12, 14: Via Bramante Via Sarpi

To shop on a budget, try Milan's Chinatown. The neighborhood's main street, Via Paolo Sarpi, is lined with more than 150 silk and leather shops as well as small boutiques selling discount fashions.

OPEN AIR MARKETS

Mercato Dei Navigli

Naviglio Grande, Navigli; 9am-6pm on the last Sun. of each month; Metro M2: Porta Genova

The Mercato Dei Navigli, set up along Navigli's Grand Canal (Naviglio Grande), is open on the last Sunday of each month. It hosts nearly 400 antique vendors that sell a variety of wares, including furniture, porcelains, jewelry, silverware, dolls, games, and comics. Despite the fact that it seems like a mile-long garage sale at first sight, each vendor is carefully selected by the market host.

Fiera di Sinigaglia (Sinigaglia Fair)

Corner of the Naviglio Grande and Via Valenza, Navigli; http://fieradisinigaglia.it; 8am-6pm Sat.; Metro M2: Porta Genova

If you're in town on a Saturday and are looking for a more frequented market that still maintains the vintage feel of Navigli, head to the Fiera di Sinigaglia near the Porta Genova metro station along the Grand Canal in Navigli. Here you'll find a smorgasbord of items: used clothing, vinyl records, knickknacks, organic cosmetics, spices, original artwork, and more.

This is known as the oldest open flea market in Milan, with roots that go back to the beginning of the 12th century, and embodies the authentic and local feel of the Navigli and Ticinese districts.

Mercato di San Marco

Via San Marco, Brera; 7:30am-2:00pm Mon. and Thurs.; Metro M2 Moscova; Bus 43, 94: Piazza Mirabello

The Brera district is home to some popular open-air street markets, such as the market on San Marco on Monday and Thursday mornings, which has an eclectic mix of imported clothing and accessories, including a stylish selection of sweaters, scarves, shoes, and purses. While most items run under €30, pay attention to the quality from stall to stall, and check out multiple stalls before making a purchase. To pick up local produce, flowers, meat, or seafood, swing by the adjacent farmer's market.

Via Fauchè Market

Via Giovanni Battista Fauchè, Brera; 8am-2pm Tues., 8am-6pm Sat.; Metro M5: Gerusalemme

This colorful market, open by 8am on Tuesdays and Saturdays, sits in the Brera district and offers everything from fresh local vegetables, cured meats, and cheeses to last season's high-fashion styles and Italian leather shoes at competitive prices. You'll find brands such as Jimmy Choo, Gucci, and more lining the stalls here. If you're looking to get the best quality products for the lowest prices, get here early in the day while the selection is still plentiful and stall owners are still in the mood to negotiate.

In addition to hosting renowned fashion and design events, Milan also serves as the headquarters of most Italian fashion or designer brands. Many iconic fashion brands have chosen Milan as the location for their Italian or international flagship stores—that is, the largest and most important store in the retail chain that typically showcases each brand's highest-level products. Most these flagships can be found in the **Golden Quadrilateral,** one of Milan's preeminent shopping districts bounded by Via Montenapoleone, Via Borgospesso, Via Della Spiga, and Via Sant'Andre These designer-laden streets are home to the flagships of such brands as Armani, Versace, and Fendi.

Others concentrations of flagships can be found in **Galleria,** which houses the Prada store, and **Piazza San Fedele,** which is home to Lavazza. In the city center, expect to find the flagship for other famous brands such as Gucci, Valentino, Givenchy, Tod's, and Just Cavalli.

CLOTHES AND ACCESSORIES

Cavalli e Nastri

Via Brera, 2; 02/7200-0449; www.cavallienastri.com; 10:30am-7:30pm daily, from 12pm Sun.; Metro M3: Montenapoleone

Cavalli e Nastri on Via Brera is one of the city's most popular vintage shops. Don't let this little shop with its cozy feel fool you; you are sure to find plenty of big labels here, including Christian Dior and Yves Saint Laurent. The shop's interior is colorful and chic, with cloth-covered tables displaying porcelain plates of jewelry and closets organized by color. You can find designer labels from the 1950s, as well as broaches, earrings, and plenty of patterned purses and dresses that you can't find anywhere else. Locals shop here for unique story pieces to add to their collections. Besides the shop on Via Brera, you'll also find another Cavalli e Nastri shop on Via Gian Giacomo Mora 12 in Ticinese.

Excelsior

Galleria del Corso, 4; 02/7630-7301; www.excelsiormilano.com; 10am-8:30pm daily; Metro M2: San Babila

Visit the seven-story Excelsior to shop both menswear and womenswear. The huge department store sells some of the most famous brands in the world, including Dries Van Noten and Yeezy, just to name a couple. Coming up on its ninth decade in Milan, Excelsior exudes glamour and glitz from the moment you walk through the door and enter its sleek, shiny interior. Similar to London's Harrods, you can find everything here, from high-end fashion to the latest technology to fine foods.

Frip

Corso di Porta Ticinese, 16; 02/832-1360; www.frip.it; 11am-2pm and 3:30-7:30pm Tues.-Sat, 3:30-7:30pm Sun. and Mon.; Bus 94: Colonne di San Lorenzo

For edgier finds, visit Frip on Corso di Porta Ticinese, where you'll come across hand-picked French, British, and Scandinavian designer label items. Everything inside is crisp white, with the only splashes of color coming from the clothes hanging on the racks or the modern shoes displayed on the shelves. You'll find brands such as Acne and Hope here, with most clothes serving as basic, high-quality staples for your wardrobe.

Biffi

Corso Genova, 6; 02/8311-6052; www.biffi.com; 10am-7:30pm Tues.-Sat., 3pm-7:30pm Mon.; Bus 94: Piazza Resistenza Partigiana

To experience both architectural and

fashion design in one place, shop at Biffi, a 2,000-square-foot space designed by famous Italian architect Gae Aulenti. The boutique is named after the Biffi family, known for their research in finding the world's best up-and-coming designers. You'll find the renovated space filled with soft tones and modern decorations, and elegant yet casual clothing. The boutique sells both high-end menswear and womenswear and features items by such fashion icons as Alexander Wang.

Wait and See

Via Santa Marta, 14; 02/7208-0195; www. waitandsee.it; 10:30am-7:30pm Tues.-Sat., 3pm-7:30pm Mon.; Tram 12, 14: Carrobbio

To find something flashy and vibrant, Wait and See on Via Santa Marta offers lots of patterns, pops of color, costume jewelry, and many more items. The place is housed in an 18th-century former convent, and the style and color inside has brought the building back to its former glory. The store focuses on womenswear and fashion and features writing accessories, with rainbow displays of dresses, bags, jewelry, stationery, and other hand-picked vintage pieces from around the world. You'll also find on display rotating exhibits by local artists.

BEAUTY
Kiko Milano

Via dell'Unione, 2; 02/7208-0336; www. kikocosmetics.com; 9am-8pm daily; Metro M1, M3: Duomo

For cosmetics and other skincare products, visit Kiko Milano, the city's most well-known Italian cosmetic brand. With multiple locations scattered throughout the city, Kiko not only offers one of the most diverse selections of products, it also offers

seasonal lines and limited-edition collections. All items are reasonably priced, so it's ideal for budget shoppers. Lipsticks and mascaras are as low as €4 apiece. Each Kiko location tends to fill up quickly due to popularity, so arrive upon opening in order to avoid the crowds.

La Rinascente

Piazza del Duomo; 02/88-521; www. rinascente.it; 9am-10pm daily; Metro M1, M3: Duomo

One of the Italy's nicer department stores that focuses on everything beauty is La Rinascente. Milan's Piazza del Duomo is home to the department store's flagship location, with 10 floors of a wide assortment of products and designer brands. Here, you'll find high-end cosmetics by Giorgio Armani, Burberry, and Mac. You'll also find departments dedicated to fashion and interior design, as well as a fine-dining food hall. Much like Harrod's in London, this place gets packed pretty quickly, especially on the weekends, so arrive early or near closing time in order to avoid the crowds.

Brian & Barry

Via Durini, 28; 02/6990-1193; www. brianebarry.it; 10am-7pm daily; Metro M2: San Babila

Offering a mega-beauty experience is Milan's Brian & Barry store, with 12 floors of both Italian and international premier beauty products. It also houses a Sephora corner where shoppers can test new products, a nail bar where you can try out new paints, and an old-style wall with raw fragrance materials used to create perfumes. The first floor offers an Eataly cafeteria for those looking for a quick bite to eat before or after shopping. You'll also find home decor, clothing, a food market, and more here.

Officina Profumo-Farmaceutica di Santa Maria Novella

Via Madonnina, 11; 02/3651-9630; www. smnovella.com; 10am-7:30pm daily; Metro M1: Cairoli Castello, M2: Lanza

Milan is home to some of Europe's most original fragrance shops, such as Officina Profumo-Farmaceutica di Santa Maria Novella (Santa Maria Novella Pharmacy and Perfume Shop), where all of the perfumes, soaps, and body lotions are packaged in hand-printed material. This store takes you to a bygone era and offers Italian delicacies such as chocolates and cappuccino liqueur for its shoppers. The place is a showroom for perfumes, and it feels like everything you touch is magical. Despite being in the city center, the shop is rather hidden (look for Via Madonnina near the corner of Via Vetero and Via Landolfo), but it's worth the effort due to its ancient charm and elegance.

Acqua di Parma

Via Gesù, 1; 02/7602-3307; www. acquadiparma.com; 10am-7:30pm daily; Metro M3: Montenapoleone

Acqua di Parma is another beauty shop specializing in fragrances and other original Italian artisanal products, such as soaps. The brand has been around for more than 100 years, originating with one of the oldest families, the Magnani family, from the city of Parma, located southeast of Milan. This family created the first true Italian cologne. Today, the brand and store are known for its graceful, lavish, yet classic Italian style, and its flagship store on Via Gesù is no exception.

HOME DECOR AND FURNITURE
Bottega Veneta

Via Borgospesso, 5; 02/7600-9934; http:// bottegaveneta.com; 10am-7pm Mon.-Sat.; Metro M3: Montenapoleone

For custom-made furniture with high-quality craftsmanship representing the true embodiment of Milanese design, visit Bottega Veneta's homewares boutique, where you'll find a variety of lighting, tableware, and furniture. Several of its stores around Milan also sell clothing and accessories, but this location near Via Montenapoleone does not. Located in the historic 18th-century Palazzo Gallarati Scotti, you'll find inside the building itself centuries-old frescoes and coffered ceilings, making the shopping experience an enchanting one, whether you walk out with anything or not.

Spazio Rossana Orlandi

Via Matteo Bandello, 14/16; 02/467-4471; rossanaorlandi.com; 10am-7pm Mon.-Sat.; Metro M1: Conciliazione

For a true taste of Milanese design and all that it encompasses, visit the gallery, social venue, and flagship store of Spazio Rossana Orlandi. The space is filled with modern and unique furniture pieces, statement art, and a variety of home decor that you won't be able to find in any other city. This colorful space has both indoor and outdoor sections, so you feel like you're in a little fairytale corner of the bustling city center. Grab a coffee, shop around, or simply soak up inspiration from the relaxed yet refined atmosphere.

BOOKSTORES
Gogol & Company

Via Savona, 101; 02/4547-0449; www. gogolandcompany.com; 9am-10pm daily; Tram 14: Via Giambellino Via Tolstoj

For works in English, Spanish, and French from emerging writers or smaller publishing companies, visit Gogol & Company, where the friendly atmosphere invites you to grab a book and enjoy a leisurely read in one of the leather armchairs. You can also get a small bite to eat at the little bistro inside the shop. Unlike most coffee shops and bookstores in Italy, this little gem offers a quiet place to study with your laptop, or to just get away from the world for a while. The staff here are extremely affable and welcoming, ready to help you find the right book or make your stay here as comfortable as possible.

Verso

Corso di Porta Ticinese, 40; 02/837-5648; www.libreriaverso.com; 10am-9pm Tues.-Sun., 1pm-9pm Mon.; Bus 94, Tram 3: Colonne di San Lorenzo

The lower level of Verso houses the bar and café with tables ideal for quiet socializing, reading, or working; WiFi is open to guests. The upper level houses the bookstore, which specializes in works by independent publishers and up-and-coming writers; you'll also find a handful of bestsellers. One of the best features of this place is the children's space, a colorful area of the store dedicated solely to children and their imaginations.

Corraini 121

Via Savona, 17; 02/3658-4119; www.corraini. com/en/librerie/milano; 10:30am-2pm and 3pm-7:30pm Tues.-Sun, 3pm-7:30pm Mon.; Metro M2: Porta Genova; Tram 14: Via Montevideo

Corraini 121 is a publishing house as well as an art gallery, so you can browse various forms of art and purchase more than just books. Known for its innovative design, the space is bright and colorful, with wooden tables and shelves stacked with books on design, art, architecture, fashion, graphics, food, and more from nearly every continent. The house and gallery also host workshops and author readings.

FOOD AND GOURMET

Eataly

Piazza Venticinque Aprile, 10; 02/4949-7301; www.eataly.it/milano; 8:30am-12am daily; Metro M2, M5: Porta Garibaldi

If you're hungry and not sure where to go, there's always Eataly, Milan's gourmet superstore in Piazza XXV Aprile. Here you'll find multiple stories of Italian specialty items, from pestos and oils from Liguria, to mozzarella from the south of Italy. There's nothing you can't find here and aromas and colors entice you from every direction, so stroll every level and grab a bite to eat at one of the several outposts within the building. If you're close to the Duomo district, you can get this experience at Brian & Berry's megastore in Piazza San Babila, which houses a much smaller Eataly.

Peck

Via Spadari, 9; 02/802-3161; www.peck.it; 9am-8pm Tues.-Sat., 3pm-8pm Mon.; Metro M1, M3: Duomo

Food lovers will enjoy some time in Peck, a gourmet shop full of beautiful fresh produce, meats, pastas, cheese, olive oils, and much more. Although your wallet may take a hit here, it's well worth a visit to simply browse the impressive varieties of edible treats on offer. Locals come here to take home some ready-made meals that are the highest quality found in the city. If all the food is making you hungry, the first floor is home to the Ristorante Al Peck, where an award-winning local

Eataly offers three levels of Italian food shopping

chef prepares traditional Milanese dishes using ingredients that you can purchase off the shelves. There's also **Piccolo Peck,** a small café where you can sample a selection of the fresh meats and cheeses, as well as appetizers and sandwiches, that are all for sale here.

Food

Italy has a vegetarian-friendly culture, and veganism and gluten-free options are also on the rise. Many first-course options are vegetarian, while second-course options usually offer some sort of salad or vegetables. For those that are tired of carb-overloading on Italian food after a few days, Milan offers more international options than any other city in Italy. From all-you-can-eat sushi to Mexican street food, the city is full of every cuisine. In recent years, a handful of fusion restaurants have popped up as well, mixing traditional Italian cuisine with international flavors, which is a direct reflection of the city's culture.

CITY CENTER AND DUOMO
MILANESE
Enoteca Regionale Lombarda
Via Stampa, 8; 02/8968-1143; http:// enotecaregionalelombarda.it; 12pm-3pm and 6:30pm-10:30pm Mon.-Sat.; entrees €12-30; Trams 2, 3, 14: Via Torino Via S. Maria Valle
Unlike most restaurants serving Milanese fare in the city, this wine shop and restaurant focus on the elegance of the atmosphere as much as on the presentation and taste of the food. The place is warm and spacious, with neutral walls, wine barrels, wooden shelves filled with bottles, and rustic wooden tables in several rooms. Most wines here

are the region's best, and you can pair them with hot or cold meals. A must-try is the traditional risotto Milanese topped with osso buco. Ask your waiter for specific wine pairings to make the most of your experience here.

Cascina Cuccagna

Via Cuccagna, angolo via Muratori, 2/4; 02/8342-1007; www.cuccagna.org; 10am-1am Tues.-Sun.; entrees €10-15; Metro M3: Porta Romana

This farm-to-table kitchen is a result of an urban regeneration project that restored a 17th-century farmhouse into a cultural meeting space. Here, you can enjoy a leisurely drink or meal from a menu specializing in organic, local, and seasonal ingredients that changes daily, with offerings such as freshly picked and grilled vegetable plates, black risotto, and gourmet burgers. Located southeast of the Duomo (about a 10-minute walk from the Porta Romana metro stop), the farmhouse serves as a quiet break from everything outside of its walls. The courtyard area is a great place for a picnic. Grab a small plate and a hot or cold beverage from the bar and enjoy some sun, take a stroll through the **small farmers market** on the grounds, or stop by for a calm *aperitivo* hour.

ITALIAN AND PIZZA
A Santa Lucia

Via S. Pietro All'Orto, 3; 02/7602-3155; www.asantalucia.it; 12pm-1am daily; first courses €15, second courses €24, pizza €10; Metro M1, M3: Duomo, M1: San Babila

For visitors wanting to eat near the Duomo, A Santa Lucia is a Neapolitan-style restaurant and one of the first pizzerias to open in Milan. The menu offers traditional Italian cuisine, from the antipasti to pizza to dessert and wine. While the food is above-average

a traditional Italian breakfast

quality for this highly touristed area, the prices reflect that, so be prepared to spend at least €20-40 per person here. During high season, the restaurant stays packed, so consider eating an early or late lunch or reserving a table, which you can do online no later than two days in advance.

Berton

Via Mike Bongiorno, 13; 02/6707-5801; www. ristoranteberton.com; 12:30pm-2:30pm Tues.-Fri., 7pm-10pm Mon.-Sat.; entrees €20-60; Metro M3: Repubblica

Berton, named after its famous acclaimed chef Andrea Berton, gives diners a Michelin-star experience with just a few simple ingredients. Berton's exquisite cuisine, which ranges from a full menu of broth-based soups to risottos to veal liver, perfectly matches the modern and minimalistic ambiance of the restaurant. You can order nothing wrong here, as every plate and its paired drink are top notch. Save room for the chocolate soufflè for dessert; it's worth it. While dressing elegantly isn't necessary, you may want to change out of your street clothes before dining here. Booking ahead here is strongly recommended, especially if you're dining in groups of three or more.

BARS AND CAFÉS
Armani Caffè

Via Croce Rossa, 2; 02/7231-8680; http:// armaniristorante.com; 8am-9pm Mon.-Fri., 9am-9pm Sat. and Sun.; drinks €5-15; Metro M3: Montenapoleone

Kickstart your walk down Via Montenapoleone with breakfast at the Armani Caffè, or sit down for a breather after finishing an afternoon of shopping. Offering a full coffee and cocktail menu all day every day and some sweet treats and pastries in the mornings, this luxurious cafe follows suit with its designer surroundings in the neighborhood. In the afternoon, select an appetizer plate along with your glass of wine. The restaurant also offers a full menu of simple Italian bites like panini, pastas, and pastries for those wanting to stop by during lunch or for an early dinner.

Terrazza Aperol

Via Ugo Foscolo, 1; 335/735-6773; www. terrazzaaperol.it; 11am-11pm daily; drinks €10-20; Metro M1, M3 Duomo

Milan's Terrazza Aperol on the second level of the Galleria is one of the most popular bars in the city, as it overlooks Piazza del Duomo, one of best views from any Milanese rooftop bar. Stop in for an *aperol* spritz cocktail and a selection of finger foods during happy hour, or during any other time of day. If you want to get a seat on the terrace during the normal *aperitivo* hour, call ahead and book a table, as this place fills up very quickly.

Bianchi Cafe & Cycles

Via Felice Cavallotti, 8; 02/2506-1039; www. bianchicafecycles.it; 7am-9pm Mon.-Fri., 8am-6:30pm Sat.; entrees €10-25; Metro M1: San Babila; Bus 54, 60, 73, 84: Cavalloti

For cycle lovers, Bianchi bikes opened this bike-themed cafè just a stone's throw away from the Duomo. You'll find the brand's bicycles and history-related decorations adorned all over the establishment. Several Bianchi bikes are on display to showcase the progress in design throughout the decades. The cafè has an extensive wine list and restaurant menu, and a separate shop selling Bianchi bike gear and memorabilia. Due to the numerous events that take place here throughout the year, book ahead if possible.

Bianche Cafe is a unique place to grab a bite to eat for cycle-enthusiasts

CASTELLO AND SEMPIONE

ITALIAN AND PIZZA

Pasta Fresca da Giovanni

Piazza Giovine Italia; 335/521-5743; 12pm-3pm Mon.-Fri.; entrees €8-9; Metro M1: Conciliazione

This little place near the castle offers exclusively fresh pasta made that day, either to eat by the portion in the restaurant itself or to take away (uncooked and without sauce). The menu changes daily, depending on the type of pasta made that morning and the housemade sauces that accompany the pasta. No menus here; simply take a look at the pastas and sauces on the chalkboard and select your pairing. Considering this place is only open a few hours on the weekdays, arrive early to snag a table if you plan on eating lunch here.

Puccia's Brothers

Piazza Virgilio, 3; 02/6666-6360; www.pucciasbrothers.it; 7am-11pm Mon.-Fri., 8am-8pm Sat.-Sun.; entrees €10-15; Metro M1, M2: Cadorna

Puccia's Brothers brings Italian street food, such as overflowing meaty sandwiches, to a restaurant setting. Choose from more than 30 different types of sandwiches, meat and cheese plates, salads, desserts, hot beverages, cocktails, and beyond. The casual atmosphere here makes it a great place for a last-minute drop for a quick bite when you're in the area.

Pizzeria Starita

Via Giovanni Gherardini, 1; 02/3360-2532; www.pizzeriestarita.it; 12pm-3pm, 7pm-12am daily; entrees €10-20; Tram 1: Arco Della Pace

For traditional Neapolitan style pizza at a decent price and low-key atmosphere, look no further than Pizzeria Starita. Open for more than 100 years, the place started as a tasting cellar for wines and has since evolved into a pizzeria and trattoria. The pizza choices are diverse and numerous, with all classic pizzas on the menu as well as specialty house pizzas, seasonal pizzas, and calzones. They don't take reservations, so come earlier to avoid a wait.

Deseo

Corso Sempione, 2; 02/315-164; www.deseomilano.com; 8am-2am daily; aperitivo €10-20; Tram 1: Arco Della Pace

Known mostly for its huge buffet and selection of cocktails, Deseo is a hot spot for a younger crowd, located right on the corner of the Arco della Pace. The *aperitivo* menu includes everything: pizza, sandwiches, cheese, meats, pasta, and a chocolate fountain. The ambiance is relaxed yet fits right in with Milan's fashion-centric and stylish atmosphere. Deseo also offers a full Italian lunch menu with vegetarian and vegan-friendly dishes, as well as brunch on the weekends.

INTERNATIONAL

Tara

Via Domenico Cirillo, 16; 02/345-1635; www.ristorantetara.it; 12pm-2:30pm, 7:30pm-11pm Tues.-Sun.; entrees €15-25; Tram 1: Arco Della Pace

ITALIAN COFFEE CULTURE

Italians take coffee seriously, from the rich flavor of each espresso down to the experience of drinking it in an ideal atmosphere. It's not unusual for an Italian to drink anywhere from 2-8 espressos every day, starting first thing in the morning and ending as a final thought after dinner.

BARS AND CAFÉS

Coffees are usually taken at bars standing up, and after each meal, which is why you'll see plenty of bars with very few seating options. Unlike coffee shops in the U.S. or the U.K., bars and cafés in Italy aren't usually places to stay for several hours, catching up with friends, or working away on your laptop. Rather, you order your beverage of choice, drink it at your own leisure, then continue with the rest of your day.

COFFEE LIKE A LOCAL

Cappuccinos and other similar coffee drinks are generally only served before 11am, but many bars in touristy areas of Milan will serve these drinks to visitors in the afternoon upon request. If you want to fit in with the local crowd, grab a sweet pastry for breakfast with a cappuccino or other coffee beverage, then take an espresso after lunch and dinner along with your dessert.

If you're burned out on Italian food and looking for something Asian and spicy, Tara focuses on northern Indian cuisine. The menu is full of various tandoori and curry dishes, with a decent portion of the menu dedicated to vegetarian plates. The low lighting and fragrant aromas here give off a romantic, intimate atmosphere. On weekends during the lunch hours, try the unique Indian brunch experience with a large and diverse selection of dishes for a fixed price of €16.50.

Cinquantadue Milano

*Foro Buonaparte, 52; 334/362-7228; www.
cinquantaduemilano.it; 8am-2am daily;
entrees €10-20; Metro M2: Lanza*

This Japanese sushi restaurant prides itself on its upscale dining experience. The mood is set the moment you walk in the door, with the lamp lighting and carefully selected Italian music playing in the background. The menu has the classic sushi offerings: tartar, uramaki, tempura, carpaccio, and nigiri, with a selection of traditional Japanese

hot dishes. All the dishes made by the locally known chef are creatively and sophisticatedly presented. If you're planning on dining here in the evening, reservations are recommended.

BARS AND CAFÉS
Verdi's

*Via Nirone 2; 02/5656-8947; verdi-s.it;
7:30am-7:30pm Mon.-Sat., 10am-8pm Sun.;
entrees €5-15; Metro M1, M2: Cadorna*

Verdi's bistro is a sunny place focused on providing all-natural, healthy food options in the heart of the city. On weekdays, you'll see this place bustling with students from the neighboring Università Cattolica. The breakfast options range from traditional Italian pastries to smoothies and fruit salads, with a full coffee bar to go along with it. For lunches, you'll find a seasonal menu with plenty of vegetarian and vegan-friendly options, pastas, sandwiches, salads, sweets, and an *aperitivo* menu with various house-recommended alcoholic beverages.

TICINESE AND NAVIGLI

MILANESE

Antica Hostaria Della Lanterna

Via Giuseppe Mercalli, 3; 02/5830-9604;
12:30pm-2:30pm Mon.-Fri., 8pm-10pm
Mon.-Sat.; entrees €10-15; Tram 15: Corso
Italia Via S. Sofia

While the official name of this small *osteria* (tavern) just south of the city's Duomo district is a mouthful, the local name is one to remember: *La Sciura*, meaning "the lady" in Milanese dialect. The owner, Paola, makes herself known by scurrying around the place chatting with guests. Anything pasta here is good, as it's housemade, but try the gnocchi with gorgonzola or pistachio pesto. Traditional Milanese second courses, including osso buco, are served as well, but make sure you save room for dessert, because you cannot leave this place without trying some of the city's richest, creamiest *tiramisù*. Prices are budget friendly, but be prepared to loosen your belts, as portion sizes for first courses are usually generous here.

La Madonnina

Via Gentilino, 6; 02/257-2998; www.
facebook.com/lamadonninamilano;
12pm-2:30pm Mon.-Sat., 8pm-10:30pm
Wed.-Sat.; entrees €10-12; Metro M1:
Precotto

For risotto Milanese, osso buco, and a *cotoletta alla milanese* (veal cutlet) so big that it overflows your plate, look no further than this local trattoria, with handwritten menus, old pictures of the city hanging on the walls, and a lively local crowd stopping by most days. If the weather is nice, sit outside under the pergola overlooking a nearby courtyard and ask the waiter for a local wine. You should be able to find a table each day, but it's not a bad idea to book ahead in the evenings.

INTERNATIONAL

Maya Bar

Via Ascanio Sforza, 41; 02/5810-5168; www.
mayamilano.it; 6pm-2am daily; entrees
€11-25; Tram 3: Corso S. Gottardo Via
Lagrange

Right along Navigli's smaller canal is this popular *aperitivo* bar with one of the largest happy hour buffets and drink menus in the city. Tables fill up fast, especially on the weekends. Both traditional Italian dishes, such as eggplant parmesan and *pasta al forno* (baked pasta dishes), and a selection of international dishes are offered all-you-can-eat style with the purchase of a drink until 10:30pm. Reservations are recommended, as this bar gets busy pretty quickly upon opening.

El Porteno

Viale Gian Galeazzo, 25; 02/5843-7593;
www.elporteno.it; 7:30pm-1am daily; entrees
€40-50; Tram 9: Viale Col Di Lana

For meat lovers, the Argentinian steakhouse of El Porteno is one of the best that the city has to offer. The large cuts of steak are accompanied by a menu full of housemade empanadas and special sauces; you can even order sashimi. El Porteno also offers a large selection of Argentinian wine to pair with each dish. The atmosphere is elegant, but not overwhelmingly so. Reservations here are recommended, especially on weekends.

MAMAStrEAT

Corso di Porta Ticinese, 77; 02/9167-9165;
www.mamastreat.com; 12pm-12am
Tues.-Sun.; entrees €10-12; Bus 94, Tram 3:
Colonne di San Lorenzo

For a quick spicy bite of something other than pizza or gelato, try

✪ APERITIVO

Internationally, Milan is known as one of the four global fashion capitals. In Italy, it's known as the capital of *aperitivo* culture. Starting at 5pm or 6pm and sometimes lasting throughout the night, *aperitivo* is a special offered by bars and cafés where buying a drink for €10-20 comes with an all-you-can eat buffet of appetizers and small bites. At any given place, you'll probably find an assortment of bite-size portions of pizzas, sandwiches, pasta dishes, chips, pickled vegetables, fruits, and chocolates.

Aperitivo usually lasts from the end of the work day until dinnertime, with many groups simply moving from the office to a bar, then straight to a restaurant or a meal at home. Other Italian cities have adopted the *aperitivo* culture as part of normal Italian life, but Milan is still the leader of this hour. The Navigli district and Via Corso Como are the most popular *aperitivo* areas, with bars filling tables quickly, especially on the weekends.

The Milanese *aperitivo* is unparalleled throughout the world, with the vibrant and robust offerings of each bar as enticing as the next.

BEST *APERITIVOS* IN MILAN

Almost every bar in Milan participates in the *aperitivo* hour, so stopping into any bar or café at this time, regardless of where you are in the city, will give you a taste of this part of Milanese culture. The number of *aperitivo* options can be daunting, so here's a list of places where you can't go wrong:

- **Bar Basso** (Via Plinio, 39) is a Milanese bar opened in 1947 that claims itself to be the birthplace of *aperitivo*. Owner Mirko Stocchetto was the first to pour the Negroni Sbagliato, now one of the most popular local drinks. Drinks here range from €8-10, with finger foods served at each table.

- **Radetzky** (Corso Garibaldi, 105), in the heart of the Brera district, is another classic hot spot for drinks (averaging around €10 each) and a plentiful finger-food buffet. The patio seating lends itself to an hour or two of people-watching entertainment.

- **Pisacco** (Via Solferino, 48), for a modern and professional *aperitivo*, is hard to beat, especially in terms of the spreads that are offered along with a glass of wine or cocktail (averaging around €10 each). Chef Fabio Gambirarsi doesn't go light for this hour—you'll see everything from homemade potato chips to veal breast to seared tuna on your happy hour plate.

- **Ceresio 7 Pools & Restaurant** (Via Ceresio, 7) hosts a luxurious rooftop *aperitivo* boasting two pools and a 360-degree view of the city from the roof of Dsquared2's headquarters. The cocktails average around €15 each, but the views and the bites are worth the extra euros.

- **Rita & Cocktails** (Via Angelo Fumagalli, 1) is where you come for the stellar original cocktails (averaging €9 or €10 apiece) and stay for the atmosphere and daily special appetizer.

MAMAstrEAT, tucked into the busy Corso di Porta Ticinese. This tiny Mexican food joint, although limited in seating space, packs a punch with its menu and flavors, all while remaining budget friendly. Traditional Mexican dishes such as tacos and burritos are served along with frozen sangria, margaritas, and Mexican beers. With such a small space, order the food to go and enjoy it in the Basilicas Park directly behind it.

BARS AND CAFÉS
Santeria Social Club

Viale Toscana, 31; 02/2219-9381; www. santeria.milano.it; 6pm-2am Mon.-Wed., 11am-2am Thurs.-Sun.; entrees €10-20; Bus 90: Viale Toscana Via Castelbarco

The Santeria Social Club is one of the most versatile spots in Milan, serving as a cocktail bar, coworking space, concert venue, theater, bistro, and shop. Come here for the casual atmosphere if you need a space to chill for a while. Food includes burgers, sandwiches, soups, and desserts along with a full selection of cocktails, wines, and beers. With events on several evenings throughout the week and almost always on the weekends, Santeria Social Club is also an ideal place for a laid-back, entertaining evening with friends.

BRERA DISTRICT
MILANESE
La Libera

Via Palermo, 21; 02/805-3603; www. ristorantelaliberamilano.com; 7pm-12:30am daily; entrees €12-20; Metro M2: Moscova

Located in the heart of the vibrant and ever-evolving Brera district is this old-style restaurant offering diners traditional Lombard dishes focused on meat, fish, and mushrooms. Everything about this place, originally opened in the earlier part of the 20th century, screams tradition: an old wooden boiserie, the original counter from when the restaurant was first built, and windows recovered from a long-gone local grocery market. Try the risotto *al salto* (fried rice pancake), a traditional Milanese rice dish that differs slightly from the risotto Milanese in that it is a crunchier, more formed dish. Reservations are recommended here and should be booked by phone.

Al Mataral

Corso Garibaldi, 75; 02/654-204; www.facebook.com/almatarelmilano; 7pm-12:30am daily; entrees €20-30; Metro M2: Moscova

If you want Milanese food that fills your entire plate (and nearly half the table), Al Matarel serves notoriously big osso buco with risotto Milanese and Milanese cutlets. The first courses focus primarily on different types of tortellini, risotto, and fresh tagliatelle (egg noodle) plates, and the second plates focus on meats and mushrooms (although a few vegetarian options are sprinkled throughout the menu). Dining here also means you'll experience the traditionally slow Italian style of enjoying a meal with friends or family, so don't expect rushed service. Reservations are recommended if you want to dine here in the evenings.

ITALIAN AND PIZZA
Pisacco

Via Solferino, 48; 02/9176-5472; www. pisacco.it; 12pm-3pm, 7pm-11pm Tues.-Fri., 7pm-11pm Sat.; entrees €30-40, aperitivo €10-12; Metro M2: Moscova

This hot spot is one of the highest-ranked restaurants amongst locals. As a collaboration between renowned chef Andrea Berton and architect Tiziano Vudafieri along with a few others, the Milanese had high expectations for this place, and it has continued to hit it out of the park with its excellent, modern bistro atmosphere paired with the second-to-none menu of dishes made from fresh, high-quality ingredients. The best part about this place is you're eating some of the finest contemporary Italian food without breaking the bank. Try a quick business lunch from a specific, daily menu on Tuesday to Friday for under €15 or stop by for one of the most gourmet and unique *aperitivo* experiences in the city. If you're coming for dinner, reservations are recommended.

Ristorante Emilia e Carlo

Via Giuseppe Sacchi, 8; 02/862-100; www. emiliaecarlo.it; 12pm-3pm, 7pm-11pm Mon.-Fri.; entrees €20-45; Metro M1: Cairoli Castello

This classic Italian restaurant is one of the more popular restaurants in Brera, with a large menu of appetizers and first courses, as well as full pages of both fish and meat second courses. All of this is matched with a lengthy wine list, which is also considered one of the highest regarded in the city.

INTERNATIONAL
Hong Kong Crossover

Via Ciovasso, 5; 02/8901-0313; www. hkcrossover.it; 12pm-2:30pm, 7pm-11pm Mon.-Sat.; entrees €15-30; Metro M1: Cairoli Castello

Following Milan's innovative style, Hong Kong Crossover's owner and chef takes traditional Asian flavors and blends them with other international tastes, hence the name. You'll find tartare and carpaccio mixed with housemade sauces and fruits, tempuras, and unique sushi rolls not found on any other menu in the city. They

also have a selection of special menus, like the tartare and *uramaki* menus. Although plenty of seating is available on the restaurant's two levels, booking is recommended on Friday and Saturday evenings.

PORTA NUOVA
MILANESE
Il Solferino

Via Castelfidardo, 2; 02/2900-5748; www. ilsolferino.com; 12pm-2:30pm, 6pm-11:30pm daily; entrees €15-30; Metro M2: Moscova

The chef and stellar maitre d' combo at Il Solferino is what puts this antique-style restaurant on the map. The menu here is quite expansive, with plenty of Milanese and other classic Italian options for every course. However, the real menu standouts are the cheese and vegetable plates, making this place very vegetarian friendly. Order a first course, then a local cheese plate, such as gorgonzola, with a plentiful plate of veggies to go along with it. Swing by if you're in the Porta Nuova area on any day of the week during lunch or dinner.

Antica Trattoria della Pesa

Viale Pasubio, 10; 02/655-5741; www.anticatrattoriadellapesa.com; 12:30pm-2:30pm, 7:30pm-11pm Mon.-Sat.; entrees €20-40; Metro M2, M5: Garibaldi

This trattoria has been operating since 1880, and you will feel like you have stepped back into a previous era with its warm lighting, simple wall decorations, 1950s brick walls, and white tablecloths. The menu offers traditional Milanese dishes, such as Lombard meats and cheese, pickled vegetables, risotto Milanese, osso buco, *cotoletta alla Milanese*, cabbage rolls, and more. Although not cheap, the dining experience is worth every euro. Reservations are recommended,

REGIONAL CUISINE AND FOOD CULTURE

Food culture in Milan follows the larger Italian food culture (with the exception of the more vibrant *aperitivo* hour).

MEALS AND MEALTIMES
Meals are divided into courses, with most people taking at least a first and second course or side dish during lunches and dinners. In general, you'll find Italians eating lunch around 1pm and dinner around 8pm. First courses are usually a pasta or rice dish, and second courses serve meat or fish and vegetables. Breakfasts usually consist of espresso or another coffee drink with a sweet pastry.

LOCAL SPECIALTIES
While the Holy Trinity of Italian food—pizza, pasta, and gelato—are plentiful in the city, Milan has its own local dishes. The most famous is **risotto Milanese,** highlighted by its use of saffron and dry white wine. Traditional Milanese trattorias will feature this dish alongside osso buco, a plate of cross-cut veal shanks cooked with vegetables, broth, and white wine. *Cotoletta alla Milanese* is another veal dish that originated from the city, similar to Vienna's Wiener schnitzel. *Tagliere* plates (plates with a mix of cold cuts, cheeses, breads, and crackers) are served during *aperitivo* or as appetizers to meals.

If you're in the city during Christmastime, getting a **panettone** from a local bakery is a must. While this sweet bread loaf is now a popular holiday dessert in much of Southern and Eastern Europe, its undisputed birthplace is Milan. Each city or region has modified the original sweet treat over the decades, but the traditional Milanese panettone is filled with tiny pieces of candied fruit.

Ask a waiter for a drink from the Lombardy region (of which Milan is the capital), and he or she will more than likely bring you a sparkling wine, such as **Franciacorta,** a prestigious Italian sparkling wines from the Lakes region.

---

as this small trattoria fills up fast, especially on the weekends.

ITALIAN AND PIZZA
STK Milan
Piazza della Repubblica, 13; 02/8422-0110; http://togrp.com/restaurant/stk-milan; 7pm-10pm Mon.-Sat.; entrees €20-50; Metro M3: Repubblica

STK Milan, near Porta Nuova, offers one of the more modern and eclectic food experiences in Milan. There are plenty of options on the menu that are internationally rooted but created using traditional Italian ingredients, such as truffle, pistachio, and gorgonzola. While the prized dishes here are the huge cuts of steaks, you can find everything from fish and beef tartare, salads, lobster mac and cheese, and various second course dishes accompanied by both Milanese and international cocktails. Reservations are recommended here, especially on the weekends, due to its limited operating hours.

Eataly
Piazza Venticinque Aprile, 10; 02/4949-7301; www.eataly.it/milano; 8:30am-12am daily; prices vary; Metro M2, M5: Porta Garibaldi

Milan's food scene wouldn't be complete without a giant Eataly dominating one of the most modern parts of the city. The internationally famous food monster boasts the title of "largest Italian marketplace in the world," with several restaurants and gourmet food and wine shops sprawled across three floors. You can purchase anything from traditional pesto Genovese, artisan pastas, cheeses, cured meats, fine wine, and sweet treats to kitchen appliances, Italian beauty products, souvenirs, and more. Each restaurant, bar, or café within the complex focuses on traditional Italian cuisine. The best sit-down meal you'll find in the emporium is in the Michelin-starred Alice, but you genuinely cannot go wrong with any decision here, as each spot is full of local, high-quality products and a bustling atmosphere.

PORTA VENEZIA

ITALIAN AND PIZZA
Gattò

Via Castel Morrone, 10; 02/7000-6870; https://gattomilano.com; 12:45pm-3pm, 7:45pm-10:45pm Mon.-Sat.; lunch €15, dinner €30-40; Bus 60, 62: Via C. Morrone Via Modena

Known for its traditional Neapolitan dishes with a northern twist, Gattò started as a hole in the wall among a group of friends who wanted to create a minimalistic and unpretentious eatery with a menu to match. This small eatery quickly grew in popularity and eventually expanded to meet customer demand. Come here for a quiet evening of simple Italian fare made from top-quality ingredients.

Dry Milano

Viale Vittorio Veneto, 28; 02/6347-1564; www.drymilano.it; 7pm-1am daily; entrees €15-30; Metro M3: Repubblica

Come here for the mile-long cocktail list and stay for the gourmet pizza. The bar offers a wide selection of wines, beers, and spirits, but the cocktail menu is the true gem here, with pages full of "vintage and forgotten" drinks, such as a vintage Negroni or a French75, as well as classic and contemporary ones. The pizzas and focaccia here are cooked in an artisanal wood oven. Its grand opening occurred during Design Week in 2013,

so you know that its chic yet welcoming interior must reflect Milanese design culture.

INTERNATIONAL
Dim Sum

Via Nino Bixio, 29; 02/2952-2821; www. dimsummilano.com; 12pm-2:30pm, 7pm-11:30pm Tues.-Sun.; entrees €15-30; Tram 19: Via Bixio

One of the best traditional dumpling places in Milan, Dim Sum has made a name for itself in the international dining scene with its variety of Chinese meat, fish, and veggie dumplings, rolls, and soups. The menu also has a fairly large selection of rice, noodle, vegetable, and meat dishes for those craving more than just dumplings. The interior of the restaurant is elegant and contemporary, and the staff is very welcoming. Reservations are recommended in the evenings.

GELATO
Gelato Giusto

Via S. Gregorio, 17; 02/2951-0284; http:// gelatogiusto.it; 12pm-8:30pm daily, €3-5; Tram 5, 33: Porta Venezia Viale Tunisia

Gelato Giusto makes housemade gelato from fresh Italian ingredients in dozens of flavors, making it a perfect stop for an afternoon snack. Both cups and cones are available, as well as large tubs to go. Flavors range from traditional vanilla to various fruits to chocolate and licorice. Sorbets and *granitas* (slushies) are also available. Because everything is made directly in house, they pay special attention to the ingredients in each product and can, therefore, tell you which ones may cause problems for those with allergies to gluten, eggs, soy, or dairy.

CHINATOWN

INTERNATIONAL

Ravioleria Sarpi

Via Paolo Sarpi, 27; 331/887-0596; 10am-9:30pm daily; entrees €8-10; Tram 12, 14 Via Bramante Via Sarpi

For homemade Chinese dumplings served in plastic bowls or on paper plates, Ravioleria Sarpi is one of the most well-known street food options in the city. The menu is quite simple, offering cooked dumplings to eat on the spot or uncooked dumplings to go. You can watch your food being made directly in the show kitchen and eat it on the streets of Chinatown (no seating other than a handful of benches available). Choose from beef, pork, or vegetarian dumplings, but know that the pork ones tend to be the most talked about here.

Chateau Dufans

Piazzale Baiamonti ang. Via Paolo Sarpi, 2; 02/3453-4113; www.chateaudufan.com; 9am-9pm daily; entrees €8-15; Tram 2 or 4: Piazzale Baiamonti

This bakery serves mostly sweet bites and pastries, but also offers gelato and a limited food menu. It is one of the best stops in Chinatown for a quick place to rest your feet for a minute or to grab yourself a sweet treat reward while continuing to roam the area. Because it's one of the few places in the city that is open for 12 hours a day every day, the place is often crowded with locals studying or getting in a few hours of work. You may have to sit at a communal table or rush to grab a free one upon entering.

Ramen a Mano

Via Paolo Lomazzo, 20; 02/3653-6559; www.ramenamano.it; 12pm-2:30pm, 7pm-10:30pm Wed.-Mon.; entrees €8-15; Tram 10: Via Procaccini Via Lomazzo

Authentic ramen dishes are few and far between in Milan, but Ramen a Mano provides. The restaurant's name translates literally to "ramen by hand," and that's exactly what they do best. The chef wanted East to meet West, so the atmosphere is similar to any other Milanese eatery but brings in Eastern influences. The kitchen is open, so you can watch the hand-kneaded dough being made into noodles from start to finish. Although the menu specializes in ramen, it also include a number of Chinese noodle dishes, many of which are vegetarian and vegan-friendly.

ISOLA

MILANESE

Ratanà

Via Gaetano de Castillia, 28; 02/8712-8855; www.ratana.it; 12:30pm-2:30pm, 7:30pm-11:30pm daily; entrees €20-30; Metro M2: Gioia

This fine-dining restaurant, which brings life and tradition to the early-1900s building in which the restaurant is located, is Milanese through and through, thanks to chef Cesare Battisti and his sommelier Federica Fabi. The chef himself is highly selective about which ingredients come into his kitchen, wanting to ensure that his guests receive nothing but the highest-quality dishes. Most ingredients come directly from small, local producers of the region. Stop by for a full tasting menu, a Milanese *aperitivo* menu, a la carte items, and more. Reservations are highly recommended here.

ITALIAN AND PIZZA

Frida

Via Antonio Pollaiuolo, 3; 02/680-260; www.fridaisola.it; 12pm-3pm, 6pm-2am Mon.-Sat., 12pm-1am Sun., closed for lunch on Sat.; entrees €10-20; Tram 22: Via Porro Lambertenghi

gelato

Frida is one of Isola's friendliest and hospitable *aperitivo* spots, with an extensive bar menu and a large outdoor courtyard surrounded by walls of ivy. Visitors often say that coming here almost feels like coming home, given its warm and laid-back atmosphere. Frequented mainly by locals and a younger crowd, the place is busy most nights, so book a table in advance for an *aperitivo* including chips and all-you-can-eat pizza.

GELATO
Artico Gelato Tradizionale

Via Luigi Porro Lambertenghi, 15;
02/4549-4698; www.articogelateria.com;
10am-11pm daily; €2-6; Tram 22: Via Porro
Lambertenghi

If you're in the Isola area, stop by the neighborhood gelato workshop (complete with its own classroom chalkboard), where several people at a time come to learn the art of gelato and try the all-natural products made out of organic ingredients. Don't be alarmed by the lack of bright and bold colors;

real handmade gelato often has a more neutral palette. The gelato is served in traditional cups or cones, as well as on crepes or as filling inside traditional Italian breakfast pastries, such as gelato-filled brioches.

SAN SIRO
MILANESE
La Pesa Trattoria dal 1902

Via Giovanni Fantoni, 26; 02/3651-4525;
www.trattorialapesa1902.it; 12pm-3pm,
7pm-11pm daily, entrees €15-25; Bus 63, 80:
Via Rembrandt Via Vapecelatro

This trattoria combines traditional Milanese dishes and highly attentive service in a modern atmosphere. Locals often recommend this place to visitors who want a true taste of authentic Milanese cuisine. The two standout dishes here are the *cotoletta*, which can be ordered either as a standard cut or as a thicker cut (not for the faint of heart), and the osso buco served over the traditional yellow rice of Milan. While the restaurant isn't as close to the city center as several others, it's a great choice for those already heading out to San Siro to see the stadium or catch a football match. Reservations are encouraged.

ITALIAN AND PIZZA
La Barchetta

Via Federico Tesio, 15; 02/4820-5118; www. labarchettamilano.com; 12pm-2:30pm, 7pm-11:30pm daily; entrees €20-30; Metro M5: San Siro Stadio

For a casual yet satisfying meal after a football match or when in the San Siro area, La Barchetta serves mostly seafood as well as traditional Italian dishes. The white and teal interior mirrors coastal restaurants, and the seafood and pasta dishes are generous in portion and beautifully plated, so it's easy to feel like you're enjoying a nice dining experience without breaking the bank. Reservations are recommended on the weekends, and tables can be booked directly on their website.

Nightlife

Milan's nightlife starts early, around 5-7pm, and kicks off with *aperitivo* hour, during which most bars in the city fill with locals gathering for after-work drinks and finger foods. If you want to dance the night away, visit Milan's several **exclusive nightclubs and discos**—many of which are frequented by university students throughout the week. As one of Italy's most populous cities, Milan also has its fair share of large and small music venues that accommodate the tastes of all kinds of music lovers. The city hosts plenty of famous international artists every year at the San Siro Stadium or the Mediolanum Forum, such as Coldplay, the Rolling Stones, and many more. Local venues cover rock, indie, blues, and jazz.

Alternatively, try one of Milan's **rooftop bars,** such as La Rinascente Rooftop or Terrazza Aperol, both located in Piazza del Duomo and open until midnight. Or you might like to try Ceresio 7. It is easier to hop between bars and venues if you stick to Navigli, particularly the **Grand Canal,** and Brera, where you will find some of Milan's trendiest and liveliest bars in **Corso Como.**

Armani Privè

Via Gastone Pisoni, 1; 02/6231-2645; http:// armanipriveclub.com; 11:30pm-3am Wed. and Thurs., 11:30pm-3:30am Fri. and Sat.; €25-35; Metro M3: Montenapoleone

If you're looking for a sophisticated club experience, consider Armani Privè. Its golden hues, accented by touches of black and gray, and soft lighting create a warm and welcoming atmosphere enjoyed by local and international club-goers of all ages. Enjoy a dance or two on the unofficial dance floor, or sip on one of the signature cocktails from its bar. You'll also find a full selection of wines, beers, and other spirits.

Il Gattopardo Café

Via Piero della Francesca, 47; 02/3453-7699; www.gattopardomilano.com; 6pm-3am Tues.-Sun.; €15 entrance fee; Metro M5: Gerusalemme

Il Gattopardo Cafè sits in an old

Milanese church with its original architecture, marbled columns, and crystal chandeliers all still intact. It is popular among those in their late 20s through 40s. The line for entry may seem intimidating, but you shouldn't have any trouble getting in if you visit during the earlier hours of the evening. When the DJ is not spinning a mix of commercial house music, singers on rotation will entertain the crowd with some live performances.

The Club

Corso Garibaldi 97; 02/3653-4005; www.
theclubmilano.it; 11pm-5am Tues.-Sat., €20
entrance fee; Metro M2: Moscova

For a casual vibe, try The Club located near Moscova in the Brera district, an area that offers some of the city's most vibrant nightlife. Its dark mirrored walls, neon strobe lights, and pulsating music make it a hot spot for university students and locals in their 20s. The music comprises a mix of hip-hop, pop, and house. Drinks cost around €10 each.

Dude Club

Via Carlo Boncompagni 44; 392/385-1779;
http://dude-club.net; 11pm-5am Fri. and Sat.;
€18 entrance fee; Metro M3: Porto di Mare

Techno music lovers will get their fill at the Dude Club. With music spun by international and Italian DJs, this place has an underground vibe and is located outside of the city center (women are advised to travel in groups via metro). Its uncomplicated interior comprises a dark room illuminated by neon lights (so visibility is minimal), a large dance floor, a DJ booth in the front, and a full bar. This place stays pretty packed on the weekends.

Alcatraz

Via Valtellina, 25; 02/6901-6352; www.
alcatrazmilano.it; 11pm-4:30am Fri. and
Sat.; €10-15; Metro M3: Maciachini

As one of Milan's largest and most popular live music and club venues, Alcatraz sees thousands of party-goers each weekend throughout the year. Artists such as Korn, Passenger, Alice Cooper, and more have taken the stage here, but evenings without major headliners are just as busy and alive, with plenty of themed events and live DJs filling in the rest of the time. The property has three levels of dance floors as well as a bar that serves a full drink menu, averaging at €10 per drink. The crowds here are generally 25 years and under, with many being university students.

Fabrique

Via Gaudenzio Fantoli, 9; 02/5801-8197;
www.fabriquemilano.it; hours and ticket
prices vary by performance; Tram 27: Via
Mecenate Via Fantoli

Housed in the old Venus headquarters, this huge venue is one of the most popular live music venues in the city, with two bars, a stage, three levels of dance floors, and a high-tech lighting and audio system. In fact, Fabrique often wins local and national awards for its top-notch and high-energy atmosphere. Several big names have performed here, including George Extra, All Time Low, and Mika. On evenings when there isn't an artist performing live, you'll find DJs spinning mixes and themed nights. Ticket prices and hours vary, and depend on what's happening that evening. You can find a full schedule and ticket prices on the club's website.

Blue Note

Via Borsieri, 37; 02/6901-6888; www.
bluenotemilano.com; 7:30pm-12:30am
Tues.-Sun., 7:30pm-1am Fri. and Sat.; Metro
M3, M5: Zara

To slow things down, visit the Blue Note, Milan's high-quality and popular blues joint located in the Isola district. This intimate venue hosts nearly 350 shows annually, so you're bound to find live jazz and blues during your time in Milan. While the place has featured such musical artists as the Blues Brothers and Dee Dee Bridgewater, it also features local jazz musicians, highlighting some of Milan's musical culture. Shows generally start later in the evenings, but arrive early for dinner and drinks to ensure you get a spot as close to the stage as possible.

Caffè Doria

Via Andrea Doria, 22; 02/6741-1411; www.
doriajazzclub.it; performances 10pm Tues.
and Thurs.; €15-30 per person for a meal and
drink; Metro M2, M3: Centrale, M2: Caiazzo,
M1, M2: Loreto

Nestled in a little corner of the Adi Doria Grant Hotel, just east of Central Station, Caffè Doria boasts classic mahogany walls and a substantial inviting bar. A breadth of musical genres is featured here, including alternative and traditional jazz, ragtime, swing, bayou blues, and quartets. Live performances take place on Tuesday and Thursday evenings. The space is rather small, so be sure to book a table in advance for dinner and drinks.

Mag Cafè

Ripa di Porta Ticinese, 43; 02/3956-2875;
http://magcafemilano.myadj.it;
7:30pm-1:30am daily; Metro M2: Porta
Genova; Tram 10, 12: Via Vigevano Viale
Gorizia

While in Navigli, stop by Mag Cafè for a relaxing, casual drink. This cozy café features antique furniture and walls decorated with wooden shelves filled with bottles and old picture frames. There's also a seating area on the outdoor patio built along the Grand Canal—a perfect spot for catching a breeze on fair-weather days. The house cocktails are made of fresh ingredients, so ask the bartender what he or she recommends. For a really unique experience, ask those working at Mag Cafè where you can find the 1930s-style speakeasy nearby, and they may just give you the address.

Ceresio 7

Via Ceresio, 7; 02/3103-9221; www.ceresio7.
com; 12:30pm-1am daily; Metro M5:
Monumentale; Tram 10: Piazzale Cimitero
Monumentale; Bus 70: Via Ceresio

Owned by internationally known design duo DSquared2, this lavish bar on the rooftop of the Enel Energy building boasts two pools, two lounges, and unparalleled skyline views of the city. Favored by locals and the occasional celebrity for its elegance and first-rate cocktails and *aperitivo*, Ceresio 7 is a great spot for a cocktail with friends or a business outing. In the warmer months, book a table for drinks and dinner to watch the sunset.

Company Club

Via Privata Benadir, 14; 02/8738-1591; www.
companyclub.org; 9:30pm-2am Tues.-Sun.;
Metro M2: Cimiano; Bus 53 Via Derna Via
Menadir

This LGBTQ bar and club attracts mostly men between the ages of 20-40 and is popular among both locals and tourists. The club is known for its lively, colorful, neon-lit dance floor, as well as its impressive *aperitivo* and beer menu. Themed nights and Thursday happy hour often invites huge crowds. In its effort to incorporate some of Milan's rich culture, the club will occasionally exhibit the photography and paintings of local artists. Note that membership in ANDDOS or ARCI (international gay associations) is required to get in here.

LeccoMilano

*Via Lecco, 5; 328/851-9783; www.
leccomilano.it; 12pm-3pm weekdays,
6pm-2am Tues.-Sun., Metro M1: Porta
Venezia, Trams 5, 33: Viale Tunisia*

This LGBTQ-friendly bar and restaurant, located in one of Milan's most vibrant LGBTQ neighborhoods, is known for its welcoming, relaxing, and affable atmosphere. Open daily for lunch, its menu comprises modern Italian food and vegetarian-friendly plates. Its sizeable *aperitivo* buffet with drinks makes the place fill up fast in the evenings and stay busy most nights. The checkered floor gives off a retro vibe, and its wooden patio seating area invites guests to take advantage of Milan's good-weather days.

Accommodations

Milan's accommodation options range in both type and price, but one thing seems to ring true for most of them: the city's design and fashion culture never seems lost. In fact, you'll find local art and Italian design incorporated into many places throughout the city. While most accommodations fall into the €80-150 per night category, several higher-priced luxury and boutique hotels are also available, especially in the Duomo, Brera, Navigli, and Porta Nuova districts. However, budget-friendly hotels focusing on design and community are also growing in popularity, with more and more of them popping up in recent years, especially near transit zones such as the airports or Central Station.

CITY CENTER AND DUOMO DISTRICT
UNDER €80
Ostello Bello

*Via Medici, 4; 02/3658-2720; www.
ostellobello.com; €40 shared, €125 private;*
*Tram 2, 3, 14: Via Torino Via Santa Maria
Valle*

Ostello Bello is considered more than just a place to crash during your stay in the city, but rather a memorable experience due to its vibrant ambiance and helpful staff. This hostel, with its 24-hour reception desk and bar, is perfectly situated between the Duomo and the Navigli district, so most of Milan's popular sights are within walking distance. Guest have a choice of private or shared rooms, all of which have air conditioning; all shared rooms have lockers. WiFi is free in all guest rooms and the common room. The price includes luggage storage, community laptops and iPads, earplugs, towels and toiletries, breakfast, *aperitivo*, and a free welcome drink.

Babila Hostel

*Via Conservatorio, 2/A; 02/3658-8490;
www.babilahostel.it; €30 shared, €89
private; Metro M1: San Babila*

As one of Milan's newest

Ostello Bello is a budget-friendly option near Piazza Duomo

accommodations (opened in 2017), Babila Hostel almost seems too chic to be a hostel. With sleek, modern furniture that highlights Milan's design culture and a top-level terrace just a stone's throw away from Piazza San Babila, it gives you an above-average hostel experience. Room offerings include unisex dorms, women-only dorms, and private rooms, with WiFi, air conditioning, and private bathrooms available in each room.

€80-150
Hotel Vecchia

Via Boromei, 4; 02/875-042; www. hotelvecchiamilan.com; €65 s, €110 d; Metro M1: Cordusio

Located strategically between the Duomo and the Università Cattolica, Hotel Vecchia is a short walk away from most landmarks in the Duomo District as well as in the Ticinese and Navigli areas. The hotel is also surrounded by dozens of local and international shops as well as a plethora of diverse food choices, from sushi to traditional Italian cuisine. Each room comes with WiFi, breakfast, air conditioning, and

a private bathroom. Some rooms also have a private balcony overlooking a quiet courtyard, and parking is available for those traveling by car.

BC Maison

Via Gonzaga, 2; 334/946-5964; www. bcmaison.it; €150 d; Metro M1, M3: Duomo

BC Maison is consistently rated as one of the most charming accommodations in the city center. With a modern and pristine interior located in a 1950s building in Piazza Diaz (a very short walk away from Piazza del Duomo), the few rooms here should be booked as far in advance as possible. Each uniquely designed room comes with a private balcony and bathroom, parquet floors, WiFi, and air conditioning. Breakfast is included in the price of the room, and guest parking is available.

OVER €150
Chateau Monfort

Corso Concordia, 1; 02/776-761; www. hotelchateaumonfort.com; €230 d; Tram 9: Piazza Tricolore

Just walking into Chateau Monfort gives you a feeling of elegance and luxury. The hotel itself has a nicely reviewed Italian restaurant, a lounge bar, a separate wine bar, and a well-appointed spa. The best parts of this hotel, however, are its fairy-tale and musical-themed rooms and suites, such as *Madame Butterfly* and *The Nutcracker*. Each room includes custom-made Italian furniture, air conditioning, and a private bathroom. The breakfast is American buffet-style and includes both vegetarian and gluten-free options.

Hotel Straf

Via S. Raffaele, 3; 02/805-081; www.straf.it; €320 d; Metro M1, M3: Duomo

Hotel Straf is considered one of the most well-designed contemporary accommodations in the city center. As a member of the Design Hotels group, Straf tries to reinvent the classic hotel experience through design, art, and good service. The 19th-century building in which the hotel is housed, located just 50 meters (164 feet) away from the Duomo itself, is completely modernized on the inside. Each room comes with soft bathrobes and slippers to go along with the spacious private bathrooms, WiFi, an organic tea selection, and air conditioning. The hotel offers a free buffet breakfast and a 24-hour gym.

TICINESE AND NAVIGLI

€80-150
My Bed (Columns)

Corso di Porta Ticinese 24; 02/8324-2224; www.mybedmilano.com; €99 d; Tram 3: Carrobbio

Located across the Colonne di San Lorenzo, My Bed Columns sits at the unofficial line dividing the Duomo and Ticinese and Navigli districts. This affords you easy access to several sights, restaurants, bars, and shopping options. A tram stops directly outside the hotel, so you can reach the heart of both districts in a few minutes, or you can walk to the center of both areas in roughly 10 minutes. Each room includes air conditioning, WiFi, Italian-made furniture, and private bathrooms. The hotel partners with a local bar nearby, Cioccolati Italiani, to provide breakfast at a reduced price.

Home BB

Via Lorenteggio, 141; 338/939-0193; www. homebbmilano.com; €107 d; Buses 50, 98: Piazza Frattini

Home BB focuses on the home-away-from-home experience, providing you with the comfort and privacy of your own space along with the usual bed and breakfast services. The accommodation is well served by buses and trams. Each room includes memory foam pillows, air conditioning, coffee machine, and private bathrooms. The hotel offers airport shuttle services and parking for guests as well as a breakfast buffet included in the price of the room.

Art Hotel Navigli

Via Angelo Fumagalli, 4; 02/89438; www. arthotelnavigli.com; €120-190 d; Tram 2, Bus 74, 169, 325: Via Valenza Alzaia Nav. Grande

The rooms at Art Hotel Navigli mix functionality and comfort with modern design. The hotel itself is roughly a five-minute walk from the Porta Genova station, near Via Tortona. The surroundings include a rooftop terrace, modern paintings and sculptures, and an outdoor garden at ground level. All rooms have air conditioning, WiFi, private bathrooms, and a coffee machine. Interconnected rooms and rooms with balconies are available upon request. Hotel services include an airport shuttle, a wellness center and spa, fitness center, and breakfast.

OVER €150
Hotel Maison Casa Borella

Alzaia Naviglio Grande, 8; 02/5810-9114; www.hotelmaisonborella.com; €180 d; Tram 9 or 10: Via Vigevano Viale Gorizia

This elegant hotel sits right along the banks of Navigli's big canal in an 18th-century building. You have Milan's most vibrant nightlife scene right outside your door, yet the hotel's space is relaxing, elegant, and quiet. Rooms vary from a classic double to suites and independent rooms with private entrances. Each room is wheelchair accessible and includes WiFi, air conditioning, and a private bathroom.

Magna Pars Suites

Via Vincenzo Forcella, 6; 02/833-8371; www. magnapars-suitesmilano.it; €225 junior deluxe suite; Metro M2: Porta Genova

The five-star Magna Pars Suites packs a lot into a small space. Its very modern, neutral-colored suites are housed in an old perfume factory—with a perfume laboratory on the premises. Each room comes with a living room and a private bathroom and is filled with elegant wood furniture. Other amenities include air conditioning, a coffee machine, WiFi, soundproofing, and a complimentary breakfast buffet each morning. Many rooms overlook the hotel's garden. The hotel has a high-tech gym that also features a Turkish bath.

BRERA DISTRICT

€80-150
Brera Prestige B&B

Via delle Erbe, 2; 393/857-8228; www. breraprestige.com; €140 d; Metro M2: Lanza

In the Brera district, sits Brera Prestige B&B. Most sights in the city center and the Brera district are just a 10-minute walk away. Each room includes WiFi, air conditioning, breakfast in the room, refrigerator, a coffee machine, and a private bathroom. The hotel also offers guest and valet parking.

OVER €150
Palazzo Parigi

Corso di Porta Nuova, 1; 02/625-625; www. palazzoparigi.com; €400 d; Metro M3: Turati

The luxurious and captivating Palazzo Parigi has of late been the hot spot for

Palazzo Parigi feels like a hidden corner in the city center

Milan's celebrity guests. It's no wonder, with its white marble interior, verdant courtyard, and floor-to-ceiling windows. Each room or suite includes a private balcony or terrace, air conditioning, a fully marble private bathroom, and beds that are generally larger than normal size. The hotel also includes a fine dining restaurant, a highly-rated spa and wellness center with a swimming pool, a bar, and breakfast.

Bulgari Hotel Milano

Via Privata Fratelli Gabba, 7b; 02/805-8051; www.bulgarihotels.com; €900 superior king room; Metro M3: Montenapoleone

The Bulgari Hotel chain is known for providing luxurious accommodations around the world, and the property in Milan is no exception. Despite its location adjacent to bustling Via Montenapoleone, the hotel, with its private courtyard and earthy and wooden tones, feels like a quiet, hidden corner of the city. Each room or suite includes air conditioning, WiFi, an iPod dock, tile or marble floors, and a private bathroom. The hotel includes a spa with glass mosaics and an indoor swimming pool.

PORTA NUOVA
€80-150
Bohemki
Via Pietro Maroncelli, 12; 347/819-5967; bohemki.com; €90 d; Metro M2, M5: Porta Garibaldi

One of Milan's most unique accommodations, Bohemki serves as a museum of contemporary art and hosts up-and-coming artists passing through Milan in exchange for work, putting you in the middle of Milan's bustling art scene. Each room includes a private balcony and bathroom, WiFi, fans, and tile or marble floor. Throughout the hotel, you'll find homey scenes of handwritten notes and art, various knick-knacks, and mismatched decor. Breakfast is included.

OVER €150
Hotel TOCQ
Via Alessio di Tocqueville, 7/D; 02/62-071; http://tocq.it; €165 d; Metro M2, M5: Porta Garibaldi

Hotel Tocq is yet another design hotel strategically located in the Porta Nuova district, near the Porta Garibaldi station and 100 meters (300 feet) from Corso Como. The light hues of its interior make the hotel welcoming and approachable, yet the furniture is sleek and modern. Guests seem to love the huge breakfast of both savory and sweet dishes. Each room includes air conditioning, WiFi, and a private bathroom. The onsite cafè offers a relaxing *aperitivo* hour with snacks and housemade cocktails. Breakfast is included.

Hotel Viu
Via Aristotile Fioravanti, 6; 02/8001-0910; www.hotelviumilan.com; €225 for twin room; Metro M5: Monumentale

The huge, contemporary Hotel Viu is another Milanese accommodation frequented by celebrities. The most beloved feature of this place is the rooftop pool with a 360-degree view of the city. Designer Nicola Gallizia is responsible for the luxurious look of the hotel: think marble bathrooms and earthy and neutral tones. Each room is wheelchair-accessible, with air conditioning, WiFi, and a private bathroom, and offers a unique view of one of the city's more famous landmarks. The restaurant boasts a Michelin-star chef serving up Italian and international dishes.

NEAR MILAN'S CENTRAL STATION
UNDER €80
43 Station Hotel
Via Fabio Filzi, 43; 02/2217-9900; www.43stationhotel.com; €75 d; Metro M3: Sondrio

The new 43 Station Hotel, which opened in 2017, has made a name for itself for its quality care and accommodation without forcing guests to dip too far into their wallets. The hotel was designed with the conveniences of modern technology in mind while remaining environmentally responsible. The 66 rooms in the hotel, which is just 100 meters (300 feet) away from Central Station, were designed by local artists and engineers. Each room includes air conditioning, WiFi, and a private bathroom.

Biocity

*Via Edolo, 18; 02/6670-3595; www.
biocityhotel.it; €70 s, €75 d; Metro M2, M3:
Centrale*

Biocity Hotel offers guests an organic and eco-friendly experience. The hotel is housed in a 1920s villa and includes a snack bar and wellness center, which you can access for €8 upon room reservation. The closest entrance to Milan's Central Station is half a kilometer (third of a mile) away by foot. Each room includes air conditioning, WiFi, and a private bathroom. This hotel is a great option for solo travelers, with single rooms starting as low as €70 per night.

€80-150
NYX Milan Hotel

*Piazza Quattro Novembre, 3; 02/2217-5500;
www.leonardo-hotels.com/nyx-milan; €116 d;
Metro M2, M3: Centrale*

The NYX Milan Hotel, which is located just next to Central Station, is a concept hotel that incorporates a combination of Milan's street art and contemporary art into its hotel and guestroom decor. Its Clash bar and restaurant was created to encourage locals and tourists to meet for food or drinks; it also includes a house DJ. The rooftop terrace gives guests a decent view of the city skyline. Rooms range in size and price, from small rooms for two people to suites for up to four people. Each room includes air conditioning, WiFi, a coffee machine and kettle, and a private bathroom.

Casa Titta

*Via Giulio Belinzaghi, 21; 347/927-3384;
www.casatitta.it; €120 d; Metro M3:
Maciachini*

This quaint and homey bed-and-breakfast is just a couple stops away from Central Station on metro Line M3 (yellow), making it close enough for convenience but just far enough away to feel like you're out of the hustle of the travel zone. The four rooms at Casa Titta are nothing short of cozy and welcoming, so guests feel right at home. A continental breakfast, which is included, is served every morning in the common room. Each double room includes air conditioning, a private bathroom, WiFi, and a tea and coffee maker.

NEAR THE AIRPORT
€80-150
Moxy Hotel Malpensa

*Via Somma Lombardo, Milan Malpensa
Airport Terminal 2; 02/9475-7100; www.
marriott.com/hotels/travel/milox-moxy-
milan-malpensa-airport; €80 d*

If you're flying into Malpensa Airport very late or you have an early flight one morning, consider staying at the Moxy. Newly opened with an extremely friendly staff, this Marriott-owned hotel offers a modernly funky common area with computers, board games, reading nooks, loungers, and more. The hotel is located directly in Malpensa's Terminal 2 parking lot and

Moxy's hip and friendly atmosphere is an ideal option for those staying near Malpensa

right outside the Malpensa Express Terminal 2 train stop.

Air Hotel Linate

Via Francesco Baracca, 2; www.airhotel. it; €80 d

Air Hotel Linate is generally considered the best option for those needing to stay near the Linate Airport for a night due to a late arrival or early departure. Each room includes air conditioning, WiFi, and a private bathroom. The buffet breakfast is included, as is access to the gym and the patio overlooking the garden. The airport shuttle is free both ways and operates frequently. You can ask the 24-hour reception desk for the official times. The restaurant located in the hotel offers traditional Italian dishes, with room service available.

Information and Services

Travel agencies and other travel information points are still quite popular in Italy, especially for Italians, so you can find a handful of information points throughout the city center, especially in the Duomo district and near Central Station.

InfoMilano

Galleria Vittorio Emanuele II, corner Piazza della Scala; www.turismo.milano.it; 9am-7pm Mon.-Fri., 10am-6pm Sat.-Sun.

Milan's city government opened an official tourist information kiosk, InfoMilano, in late 2014 in anticipation of the flood of visitors coming to the city for the World Expo the following year. Visitors can get information about attractions, experiences, landmarks, and more. Find it at the corner of Piazza della Scala in the Galleria, a prominent and easily accessible location.

Getting There

Milan is the most strategically placed city in Italy, and arguably in southern Europe, as it sits in the north central part of Italy, connecting the rest of Europe to the southern half of the country. With three international airports nearby and a number of domestic and international trains from surrounding countries, the city is accessible via direct flights from nearly every continent as well as from all other major European cities.

BY AIR

If you're traveling by plane to Milan, you're more than likely flying into Milan's Malpensa or Linate Airports. Most flights arrive at Malpensa, as the airport is larger and offers more international and intercontinental connections. Keep in mind that some airlines only fly to one of these two airports, while others fly to and from both. If you're planning to travel to or from Milan from the area's lakes, your best bet is traveling by car or train, as none of them are more than an hour and a half away using either mode of transportation.

FROM MALPENSA
By Train
The quickest and easiest way to get from either terminal at Malpensa to Milan is via the Malpensa Express train, a roughly 45-60 minute trip that starts at Malpensa's Terminal 2, stops at Terminal 1, and ends in two destinations in Milan: Central Station and Cadorna Station. Trains from Central Station also stop at Milan's Porta Garibaldi train station. Trains depart both ways every half hour 5am-12am (trains start slightly earlier and run a little later to and from Cadorna than they do along the Centrale-Malpensa route).

Tickets can be purchased online in advance at Malpensa Express (www.malpensaexpress.it) or directly at any of the departing train stations, including both terminals at the airport. One-way tickets are €12, with roundtrip tickets available at €21. While you must select a departing time for each train, tickets are valid to use up to four hours after the selected time. If you purchase tickets using the machines at the terminals or at one of the train stations, note that you will need to validate them using the stamping machines at the platforms before boarding the train.

By Bus
Alternatively, you can take one of the buses that run between Malpensa's Terminal 1 and Milan's Central Station. No matter which bus company you travel with, all offer prices between €5-8 for the one-hour one-way trip. These services are nearly

identical, so selecting a bus upon arrival shouldn't take much thought. The timetables are nearly the same as the Malpensa Express. For those arriving or departing from Malpensa's Terminal 2, consider using the Terravision bus line, which runs to and from Terminal 2. Alternatively, you can hop the free shuttle bus that runs approximately every 10-15 minutes between the two terminals. At the airport or at Milan's Central Station, follow the signs to the bus parking lot. Tickets can be purchased directly on the spot using cash, or you can purchase Terravision tickets online in advance at www.terravision.eu.

By Taxi
A taxi ride from Malpensa to the center of Milan will take about an hour, and most taxi companies have a flat rate of €80-100, depending on the company. Some companies also add minor supplementary charges, such as fees for night trips, luggage, pets, or holidays. Taxis stands can be found directly outside both terminals.

Car Rental
You can also rent a car from the Terminal 1 Arrivals hall, or directly online at www.airportmalpensa.com/car-hire. Rental car companies running out of Malpensa include Budget, Dollar, Goldcar, Hertz, Thrifty, and others.

FROM LINATE
Getting to and from Milan's Linate Airport takes roughly half an hour by bus from the city center. You can take one of the several private bus lines or shuttles directly from Linate to Central Station, or viceversa, for €5 each way. Between the few different companies, all of which are fairly

equal in service, buses depart each way every 15-20 minutes 5am-12am. Finding a bus is relatively easy, as the airport is rather small; simply follow the signs leading you to the bus parking lot from the arrivals hall. Each bus platform tells you which buses arrive and depart from that platform as well as when. Tickets can be purchased directly from the driver but note that they usually only take cash.

Alternatively, there is the public Line 73 city bus that runs between Piazza Diaz, which is just a stone's throw south of the Duomo, and Linate every 10 minutes for €1.50 each way, 5:35am-12:30am. The trip takes about half an hour, give or take a few minutes based on requested stops and traffic. Tickets can be purchased as regular public transportation tickets, and from any tobacco shop, kiosk, or ticketing machine in metro stations.

A taxi ride from Linate to the center of Milan will take about 20-30 minutes, and most taxi companies have a flat rate of about €15-30. Some companies also add minor supplementary charges, such as fees for night trips, luggage, pets, or holidays. Taxis stands can be found directly outside the terminal.

BY TRAIN

Milan can be reached by high-speed trains from a number of cities both in Italy or from surrounding countries, with most trains arriving at Central Station. In Italy, *freccia* (fast) trains run between Milan and Turin, Venice (with a stop in Verona), Bologna, Florence, Rome, Naples, and other cities.

- Florence to Milan: 1h 40m, €36
- Rome to Milan: 3h, €60
- Venice to Milan: 2h 25m, €25
- Turin to Milan: 1h, €17-22

- Bologna to Milan: 1h, €35
- Naples to Milan: 4h 15m, €58-68

All tickets for Italian trains can be purchased online from Trenitalia (http://trenitalia.com), the main Italian rail company. For fast trains, you should book as far in advance as possible online to get the best prices and reserve your seats.

International trains to Milan include those from Zurich, Geneva, Bern, Paris, Munich, Frankfurt, Basel, Lugano, Marseille, Nice, Cannes, and Monte Carlo. Most of these trains have quite long trips (5-12 hours) and may be pricier than arriving by plane or coach, but they will also give you an amazing view of the landscape between the cities. Night trains are available to and from Paris (via the Thello EuroNight train) as well as Munich and Vienna (via the DB City Night Line). These tickets should be purchased in advance directly on each company's website at www.thello.com and www.bahn.com, respectively.

If you're traveling between the regional lakes to and from Milan, you will either take a Trenitalia regional train, or a Trenord regional train. Trenord is a smaller train service that works in conjunction with Trenitalia and serves the northern part of Italy, and tickets for both companies can be purchased on http://trenitalia.com.

Lake Como

- Lake Como (east) from Varenna: 1h, €6.70 to Milan Central Station
- Lake Como (east) from Lecco: 40m or 1h, €4.80-5.50 to either Milan Central Station or Milan Porta Garibaldi
- Lake Como (west) from Como: 37m or 1h, €4.80 to either Milan Central Station or Milan Porta Garibaldi

Lake Maggiore
- Lake Maggiore from Verbania: 1h 18m or 1h 45m, €9.80
- Lake Maggiore from Stresa: 1h 10m or 1h 35m, €8.60 to either Milan Central Station or Milan Porta Garibaldi

Lake Lugano
- Lake Lugano from Lugano: 1h 10m, starting at €24 to Milan Central Station

Lake Garda
- Lake Garda from Desenzano del Garda: 52m, €20 using the *freccia* train
- Lake Garda from Peschiera del Garda: 1h 07m, €20.90 to Milan Central Station using the *freccia* train

MILAN'S CENTRAL STATION
Piazza Duca d'Aosta, 1; Metro M2, M3 Centrale; www.milanocentrale.it

If you're traveling to and from other major cities in Italy or Europe, Milan's Central Station will almost always be both the starting and ending points of your journey. With 24 tracks, the station sees approximately 500 departures and arrivals per day. The trains themselves are located on the third level of Centrale, with all levels offering a range of services including banks, restaurants, currency exchange kiosks, and shopping outlets.

All buses and taxis are found on the ground level on either side of the station. You can follow the signs from the trains directly to each piazza for ground transportation services. Metro Lines M2 (green) and M3 (yellow) also arrive at Central Station. You can follow the signs between the metro and the trains to reach either one. Tickets can be purchased throughout the

various ticketing machines in the station, or at the Trenitalia office on the first floor. Milan's train platforms are guarded with a security gate, so you must present your purchased train ticket to the security guards before entering the platforms.

BY BUS
If you're traveling to Milan from within Italy, you best bet is to stick to the efficient and frequent train system, especially if you're coming from one of the surrounding lakes in the area or another city in northern Italy. However, if you're coming from the nearby countries of Switzerland, Austria, France, or Germany, there are a few relatively cheap bus lines you can take that may help you save a few euros and travel just as comfortably as on a train. Flixbus (www.flixbus.com) offers routes to and from five different bus stations in Milan: Milano Sesto San Giovanni (M1), Lampugnano (M1), San Donato (M3), and both terminals at Malpensa. You can find routes from most major cities in Switzerland, Germany, and France. Tickets should be purchased online in advance directly on the Flixbus website and should be printed out or available for display on your phone before boarding the bus. Flixbus also offers a free mobile app for travelers.

BY CAR
If you're traveling to Milan by car, note that just as any other major European city, you'll run into plenty of traffic within city limits, and although there are several parking garages sprinkled throughout the city and marked with a blue "P" sign, you may not always find convenient parking near your accommodation. If you're dead set on getting

here by car, consider parking your car at the large, car parks at the **Cascina Gobba** (M2, south Milan) or **Sesto San Giovanni** (M1, north Milan), both of which have corresponding metro lines that can take you directly into the city center.

Milan is served by major Italian highways from every direction, making it easily accessible from other large cities in Italy as well as the surrounding lakes. From Lake Como, take the A36 (from the western side of the lake) or the A51 (from the eastern side of the lake) highways to reach northern Milan. From Lake Maggiore, you'll take the A8/E62 highway southeast to head towards Milan, which will eventually take you to the northwest part of the city. From Lake Como, regardless of which area you're coming from, you'll eventually have to get on the A4 highway heading directly west towards Milan.

Getting Around

Milan's public transportation system is arguably the best and most efficient of its kind in Italy and is by far the most economical way to travel around. The city is covered by metro, buses, and trams, so getting where you want to go is relatively fast and reliable. The metro is the quickest way to travel. All public transportation generally begins at 6am and finishes around midnight on weekdays.

A single ride via any public transportation mode within city limits is **€1.50,** with a ticket lasting 90 minutes. This means that you can use a single ticket as many times as you want on as many buses or trams as you want within 90 minutes of the time you validate the ticket, with the only restriction being that you can only have one metro ride per ticket. Milan also offers a whole day pass (€4.50), two-day passes (€8.25), week passes (two tickets per day for six days; €10), and single tickets to areas and attractions beyond the normal city limits (€1.80+). If you plan on using public transportation more than one or two times throughout a day, grab a day pass.

METRO

The metro is the quickest way to travel around Milan, with four different metro lines sprouting into every direction of the city and trains arriving at each stop every three minutes or so. The metro system has a total of 113 stations (marked by red M signs on the streets) and covers 101 kilometers (63 miles) in length, which is about 20 percent of Milan's total area. Most neighborhoods in Milan's city center are serviced by the metro, especially the Duomo district, Porta Nuova, Brera, the Castle district, and Porta Venezia. However, the Navigli and Ticinese districts are only served by one metro station, the M2 Porta Genova metro stop, meaning if you planned on using public transportation, you may want to rely on the trams weaving through this neighborhood.

Metro lines are identified by number as well as color: Line M1 (red), Line M2 (green), Line M3 (yellow), and Line M5 (purple). The **M1 Red line** runs horizontal through the city's main core, but branches into one northern and one southern branch on the western end of the line. On the eastern end, the line runs north out of the city limits. On this line, you can easily navigate the historic Duomo district as well as most shopping areas such as the Galleria and Corso Buenos Aires in Porta Venezia. The M2 Green line runs from the southern suburbs of Milan, up through Navigli and into Brera, then starts heading east at Central Station. Once it reaches the eastern edge of the city, it heads northeast out of the city. The M3 Yellow line runs primarily north and south, serving many of the city's more residential areas. The most important stops on this line are between Central Station and the Duomo, where you'll find several of the city's nicer hotels and shopping areas, including Montenapoleone. Milan's newest line, the M5 Purple line, is unique in that the trains have driver-less, modern cars. This line runs from the western part of the city, with a stop at San Siro stadium, and runs north into some of the residential areas. From here, you can reach the Porta Garibaldi station in Porta Nuova as well as the Isola district.

All stations have signs telling you which way the trains run on either side, as well as maps with each stop in that direction. Most stations also provide monitors showing the destination of the train as well as the wait time for the next train. Each individual ticket for Milan's public transportation grants you one ride within a 90-minute period, so you will need to purchase one ticket per ride.

Seven metro stops have intersecting lines: Centrale (M2 and M3), Duomo (M1 and M3), Loreto (M1 and M2), Cadorna (M1 and M2), Zara (M3 and M5), Garibaldi (M2 and M5), and Lotto (M1 and M5). The Centrale, Garibaldi, and Cadorna stations are also linked to the important railway stations that you may need when traveling to and from the city.

BUS

Eighty bus lines weave throughout the narrow streets and run along the concentric circles encompassing the city center, with buses arriving at each stop anywhere from every 4 minutes to every 20 minutes, depending on which areas the buses are serving. Unlike most other Italian cities, the buses in Milan generally run on time, and the more popular bus stops often have screens letting you know when the next bus will arrive. Bus stops are marked by poles with signs on them informing you of the bus line and schedule for each day, so you can easily see where the bus goes and at what time you should expect the next bus. The sign will only tell you the stops for the direction in which the bus is headed, so if you don't find your stop in that direction, look across the street, where you should find the same bus stop for the bus headed in the opposite direction nearby. Some bus stops have covered benches as well.

The most useful bus route for visitors is the 94 line, which runs the ring around the city center, stopping by Cadorna, Sant'Ambrogio, Università Cattolica, Corso di Porta Ticinese, and more.

When on the bus, make sure that you press the button alerting the driver that you would like to get off at the next stop *before* arriving at the stop. It's a good idea to track for how many stops you'll be on the bus before boarding, as stops are not always announced. An individual ticket of €1.50 will grant you as many bus rides as necessary within the 90-minute validity period from when the ticket was first validated on any means of public transportation. Validate your ticket using the machines in the bus upon each trip, even if the ticket is already validated, as some ticket controllers are picky about this.

TRAM

The Milanese trams are especially unique to the city; this mode of transportation dates back to the late 1800s, when the same routes were being traveled by horse and buggy. The old-style rail cars hit most major attractions and districts in the city and give visitors a slow-motion view of the city itself. The trams, which are made up of 18 different lines, are similar to buses, in that the most popular routes arrive every 10 minutes or so and you'll need to press the button in advance to let the driver know you want to get off at the next stop, otherwise the tram will not stop if no one requests the stop or if the driver sees no one waiting at the next stop.

The most popular tram routes for visitors are lines 2, 3, 14, and 16, all of which pass near Piazza del Duomo. Tram 2 passes through Isola, Porta Garibaldi, Lanza in the Brera district, near Piazza Duomo and ends near Porta Genova along the big canal in Navigli. Tram 3, instead, starts near the Piazza del Duomo and runs through Ticinese and then runs south, parallel to the small canal in Navigli. Tram 14 starts in the north, then passes near Parco Sempione and the castle, and eventually runs past Porta Genova and south, parallel to the big canal in Navigli. Tram 16 starts in the western part of the city, starting near the San Siro Stadium and passing through Corso Magenta through downtown, near Piazza Duomo.

Trams stops are marked like bus

Trams are a special mode of transportation emblematic of Milan.

stops in the city, with poles that have signs on them informing you of the tram line and schedule for each day, so you can easily see where the tram is headed and at what time you should expect the next one. The sign will only tell you the stops for the direction in which the tram is headed, so if you don't find your stop in that direction, look across the street, where you should find the same stop for the tram headed in the opposite direction.

While the old-style rail cars are charming, several trams have been updated in terms of service and appearance, so you may not always ride on one of the older trams, especially on some of the more popular lines, as the newer trams are built to hold more passengers. However, if you want to experience the old-style cars, take the Tram line 1 from Milan's Central Station, which will also take you past the Galleria, Piazza Duomo, the Castle, Parco Sempione, and the Arco della Pace.

An individual ticket of €1.50 will grant you unlimited tram rides within the 90-minute validity period from when the ticket was first validated on any means of public transportation. Validate your ticket using the machines in the tram upon each trip, even if the ticket is already validated.

TAXIS AND RIDE-HAILING

Taxis in Milan are white and marked officially with the taxi company along the sides. Instead of flagging down taxis on the street, you should go to a taxi stand or call to book one in advance. Taxi stands can be found directly outside the terminals at both Malpensa and Linate Airports, as well as outside the most-served train and metro stations: Centrale, Porta Garibaldi, Cadorna, Lotto, Loretto. Two stands are found on Corso Buenos Aires, one at Piazza del Duomo, Piazza Cavour, and Corso di Porta Ticinese, amongst others.

Taxis have a minimum fare of €3.30 on weekdays, €5.40 on weekends and public holidays, and €6.50 in the evenings. There is a cost of €1.09 per kilometer (0.5 miles) and €28 for each hour of waiting. Once a taxi reaches €13, the cost of the kilometer goes up to €1.50, and it goes up to €1.70 per kilometer if the taxi drives over 50 kilometers (30 miles) per hour for more than 60 seconds. Given all of this, taxis can be a fairly expensive way to travel in the city, as you won't find a taxi ride under €10 in most situations.

You will generally find taxis at all times of the day and night at the airports and main train stations. If you want to book a taxi in advance, you can call one of these companies: Autoradiotaxi (02-8585), Taxi Blu (02-4040 or 39/02-6767), or Radio Taxi (02-4000). Remember that some companies may not have dispatches that speak English that well, so speak your address and time of pickup slowly and clearly.

Other ride-hailing services are not popular in Milan and the surrounding area, although Uberblack, Uberlux, and Ubervan do run unofficially in the city, despite many attempts by local taxi companies and lawmakers to shut them down. However, note that Uber rides cannot be pre-scheduled in this area, so if you want to book a trip in advance, you need to call a taxi.

MONZA

Monza, approximately 15 kilometers (9 miles) northeast of Milan, is one of the city's most influential and historic suburbs. From the Middle Ages onward, royal families from various empires have chosen Monza as their temporary residence. The Villa Reale, built by Empress Maria Theresa in 1777, brought even more prominence to the city. From that point forward, Monza's history has become increasingly intertwined with that of Milan's.

Internationally, Monza is best known as the host city of the Formula One Italian Grand Prix,

HIGHLIGHTS

✪ **ROYAL VILLA:** For a taste of royalty, explore the halls of Monza's Villa Reale and admire the colorful, manicured grounds around the giant villa (page 108).

✪ **MONZA PARK:** Spend an afternoon exploring Europe's largest walled park, with a handful of villas, large grassy knolls, and plenty of paths for walking or cycling (page 108).

✪ **ITALIAN GRAND PRIX:** Get revved up for the buzzing atmosphere at Italy's largest racing event in September (page 110).

an event that draws thousands of racing fans to this small city. Although the primary attractions are the villa, the park, and the racetrack, there is plenty to see in the city center, so you can easily make a day or afternoon trip from Milan.

ORIENTATION

The small city of Monza is structured much like its big sister city to the south, Milan, with a circular road making up the city's core. Via Andrea Appiani makes up the northern half of the circle, Via Alessandro Manzoni makes up the southwestern part, and Via Ozone Visconti makes up the southeastern part. The **Lambro River** splits into two branches in the city's center, with the western branch running directly through the middle of town and the eastern branch hugging the eastern side of the center circle, just outside Via Ozone Visconti. **Corso Milano** is one of the most important roads in Monza, running from Sesto San Giovanni to the south directly to the city center, with the train station just off of this road.

Villa Reale and **Monza Park** are just north of the city center, starting at the roundabout where Via Andrea Appiani meets Viale Regina Margherita. While the Lambro River runs through the southern end of the park, it eventually exits and runs parallel the park on the eastern side. The park itself expands beyond Monza's city limits, running north past the villages of Vedano al Lambro to the west and Villa Santa to the east, capped off by the village of Biassono on the northern end.

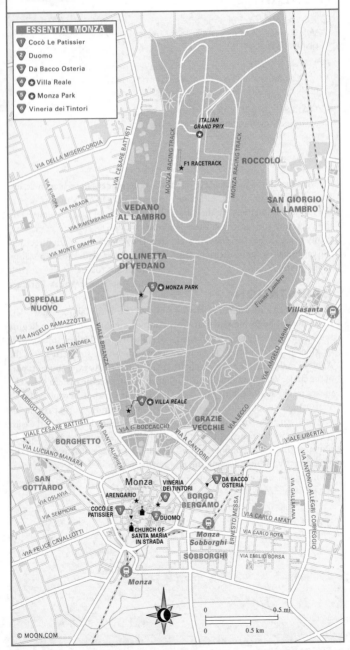

Monza

ESSENTIAL MONZA
1. Cocò Le Patissier
2. Duomo
3. Da Bacco Osteria
4. Villa Reale
5. Monza Park
6. Vineria dei Tintori

ITALIAN GRAND PRIX

F1 RACETRACK

MONZA RACING TRACK

MONZA RACING TRACK

ROCCOLO

SAN GIORGIO AL LAMBRO

VEDANO AL LAMBRO

VIA DELLA MISERICORDIA

VIA CESARE BATTISTI

VIA EUROPA

VIA PARADA

VIA RIMEMBRANZE

VIA MONTE GRAPPA

COLLINETTA DI VEDANO

MONZA PARK

Fiume Lambro

Villasanta

OSPEDALE NUOVO

VIA ANGELO RAMAZZOTTI

VIA SANT'ANDREA

VIALE BRIANZA

VIA ANGELO FARINA

VIA ABRIGO BOITO

VIA LECCO

VILLA REALE

GRAZIE VECCHIE

VIALE CESARE BATTISTI

VIA G. BOCCACCIO

VIA A. CANTORE

VIALE LIBERTA

BORGHETTO

VIA DANTE ALIGHIERI

VIA LUCIANO MANARA

VIA ANTONIO ALLEGRI CORREGGIO

SAN GOTTARDO

Monza

VINERIA DEI TINTORI

DA BACCO OSTERIA

VIA GALLARANA

ARENGARIO

BORGO BERGAMO

VIA OSLAVIA

VIA CARLO AMATI

VIA SEMPIONE

COCÒ LE PATISSIER

DUOMO

ERNESTO MESSA

VIA CARLO ROTA

CHURCH OF SANTA MARIA IN STRADA

Monza Sobborghi

VIA FELICE CAVALLOTTI

SOBBORGHI

VIA EMILIO BORSA

Monza

0   0.5 mi

0   0.5 km

© MOON.COM

Itinerary Ideas

ESSENTIAL MONZA

One day in Monza is enough time for you to see most of what Monza has to offer and get a general feel of the city:

1 Start your morning off by grabbing a sweet pastry and cup of coffee at **Cocò Le Patissier** on Via Teodolinda Regina.

2 Spend a few hours meandering around Monza's city center, stopping into the **Duomo di Monza** and the **Church of Santa Maria in Strada**. In between the churches, you'll find plenty of local shops and boutiques to pop into and browse.

3 For lunch, make your way to **Da Bacco Osteria** for a classic Italian meal with a Monza twist. You'll find plenty of delicious meat and risotto dishes here but be sure to save room for dessert.

4 Make your way to **Villa Reale**, Monza's most prized possession, and admire its neoclassical facade and immense grounds from the outside.

5 Spend a couple hours around Europe's largest enclosed public park, **Monza Park**. Rent a bike and cycle around the park or simply walk around the large grassy knolls and villas.

6 After a nice afternoon in the park, make your way back to the city center and unwind with a glass of wine and a large *aperitivo* plate at **Vineria dei Tintori**.

Sights

CITY CENTER

The center of Monza is home to several centuries-old churches and villas, making it a pleasant area to wander around.

DUOMO DI MONZA

Piazza Duomo; 039/389-420; www.
duomomonza.it; 8am-6pm Mon.-Fri.;
cathedral free, Iron Crown €4, museum €6,
combination ticket €8

The most notable building in the center is the Duomo di Monza, also known as the Cathedral of Saint John, which is a Romanesque-Gothic church. The church's interior is covered with frescoes and stuccowork, with a large bell tower to the left of the west-facing entrance. The church is also home to the frescoed chapel containing the reliquary **Iron Crown of Lombardy**, which is said to include one of the nails used during Jesus' crucifixion. Along with the crown are several other historical treasures, including the golden comb of Theodelinda (the 6th-century the queen of Lombards), a golden hen, and more. You can also visit the cathedral's **museum** (9:00am-1:00pm, 2:00-6:00pm Tues.-Sun.), which gives you historical context of the church and its importance to Northern Italy.

ARENGARIO

Piazza Roma; 039/329-541; www. lombardiabeniculturali.it/architetture/ schede/MI100-04649; 10am-1pm and 2pm-7pm, Tues.-Sun., closed Mon; free

The Arengario served as Monza's town hall in the 13th century, and it was the starting point for most of the historic roads in Monza. Today, this historic building is now owned by the city and is primarily used for art exhibits and other civic events. Its square tower with a large, sharp cone at the top, serve as reminders of the civic autonomy and history of Monza throughout the centuries. You can walk under the archways at any time, but the main room, which you can access via stairway is only open at certain hours or for certain events with a private guest list.

CHURCH OF SANTA MARIA IN STRADA
(Chiesa di Santa Maria in Strada)

Via Italia; 039/326-383; 7:30am-12pm, 4:45pm-6:30pm daily; free

This medieval church, known for its terracotta façade, is named after its location on the street that once connected Monza to Milan. Its construction began in the 1300s, but has undergone several reconstructions and expansions over the centuries.

Each renovation introduced more Baroque-style elements: a large pointed bell tower, a choir and a sacristy, frescoes, and mullioned windows as tall as the high altar made of marble and bronze. The atmosphere inside is quiet and still.

PARK OF MONZA
✪ ROYAL VILLA
(Villa Reale)

Viale Brianza, 1; 039/224-0024; /www. villarealedimonza.it; 10am-7pm Tues.-Sun., closed Mon.; tickets from €10 to €19

Monza's neoclassical Villa Reale was built in 1790, when the region of Lombardy was then a part of the Austrian Empire. Once the Kingdom of Italy was established in 1861, it then became the Italian Royal House of Savoy before the family abandoned it in 1900 after the murder of King Umberto I near the entrance of the building.

The building's campus includes a royal chapel, horse stables, courtyard theatre, and an orangery. Behind the villa is Monza Park. Today the villa serves as a location for temporary art exhibits. Ticket prices vary, depending on whether you want to see the **royal apartments** on the first floor or the **art exhibits** on the second floor. If you're an art or history lover, definitely spend an hour or two of your time exploring the villa itself. If you're short on time, then stick to admiring the grounds and the park.

✪ MONZA PARK
(Parco di Monza)

Viale Mirabellino, 2; 039/394-641; www. turismo.monza; 7am-7pm daily Nov.-Mar., 7:00am-9:30pm Apr.-Oct.; free

Parco di Monza is one of the largest enclosed urban parks in Europe, and the first of its kind upon its creation in the early 1800s. Its area of 7 square kilometers (2.7 square miles) includes the national race track Autodromo Nazionale Monza, a swimming pool, walking and biking paths, horse stables, ponds, and manicured lawns and gardens.

In the area nearest to Villa Reale, the garden walking paths lead to the rest of the park. To the north, you'll find the **Bosco Bello** (Beautiful Forest), an area originally created as a hunting reserve by Napoleon. The Lambro River runs through part of the park as well. Today, you can walk, run, cycle, and even trail ride in the park. Bicycles and tandem cycles are available for rent from **Cascina Bastia** (347/486-4569, http://www.reggiadimonza.it), located near the villa. A singles bike can be rented at €3 per hour, with a tandem bike at €7.50 per hour.

F1 Racetrack (Autodromo Nazionale Monza)

Via Vedano, 5; 039/24-821; www.monzanet.it; 10am-6pm daily; free on days with no events

Located in the northern part of Monza Park is the Autodromo Nazionale Monza, the historic racetrack and the home of the Formula One Italian Grand Prix. In the beginning of September every year, Monza and the small towns just north of it are flooded with international racing enthusiasts for a weekend full of racing and other entertainment. The track itself is known for its unique and difficult curves, making it a challenging track for drivers. Although there are multiple smaller races held at the racetrack throughout the year, the Grand Prix is the one that attracts the most visitors.

You can visit the racetrack during opening hours for free every day.

Monza's Villa Reale

There are also guided **English and Italian tours** available, which you can purchase directly at the racetrack. Tours start at €10 per person, but you can add segments to the tour, such as a walk around the race track, for €15 and up. To ensure that the track is open on the day you want to go (they close on random days throughout the summer and fall in preparation for events), check the website. Booking a tour is recommended in advance, either through the website's contact form or by phone.

Festivals and Events

✪ ITALIAN GRAND PRIX

F1 Racetrack, Via Vedano, 5; 039/24-821; www.monzanet.it; Sept.; tickets from €150

Motor racing has always been a beloved sport in Italy, and the annual Italian Grand Prix is one of the most followed sporting events in the country. Taking place every September since its 1950 inaugural season, the Italian Grand Prix, as well as the British Grand Prix, are the only Formula One World Prix that take place each year. The event draws thousands of racing fans to Monza and the small surrounding villages, **Vedano al Lambro** and **Biassono**. The grand prix race takes place on the Sunday afternoon of the race weekend, but throughout the

the Italian Grand Prix

weekend you can enjoy live music, festivals, and parades, and eat from a variety of food trucks. Be sure to book tickets and arrange accommodations far in advance.

Food and Drink

ITALIAN
Da Bacco Osteria

Via Enrico from Monza, 26; 039/230-8969; www.dabacco.it; 12pm-2:30pm Mon.-Fri., 7:30pm-10pm Mon.-Sat., closed Sun.; €25-40

This *osteria* (tavern) offers one of the more refined dining experiences in Monza. With limited options for each course, the focus here is on providing the utmost quality in terms or taste, ingredients, freshness, and ambience. Dishes such as yellow rice (don't miss any of the rice dishes here) and hearty meats are cooked and presented with modern flare but still maintain their northern Italian roots. Portions aren't huge, as the flavor is the most important aspect. Bring a full wallet and save room for dessert, such as the chocolate mousse, which is some of the best you'll find in the city. Reservations are highly recommended here for both lunch and dinner.

CAFÉS AND BARS
Cocò Le Patissier

Via Teodolinda Regina, 1, 20900 Monza MB; 039/230-1814; 7am-7:30pm Tues.-Sat., 7am-12:30pm Sun., closed Mon.; €2-10

Nestled in a cobblestone alleyway in the center of Monza is this local bakery, with its enticing aromas of coffee and confections wafting out to the street. Start your morning here with a sweet pastry filled with honey, fruit jam, Nutella, or chocolate, or swing by in the afternoon for one of its colorful, fruit-topped mini custard tarts or unique, variously shaped chocolate confections. Or, try one of the many different flavors of bite-size pastries or handmade macaroons. To drink, enjoy a coffee, a smoothie, an alcoholic beverage, and more. Grab one of the small tables and settle in to enjoy this bakery's bright and friendly atmosphere.

Vineria dei Tintori

Via Gerardo dei Tintori, 2; 039/937-2406; www.vineriadeitintori.it; 6pm-2am Mon.-Thurs., 11am-2am Fri.-Sun.; aperitivo €10

This small wine bar tucked away on one of the charming streets along the Lambo River is beloved and highly touted by locals, so you should book a table for the *aperitivo* hour, as you'll be fighting the crowd on weekends just to get a seat. The low lighting and hundreds of wine bottles lining the walls give off a very low-key, intimate atmosphere. You're presented with a wine list so thick that it likens to a novel, and the finger foods that come with your wine range from fresh veggies and fruits, meats, sandwiches, chips and dips. The staff is very knowledgeable, so if you're overwhelmed by the amount of choices, feel free to ask for suggestions.

Getting There

FROM MILAN
BY TRAIN
The easiest way to travel between Milan and Monza is via the suburban train lines. Milan's Central Station and Porta Garibaldi Station both have frequent trains to the Monza Railway Station. From Porta Garibaldi, take the S8 or S11 trains to Monza. Both are the same price, roughly €2, with trains departing Porta Garibaldi for Monza about every 10-20 minutes beginning around 6am. From Garibaldi, the trip usually lasts between 15-20 minutes. The last train back to Milan heads to Porta Garibaldi just before midnight each night.

Alternatively, you can take the regional or international TILO trains (www.tilo.ch) heading toward Switzerland from Central Station for the same price, although these trains usually run only once near the top of the hour every hour, beginning at 1:10pm each day. The trip from Central Station to Monza usually lasts 10-15 minutes. The last scheduled train from Monza to Central station leaves at just past 11pm every evening.

All tickets can be purchased online in advance at Trenitalia (www.trenitalia.com), where you'll also find a full timetable between the two cities. Otherwise, tickets can be purchased directly at the train stations in Monza or Milan.

BY CAR
It's about a 30-minute drive from the center of Milan to the center of Monza. Follow Viale Fulvio Testi north through the Biccoca and Sesto San Giovanni districts until you reach SS36. Once you've arrived, look for white signs marking Monza's city limits, at which point you can follow the marked directions to the centro (center), or Villa Reale, if you want to visit the villa and Monza Park.

BY BUS
You can take the z221 bus from Milan's Sesto San Giovanni train station to Monza. The journey takes about 45 minutes from Milan to the Villa Reale. It does stop at Monza's train station right by the city center, but if you want to go to the city center, it makes more sense to just take the train. The exact schedule depends on the day and the season, but you'll generally find buses running frequently from 7am-10pm daily. Official timetables can be found at http://autoguidovie.it. Tickets can be purchased directly on board from the driver, but note that drivers only accept coins. Ticket inspectors frequent this bus line, so be sure to validate your ticket after purchase using the machines at the front of the bus.

FROM THE LAKES
BY CAR
Monza is fairly easy to get to, especially from Lake Como. If you're coming from the western side of Lake Como, follow SP342 southeast until you get to SS36, then follow that directly south, which leads you directly to Monza. From Lecco in Lake Como, you can simply follow the SS36 south until you reach Monza. Once you get closer to Monza, you'll see signs leading you directly to the centro (center). From both Como and Lecco, the trip is roughly 40 kilometers (25 miles), although it's about

a 30-minute drive from Lecco and a 50-minute drive from Como.

To get to Monza from Lake Maggiore, take the **A8/E62** south until you get to the Milan area, at which point you'll take the **E64** east until you reach Sesto San Giovanni. Then, take the **SS36** north toward Monza. All interchanges are clearly marked, and will direct you to Monza. It's about 90 kilometers (56 miles), or an hour and a half drive.

From Lake Garda, take the **A4** west toward Milan, through Brescia and Bergamo, until you've reached Sesto San Giovanni, at which point you can easily follow the signs toward Monza. From the southwestern part of Lake Garda, you'll drive about 1.25 hours to Monza over a span of 114 kilometers (71 miles).

BY TRAIN

Most trains that depart from Lake Como on both the western and eastern sides almost always stop in Monza on their way to Milan. From the Como San Giovanni station, you can catch a train that is roughly an hour long and costs about €5 each way. The trains usually run each hour, and tickets can be purchased directly at the station. From Lecco, you can take the train to Monza for around €4, with a trip lasting from 30 minutes to an hour, depending on whether you take a regular regional train or a fast regional train with fewer stops. Trains depart about every hour from the Lecco station, and tickets can also be purchased directly at the station. All tickets can be purchased online in advance at Trenatalia (www.trenitalia.com), where you'll also find a full timetable between each destination.

If you're traveling by train from Lake Maggiore or Lake Garda, travel to Milan first, then grab a train from Milan's Porta Garibaldi or Central Station.

Getting Around

Monza city center is very walkable, so you won't need to use any mode of transportation to get around if you're sticking to that area. The Monza train station is located on the edge of the city center, and you can walk from the station to all bars, restaurants, shops, and sights. Regardless of where you're headed in Monza city center, it shouldn't take more than a 10-20 minute walk to get there.

To reach Monza Park or Villa Reale, take the **z221** bus from Monza's train station to the villa, which is an approximately 10-minute ride. Buses run frequently from 7am-10pm daily. Official timetables can be found at http://autoguidovie.it. Tickets can be purchased at the bar in the train station or directly on board from the driver. Drivers only accept coins, so be sure you have some handy. Ticket inspectors frequently monitor this bus line, so once you purchase your ticket, be sure to validate your ticket using the machines at the front of the bus.

LAKE COMO

If you only know one lake in Italy, it's more than likely Lake Como—not because it's the third-largest lake in the country, but because it's known as the destination for the wealthy and has been since the Roman age. As one of the most accessible and alluring lakes of this region, Lake Como sees its fair share of both local and international visitors year after year.

The lake is not only popular for its villages and celebrity vacation homes, but also for its spa getaways and spectacular landscape, its shores tucked amidst the backdrop of the towering Alps.

HIGHLIGHTS

✪ **GARDENS OF VILLA CIPRESSI, VARENNA:** This hotel situated near Varenna's shoreline is known for its surrounding and intricately designed public gardens, which feature contemporary statues placed in a lush greenery of indigenous plants (page 123).

✪ **VILLAGE-HOPPING:** Lake Como is filled with so many beautiful villages in such close proximity to each other that you would be hard-pressed sticking to just one. Whether you want to stay on one coast or jump around each shore, you can see many of these little villages in just a few days (page 130).

✪ **VILLA SERBELLONI, BELLAGIO:** Villa Serbelloni, home to a luxury hotel filled with one of the more exquisite art and furniture collections on the lake, is surrounded by beautiful, well-manicured gardens that are open to the public by tour (page 132).

✪ **PUNTA SPARTIVENTO, BELLAGIO:** At this centermost point on Lake Como, you can see all three branches of the lake at once. Sit awhile at one of the benches and just take in the breathtaking views of the mountains and lake (page 133).

✪ **VILLA CARLOTTA, TREMEZZO:** This villa has nearly 20 acres (8 hectares) of blooming, colorful gardens featuring terraces, fountains, statues, and several different types of plants and trees, all designed to create a classic, luxurious Italian garden experience (page 150).

✪ **DUOMO DI COMO:** Arguably the most important church on Lake Como and one of the most prestigious churches in Lombardy, the Como Cathedral with its stunning exterior and interior is the city's heart. It is said to be the last-known Gothic-style cathedral built in Italy (page 155).

Despite its luxurious and posh reputation, there's plenty for the average visitor to see and do, from sailing to hiking to drinking local wine and eating seafood by the lakeshore.

Roughly an hour away from Milan, Lake Como is the ideal getaway for those looking for a quick and easy escape from the hustle and bustle of the city, with its quaint villages of quiet churches and historic villas, narrow winding alleys lined with boutiques and bars, and lush gardens hugging the shore.

GETTING TO LAKE COMO
FROM MILAN

Trains from Milan's Central Station run frequently to **Como** on the western shore of Lake Como and to **Lecco** and **Varenna** on the eastern shore. If you're coming from Milan, I recommend you that you take the train rather than drive, especially during high season. Otherwise, you'll find yourself contending with all the locals and other European visitors driving toward the lake each weekend, often backing up traffic for an hour or more.

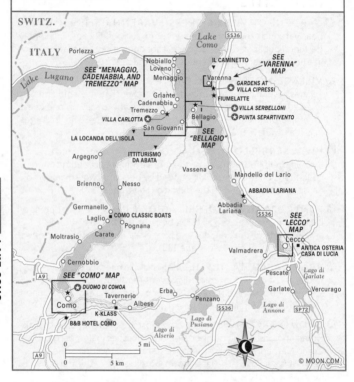

Lake Como

SWITZ.

ITALY   Porlezza

Lake Lugano

Lake Como

SS36

SEE "MENAGGIO, CADENABBIA, AND TREMEZZO" MAP

Nobiallo
Loveno
Menaggio

IL CAMINETTO

SEE "VARENNA" MAP

Varenna

GARDENS AT VILLA CIPRESSI

Griante
Cadenabbia
Tremezzo

FIUMELATTE

VILLA SERBELLONI

VILLA CARLOTTA

Bellagio

PUNTA SEPARTIVENTO

San Giovanni

SEE "BELLAGIO" MAP

LA LOCANDA DELL'ISOLA

Argegno

ITTITURISMO DA ABATA

Vassena

Mandello del Lario

Brienno

Nesso

ABBADIA LARIANA

Germanello

Abbadia Lariana

SS36

Laglio

COMO CLASSIC BOATS

SEE "LECCO" MAP

Pognana

Moltrasio

Carate

Lecco

ANTICA OSTERIA CASA DI LUCIA

Cernobbio

Valmadrera

A9

SEE "COMO" MAP

Pescate

Lago di Garlate

DUOMO DI COMOA

Tavernerio

Erba

Garlate

Vercurago

Como

Albese

Penzano

SP72

K-KLASS

SS36

Lago di Annone

B&B HOTEL COMO

Lago di Pusiano

Lago di Alserio

0   5 mi

A9   0   5 km

© MOON.COM

But if you really want to drive, to get to the city of **Como** from Milan, head north outside of the city on A8 (follow signs toward Malpensa airport and the autostrada). Once you're on the A8 heading out of Milan, drive roughly 10 kilometers (or roughly 6 miles) before merging onto A9/E35. Drive about 22 kilometers (14 miles) on this highway until you see signs to exit for Como Centro. From there, follow the signs to Como Centro (Como city center). The trip takes an hour, give or take.

Depending on the traffic flow, a road trip from Milan to the town of **Lecco** on the eastern side of the shore is about an hour, give or take a few minutes depending on the day. Head

northeast out of the city toward Sesto San Giovanni on the SS36, following the signs to Lecco the whole way. The total drive is 55 kilometers (34 miles).

FROM THE OTHER LAKES

From the other lakes in the region, traveling by train is more complex and usually involves heading back to Milan, so driving is your best bet. From **Lake Garda,** the easiest and quickest route is to make your way to the major A4 highway, just below the southernmost part of Lake Garda, going west toward Milan. You'll stay on A4 for approximately 65-85 kilometers (40-53 miles), depending on where you got on the highway, driving past

Brescia and Bergamo. Take the exit past Bergamo for **SS36** toward Lake Como. You'll stay on this state road for roughly 30 kilometers (18 miles) until you reach the Lake Como area, close to Lecco. From here, follow the road signs directing you to your city or village of choice. From the southwestern area of Lake Garda (Desenzano del Garda) to the southeastern branch of Lake Como (Lecco), the drive is about 1.5 hours (120 kilometers/75 miles).

From **Lake Maggiore**, take the E62 highway south toward Milan until you reach A36 (roughly 75 kilometers/46 miles). Take the exit for A36, stay on this highway for about 16 kilometers (10 miles), then exit toward A9/E35 and follow the signs to Como Centro. This road will lead you toward the city of Como. Once you're in the Lake Como area, follow the road signs directing you to your village or city of choice. From Stresa to the town of Como, the trip takes about 1.5 hours (89 kilometers/55 miles).

While driving to the lake ensures that you don't need to worry about the constraints of public transportation (paying attention to train and ferry schedules, for example), keep in mind that the smaller villages often have very limited public parking, and the streets that wind along the shores are often narrow and busy. Italian driving culture is generally more chaotic and less structured than in the U.S. or U.K., so go this route only if you feel confident and comfortable driving in this kind of environment.

GETTING AROUND LAKE COMO
BY PUBLIC FERRY
Taking the ferry is one of the most accommodating travel options for those wanting to hop shores around

the lake. Each village in this chapter (Varenna, Bellagio, Menaggio, Tremezzo, Cadenabbia, Como, and Lecco) has its own ferry station in the middle of town. Ferries run year-round, but more frequently during the spring and summer months. Service begins at 7:30am and ends at 7:30pm.

You can take a fast ferry (*aliscafo*) or slow boat (*battello*) to and from each village, or opt for the car ferry (*traghetto*) that runs between Bellagio, Menaggio, and Varenna, allowing you to avoid having to drive around the circumference of the lake to get from one branch to the other. The latter of the three ferries is by far the most popular ferry route on the lake. Tickets range €2-16, depending on where you're heading, and you can purchase a one-way ticket, round-trip ticket, or a daily pass. If you're planning on visiting three or more villages, opt for the pass. All up-to-date fares and timetables can be found at www.navigazionelaghi.it, but here are a few of the most popular routes:

- **Como to Tremezzo:** 45min on the fast boat, 1h 30min by slow boat
- **Tremezzo to Menaggio:** 10min on the fast boat, 30min by slow boat
- **Menaggio to Varenna:** 12min by the slow boat or car ferry
- **Varenna to Bellagio:** 15min by slow boat or car ferry
- **Bellagio to Menaggio:** 25min by slow boat or car ferry
- **Bellagio to Tremezzo:** 16min by slow boat
- **Lecco to Bellagio:** 1h 30min by slow boat

BY WATER TAXI
While jetting around the lake in a private water taxi is way more costly than opting for a ferry, it's a convenient option for those wanting something

WHICH LAKESIDE VILLAGE?

- **If you like a bustling scene:** Head to Bellagio, a small village with picturesque alleys full of boutiques and local artisan shops. As one of the lake's most popular villages, you'll be hard-pressed to find this spot empty.

- **If you want a convenient hub:** Stick to the town of Como, which has a little bit of everything. The town is also the most convenient spot from Milan, with direct trains running frequently between Milan and Como's train stations a few times each hour.

- **If you want a hidden gem:** Try the small but charming villages of Tremezzo or Cadenabbia. Although you won't find as many prominent sights or dining and shopping options here, the natural and low-key feel of both places make for a tranquil afternoon.

- **If you like gardens:** Visit Tremezzo, home to Villa Carlotta, one of the most spectacular villas and gardens on Lake Como.

- **If you like outdoor recreation:** Visit Lecco and take advantage of one of the many cycling or trekking trails that start in Lecco, such as the circular bike trail along the Adda River.

more private and quicker than the public ferry services. Water taxis should be booked in advance whenever possible, as there is no guarantee that you'll always find one waiting on the shores of the village that you're visiting. You usually won't find a water taxi to be any cheaper than €30 between villages, and most ferry services run around 8am-6pm daily.

Companies such as **Taxi Boat Varenna** (www.taxiboatvarenna.com, 349/229-0953) and **Taxi Boat Service** (www.taxiboat.it, 031/950-201) offer personalized trips from every corner of the lake, including private tours and group tours of up to 20 or so people. Many companies also offer tour packages that include drinks or *aperitivo* on the boat, lunches, full-day cruises, and more.

BY CAR

There are a few main roads that hug the shores of the lake, for those getting around by car. Although, keep in mind that these roads clog up with tons of traffic during high season, especially on the weekends. Parking is also limited, so stick to public transportation when you can. The **SS36** runs from Lecco to Verceia up the eastern shore, while the **SS340** runs from Como to Ponte del Passo up the western shore. In between the two southern branches, the **SP583** connects Como, Lecco, and Bellagio. Find a few times and distances below:

- **Como to Lecco:** 40min, 31 kilometers (19 miles)
- **Como to Bellagio:** 50min, 31 kilometers (19 miles)
- **Lecco to Bellagio:** 30min, 22 kilometers (14 miles)
- **Lecco to Varenna:** 30min, 22 kilometers (14 miles)
- **Como to Menaggio:** 50min, 36 kilometers (22 miles)

BY TROMBETTA EXPRESS

To travel easily between the main villages and sights on the western shore, take the Trombetta Express (www.trombettaexpress.com) *trenino* (little train) that chugs along Via Regina between Menaggio and Lenno. The train starts running daily from 8:50am from the center of Menaggio and ends at Villa Balbianello at 9:23am, when the first journey back to Menaggio begins. The circuit runs until 11pm from Menaggio and until 11:30pm from the villa. The train stops at the beach area of Menaggio as well as at the ferry stations in Menaggio, Cadenabbia, Tremezzo, Villa Carlotta, and Lorenzo Church before reaching Villa Balbianello. Tickets can be purchased from the driver upon boarding the little train, with a one-way journey starting at €5 per person. The best way to use this train is by purchasing a full day pass for €15 per person, or a daytime pass (valid until 5:30pm) for €12 per person, with both tickets allowing you to hop on and off the train in either direction for the entire day. Passes for children under the age of 8 are only €5.

ORIENTATION

The southern shores of Lake Como are about an hour directly north of Milan. The lake itself is shaped like an upside down Y, with Como sitting at the end of the western branch and Lecco sitting at the end of the eastern branch, and the small town of Colico sitting at the very top of the lake. The triangle right where the two branches of the Y meet is known as the Larian Triangle, and right in the center is the town of Bellagio. To the east of Bellagio, and about a 15-minute ferry ride across the water, you'll find the town of Varenna. West of Bellagio, across the lake, are the towns of Menaggio, Cadenabbia di Griante, and Tremezzo (from north to south). The lake's sole island, Isola Comacina, sits just off of the southern edge of Tremezzo's shore.

Lake Como is fed primarily by the Adda River, which flows into the lake near Colico in the north and flows out near the city of Lecco. The lake is 46 kilometers (29 miles) at its longest and 4.5 kilometers (2.8 miles) at its widest, making it the third largest lake in Italy in terms of geographic size.

PLANNING YOUR TIME

Due to the close proximity of the villages dotting the shores of Lake Como, it's fairly easy to see most of the lake's best tourist spots in a few days. If you're staying at the lake, consider staying in Varenna, Bellagio, Menaggio, or Como, as all are well-connected to other villages on the lake by ferry, and all offer plenty of accommodation, dining, and recreation options. If you're just taking a day trip from Milan, your best option is to take the train to Varenna or Como, where you can stop to do some shopping and dining, and then taking a ferry to Bellagio or Menaggio if you want to see another village on the lake. Except in Como, there is little nightlife to speak of in the villages.

Lake Como's climate is similar to that of Milan's, and the lake sees all four seasons: Spring temperatures are between 15°C (59°F) and 19°C (66°F) and summer temperatures range 18-25°C (64-77°F). In the fall temperatures range 12-15°C (54-59°F). The winters can get quite cold, with lows of 3°C (37°F) and highs of 8°C (46°F).

Many shops, businesses, and restaurants close November-February during the low season, so consider visiting in the spring or summer, when all businesses are open and the gardens around the lake are in full bloom.

Itinerary Ideas

LAKE COMO ON DAY 1

If you have just one day to explore Lake Como, stick to the "holy trinity": Varenna, Bellagio, and Menaggio.

1 Start your morning off at **Cafe Il Binario** in Varenna with a cappuccino or espresso paired with a sweet brioche. Afterward, walk down the hill to the lake, and buy a ferry pass for trips between the villages. Check the posted timetables for the ferry to Bellagio.

2 Spend a couple hours exploring the streets of Varenna and wandering around the **Villa Cipressi** gardens, which will be bursting with cypress trees and other colorful flora.

3 Catch a ferry to **Bellagio,** then grab a delicious, filling lunch at **Terrazza Barchetta.**

4 Spend your afternoon exploring the Bellagio's charming, colorful village, popping into the **Basilica of St. James** and browsing the many local shops. Don't leave without purchasing something handmade as a souvenir.

5 Grab the next ferry to your final village of the day, Menaggio. Wander around the small streets and piazzas, and when you're tired, stop into **Il Gabbiano** for a sorbet or gelato to enjoy while people-watching by the lakeshore.

6 Eat an early dinner at **Osteria Il Pozzo** in the middle of the village, then call Menaggio home for the night, or grab the last ferry back to Varenna.

LAKE COMO ON DAY 2

If you have another day on the lake, consider spending it in the town of Como.

1 Start your day off with a hearty breakfast at your hotel. Then, head down to the dock near the Como Nord train station for a quick two-hour tour of Como's shores with **Como Classic Boats.**

2 For a quick dose of history, step inside Como's Gothic-style **Duomo** and admire the frescoes and various altars around the large interior.

3 Stop for lunch at **Bar Delle Terme at Terminus.**

4 Pop into a local wine shop and buy a bottle of wine, then take the **Brunate funicular** up to the top. Crack open the bottle of wine, and enjoy it while admiring the panoramic views of the lake below.

Lake Como Itinerary Ideas

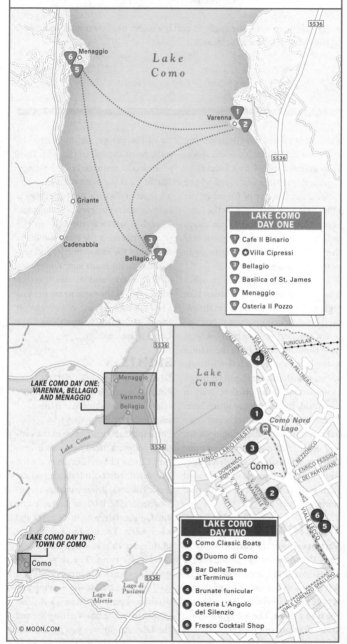

LAKE COMO DAY ONE

1. Cafe Il Binario
2. ⭐ Villa Cipressi
3. Bellagio
4. Basilica of St. James
5. Menaggio
6. Osteria Il Pozzo

LAKE COMO DAY ONE: VARENNA, BELLAGIO AND MENAGGIO

LAKE COMO DAY TWO: TOWN OF COMO

LAKE COMO DAY TWO

1. Como Classic Boats
2. ⭐ Duomo di Como
3. Bar Delle Terme at Terminus
4. Brunate funicular
5. Osteria L'Angolo del Silenzio
6. Fresco Cocktail Shop

© MOON.COM

5 Back down in Como, head to Osteria L'Angolo del Silenzio for a traditional northern Italian dinner.

6 If you're not quite ready to call it a night, head next door to Fresco Cocktail Shop for a nightcap.

Varenna

Varenna is an unpretentious fishing village on Lake Como's eastern shore. First founded in 769 by a local fisherman, it was later destroyed by the residents of the city of Como in the 1100s before being rebuilt by the refugees of Comacina Island, Lake Como's only island. The town has grown over the centuries, but still remains quite peaceful and quaint.

Like the houses you see in other small villages around the Italian lake region, Varenna's houses are multicolored and stacked up against one another. Travelers visiting by train must walk the stairs down from the station to the lake's shore. With two historic villas, a castle, and tranquil churches as well as one of the smallest rivers in the world, there is plenty to see here. The village center hosts a few cozy bars, restaurants, shopping options, and other leisurely activities. As one of the most easily accessible villages from Milan, Varenna is often flooded with visitors during the spring and summer.

ORIENTATION

Varenna sits on the eastern shore of Lake Como, about 20 kilometers (12 miles) north of Lecco. The town itself is spread out over a few kilometers running north to south against the lake's shore. The Varenna-Esino train station sits on the northern tip of the village, so you'll need to walk down the hill to the lake, then south to the main part of the village. The SP72 is the main road connecting most of the area, but the village is entirely walkable, even with luggage. There's a walkway directly on the water connecting the ferry station to the rest of the shops, hotels, and restaurants in the main hub. The village of Fiumelatte and its small, milky white river of the same name sits just a few kilometers south of Varenna on the SP72 road that runs along Lake Como's eastern shore.

SIGHTS
CHIESA DI SAN GIORGIO
Piazza S. Giorgio, 25; 0341/830-228; www.varennaturismo.com/portfolios/chiesa-di-san-giorgio; 8:30am-7pm daily

For a spiritual experience in the center of Varenna, head to the 13th-century Chiesa di San Giorgio, a church decorated with both interior and exterior frescoes. It was partially reconstructed in the 1600s in Romanesque and Gothic style, with three naves and a bell tower. The most unique feature of this church is its completely black marble flooring. The stone facade gives the church a naturally medieval feel, with the bell tower serving as a prominent piece of Varenna's skyline, visible from the boats jetting around the lake. As soon as you go into the

Varenna

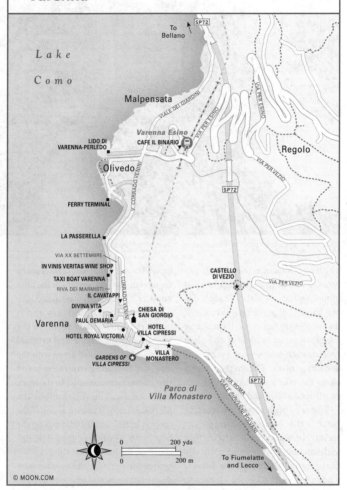

church, a sense of peace and tranquility washes over you; its stone columns and white walls add to the serenity. Stop by here for a nice break from the bustling groups of tourists outside.

✪ GARDENS OF VILLA CIPRESSI

Via 4 Novembre, 18; 0341/830113; www. hotelvillacipressi.it; 9am-7pm daily; €5

Villa Cipressi sits adjacent to Villa Monastero and is surrounded by terraced gardens that lead directly to the lake's shoreline. The name of the villa comes from the surrounding cypress trees, and the villa itself is now home to the upscale hotel of the same name. The gardens of indigenous plants outside the hotel are known for their intricate, appealing design. The gardens,

123

a path leading further into the botanical garden at Villa Monastero

which are in bloom in the spring (Apr.-June), are open to the public, not just to hotel guests. A walk through one of a handful of garden paths is worth the small entry fee, as you'll encounter dozens of varieties of trees and plant species, such as towering evergreens and magnolias. The path directly along the lake's shore is simply unparalleled in color and beauty.

The villa prides itself on creating gardens that balance contemporary architecture and modern sculpture with ancient features and naturally lush greenery. Although the hotel is a popular destination for visitors to Varenna, the gardens stay rather under the radar, so you shouldn't ever find them overcrowded with tourists, even during high season.

VILLA MONASTERO

Viale Giovanni Polvani, 4; 0341/295-450; www.villamonastero.eu; 9:30am-7pm daily; gardens €5, combination ticket €8

Villa Monastero is one of the most visited villas on the lake. The original grounds were home to a 12th-century Cistercian convent, on which the villa now sits. The convent was turned into a manor in the 17th century and is now a museum. The 14 rooms in the manor, all with unique and original decor, can all be visited along with the long, narrow garden stretching nearly two kilometers (one mile) to the town of Fiumelatte. The villa, built by the Mornico family, is known as one of the more eclectic historic buildings on the lake for its Nordic design, a style uncommon for Italy at that time.

Outside the villa, the verdant **gardens** offer a peaceful refuge away from other travelers hopping on and off the ferries; here, it's easy to feel secluded from the rest of the bustling village. If you're looking for an off-the-beaten-path experience, this place fits the bill while still giving you a good taste of the lake's history.

CASTELLO DI VEZIO

Via del Castellano, Perledo; 333/448-5975; www.castellodivezio.it; 10am-5pm Mar.-Oct.;

adults €4, students and 65 and over €3 ,
children 12 and under €2

For aerial views of Varenna, head to Castello di Vezio, which is a 20-minute walk uphill from Varenna. The castle has gazed down upon the village for centuries, and today it is home to several bird species, including owls and falcons. While most of the castle has been ruined over time, the original main tower still stands tall, serving as the watch guard for the lake. The castle itself isn't much to look at; however, it does offer stunning views over the lake. The views alone are what motivate most travelers to hike up the hill. The path starts at the Church of San Antonio in Varenna, where you'll walk through a green gate and continue on the steep path continuously up toward the castle. Bring comfortable walking shoes and stop along the way, if needed.

FIUMELATTE

Nature lovers should visit the river of Fiumelatte, where the springs of the same name flow. This spot is just far enough away from Varenna that it feels like you're in a secluded, green corner of the world. The short river only flows freely March-September, and its name translates to "milk river," which comes from the peculiar milky white water of the stream. The village of the same name also has a public beach for those wanting to lay around in the sun for a few hours. The village is just a few kilometers south of Varenna on the SP72 road that runs along Lake Como's eastern shore, so it's easily accessible by car. Alternatively, you can walk roughly 25 minutes south on Via Roma from Varenna to reach the river, following the steps until you see the milky white waters.

RECREATION

Varenna offers a few recreation options both on the lake and nearby, such as canyoning excursions in a local river as well as private boat tours from the shoreline.

BEACH
Lido di Varenna-Perledo

Via al Lido, 2, Perledo; 0341/815-370; 9:30am-12am Wed.-Mon.; €2 entrance, sun bed with umbrella €6

The Lido di Varenna-Perledo is a small beach on the lake shore with sun beds with umbrellas, a bar and restaurant, dock, and swimming area free of motorboats. This beach is undergoing an upgrade, which will include a swimming pool and a larger pier. The restaurant has a full menu for lunch as well as snack items throughout the day and a full bar, with both indoor and outdoor seating.

CANYONING
Alto Lario Guide

333/673-5419; www.altolarioguide.com; tours run 7am-11pm Apr.-Sept.; €60 per person, equipment included

To put a little outdoor adventure in your agenda, you can try a guided canyoning excursion. The roughly two-hour excursion is classified as easy, so beginners are welcome. You must be at least 10 years old to participate, and you should book online in advance. The same company also offers guided climbing, hiking, ski mountaineering, waterfall climbing, and spelunking in various locations near the lake throughout the year.

BOAT TOUR
Taxi Boat Varenna

Contrada del Porto 1; 349/229-0953; www. taxiboatvarenna.com; €15-100 per person, depending on the tour

The Taxi Boat Varenna company, operating for over 10 years, takes pride in its knowledgeable, professional, and friendly boat captains. Various tours are offered, ranging from trips around the central part of the lake to tours expanding to the outer parts of the lake and hitting most of the beautiful villas along the shore. Boats can fit up to 16 people, but there are smaller boats for a more private, tailored experience. An *aperitivo* is offered for private tours.

Varenna's quiet center tucked into the mountains

SHOPPING
Paul DEMARIA

Ctr. Del Prato, 6; 335/608-6530; http:// pauldemaria.com; 3pm-7pm daily Apr.-Oct.

The Paul DEMARIA art studio is one of the most beloved spots in Varenna. The artist Paul Demaria Guaitamacchi's wife, Melita, runs the gallery, selling his landscape oil paintings, still life, and other pieces. Demaria Guaitamacchi's work is displayed in a handful of locations in Italy, the United Kingdom, and in the United States, but you'll find the largest collection right here in Varenna.

In Vinis Veritas Wine Shop

Via XX Settembre, 7; 331/912-2990; www. invinisveritas-shop.com; 12pm-10pm Mon.-Sat., 5pm-10pm Sun.; €5-8 per glass with appetizers

For another Italian shopping experience, try the In Vinis Veritas wine bar and shop on Via XX Settembre. This small corner shop perched on a hilltop boasts a huge and diverse selection of Italian wine for both tasting on the spot and for purchase. The staff is incredibly knowledgeable, making it a point to help you find exactly what you're looking for and doing their best to ensure you have a relaxing experience while drinking and nibbling on appetizers.

FOOD
ITALIAN AND PIZZA
Il Cavatappi

Via XX Settembre, 8; 341/815-349; www.cavatappivarenna.it; 12pm-2pm, 6:30pm-9:30pm Thurs.-Tues., closes at 9pm Mon. and Tues.; €15-30

This little family-run restaurant off the beaten path offers traditional dishes of the lake region, including white coregone fish and smoked trout tartare. With only seven tables, the atmosphere is quiet and intimate and the service attentive. Soft opera music plays in the background while you dine. A handful of vegetarian-friendly dishes are also available on the menu. Due to limited space, book ahead in order to ensure a table here. You can reserve a table until 1:30pm for lunch and until 8:30pm for dinner.

Il Caminetto

Viale Progresso, 4, Perledo; 341/815-225; www.ilcaminettoonline.com; 12:30pm-2pm, 7:30-9pm Thurs.-Tues.; €15-30

The tradition of cooking runs deep at Il Caminetto, with a family taking

romantic sunset dining in Varenna

over and renovating the space and creating the restaurant hand in hand, passing down recipes and skills from one generation to the next. Today, the restaurant is not only a dining stop in Varenna, but also a cooking school for travelers who want to learn the art of Italian cuisine. Classes are taught in English. The menu is straight and simple, featuring fresh pasta, risotto, lake fish, and a handful of classic Italian desserts and cheese plates. Call ahead to book a table for dinner.

CAFÉS
Café Il Binario

Piazza Stazione, 1, Perledo; 341/830-546; www.terzobinariostazione.com; 6am-10pm daily; €2-7

Conveniently located in an old 19th-century station building at the train station in Varenna, this café has a full bar menu and plenty of finger foods to nibble on throughout the day. Take a seat and grab a hot chocolate or glass of prosecco while waiting for your train. The illuminated display of fresh pastries as soon as you walk in the door is an enticing enough reason to stay. Head here after a long day on the lake or pick up a cappuccino and croissant before catching an early train elsewhere.

GELATO
La Passerella

Contrada del Porto Varenna, 14; 341/830-369; 11:30am-7:45pm daily; €2-5

Stop by La Passerella for a sweet treat of artisan gelato and sorbet. The little place is housed inside an old stone building, which gives it the comfortable feeling of home. The shop offers everything from dairy-free dark chocolate sorbet to classic fruity gelato to vegan options served on waffles and crepes. Grab a cone and head to the stairs next to the gelateria to catch a nice view of the sunset or enjoy the soft sun glistening off of the lake top in the summer.

ACCOMMODATIONS

Accommodations in Varenna are generally a little cozier than those in other popular villages on the lake, giving you a more local feel than some other towns. You can find a handful of apartments available for short-period rent as well as two of the most luxurious hotels on the eastern side of Lake Como.

€150-250
Divina Vita

Contrada Guasta, 4; 341/830070; www. barilmolo.it; €160

The lovely little B&B situated above a local bar directly on the Varenna shoreline consistently garners positive reviews for its location and setup. The apartment, equipped with a kitchenette, air conditioning, WiFi, and a huge luxury bathtub, is modern yet quaint and welcoming. A full American or Italian style breakfast of your choice is served every morning at the bar below the apartment and is included in the price of the room. Due to the popularity of this place, book as far in advance as possible, as dates fill up fast.

Hotel Villa Cipressi

Via 4 Novembre, 18; 341/830113; www. hotelvillacipressi.it; €240

This timeless and historic villa makes you feel like royalty during your stay here, with the parquet floors, suites flooded with natural lighting, grand staircase, and botanical gardens running along the lake. The classic double rooms can come with a lake view or garden view, each including a private bathroom, air conditioning, and WiFi. A large breakfast with plenty of both sweet and savory options is included.

OVER €250
Hotel Royal Victoria

Piazza S. Giorgio, 2; 341/815-111; www. royalvictoria.com; €350

Peaceful luxury best defines the Hotel Royal Victoria, which is located in a beautiful 19th-century building surrounded by lush, green gardens and a private dock with lake access just a short minute away. With a swimming pool open every day during high season and a modern spa and wellness center, the place is so relaxing that it's almost hard to get out and explore the surrounding town.

INFORMATION AND SERVICES

The main tourist office in Varenna (Via 4 Novembre 3; 0341/830-367; www.varennaitaly.com; 10am-6pm Tues.-Sun., until 3pm Mon.) can be found on the southern side of the village. The office provides tons of English materials and support for those interested in Varenna's offerings, including hotels, restaurants, and recreational activities.

The closest hospital, Ospedale Di Bellano Azienda Ospedaliera Provinciale Del S.S.N (Via Carlo Alberto, 25, Bellano; 0341/829-111), is in Bellano, about 5.5 kilometers (3.5 miles) north of Varenna following the SP72. The hospital is open 24 hours a day, and English-speaking staff should be available to assist you. Local police (0341/830-119) can be found at city hall at Piazza Venini, 2. In case of emergencies, you should call 112. Local police usually have conversational English skills, but its not a bad idea to have a translating app on hand.

GETTING THERE AND AROUND

Varenna is one of the few villages on the lake that is accessible by train directly from Milan. From the other villages around Lake Como, it's best to travel to Varenna by boat or car. As with most lake villages, the best way to see the true Varenna is by walking the winding pathways that make up the center and strolling along the shore.

TRAIN

The easiest way to get to Varenna from Milan is by train, with several trains running both ways each day. All trains depart from Milan's Central Station, with the direct trip to Varenna lasting roughly one hour. Tickets are €6.70 each way, and can be purchased in advance either at a ticketing machine at Central Station or online at www. trenitalia.com.

From Lecco, you can grab one of the frequently running trains (2-3 per hour, 6am-10pm daily) for €2.90. The trip is approximately 20-35 minutes.

Purchase your return ticket back to Milan or Lecco online because the train station in Varenna does not have a ticket machine. However, there is a small tobacco shop that is reachable by foot as you're walking from the ferry station up to the train station that sells train tickets during opening hours, and travelers can usually purchase return tickets directly from the ticket controller on the train. You'll also find a sign on the single platform at the train station directing you to a local travel agency selling train tickets.

BOAT

Varenna is reachable via the public ferry system from Menaggio, Cadenabbia di Griante, and Bellagio, with both slow boats and car ferries running between these villages. You

Varenna-Esino train station

⭐ VILLAGE-HOPPING AROUND LAKE COMO

Village-hopping is one of the best experiences on Lake Como, as most villages are small enough for you to get a good feel for in just half a day. They're close enough to each other that you can jump on a ferry or another mode of transportation and be on to the next village in just 20 minutes or less.

BY FERRY

The most popular village-hopping strategy is to take the ferry between the "holy trinity" villages: **Varenna, Bellagio,** and **Menaggio.** Each village sits on different shores of the lake: While it's easy to catch a glimpse of all three villages in a long day, it may be best to travel to one, spend the night there, then see the other two the next day. For example, take the train from Milan to Varenna (the only one of these three villages that is accessible by train), spend the evening in Varenna,

ferry connecting the villages of Bellagio, Varenna, and Menaggio

then explore Bellagio and Menaggio the next day. However, you can make any one of these villages your starting and ending points, as ferries run about every hour during daylight hours in high season.

BY TRENINO

You can take the **Trombetta Express** (www.trombettaexpress.com) *trenino* up and down the western shore of Lake Como between the villages of **Menaggio, Cadenabbia,** and **Tremezzo.** The small trolley train is driven up and down the main road connecting the three villages many times a day during high season, making them easily accessible without needing to drive. The best way to use this train is by purchasing a full-day pass (€15 per person) or a daytime pass (valid until 5:30pm, €12 per person). Both tickets allow you to hop on and off the train in either direction. Passes for children under the age of 8 are only €5.

can also take the fast ferries *(aliscafo)* from Como or Colico. Ferries usually run 7:30am-8pm, usually once per hour. Tickets, ranging €7-20, can be purchased directly from each of the town ferry stations. Timetables can be found at the stations or online at www.navigazionelaghi.it. A trip from Bellagio to Varenna is about 15 minutes, and from Menaggio about 12 minutes.

CAR

The quickest way to reach Varenna by car from Milan is to drive to Lecco on the western shore, then on to the village of Varenna. From Lecco, continue to take the SS36 highway until you reach the Abbadia Lariana exit. From there, follow the signs to Fiumelatte. Before reaching the tunnel, take a left turn, following the signs to Varenna. Note that as with most small villages on the lake, public parking is limited, especially near the lake. If you're staying in Varenna, make sure that your hotel offers parking for guests. From Lecco to Varenna, the drive is about 22 kilometers (14 miles), and takes approximately half an hour. The whole journey from Milan to Varenna is 76 kilometers (47 miles) and takes approximately an hour and a half.

From Como, take the SP72 east toward Lecco until it turns into SS36 in Civate, then follow the SS36 north through Lecco and on to Varenna. From Como, the trip is just over an hour for a total of 53 kilometers (33 miles).

To reach Fiumelatte from Varenna, drive a few kilometers south on the SP72 road that runs along Lake Como's eastern shore. It's just a quick five-minute drive.

Bellagio

Often referred to as "the pearl" of Lake Como, Bellagio is a picturesque, idyllic Italian lake village: cobblestone steps leading up to a beautiful but small, quiet church at the top of a hill, local boutiques tucked in between wine bars and restaurants that are nearly 100 years old, colorful gardens providing leisurely walkways along the shoreline. It's no wonder that Bellagio is one of the most visited spots in northern Italy year after year. Its charm is timeless.

While this little village can easily be seen in a day, it's also a great, quiet place to call home during your trip to Lake Como, with several accommodation options and plenty of dining options, water sports, and shopping. If you're traveling by train, you'll need to take a ferry from Como or Varenna to reach this corner of paradise. For visitors coming by car, make sure that your hotel offers parking for guests, or find one of the few public parking spots just outside of the center.

ORIENTATION

Bellagio is located at the point where the two bottom branches of Lake Como meet, in the middle of the Y. The center of the village sits on the western side of this point, with two ferry departure stations found along **Via Roma** and **Piazza Mazzini.** These two streets connect to form the shoreline of Bellagio, filled with waterfront restaurants, shops, and benches to stop and rest all surrounded by colorful flowers—lots of options for a perfect, leisurely afternoon. Tucked in between the colorful buildings, you'll find winding stairways lined with local shops and eateries, all leading to the village's second main road, **Via Garibaldi.**

This road runs parallel to Via Roma, just at a higher altitude, except in the northern part of the village center, where Via Roma loops near Villa Serbelloni and meets Via Garibaldi. The main staircase connecting the two roads is **Salita Serbelloni,** the top of which is from where you'll find one of the most picturesque views of the lake.

SIGHTS

BASILICA OF ST. JAMES
(Basilica di San Giacomo)

Piazza della Chiesa, 27; www.comune. bellagio.co.it; free

If you're walking along Via Garibaldi and in the Piazza della Chiesa, stop to explore the Basilica of St. James, a Romanesque church at the top of the village's center originally built in the beginning of the 1100s. Inside the small church is a 12th-century cross and a 16th-century altarpiece, as well

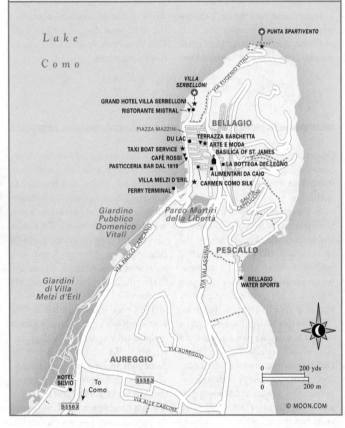

Bellagio

Lake Como

★ PUNTA SPARTIVENTO

VILLA SERBELLONI ★

GRAND HOTEL VILLA SERBELLONI ★
RISTORANTE MISTRAL

PIAZZA MAZZINI

BELLAGIO

DU LAC
TAXI BOAT SERVICE ★
CAFÈ ROSSI ★
PASTICCERIA BAR DAL 1919

VILLA MELZI D'ERIL
FERRY TERMINAL

TERRAZZA BARCHETTA
★ ARTE E MODA
BASILICA OF ST. JAMES
★ LA BOTTEGA DEL LEGNO
ALIMENTARI DA CAIO
★ CARMEN COMO SILK

SALITA CAPPUCCINI

VIA EUGENIO VITALI

Giardino
Pubblico
Domenico
Vitali

Parco Martiri
della Libertà

PESCALLO

Giardini
di Villa
Melzi d'Eril

VIA PAOLO CARCANO

VIA VALASSINA

★ BELLAGIO
WATER SPORTS

AUREGGIO

VIA AUREGGIO

0   200 yds
0   200 m

HOTEL
SILVIO ●

To
Como

SS583

VIA ALLE CASCINE

SS583

© MOON.COM

as a handful of artwork from both Lombardy and Umbria. The pulpit is made completely of marble, including the four pillars holding it up. Due to its proximity to the rest of the village, it is popular among tourists, but remains a quiet, low-lit spot among a bright and bustling area of the lake. Stop in to enjoy a few peaceful moments and to admire one of the important centerpieces of Bellagio's history.

✪ VILLA SERBELLONI

Via Roma, 1; 031/950-216; www.
villaserbelloni.com; 11am and 3:30pm
Tues.-Sun. mid-Mar.-Oct.; tours €9

Bellagio's "belle of the ball" is Villa Serbelloni, a historical villa commanding the village's center. Replacing what used to be an ancient castle, the villa complex was built in the 15th century, and was subsequently reconstructed multiple times before it took its modern-day shape. Alessandro Serbelloni, after whom the villa is named, took control of the villa in the 1700s, filling

the bright pool of Villa Serbelloni overlooking the shores of Lake Como

it with art and fine decorations. The villa now houses a five-star hotel, so the beautiful and welcoming gardens can only be viewed by hotel guests and on guided tours. The gardens are full of towering evergreens and vibrant flowers, such as tulips. The trails surrounding the villa lead to an old 16th-century monastery, which you are invited to explore.

Today, the park can only be visited via guided group tour of 6-30 people, and English guides must be booked in advance (shoot for at least a week or two in advance) by contacting the hotel. Tours run twice a day at 11am and 3:30pm, and last about an hour and a half. For nature enthusiasts and admirers of manicured gardens, Villa Serbelloni is definitely worth the time.

VILLA MELZI D'ERIL
Via Lungolario Manzoni; 333/487-7427; www.giardinidivillamelzi.it; 9am-6:30 daily Mar.-Oct.; €6.50
Another historic building overlooking the lake in Bellagio is Villa Melzi

d'Eril, commonly referred to as Villa Melzi. Originally built as political housing during the Napoleonic period of the Italian Republic, the villa is now an elegant reminder of the town's political history, furnished with paintings from famous artists. Today, like Villa Serbelloni, only the gardens are open to visitors, but the villa itself is closed to the public. Because this villa sits outside of Bellagio's village center, you won't find as many tourists here, so take the opportunity to visit the gorgeous gardens, which include Japanese-style fish ponds and Napoleonic memorabilia. You can get to the villa by walking approximately a kilometer south of the main part of Bellagio's waterfront, past the ferry stations and along the gravel walking path that hugs the lake.

✪ PUNTA SPARTIVENTO
Via Eugenio Vitali
For a natural, scenic view of the point where all three branches of the lake meet, head to Punta Spartivento.

133

Roughly a 10-minute walk from the ferry docks in Bellagio, this point gives you unparalleled views of the water and the mountains hugging the lake. The restaurant provides patio seating overlooking the point, so you can grab a bite to eat while taking in the views. If you're wanting something a little more low key, grab a few snacks and a bottle of wine from one of the local Bellagio shops, and enjoy them while sitting along the wall or on the benches. You can easily spend an hour or two admiring the spectacular view.

RECREATION

While most visitors come to Bellagio for a little relaxation and a taste of *la dolce vita,* there are a handful of sports and recreation activities for those looking for a bit more adventure.

KAYAKING AND PADDLE BOARDING
Bellagio Water Sports

Via Sfondrati, 1; 340/39-49-375; www.bellagiowatersports.com; 8:30am-4:30pm daily, last tour at 2:30pm Sun.; €59-120

Bellagio Water Sports Club is one of the best kayaking outfits on Lake Como, offering private kayak tours every day of the week, including a private sunset tour. Most tours paddle by Villa Serbelloni, Punta Spartivento (the "center" of Lake Como), and Villa Marescalchi; you can also catch a glimpse of the Bellagio skyline from the water. Tours have a minimum age of 8 and a maximum age of 65, with a minimum booking of at least two people.

The same company also offers paddleboarding tours; beginners to experts are welcome to join. The paddleboards are equipped with additional rowing equipment for those that can't quite get the hang of standing but still want to take in the views of the lake from the

water. Reservations for all tours must be made in advance online.

BOAT TOURS
Bellagio Water Limousines

Piazza Mazzini; 338/524-4914; http://bellagiowaterlimousines.com; daily while the sun is up; from €55 per person

For private or group tours on water taxis or water limousines, head to Bellagio's Piazza Mazzini, where you'll find a handful of private boat companies offering a variety of tours ranging from one hour to a full-day tour. The Bellagio Water Limousines company is a popular choice amongst visitors, offering tours from one to three hours as well as half-day and full-day tours. A popular group tour option is the Villa Balbianello tour (2.5 hours), which includes a tour of the lake and this popular villa in Tremezzo, which was featured in a number of Hollywood films, including *Casino Royale* and *Star Wars: Episode II Attack of the Clones.* Or you could opt for the semi-private lunch tour, which includes roughly two hours on the water cruising around various important villas and villages dotting the lake as well as a stop at Isola Comacina, Como's lake island for lunch. Tours are offered every day while the sun is up, and can be booked in advance via their website.

BIKING
Bike It! Bellagio

Via Valassina 103; 334/975-1604; www.bikeitbellagio.com; 8:30am-6pm daily Mar.-Oct.; €35-50

Bike It! Bellagio offers road bikes, mountain bikes, and electric bikes for rent, with helmets included. Each type of bike comes in various sizes and speeds; children's bikes are available as well. The website has a really handy online booking form, which allows you to rent in advance. Renting online saves you time and ensures that even on days when bikes sell out (which is common during high season), there will be a bike waiting for you.

Bike It! Bellagio also offers the **Ghisallo Experience** (9am or 9:30am daily Mar.-Oct.; €65 per person) guided electric bike tour, which is a friendly option for families or groups who want to enjoy biking through the mountains around Bellagio without battling any steep climbs. You'll start at the Bike It! Bellagio office, then make your way to the locally known **Ghisallo Cycling Sanctuary**, which offers beautiful aerial views of Lake Como once you reach the top. Throughout the ride you'll be surrounded by greenery and trees, making for a peaceful trip. The total distance is 18 kilometers (11 miles), approximately 2-3 hours with rest stops, and over a total elevation of 550 meters (1,804 feet). Book in advance online.

SHOPPING

Shopping local is a must in Bellagio. Whether you're shopping for silk scarves or ties, local crafts or wines, leather bags or art, Bellagio's many local shops and boutiques makes for a one-of-a-kind shopping experience.

ACCESSORIES
Arte e Moda
Salita Mella 19; 031/950-067; www. pmartemoda.com; 10am-7pm daily
Visit Arte e Moda for the intricately detailed scarves and ties (that have been purchased by U.S. presidents and celebrities) made of local silk, as well as for the Murano glass jewelry. The owner, Pierangelo Masciadri, makes himself known and is the chief designer of the shop's products, so stop in and say hello to the man that designed ties for George Bush and Bill Clinton.

Carmen Como Silk
Salita Serbelloni 8; 031/950-101; 10:30am-6:30pm daily
Even more fine silk products can be found at Carmen Como Silk, just a quick walk up the steps of Salita Serbelloni in the village center. All ties, scarves, and other silk products are handmade from local material, and prices are affordable.

FOOD AND GOURMET
Alimentari da Caio
Via C. Bellosio, 1; 031/950-570; 7:30am-7:30pm daily
For food shopping, look no further than the Alimentaria Gastronomia, where you can find plenty of local cheeses, fish, porcini mushrooms, olive oil, and limoncello. The aromas are enough to lure you in from the street. Some sort of food product fills up nearly every inch of this place, and freshly made lunches can be taken to go and eaten near the waterfront.

ARTS AND CRAFTS
La Bottega del Legno
Via Giuseppe Garibaldi, 22; 031/950-836; www.bellagio.co.nz/tacchi; 10:30am-7:30pm daily
To browse artisanal souvenirs that you can't find anywhere else, such as handcrafted and hand-painted bowls, vases, cutting boards, and many other wood items, try La Bottega del Legno, one of Italy's oldest shops, dating back to 1855.

FOOD
ITALIAN AND PIZZA
Ittiturismo da Abata
Frazione Villa, 4 - Villa; 031/914-986; www.ittiturismodabate.it; 7am-11pm Tues.-Sun.; €10-20
Specializing in lake fish, this restaurant's menu changes daily, but the

Most waterfront restaurants in Bellagio offer beautifully covered seating.

cuisine is consistently high in quality and innovation. Local fishermen spend all night until the sunrise securing the daily catch, so the fish brought in every morning is fresh and ready for both lunch and dinner. Considering that the place is about 8 kilometers (5 miles) south of the village center, this place is best reached by car. Reservations are recommended, as the restaurant fills up quickly, especially on the weekends.

Terrazza Barchetta

Salita Antonio Mella, 15; 031/951-389; www. ristorantebarchetta.com; 12pm-2:30pm, 7pm-10:30pm Wed.-Mon.; €20-40

One of Bellagio's most beloved and charming eateries, this century-old restaurant prides itself on top-notch local dishes, but you'll also find traditional Italian plates such as risottos and carbonaras. The boneless lake trout is a must-try for fish lovers, but the wood-fired pizzas served on the restaurant's lower level also garner consistent rave reviews. Although the place has expanded over the years,

it's still quite small compared to the demands of hungry tourists, so book your table a day ahead, if possible.

Salice Blu Restaurant

Via per Lecco, 33; 339/834-3067; http://ristorante-saliceblu-bellagio.it; 12:30pm-2:30pm, 7pm-10:30pm Wed.-Mon..; €20-50

The family-owned and operated restaurant combines fine dining with local flavor. The fireplace in the corner of the dining room and the stonework-accented wood walls create a warm and inviting ambiance. The owners' son, Chef Luigi, has won plenty of cooking competitions, earning him international recognition for his unique combinations of simple, fresh ingredients. Try the tuna and king prawn carpaccio with mango sorbet, a house favorite, or split a catch-of-the-day platter between the table. Like most restaurants in Bellagio, book in advance to ensure a spot here in the evenings.

✪ Ristorante Mistral

Via Roma, 1; 031/956-435; http:// ristorante-mistral.com; 7:30-10pm daily, also 12:30-3:30pm Sat. and Sun.; €30-60

This Michelin-star restaurant, housed inside the luxurious Villa Serbelloni, serves some of the most modern Mediterranean cuisines on Lake Como, with Chef Ettore Bocchia focusing on local, high-quality ingredients. If you're feeling like splurging, opt for the €170 tasting menu with seven courses prepared by the chef himself. Otherwise, you'll find a full a la carte menu of appetizers, first courses, fish and meat dishes, sweets, cheese plates, and a robust wine menu. Expect to empty your wallet but leave feeling fully satisfied.

CAFÉS AND LIGHT BITES
Pasticceria Bar Dal 1919
Piazza Giuseppe Mazzini, 22; 031/950-196;
6:30am-11pm daily; €2-6

For some sweet treats, head to Pasticceria Bar Dal 1919, a nearly 100-year-old bakery that sells a variety of sweet treats, coffees, and other local food items. Open nearly all day year round, you can stop in for an early-morning pastry as well as a coffee or glass of wine at any time throughout the day.

cafés of Bellagio

Café Rossi
Piazza Giuseppe Mazzini, 22; 031/950-196;
6:30am-11pm daily; €2-10

Opening at 6:30 am, Café Rossi is a classic bar and bakery that welcomes early risers with traditional Italian pastries and a full-service coffee bar all day every day. From croissants, brioches, small cakes, sandwiches, happy-hour treats, and more, you can get just about every type of quick bite and drink imaginable here. Take a seat in the elegant art nouveau dining area or under the arches outside that overlook the lake.

ACCOMMODATIONS

As one of Lake Como's most popular villages, there are plenty of accommodation options in Bellagio, but expect to see a slight price increase compared to other villages due to the high demand of rooms here, especially during high season. If you're set on staying in Bellagio, be sure to book as far in advance as possible and check if your hotel offers free parking if you're traveling by car.

€85-150
Hotel Silvio
Via Paolo Carcano, 10-12; 031 950322; www.
bellagiosilvio.it; €88

This low-key, unpretentious, family-run hotel is located just outside the center of Bellagio, so you can enjoy a stay away from the crowds. The property includes a local restaurant serving fresh lake fish and other Northern Italian cuisine. Each room includes air conditioning, a private bathroom, and a balcony. Parking and breakfast are included in the price of the room. The hotel is about a 15-minute walk from the center of Bellagio, or you can hop on the bus at the San Giovanni al Ponte stop directly outside the hotel to catch a life to the village.

€150-250
Du Lac
Piazza Giuseppe Mazzini, 32; 031/950-320;
www.bellagiohoteldulac.com; €200

This charming, family-run lakefront hotel is located in the heart of Bellagio, making it a convenient and affordable option in the center of village life. Several rooms offer a panoramic view of the lake, and staff is known to be extremely helpful and friendly in order to ensure your stay is as comfortable as possible. Each room offers air conditioning and a private bathroom.

Hotel services include a restaurant with panoramic views and a full bar, guest parking, and breakfast with the room rate.

OVER €250
Grand Hotel Villa Serbelloni

Via Roma, 1; 031/950-216; www.villaserbelloni.com; €500

This historic villa-turned-luxury-hotel is one of the most revered establishments on Lake Como, with guests enjoying 100 years of five-star accommodation and services. The villa, owned by the Bucher family for three generations now, includes two lush gardens, an indoor and outdoor swimming pool, a world-class spa, and amazing views of the lake and the surrounding Alps. Guest rooms come with either a lake view or a park view, and each one includes air conditioning, WiFi, and private bathroom.

INFORMATION AND SERVICES

Bellagio's official tourism office, **Office du Tourisme-Bellagio** (Piazza Giuseppe Mazzini, 48; 031/950-204; www.bellagiolakecomo.com; 9:30am-12:30pm, 1:30-6pm Mon.-Sat., 10am-2pm Sun. Apr.-Sept.) offers information related to hotels, restaurants, and activities in the Bellagio area, as well as maps and other material that may interest you. The staff speaks English, French, and Spanish.

The **local police station** (Via Garibaldi, 1; 031/951-110; 11am-12am Mon.-Fri.) is located at the town hall, but you can always call 112 in case of emergencies.

GETTING THERE AND AROUND

Bellagio is a very small village, so it's best seen by foot, as roads are few and narrow, and the best restaurants,

view from Lake Como of the Grand Hotel Villa Serbelloni

shops, and sights are along the cobblestone alleys in between the streets. Public parking is very limited in the center of the village, especially near the lake, but some hotels offer parking for guests. Bellagio does not have a train station, so first you'll need to take a train to Varenna then head to Bellagio by ferry.

BY BOAT
Bellagio is reachable via the public ferry system from Menaggio (25 minutes), Cadenabbia di Griante (16 minutes), and Varenna (15 minutes), with both slow boats and car ferries running between these villages. Ferries usually run 7:30am-8pm, usually once per hour. Tickets (€7-20) can be purchased directly at the ferry stations at each of these towns, and timetables can be found there as well or online at www.navigazionelaghi.it.

BY CAR
You can reach Bellagio from Como and Lecco using SP583, which runs along the lake's shore. The drive from Lecco is roughly half an hour, with 23 kilometers (just over 14 miles) of travel, while the car trip from Como is roughly an hour, with 31 kilometers (roughly 19 miles) of road. Keep in mind that the SP583 road is often curvy and narrow, and hugging the shore of the lake. The road is full of travelers during high season, so expect traffic delays and consider traveling by public transportation if you want to get there as quickly as possible.

BY BUS
Travelers can take a bus from Como's San Giovanni bus station directly to Bellagio via **Bus C30** (once an hour, 6am-8:20pm daily; €2.75 one-way; 1 hour). You can also take **Bus D10** (few times a day, 7:30am-7:15pm; €2.80 one-way; 45min) from the train station in Lecco. More information can be found at www.lineelecco.com.

BY TAXI
You won't find many taxis in the small village of Bellagio, as the ferry service is reliable and the distances in between places are rather short. However, if you need a taxi, services such as **Bellagio Taxi** (www.bellagiotaxi.com, 329/703-2702) are available. Taxis can be booked by calling or text message. Taxis should be booked at least a couple hours in advance, as there are a limited number of cars available.

Menaggio

As one of Lake Como's "Holy Trinity" villages along with Bellagio and Varenna, Menaggio draws in thousands of travelers each summer with its quiet, colorful charm. Although not as large as some of the other villages lining the lake, Menaggio is lively with plenty to do. Step inside the lovely churches just outside the main promenade, grab a gelato and park yourself on a bench overlooking the lake, take a swim at the pebble beach, and eat lake fish at one of the local restaurants along the shore. Or just simply wander around. A walled city in Roman times, you can still find pieces of those walls scattered around the village today.

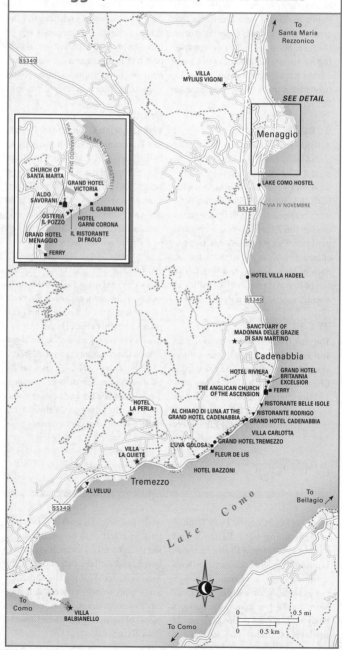

Menaggio, Cadenabbia, and Tremezzo

To Santa Maria Rezzonico

SS340

VILLA MYLIUS VIGONI

SEE DETAIL

Menaggio

LAKE COMO HOSTEL

VIA IV NOVEMBRE

SS340

Detail inset

VIA BENEDETTO CASTELLI

VIA ARMANDO DIAZ

CHURCH OF SANTA MARTA

GRAND HOTEL VICTORIA

ALDO SAVORANI

IL GABBIANO

OSTERIA IL POZZO

HOTEL GARNI CORONA

IL RISTORANTE DI PAOLO

GRAND HOTEL MENAGGIO

FERRY

HOTEL VILLA HADEEL

SS340

SANCTUARY OF MADONNA DELLE GRAZIE DI SAN MARTINO

Cadenabbia

HOTEL RIVIERA

GRAND HOTEL BRITANNIA EXCELSIOR

THE ANGLICAN CHURCH OF THE ASCENSION

FERRY

RISTORANTE BELLE ISOLE

HOTEL LA PERLA

RISTORANTE RODRIGO

AL CHIARO DI LUNA AT THE GRAND HOTEL CADENABBIA

GRAND HOTEL CADENABBIA

VILLA CARLOTTA

L'UVA GOLOSA

GRAND HOTEL TREMEZZO

VILLA LA QUIETE

FLEUR DE LIS

HOTEL BAZZONI

Tremezzo

AL VELUU

SS340

To Bellagio

Lake Como

To Como

0   0.5 mi

0   0.5 km

To Como

VILLA BALBIANELLO

ORIENTATION

Menaggio sits on the western shore in the central part of Lake Como. The center of Menaggio sits right on the waterfront, divided into two squares: **Piazza Garibaldi** and **Piazza Grossi**, with the latter sitting just north of the former. Most restaurants, shops, and sights sit just outside of these two piazzas, both with beautiful views of the Lake Como waters. **Via Regina** runs just behind these piazzas, connecting the town to the rest of the villages along the western shore of the lake. Along the lake, you'll find **Viale Castelli** running parallel to Via Regina and the shore. The small pedestrian street of **Via Calvi** connects these streets near Piazza Garibaldi in the middle of town. Menaggio's **ferry station** is just a short walk south of the main piazzas along Viale Castelli.

SIGHTS

CHURCH OF SANTA MARTA

Via Calvi, 15; free

Peek into the very small Church of Santa Marta on Via Calvi, directly off of Menaggio's main promenade along the lake. Tucked between the local shops and bars along this road, the church is known for its tranquil interior that includes a **Roman memorial** and a coat of arms on the facade of the church. The bright, tiny room may seem like just a little sliver of space between local shops in the center of town, but it serves as a peaceful cornerstone for the village, beloved by locals and admired by thousands of visitors every year.

VILLA MYLIUS VIGONI

Via Giulio Vigoni 1; 344/361-232; www.villavigoni.eu; guided tours 2:30pm Thurs. Mar.-July, Sept.-Oct.; €10

Another tourist favorite in Menaggio is Villa Mylius Vigoni in Lovemo, which is a hamlet of Menaggio. The 19th-century building served as a place for German and Italian artists to convene in the 1800s and 1900s, and it is known today for its surrounding **garden** full of cypresses, pines, cedars, and a variety of smaller plants, and from where you can enjoy an aerial view of the lake. While most travelers on Lake Como's western shore opt to visit Villa Carlotta in Tremezzo, this quiet and elegant villa offers a similar experience with fewer crowds and stunning aerial views of the western branch of the lake.

You can visit the gardens of the villa every Thursday afternoon from March to October, but you must book online in advance. The best way to arrive is by car following the SP7 off of Via Cadorna for about 10 minutes, as the villa sits on top of a hill overlooking Menaggio.

SHOPPING

Aldo Savorani

Via Calvi, 7; 034/431-161; www.aldosavorani.com/dove-aldo-savorani; 9:30am-12:30pm, 3pm-7pm daily

A shopping excursion in Menaggio isn't complete without a stop in Aldo Savorani on Via Calvi, just next to the Church of Santa Marta. The store is known for its curated and posh selection of brands for both women's and men's modern fashion. While most brands are Italian, you'll also find a handful of international brands.

FOOD

Menaggio's best dining options are all located in or close by the main square along the waterfront. Due to the number of visitors that flock to this small village during high season, book a dinner table in advance for any restaurant.

ITALIAN
Osteria Il Pozzo

Piazza Giuseppe Garibaldi; 034/432-333;
www.osteriadelpozzo.com; 12pm-2pm,
7pm-9:30pm Thurs.-Tues.; €20-40

Osteria Il Pozzo is tucked into a corner of
Menaggio's main square

Osteria Il Pozzo is known for its comfortable, homestyle atmosphere and generous portions. Tucked away in a corner of the main piazza, this place fills up quickly with hungry travelers looking for fresh pasta, meats and cheeses, local fish, polenta, and other Lombardy dishes such as osso buco and veal. The friendly staff is both attentive and knowledgeable, ready to suggest wine and food pairings. Try the house wine with your meal.

Il Ristorante di Paolo

Largo Cavour, 5; 034/432-133;
12pm-2:30pm, 7pm-10pm Wed.-Mon.;
€35-50

Il Ristorante di Paolo is situated along the shore of Lake Como, with a spacious outdoor seating area that offers a peaceful view of the water to accompany the menu of traditional Italian dishes and local fish. Presentation is just as important as quality and flavor here, so expect beautifully plated dishes, from the appetizers to the pastas and risottos filled with fish to the classic Italian desserts. While you will more than likely find a spot on the patio for lunch without reservations, you should book ahead for dinner here.

GELATO
Il Gabbiano

Lungo lago; 0344/32-608; 7am-10pm
Thurs.-Tues.; €3-10

For a refreshing dessert or snack directly on the lake, Il Gabbiano's gelato and sorbet hit the spot. All products are handmade directly in the lab attached to the restaurant using all-natural ingredients without preservatives or artificial coloring. The gelato and sorbet come in cups or cones; you can also add fresh fruits or liqueurs. A selection of teas and hot chocolates is available for those visiting in the colder months.

ACCOMMODATIONS

If you're set on staying on the western shore of Lake Como, you will find the most accommodation options in Menaggio, ranging from affordable, modern hostels to luxurious all-inclusive hotels.

UNDER €85
Lake Como Hostel

Via IV Novembre, 106; 034/432-356; www.
lakecomohostel.com; €20-70

As one of Lake Como's only hostels, this budget-friendly solution is bright, clean, and comfortable and offers both shared and private options. The shore is just a one-minute walk away. The hostel grounds include a private garden, restaurant and bar, a terrace, and a free private beach. Breakfast is included in the price of every room. The cost for a single bed in an eight-person mixed dorm and a shared bathroom starts at €20 per night.

€150-250
Hotel Garni Corona
Largo Cavour, 3; 034/432-006; www.hotelgarnicorona.com; €140
This family-run hotel is just a stone's throw away from the shoreline, with 17 of the 24 rooms offering lake views, and all rooms modestly priced for the area. Rooms are bright, spacious, comfortable, and modern. Each room includes air conditioning, private bathroom, and WiFi.

Grand Hotel Victoria
Viale Ingegner Benedetto Castelli, 9/13; 034/432-003; www.grandhotelvictoria.it; €250
Despite just being 100 meters (109 yards) from the village's main square,

Grand Hotel Victoria resides in a quiet, untouched corner of Menaggio, providing a perfect mix of serenity and elegance for those looking to catch a little R&R during their time on the lake. The art nouveau building is surrounded by private gardens and a swimming pool, while the interior is timelessly and classically decorated. Rooms come with either a garden or lake view as well as air conditioning, WiFi, and private bathroom.

OVER €250
Grand Hotel Menaggio
Via IV Novembre, 77; 034/430-640; www.grandhotelmenaggio.com; €270
The Grand Hotel Menaggio sits just a few-minutes walk away from Menaggio's main square directly on the lake. The hundreds of windows flood the large building with plenty of natural sunlight, giving it a bright and welcoming atmosphere on every

Grand Hotel Menaggio sits directly on the village's shoreline level. The hotel is situated just next to the village's ferry area and boat dock, where you can quickly catch a ride to other parts of the lake. Each guest room has air conditioning, WiFi, and a private bathroom, and the breakfast buffet is included. Live piano music is offered on the terrace most evenings as well. Rooms with lake views are more expensive.

INFORMATION AND SERVICES

Menaggio's tourism office, **Infopoint Menaggio** (Piazza Garibaldi, 3; 0344/32-924; www.menaggio.com; 9am-12:30pm, 1:30pm-5:30pm daily, until 6pm Jul.-Sept.) is right in the middle of town and is full of material and maps that you may find useful during your stay. The English-speaking staff is incredibly helpful.

The hospital in Menaggio, **Ospedale di Zona** (Via Virginia Casartelli 7; 0344/33-111), offers 24-hour emergency services. You can also reach the **local police station** (Via Foppa, 38; 0344/32-142) at all hours of the day or evening, but in any emergency situation, call 112. At both the hospital and the police station, you shouldn't have trouble finding someone that speaks English.

GETTING THERE AND AROUND

Due to its small size, Menaggio can be easily explored on foot. Note that Menaggio has no train station, so the best way to reach the village is by car, boat, or the *trenino* running on the most popular area of the lake's western shore.

BY BOAT

Menaggio can be easily accessed via public ferries from Bellagio (25min),

Como (50min), and Varenna (15min). Ferries usually run 7:30am-8pm, once per hour, with both slow boats and car ferries from these villages to Menaggio. Tickets (€7-20) can be purchased directly at the ferry stations at each of these towns, and timetables can be found there as well or online at www.navigazionelaghi.it.

BY CAR

From Como, follow Via Regina up the western shore of the lake to reach Menaggio (35 km/21 mi, 55 min). Note that public parking is limited, so you may not find available space in the center of the village. If you're staying in Menaggio, confirm with your accommodation before your arrival that they offer free parking for guests.

From Lecco, you need to first reach Como by taking the SS36 southwest until it becomes SP342, then follow that west until you reach Como. Once you get to Como, follow the signs leading you to Menaggio and Tremezzo along the SS340. You can take this road until you reach Menaggio. The total trip is about 67 kilometers (41 miles) and a little over 1.5 hours.

BY BUS

Bus C10 (about once an hour, 7am-8:20pm daily; €3.60 one-way; approx. 1 hour) runs from Como San Giovanni and the Como Nord Lago station in Como to Menaggio. Tickets can be purchased at the trail station or directly on board.

BY TROMBETTA EXPRESS

Alternatively, you can take the Trombetta Express (www.trombetta-express.com) *trenino* from Cadenabbia (12 minutes) or Tremezzo (15 minutes). The small train is driven up and down the main road connecting the

The San Martino Church in Cadenabbia di Griante is tucked into the mountains overlooking the lake

three villages many times a day during high season. A one-way ticket is €5 per person, but you can also purchase a full-day pass for €15, or a daytime pass (valid until 5:30pm) for €12 per person.

Cadenabbia di Griante

Tucked in between Tremezzo to the south and Menaggio to the north is the tranquil little village of Cadenabbia, which is officially part of the Griante commune. Due to the greenery and plants around the village, it's a well-known destination for travelers in the springtime and the fall, as the foliage changes into a variety of beautiful colors. Since the 19th century, Cadenabbia has been a popular destination for British travelers, so much so that the first Anglican Church in Italy was built in the village. Today, this fishing village's hot spot is the grand resort dominating its shoreline.

The town is quite small, sitting right up against the western shore and taking only a couple minutes to drive from the southern to northern village borders on Via Regina, the main road connecting Cadenabbia to other western villages of Lake Como. Along this road, you can reach the Anglican Church, most hotels, restaurants, and the beach. On the southern side of the village's waterfront, you'll find the ferry station.

SIGHTS

Due to its small size, Cadenabbia's top sight is its natural surroundings—the flora-lined shore that leads back to the towering mountains is itself a

145

breathtaking view. If you are looking for some sights, a couple of notable churches are worth visiting during your time in the village.

SANCTUARIO MADONNA DELLE GRAZIE DI SAN MARTINO

Piazza S. Rocco, 5, Griante

To see the greenery and foliage on local farms, visit the small but lovely mountainside church of Sanctuary of Madonna delle Grazie di San Martino, which takes you through winding back roads and up a mountain.

Locally known as just San Martino, this church is set against the backdrop of spectacular views of the mountains and lake, which you can see from inside the church as well as out. While you can take a roughly 45-minute walk up to the church by following the signs from the shore, or by simply asking the locals, San Martino is also accessible by car. Be careful, however; the roads are very narrow, barely fitting two cars side-by-side. Note that the church is often closed, so consider yourself lucky if you are able to get a peek inside. The trip itself is worth it for the stunning views of the surrounding Alps pressed against the shore, punctuated by the rolling hills and deep blue lake waters sparkling in the distance.

ANGLICAN CHURCH OF THE ASCENSION

Via Statale, 31, Griante; 02/655-2258; www. churchonlakecomo.com; daily Easter-Oct.

Cadenabbia is also home to Italy's first official Anglican church, the Anglican Church of the Ascension. Situated just opposite of the ferry terminal in the town, this church was first built in 1891 on the grounds of the Hotel Bellevue, today known as the Grand Hotel Cadenabbia, by British settlers. While most the original congregation returned to England during and after World War II, the church was reconstructed after minimal war damage and remains one of most popular sights along Lake Como. Services are held every Sunday in English, with English-speaking priests rotating in and out of the church each year. While the church may differ in religious practices, the interior and exterior are much like the surrounding Catholic churches, with a peaceful dusty interior marked by a gold-hued altar at the front and large stained-glass windows that glow with streaming light.

FOOD

Despite being such a small village, Cadenabbia di Griante has plenty of cafés, bars, and Italian restaurants along the small squares lining Via Regina.

ITALIAN AND PIZZA

Ristorante Rodrigo

Via Regina, 7, Griante; 0344/42-290; www. ristoranterodrigo.webs.com; 10am-12am daily; €7-20

Visitors will tell you that this place is reliable, open, consistent, and satisfying all without breaking your budget. The menu at Ristorante Rodrigo is expansive and includes local dishes and plates with lake fish, but most guests seem to love the wood-fired pizzas. With nearly 100 years of service, this family-run establishment grew in popularity as the village grew in size following the first world war. While you're bound to find a table during lunch hours, book ahead to ensure a table for dinner.

LAKE COMO INTERNATIONAL MUSIC FESTIVAL

The Lake Como International music festival is a concert series held from February to September every year in a handful of locations scattered on the shores of the lake, from the Villa Carlotta in Tremezzo to the Civic Art Gallery in Como. Produced by Amadeus Arte, a local non-profit art and cultural association, the festival hosts 15-20 concerts featuring soloists and small ensembles from both Italy and other parts of the world. Performances range from guitar to piano, cello, flute, and more.

Locations are carefully curated to ensure that the acoustics and the atmosphere maximize the concert experience, which mixes casual with a touch of sophistication. Due to the high number of visitors that have taken interest in the festival in recent years, programs for every concert are now offered in both English and Italian.

Most concerts are €10 each, though some are free. If you're planning to see a few concerts, purchase a €20 festival card that will grant you entry to all concerts. Most concerts start in the early evenings, around 6:30pm, but there a handful each year that start in the early afternoon or late in the evening. The program for the festival year can be found at https://lakecomofestival.com.

Ristorante Belle Isole

Via Regina, 25, Griante; 0344/41-003; www.ristorantebelleisole.it; 10:30am-11pm daily; €7-20

This traditional Italian restaurant focusing on classic flavors with a local twist pairs comfort and hospitality, with plenty of customers coming back for more once they dine in the relaxed atmosphere overlooking the water. Directly across the street from the lake, Ristorante Belle Isole is convenient for those wanting to stay local while grabbing a fulfilling bite to eat. The place is family owned and operated, so they pride themselves on their friendliness and knowledge of local cuisine and history. Both indoor and outdoor seating is available, with the covered patio seating open to calming views of the lake.

Al Chiaro di Luna at the Grand Hotel Cadenabbia

Cadenabbia, di, Via Regina, 1, Griante; 0344/40-418; www.grandhotelcadenabbia. it; 8am-10pm daily; €25-60 per person

The Al Chiaro di Luna restaurant is on the rooftop terrace of the Grand Hotel Cadenabbia, giving diners an amazing, unobstructed view of the lake and the village of Bellagio across

the water. Most visitors choose to dine here around sunset when the weather is nice, and the intimate setting and attentive service often makes it feel like you've found a corner of paradise. The most popular dishes are the risottos and flambés. While you shouldn't have trouble finding a table, book ahead for dinner to play it safe.

ACCOMMODATIONS

Despite being a small stop on the lake's western shore, you will find a handful of accommodations here. The centerpiece, however, is the luxurious Grand Hotel Cadenabbia. Most other hotels are located directly on or close to the shore.

€85-150

Hotel Riviera

Via Statale, 43, Cadenabbia; 0344/40-422; www.rivierahotel-como.com; €95

This small 19th-century establishment offers excellent views of both the lake and the village of Bellagio across the water. The outdoor terrace is open for breakfast, lunch, and dinner each day, with breakfast comprising traditional Italian coffee and pastries. There is also an Internet access point available for guests in the common area. Each guest room includes a private bathroom and cooling fan.

Hotel Villa Hadeel

Via Regina, 87, Griante; 0344-42126; www. hotelvillahadeel.com; €110

The family-owned and operated Hotel Villa Hadeel combines 18th-century architecture with modern and Venetian-style design. The building was originally built as a house for a wealthy family and has since turned into one of Cadenabbia's most prized accommodations. Each guest room comes with air conditioning, sound-proofing, WiFi, and private bathroom. Some rooms have balconies with both lake and mountain views. Breakfast for an additional €5 per person per night is also available, and parking is free.

Grand Hotel Britannia Excelsior

Via Regina, 41, Cadenabbia; 0344/40-413; www.comovita.com/en/britannia; €126

The 19th-century Grand Hotel Britannia Excelsior is located directly on the water, with large classically decorated rooms full of antique furniture. The huge pool is one of its best features, with its pool deck lying just a few feet above the waters of the lake and sun beds and lounge seating nearby. Each guest room comes with air conditioning, private bathroom, and minifridge. Breakfast is an additional €5 per person.

€150-250
Grand Hotel Cadenabbia

Via Regina, 1, Cadenabbia di Griante; 0344/40-418; www.grandhotelcadenabbia. it; €200

The Grand Hotel Cadenabbia is a dominating presence, taking up a huge part of Cadenabbia's shoreline

The Grand Hotel Cadenabbia is one of Lake Como's most luxurious hotels

and exuding elegance and grandeur from the inside out. Although it's situated right next to Villa Carlotta, the hotel's gardens stack up well, bursting with just as much color and beauty. Each room includes floor-to-ceiling curtains and antique furniture, giving off a royal vibe, and is equipped with air conditioning, WiFi, and private bathroom. Guests can dine in the rooftop terrace restaurant or swim in the peaceful pool, surrounded by blooming green in every direction. Breakfast and parking are included.

GETTING THERE AND AROUND

Cadennabia di Griante is very small, so you can explore the entire village in a day on foot.

BY BOAT

Cadenabbia can be reached via public ferry from both Bellagio (20 minutes) and Varenna (30 minutes). Ferries generally run from 7:30am-8pm during high season and usually once per hour. Tickets (€3-10) can be purchased directly from each village's ferry stations, where you can also find the timetables. They are also available online at www.navigazionelaghi.it.

BY CAR

From Como, take Via Regina up the western shore of the lake to reach Cadenabbia. The trip is roughly 30 kilometers (19 miles) to Cadenabbia and takes about 45 minutes.

From Lecco, you need to first reach Como by taking the SS36 southwest until it becomes SP342, then follow that west until you reach Como. Once you get to Como, follow the signs leading you to Menaggio and Tremezzo along the SS340. You can take this road until you reach Cadenabbia. The total trip is about 63 kilometers (39 miles) and takes 1.5 hours.

From Menaggio, head south of Via Regina hugging the shore for 3.7 kilometers (2.3 miles), which is about a five-minute trip.

Note that public parking is really limited in Cadenabbia, so you may have trouble finding a free spot along the shore. Make sure that your accommodation offers free parking for guests.

BY BUS

Bus C10 (about once an hour, 7am-8:20pm daily; €3.60 one-way; approx. 50min) runs from Como San Giovanni and the Como Nord Lago station in Como to Cadenabbia. Tickets can be purchased at the train station or directly on board.

BY TROMBETTA EXPRESS

Alternatively, you can take the Trombetta Express (www.trombetta-express.com) *trenino* from Menaggio (12 minutes) or Tremezzo (10 minutes). The small train is driven up and down the main road connecting the three villages many times a day during high season, making them easily accessible without needing to drive. A one-way ticket is €5 per person, but you can also purchase a full-day pass for €15, or a daytime pass (valid until 5:30pm) for €12 per person, with both tickets allowing you to hop on and off the train in either direction for the entire day.

Tremezzo

The tiny but wildly beautiful town of Tremezzo, with a population of 1,300, sits on Lake Como's western shore in the central part of the lake. In the last decade, the small community merged with a few other surrounding villages to create the Tremezzina village. Today, it's known mostly for its luxurious villas where a handful of blockbuster movies, such as *Casino Royale* and *Star Wars Episode II,* were filmed. Its 8.4 square kilometers (2.3 square miles) mostly stretches away from the lake, meaning there isn't as much shoreline in Tremezzo as in some of the other villages along the lake, such as Bellagio and Menaggio. But a visit here will not disappoint, as Tremezzo manages to fit plenty of elegance and charm into a small space.

The main road of Via Regina runs through the village, and connects it to the other villages on the western shore. Nearly every restaurant, hotel, church, or villa that you'll want to visit in Tremezzo sits directly on this road or just off of it, so you'll rarely have the need to go more than a few dozen meters or so away from the waters of the lake while visiting this area. Villa

Carlotta, Tremezzo's most prized possession, sits on the northern end of the village.

SIGHTS
✪ VILLA CARLOTTA

Via Regina, 2, Tremezzina; 0344/40-405; www.villacarlotta.it; 9am-6:30pm daily late Mar.-early Nov.; gardens and museum €10, with discounts for travelers over the age of 65 or students with ID

This prominent building on the lakeshore was built in 1745 by an unknown architect for the Clerici family, who made a name for themselves in the area as successful silk merchants. The villa has been publicly owned since the end of World War I, and is now one of the most famous spots to visit on Lake Como.

Today, the villa's **botanical gardens** are one of its main draws, with roughly 8 hectares (20 acres) of multilevel and multicolored beauty. The Italian-style garden boasts several terraces of camellias, papyrus, azaleas, citrus trees, statues, stairs, fountains, and more. For nature enthusiasts, this place should not be skipped, especially in spring when the colors are in full bloom. Every turn on the paths throughout the gardens completely awakens the senses, with picture-worthy corners in every direction.

The villa houses an **art museum**, with works from Adamo Tadolini, Antonio Canova, and Francesco Hayez. Unlike several art museums in Italy that focus on one particular time period, genre, or form, this museum showcases a variety of styles—statues, marble works, silk tapestries, paintings, and decorative furniture, just to name some. Don't skip the upper level of the villa with its beautiful vistas of Bellagio and the mountains surrounding the lake.

Villa Carlotta is known for the interior art galleries and colorful gardens

VILLA LA QUIETE

Via Statale, 36; 0344/42-491; www. villasolacabiati.com

Another worthwhile villa to stroll by is Villa La Quiete (formally known as Villa Sola Cabiati), originally built in the 1500s and eventually turned into the summer residence of the family of Serbelloni dukes. The private villa is surrounded by gardens leading up to SS Regina road, and a large staircase leads directly to the lake. While the villa is not open to the public, it can be rented out as a luxury residence; it is also a popular site for weddings. The villa is located right on the main road running along the western shore of the lake, so be sure to take a few minutes to admire the elegant facade and well-manicured lawn through the entry gates.

VILLA BALBIANELLO

Via Guido Monzino, 1; 0344/56-110; www. fondoambiente.it/luoghi/villa-del-balbianello; 10am-6pm Tues., Thurs.-Sun.; €10

Another lovely villa is the Villa Balbianello, which may look familiar to anyone who has seen the 2006 film *Casino Royale* or the 2002 *Star Wars: Episode II Attack of the Clones*. While this villa is actually in the tiny town of Lenno, on the western shore of the lake near Como, it's easily accessible for those traveling by car. The grand 18th-century villa is located on a secluded, shady peninsula, surrounded by terraced gardens visible from the water. Although the villa is not as highly touted by locals, it is a peaceful escape with its tall green trees and remnants of Italian history. To get here from the main part of Tremezzo, follow the SS340 south to Lenno, then take a left following the signs to the

Villa Balbianello from the waters of Lake Como

villa. From the center of Tremezzo, it's about five kilometers (three miles) and a 5-10 minute drive.

SHOPPING

Fleur de Lis

Portici Sampietro 4a; 331/232-7697; 9:30am-7:30pm daily

Pick up a souvenir from Fleur de Lis, where you'll find everything from locally made scarves, hats, jewelry, trinkets, soaps, food items, and more—all of which can be gift wrapped by the warm and congenial staff.

L'Uva Golosa

Portici Sampietro, 4/B; 0344/40-018; 9am-8pm daily

For locally sourced gourmet food items, head to L'Uva Golosa on Portici Sampietro. While primarily a wine cellar, you will also find soaps, pastas, sauces, spices, oils, and more.

FOOD

Although Tremezzo might be small, its restaurants are frequented often by both locals and tourists. You'll find a couple of bars that double as cafés as well as traditional Italian restaurants with killer views.

Al Veluu

Via IV Novembre, Tremezzina; 0344/40-510;
www.alveluu.com; 12pm-2pm, 7pm-9:30pm
Wed.-Mon.; €20-40

Whether you're seated on the outdoor terrace or in the indoor space accented by floor-to-ceiling windows, Al Veluu offers one of the best panoramic views of the lake and mountains, which you can enjoy while dining on traditional Italian dishes rich in local flavors. Many ingredients come directly from the kitchen's seasonal garden; its fish come from the lake, and its extensive selection of wines hail from different regions around Italy. Book ahead if you want a table outside during fair-weather seasons. The restaurant is situated on a hilltop, so it is recommended that you arrive by car.

La Locanda dell'Isola

Isola Comacina; 0344/55-083; www.
comacina.it; 12pm-2:30pm, 7pm-9:30pm
daily, Wed.-Mon.; prix fixe €77

This lakeview establishment located on Isola Comacina, Lake Como's most popular island, offers a prix-fixe menu, which the owners and staff take great pride in preparing. Each course of their five-course meal is precisely crafted, beautifully presented, and made from the highest quality ingredients—from the appetizers to the brandy and coffee served at the end. White wine is also covered in the set cost (which includes tax and cover charge). Since it is a limited menu, take caution if you have certain food allergies or intolerances. Reservations are highly recommended, and credit cards are not accepted. To get to the island, you will need to take a water taxi or boat from Tremezzo's pier for roughly €10 per round-trip.

ACCOMMODATIONS

€85-150

Hotel Bazzoni

26, Via Regina; 0344/40-403; https://
hotelbazzonitremezzo.com; €90

Hotel Bazzoni is located on the main road hugging the shore in Tremezzo. You can enjoy a large and highly-rated large breakfast, then work it all off at the gym or swimming pool, and reward yourself later with a cocktail at the bar. Each modernly decorated guest room comes with air conditioning, private bathroom, and refrigerator. Some rooms have balconies with lake views. Free WiFi is available in the public areas of the hotel, but not in the room, although you can ask the front desk for Internet options available in your room. Breakfast is available for €10 per person.

Hotel La Perla

Via Avvocato Romolo Quaglino, 7;
0344/41-707; www.laperlatremezzo.com;
€120

Run by a pair of twin sisters and their husbands, Hotel La Perla combines elegance with comfort. The space is bright, clean, and homey, so you feel comfortable whether you're taking a dip in the outdoor pool or eating breakfast on the terrace overlooking the lake. Most guest rooms here have their own balcony, and all include air conditioning, WiFi, and private bathroom. Access to the pool, parking, and the hearty breakfast are included.

OVER €250

Grand Hotel Tremezzo

Via Regina, 8; 0344/42-491; www.
grandhoteltremezzo.com; €880

This five-star luxury hotel dominates Tremezzo's shoreline and is known as one of the most elegant and majestic hotels on Como's western side. The

The Grand Hotel Tremezzo towers over the waterfront

interior is classically designed, but accented with modern details here and there. Most guest rooms have a stunning balcony view of the lake as well as air conditioning, WiFi, and private bathroom. Board games and other entertainment for children are also included. Some rooms also have terraces and hot tubs. During your stay, you can enjoy the outdoor pool, wellness center with sauna and hot tub, or tennis court. The hotel also has private water taxis that you can rent for jetting around the lake.

GETTING THERE AND AROUND

Tremezzo is best reached by car or by the Trombetta Express. While the villas and a few hotels are right along the shore and thus walkable, note that some restaurants and hotels are located up the small, winding roads leading away from the shore and up the mountains, which may be dangerous to reach by foot (especially at night), so getting around by

motor vehicle may be your best bet in Tremezzo.

BY BOAT

Tremezzo can be accessed by Lake Como's ferry service from both Bellagio (20 minutes) and Varenna (25 minutes). Ferries usually operate once an hour 7:30am-8pm during high season. Tickets (€3-10) can be purchased directly at each town's ferry stations, where timetables can also be found. You can check online as well at www.navigazionelaghi.it.

BY CAR

From Como, follow the Via Regina up the western shore of the lake to reach Tremezzo. The trip is roughly 28 kilometers (17 miles) and takes 45 minutes. Public parking is limited in Tremezzo, so you may have trouble finding a free spot along the shore, especially during high season. If you're staying overnight in town, find an accommodation that offers free parking for guests.

To head into the mountains away from the lake in Tremezzo, turn off of Via Regina and onto Via Peduzzi, which takes you past town hall and back into an area with quiet hotels and local restaurants in every direction.

BY BUS
Bus C10 (about once an hour, 7am-8:20pm daily; €3.60 one-way; approx. 45min) runs from Como San Giovanni and the Como Nord Lago station in Como to Tremezzo. Tickets can be purchased at the train station or directly on board.

BY TROMBETTA EXPRESS
You can take the Trombetta Express (www.trombettaexpress.com) *trenino* from Cadenabbia (10 minutes) or Menaggio (15 minutes). A one-way ticket is €5 per person, but you can also purchase a full-day pass for €15, or a daytime pass (valid until 5:30pm) for €12 per person.

Como

The city of Como is Lake Como's version of a metropolis, with plenty of historic sights, museums, gardens, shopping, dining, accommodation options, and nightlife. In recent years, it has outgrown its previous reputation of just being the transportation hub for the lake, turning into one of the most popular tourist destinations in Lombardy. The city of Como remains one of the most easily accessed lake points for those coming from Milan, with plenty of trains running in between the two cities each day.

As far as appearances go, Como's makeup is far more industrial than the other, smaller villages dotting Lake Como's shores. However, the cobblestone streets that make up the historic center from the shoreline and around the beautiful Duomo cathedral offer plenty of leisurely ways to fill up an entire day. Start at the waterfront and work your way into the heart of the city to find some of the most diverse sights on the lake.

ORIENTATION
Como sits on the southwestern-most point of Lake Como, at the very end of the western branch of the lake. The city itself is organized as a grid, so you'll have parallel and perpendicular roads creating piazzas and blocks throughout the main part of town. However, a large part of the city center is taken up by a large square, Piazza Cavour. Como's city center is loosely bounded by the southern shore of the lake to the north, Via Innocenzo XI to the west, SP342 to the south, and Via Alighieri to the east.

Como's main train station, Como San Giovanni, is located on the western side of Via Innocenzo XI, meaning you'll need to head east down the steps and across Via Innocenzo XI to walk to the center of town. On the opposite end of this large square, on the eastern part of the town center, just inside Via Alighieri and a quick walk to the shoreline, is the Como Nord Lago train station. The two main squares of Como are Piazza Cavour, which sits directly on the lake, and Piazza del

Como from the top of the city of Como

Duomo, site of Como's most important cathedral.

The small mountaintop village of **Brunate** lies northeast of Como by just a couple kilometers and is easily accessible via cable car or car—just follow the curves of Via per Brunate.

SIGHTS

Compared to the other villages, the city of Como offers the most diverse and extensive attractions on Lake Como—a mix of history with modernism, with everything from museums to Roman ruins to elegant villas.

VILLA OLMO

Via Simone Cantoni, 1; 031/57-6169; www.villaolmocomo.it; villa 10am-6pm Tues.-Sun., park 7am-11pm Tues.-Sun. Apr.-Sept. until 7pm Oct.-Mar.; free

Villa Olmo, a neoclassical structure built in 1797, has colorful lakeside gardens with verdant, well-manicured lawns dotted with statues and groomed trees. Although the gardens don't compare to those of other villas in the northern areas of Lake Como, they nonetheless make a lovely escape for an hour or so from the hustle and bustle of the lake's largest, busiest town. While the entire villa is only accessible during temporary art exhibitions, visitors can see the first floor, the Sala del Duca, free of charge.

✪ DUOMO DI COMO

Via Maestri Comacini, 6; 031/304-137; www.cattedraledicomo.it; 10am-6pm daily; free

Anyone that has visited Como will tell you that the absolute not-to-be-missed sight in the city is the cathedral, also known as the Duomo di Como. Its presence is dominating, and just like the Duomo in Milan, it is the heart and soul of the city. Today, it's known as one of the most important churches in the Lombardy region as well as the last known Gothic cathedral to be built in the country. Construction began in 1396 and completed in 1770. The west-facing front features a rose window and statues of two famous

155

Como

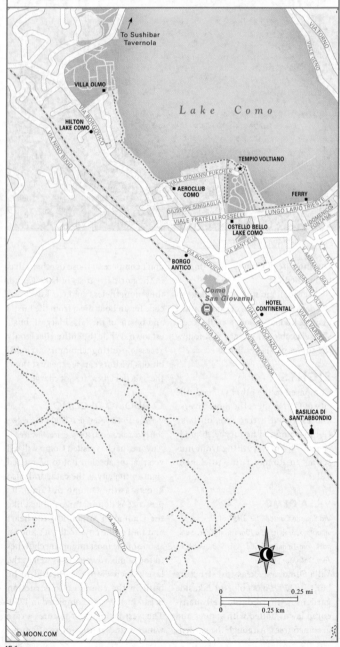

Lake Como

To Sushibar
Tavernola

VILLA OLMO

HILTON
LAKE COMO

VIA NINO BIXIO

VIA BORGOVICO

TEMPIO VOLTIANO

VIALE GIOVANNI PUECHER

AEROCLUB
COMO

GIUSEPPE SINIGAGLIA

VIALE FRATELLI ROSSELLI

LUNGO LARIO TRIESTE

FERRY

N. DOMENICO
FONTANA

OSTELLO BELLO
LAKE COMO

VIA SANT'ELIA

VIA BORGOVICO

BORGO
ANTICO

Como
San Giovanni

VIA SANTA MARIA

HOTEL
CONTINENTAL

VIALE INNOCENZO XI

VIALE REGINA TEODOLINDA

V. ALESSANDRO VOLTA

V. ADRIANO DIAZ

V. P. TATTI

VIALE VARESE

BASILICA DI
SANT'ABBONDIO

VIA RONCHETTO

0   0.25 mi

0   0.25 km

© MOON.COM

LAGHETTO

CARESCIONE

BRUNATE

FUNICULAR

VIA ALESSANDRO VOLTA

V. PER COMO

BRUNATE FUNICULAR

SALITA PELI BRERA

GELATERIA CECCATO

Como Nord Lago

TERMINUS
BAR DELLE TERME
AT TERMINUS

V. BEZZONICO

V. ENRICO PESSINA

VIA FRANCESCO CRISPI

SAN DONATO

DUOMO

PALAZZO TERRAGNI

V. VITTORIO EMANUELE II

VIA SANTO GARIBALDO

VIA VOLTO

TEATRO SOCIALE

COMO

V. BOLDONI

A PICCI

FRESCO COCKTAIL SHOP

OSTERIA L'ANGOLO DEL SILENZIO

VIA TOMMASO GROSSI

GARZOLA

ENOTECA DA GIGI

TERME DI COMO ROMANA

VIALE LECCO

VIA DANTE ALIGHIERI

VIA DON LUIGI GUANELLA

VIA FIUME

VIA PER BRUNATE

AVENUE

V. NATTA

V. GIUSEPPE ROVELLI

PAOLO GIOVIO ARCHAEOLOGICAL MUSEUM

VIALE LORENZO SPALLINO

MERCATO COPERTO

V. GIOVIO

V. GIUSEPPE PARINI

VIA GIUSEPPE SIRTORI

VIA FRANCESCO PETRARCA

VIA SAN MARTINO DELLA BATTAGLIA

VIA BRIANTEA

VIA TERESA CICERI

Como Borghi

ENOTECA 84

V. XX SETTEMBRE

V. MILANO

V. MENTANA

VIA PIAVE

LUIGI CADORNA

V. JACOPO REZIA

L'ANTICA TRATTORIA

V. MORAZZONE

VIA ITALIA

VIA LIBERA

MADE CLUB

VIA ACHILLE GRANDI

VIA LEONE LEONI

VIA FRANCESCO ANZANI

VIA PALESTRO

VIA MAGENTA

VIA VALLEGGIO

VIA REGINA TEODOLINDA

VIA MILANO

VIA DEI MILLE

VIA FRANCESCO CIGANO

VIA NAPOLEONA

VIA CARSO

CASTELLO BARADELLO

The inside of the Duomo gives visitors a peaceful break from the busy streets of Como

Como natives, Pliny the Elder and Pliny the Younger.

The interior's Latin cross floor plan is spacious and flooded with natural light. Inside, you'll find several Italian tapestries as well as a number of 16th-century paintings. There's really no excuse not to take a full loop around this overwhelmingly beautiful and extensive interior, from behind the pews to around each of the altars. Spend at least a full half hour here reading the English placards outlining various details of the church's history and importance.

BASILICA DI SANT'ABBONDIO

Via Regina Teodolinda, 35; 338/258-3328; www.diocesidicomo.it; 8am-4:30pm daily; free

The Basilica di Sant'Abbondio is yet another beautiful church found in Como. Originally built in the 5th century, the church has been reconstructed over time and now comprises two tall towers in the middle of the nave as well as a collection of choir windows. Inside, the four aisles and arches are both serene and welcoming. With most travelers sticking to the Duomo, this beloved church is often overlooked, despite its dominating stone facade near the center of Como. The interior of the narrow nave is lined with stone pillars. The tall windows streaming with natural light draw you to the long altar in the front, with its blue-painted ceiling serving as the main source of color.

PAOLO GIOVIO ARCHAEOLOGICAL MUSEUM (Museo Archeologico Giovio)

Piazza Medaglie D'Oro, 1; 031/252-550; www.visitcomo.eu; 10am-6pm Tues.-Sun.; €4

The Paolo Giovio Archaeological Museum in the beautiful Palazzo Giovio focuses on the history of the Como area up to the Middle Ages. The museum also includes sections for Egyptian, Greek, and Magna Grecia artifacts. Roam around the historic building to admire the green gardens, which date back to the Middle Ages, then take a look at the colorful frescoes on the main floor inside the building throughout the various ballrooms. For history buffs, this museum is a must-see. Entrance on the first Sunday of every month is free for everyone.

TEMPIO VOLTIANO

Viale Guglielmo Marconi, 1; 031/574-705; 10am-6pm Tues.-Sun.; €10

Science lovers can visit Tempio Voltiano, a museum dedicated to scientist and inventor Alessandro Volta, famous for inventing the electric battery. Volta was a Como native born in 1745, and he eventually retired in the city decades later in the 1800s. The building has a neoclassical style and was built in 1927 to commemorate the 100th anniversary of Volta's death. Inside you'll find several instruments, tools, and activities related to the creation of the battery. If you're looking for an educational way to spend a few hours in Como, this is your best bet. However, if your time is limited, skip it and stick to some of the bigger sights in the center of town.

Tempio Voltiano, dedicated to Alessandro Volta

PALAZZO TERRAGNI

Piazza del Popolo, 2; 031/304-466; www. comune.como.it

For an alternative experience, stop by the historically significant Palazzo Terragni, also known as the Casa del Fascio (Fascism House). Today the ordinary-looking building houses the headquarters and small museum of the financial police force, but you need to call ahead to arrange a time to see it. The structure was originally built in 1936, during Mussolini's regime, as the seat of the local branch of the National Fascist Party and was the site for large fascist gatherings and rallies. For those interested in the darker moments of Italy's history, stop by for an hour of so to learn more about fascism in the Lombardy region.

CASTELLO BARADELLO

Via Castel Baradello; 031/211-131; www. spinaverde.it/main; 2pm-6pm Sat. and Sun.; €4

Take a nature walk from Piazza San Rocco or Piazzale Camerlata in Como and follow the signs along the path to Castello Baradello, a 6th-century fort overlooking the city from a hilltop. The walk takes about an hour, with the first half relatively flat and the second half a steeper dirt-paved trail. From here, you can see unparalleled panoramas of the city, the lake, and the surrounding Alps. While many of the castle's walls no longer remain, the Romanesque square tower still stands tall at 19.5 meters (64 feet). (It was originally 28 meters tall, or nearly 92 feet.) While on top of the hill, head to the area of Sant'Eustachio, where you'll find a huge iron cross and views of the entire western branch of the lake. Come here as an alternative to the often busy Brunate Funicular if you want to skip the crowds for beautiful views from up high. Do note the limited opening hours, however.

TERME DI COMO ROMANA

Viale Lecco; 338/200-4670; 10am-2pm Tues. and Thurs., 10am-6pm Sat.; free

Explore the Terme di Como Romana, known in English as the Roman baths of Como. Primarily used in the 1st-3rd centuries, this thermal complex is situated between Viale Lecco and Via Dante. The baths were created by a donation of Pliny the Younger, a Como politician during the Roman Empire. They were covered for several centuries until the 1970s. Today, you can see the walls of eight different thermal rooms, but the true size of the original thermal complex is still to be determined. Visitors can see the baths up close using an elevated walkway for free certain days of the week. Slowly walk through each room, reading the placards that describe the purpose each bath served and enjoying the now-underground layout that was once a surface-level part of the Roman city.

BRUNATE FUNICULAR

Piazza Alcide De' Gasperi 4; 031/303-608; www.funicolarecomo.it; 6am-10:30pm daily; €5 one-way

Take a ride on the Como-Brunate funicular train to reach the charming hilltop village of Brunate, from which you can see a stellar aerial view of Lake Como. The Como funicular station is just a short 400-meter (437-yard) walk from the Como Nord train station. The funicular line runs 1,084 meters (3,556 feet) long, with the first 100 meters (328 feet) near the bottom of the hill going through a tunnel. Once at the station in Brunate, don't miss the **viewing gallery**, where you can see a panoramic view of the lake. Bring a bottle of wine to the top and make an

The funicular train from Como to the village of Brunate is one of the top activities in the city

afternoon out of it, as the views definitely merit carving time out of your schedule.

RECREATION

Como's waterfront is bustling with ferries and other boats jetting in and out, so water sports are generally reserved for the less-crowded areas of the shore. Likewise, other athletic outdoor experiences are found in the smaller villages dotting the lake. However, you'll find some of the more elegant and upscale recreation options in Como, including views of the lake by private plane as well as plenty of boat companies offering a variety of tours on the water.

FLIGHT TOURS
AeroClub Como
Viale Massenzio Masia, 44; 031/574-495; www.aeroclubcomo.com; starting at €90 per person

While most activities on Lake Como are water-based, you can also fly directly above the lake and villages to combine adventure with scenic views of the lake. AeroClub Como, which is one of the oldest seaplane clubs of its kind in the world, offers lessons for both beginners and experts as well as private and group tours of the lake by air. To book a lesson or tour in advance use the contacts on the club's website.

BOAT TOURS
Como Classic Boats
Pickup at Villa D'Este (Via Regina, 40); 392/258-1535; www.comoclassicboats.com; 9am-8pm daily; €60-400

As with most waterfront towns and villages, you can find several motorboat companies offering private and group tours in Como. Como Classic Boats is one of the best companies for a quality private tour of Lake Como.

Their tours range from two-hour tours of the major villas, to Hollywood-themed tours of Villa Balbianello, to six-hour tours including champagne, lunch at a local restaurant, and stops at various villas along the lake. Choose among any of the four boats, which hold from 2-6 passengers. Book a tour in advance using the contact form on the website, or by emailing info@comoclassicboats.com

ARTS AND ENTERTAINMENT
THEATER
Teatro Sociale
Via Vincenzo Bellini, 3; 031/270-170; www.teatrosocialecomo.it; €10-40

For theater lovers, Como's Teatro

The Teatro Sociale in Como hosts a variety of classical music concerts, ballets, plays, musicals, and more

Sociale, built on the site of an old medieval castle, frequently stages operas, modern and classical dance performances, symphonies, musicals, and more. Just a stone's throw away from the Como Nord train station. The theater is easily accessible and tickets can generally be purchased online in advance at www.teatrosocialcomo.com. There are also a handful of free events hosted here throughout the year; a full schedule as well as the opening times for the box office is available on the theater's website.

SHOPPING

The city of Como boasts the most robust and diverse shopping experience on Lake Como. The historic city center is home to several popular chains (Zara, H&M, United Colors of Benetton, etc.) as well as a collection of local shops and specialty boutiques. One can easily pass an entire day shopping in the city.

SILK GOODS
A Picci

Via Vittorio Emanuele II, 54; 031/261-369; http://apicci.it; 9am-7:30pm daily

If you want to purchase some world-famous Como silk, head to A Picci on Via Vittorio Emanuele II, one of the most well-known and historic Como silk shops in the region. The store turns 100 years old in 2019, and locals will tell you that it's one of the only stores left in the city that still sells exclusively Como-made silk. The shop is well organized, grouping items such as square scarves and ties not by type but by price category, making it easier for customers to shop according to their budgets.

SPECIALTY FOOD AND DRINK
Mercato Coperto

Via Sirtori Giuseppe, 1; https://digilander. libero.it/felice/Mercato.htm; 8am-7pm Tues., Thurs.-Sat.

For a shopping experience unique to Como, explore the covered food and produce market, Mercato Coperto, on Via Sirtori Giuseppe. While the building doesn't look like much on the outside, upon entering, you'll be greeted by stalls brimming with local fruits and vegetables (don't miss the porcini mushrooms), refrigerators stocked with Italian cheeses and cold cuts, and dozens upon dozens of flower bouquets picked from local gardens.

Enoteca da Gigi

Via Bernardino Luini, 48; 031/263-186; www. enotecagigi.com; 11am-8pm Mon., 9am-8pm Tues.-Sat.

If you're looking for a more refined gourmet shopping experience, Enoteca da Gigi on Via Bernardino Luini is your place. Open since 1930, the wine bar sells more than 700 labels from all over the world, with the largest selection obviously from Italy. The staff is very knowledgeable about their products, so if you don't have a specific label in mind, tell them your preferences and let them find the best selection for you. Along with wine, you can find Italian olive oils, vinegars, cheeses, and more available for purchase. They also ship several of their products, including wine, internationally upon request.

FOOD

The city of Como provides the largest and most diverse selection of dining options on the lake. You'll find a bar or restaurant on nearly every corner, ranging from Italian fine dining to sushi to hole-in-the-wall wine bars.

ITALIAN AND PIZZA
Bar delle Terme

Lungo Lario Trieste, 14; 031/329-111; www.albergoterminus.it; 12pm-1:45pm, 7pm-9:45pm daily; €20-40

Dining at the Bar delle Terme is an intimate experience, with only 20 seats available inside the restaurant and a handful of tables on the hotel's terrace. The decorated walls and candle lighting make it feel cozy while remaining elegant and tasteful. The menu isn't huge, with a few traditional Italian options for each course as well as a selection of salads. Large windows provide a beautiful view of the lake while dining. Reservations are strongly recommended in the evenings, but you should be able to find a table without trouble during lunch hours.

✪ Osteria L'Angolo del Silenzio

Viale Lecco, 25; 031/337-2157; www. osterialangolodelsilenzio-como.com; 12pm-3pm, 7pm-12am Thurs.-Tues.; €20-40

Serving classic Italian plates from nearly every region of the country, Osteria L'Angolo del Silenzio is known as one of the tried-and-true restaurants of Como by both locals and returning travelers. You'll find everything from homemade pasta to traditional Milanese veal cutlet to fresh lake fish, all without breaking the bank for a good bite. Reservations are recommended for dinner during high season. Due to the late hours, this is also an easy choice for those wanting to dine a little later for a quieter atmosphere.

L'Antica Trattoria

Via Luigi Cadorna, 26; 031/242-777; www. lanticatrattoria.co.it; 12:15pm-2:30pm, 7:30pm-10:30pm Tues.-Sun.; €20-40

As one of the official Michelin Guide's restaurants to watch, the food here is plated so beautifully that you almost feel guilty eating it. Ingredients are selected with the utmost attention and dishes prepared with great effort and care, so you'll be hard pressed to find anything negative about the dining experience here. The second courses are huge, with meats taking up your entire plate and cooked exactly as you request. Recently, the restaurant also adopted a gluten-free specialty menu, available on request. Reservations are

strongly recommended here during high season.

WINE BAR
Enoteca 84

Via Milano, 84; 333/427-6812; www. enoteca84.com; 9am-7:30pm Mon.-Wed., 9am-9:30pm Thurs.-Sat.; €8-20

This little wine bar is low key, with everything from the food to its authentic atmosphere. All dishes are homemade with hand-selected ingredients. Try the proscuitto and lard with pickled vegetables as a starter before moving to a first or second course. Alternatively, select from one of the 130 or so wine options that you can order by the glass or bottle and pair it with a cheese plate or housemade dessert. They also offer a selection of craft beer and high-quality spirits for those that stay away from wine. This place is quite small and fills up fast, so book a table in advance or stop by for a mid-afternoon treat.

Enoteca 84 has one of the widest and best wine selections in the city of Como

GELATO
Garden Bar Ceccato (Gelateria Ceccato)

Lungo Lario Trieste, 16; 031/23-391; www. palacehotel.it; 2pm-10pm Sun., 2pm-11pm Thurs. and Fri., 2pm-12am Sat.; €3-15

Gelateria Ceccato, located in front of the Palace Hotel, has been around since the early 20th century. Come here to enjoy a sweet treat amongst charming green gardens near the waterfront. Order a cocktail with finger food or one of the several flavors of gelato, and relax on the terrace or at one of the inviting patio tables. If you're looking for something a little more than a drink and quick bite, consider one of the full-dish options of vegetables, salads, or pizzas.

BARS AND NIGHTLIFE

As Lake Como's largest city, the entertainment and nightlife scene in Como is more robust than that of the other villages scattered around the lake.

BARS
FRESCO COCKTAIL SHOP

Viale Lecco, 23; 393/731-5649; www. frescococktailshop.it; 6pm-1am daily, until 3am Fri. and Sat.; drinks and small bites €5-15

The Fresco Cocktail Shop is one of Lake Como's most renowned bars. Hit this place right as it opens to snag a table during happy hour or stop by for a late-night drink after dinner. The cocktail recipes are original, so prepare to see traditional Italian cocktails such as the Aperol Spritz with some twists. Each drink on the extensive menu is described in paragraph-long detail, and the small bites that pair with each drink are just as high quality in terms of taste and presentation.

DANCE CLUBS
Made Club

Via Sant'Abbondio, 7; 031/268-356; www. madeclubcomo.com; 9:30pm-4am Tues., Fri., and Sat.; €10-18

For a night of dancing and drinks, hit Made Club or K-Klass, described next. Made Club is one of the better-known dance clubs of the city. Those that

arrive early can enjoy a buffet of finger foods, included in the entrance price, accompanying a full bar. Nights here are full of live music and local DJ rotations. The club also offers a catered dinner from a local restaurant starting at 10pm for €35 a person. Tables at the club can also be reserved for entire evenings for €120, with the price including entrance for five guests as well as one bottle of spirits, two bottles of sparkling Italian wine, and a selection of fruit.

K-Klass

Via Provinciale, 73, Tavernerio; 338/239-4816; 11pm-4am Tues., Fri., and Sat; €10-18

K-Klass is another hot option for both locals and visitors wanting a night of dancing and cocktails on Friday and Saturday nights. The low lighting and house music draw in plenty of guests, mostly the 20-35 set. The atmosphere is luxurious, but friendly and comfortable for everyone. You can book tables of five for an entire evening for €130 on Fridays and €160 on Saturdays, with prices including a bottle of spirits and a bottle of champagne along with a selection of fruit.

ACCOMMODATIONS
UNDER €80
Ostello Bello Lake Como

Viale Fratelli Rosselli, 9; 031/570-889; www. ostellobello.com; €45-50 bed, €165 double with private bath

Ostello Bello on Lake Como, opened in 2011, has it all: mixed or gender-specific dorms, private rooms for 2-4 people with private bathrooms, a bar, barbeque facilities, a playground for children, a garden with patio seating and a hammock, luggage storage, and more. Each guest room comes with a private bathroom as well as air conditioning and WiFi. Some rooms also come with a balcony or a garden view. Breakfast and *aperitivo* as well as a free welcome drink each night are included in the price of the room.

B&B Hotel Como

Via Pasquale Paoli, 21; 031/339-0034; www. hotel-bb.com/it/hotel/como; €75

This American-style hotel, located just a short walk away from the Como Nord train station, is modern, quiet, and reasonably priced. Guest rooms are simply decorated, clean, and bright. Each room comes with air conditioning, WiFi, and a private bathroom. A continental breakfast can be added for €7.20 for each double room per night. You can also book rooms with access for travelers with motor disabilities.

€80-150

Hotel Continental

Via Innocenzo XI, 15; 031/260-485; http:// newopeningsbyhotelbb.com; €90

Yet another option by the B&B Hotels chain, Hotel Continental is a convenient option for those wanting to stay near a train station, with the Como San Giovanni station just a few minutes away by foot. The hotel has a classic interior, with simple furniture and carpeted floors. Each guest room includes air conditioning, WiFi, and private bathroom. Breakfast can be added for €7 per room. Covered parking for guests and airport shuttle service are also available upon request for an additional fee.

Borgo Antico

Via Borgo Vico, 47; 031/338-0150; www. borgoanticohotelcomo.it; €124

The classic style, exposed stone walls, and wood-beamed ceilings of Borgo Antico make you feel comfortable from the minute you walk through the door. Despite being a hotel with 24 rooms, the coziness and large continental breakfast make it seem as if you're staying at a family-run bed and breakfast. Each room includes air conditioning, WiFi, and private bathroom. Reception is 24 hours a day, and parking is free for guests.

€150-€250

✪ Avenue

Piazzolo Giuseppe Terragni, 6; 031/272-186; www.avenuehotel.it; €180

Located in an old city building, the completely modern Avenue hotel is known for its creative and colorful interior. Each room features a unique color palette, upon which the rest of the interior is designed. All rooms are bright and welcoming, and guests will feel right at home. The hotel is about a five-minute walk from the waterfront, right in the midst of plenty of designer shops and local restaurants. Each room includes air conditioning, WiFi, and private bathroom. A hearty breakfast can be added for €12 per every two people. The hotel also offers shuttle services between the property and each regional airport upon request.

✪ Terminus

Lungo Lario Trieste, 14; 031/329-111; www. albergoterminus.it; €210

This 19th-century hotel, which was renovated about a decade ago, is situated near the Como Nord train station right along the lake. Guest rooms have classic, elegant decor set against a bright, neutral color scheme, and include air conditioning, WiFi, and private bathroom. Some rooms also offer a lake view. Breakfast is included. The hotel also features a bar and restaurant with terrace seating, sauna, gym, and private parking for guests.

OVER €250
Hilton Lake Como

Via Borgo Vico, 241; 031/338-2611; www. hilton.com; €380

The Hilton Lake Como hotel offers an all-inclusive luxurious and relaxing experience for those wanting to make the most of a lake holiday. The most popular feature is the rooftop infinity pool overlooking the lake, accompanied by the Terrazza 241 restaurant and bar. Each guest room is sleek and simple, with a neutral, calming color palette. The wellness center also includes an indoor pool, a Finnish sauna, and a Turkish bath. Each room includes air conditioning, WiFi, and private bathroom. Continental breakfast is included.

INFORMATION AND SERVICES

For any tourism information you may need or desire during your time in Como, head to the Tourist Information Office - IAT Como (Via Giocondo Albertolli, 7; 031/449-3068; www.provincia.como.it; 9am-6pm daily) in the middle of town. The English-speaking staff can offer plenty of advice on how to spend your time in the area, as well as maps and other useful material.

You'll find a handful of police stations around Como, with the most convenient and easiest to remember being directly next to the Como San Giovanni train station at Piazzale S. Gottardo, 7. You can contact them at 031/541-263 during all hours of the day, but call 112 in case of emergencies. They usually have an English-speaking policeman on duty.

If you seek medical assistance, you can head to the Ospedale Generale Di Zona Valduce (031/324-111) on Via Alighieri Dante 11. They almost always have an English-speaking member of staff around, and are open for emergencies 24 hours a day. Call 112 if you need emergency medical help.

GETTING THERE AND AROUND

The city of Como is the lake's main transportation hub, so you'll find more transportation options to and from Como than in any other spot on the lake. Of course, as with all villages and towns on Lake Como, the best way to explore the city is by foot.

BY TRAIN

The city of Como is the largest stop for trains on the western side of the lake. You will find several trains running between Como San Giovanni and Como Nord stations from Milan's Central Station. Train tickets can be purchased directly at either train station in Como or in Milan, or online at trenitalia.com. Trains run about once each hour 6am-9:10pm daily for a price of €4.80 each way.

BY BOAT

You can take slow boats (*battello*), the rapid-service boats (*aliscafo*), or the car ferry (*traghetto*) run by Navigazione Lago di Como (www. navigazionelaghi.it/lago-como) from most other villages along the lake to Como. The ferry line from Colico to Como stops in Tremezzo (45min), Menaggio (55min), Bellagio (1h 25min), and Varenna (1h 10min), and stops at Como's ferry station, which is located in Piazza Cavour along the Lungo Lario Trento. Ferries run 7:30am-8pm or so and tickets can be purchased directly at each village's ferry station or online. Timetables are posted at the station or online at www.navigazionelaghi.it.

BY BUS

Run by **ASF Lines** (www.asfautolinee.it), Como's public bus system has both urban and extra-urban lines and bus stops at all major piazzas and train stations. To get from Bellagio to Como, take **Bus C30** (once an hour, 6am-8:20pm daily; €2.75 one-way; 1 hour), which stops at the Como San Giovanni train station. Along the western shore of the lake, you can take **Bus C10,** running from Colico to Como and passing through Cadenabbia (45min Como), Tremezzo (50min) and Menaggio (1hr). These extra-urban tickets generally cost around €3.60 per person and per journey.

Within the city of Como, tickets start at €1.30, and timetables and routes can be found on the ASF Lines website, although Como is best explored on foot.

Although Como is not a large town, it is the biggest city on Lake Como and serves as the lake's transportation hub

BY CAR

From Milan, head out of the city on the A8, following signs toward Malpensa airport and the autostrada. Drive roughly 10 kilometers (or roughly 6 miles) before merging onto A9/E35. Drive about 22 kilometers (14 miles) on this highway until you see signs to exit for Como Centro. From there, follow the signs to Como Centro (Como city center). The trip will take about an hour, depending on traffic.

From Lecco, take the SS36 west until it turns into SP342, which takes you directly to the center of Como. From Lecco, the journey is about 35 minutes over 31 kilometers (19 miles). From Bellagio, it's about a 50-minute drive over 31 kilometers (19 miles) straight southwest on SP583.

If you're on the western shore of the lake, follow the SS340 down to Como from Menaggio for 35.5 kilometers (22 miles), roughly one hour; from Cadenabbia for 32 kilometers (20 miles), roughly 50 minutes; or from Tremezzo for 31 kilometers (19 miles), 45 minutes.

Due to its size, Como is the easiest area of the lake to drive around, with street parking and a handful of parking garages in the center of town. Most hotels also offer free parking for guests. Note that during high season, locals are also rushing to the lake on the weekends, so be prepared to encounter congested roads in the Como area as well as on the shoreline roads.

BY TAXI

You'll find a handful reliable, official taxi services near the train station as well as near the lake's shoreline. Services such as Radio Taxi Como (www.radiotaxicomo.com, 031/261-515) have been operating in the city for several years. You can book a taxi at any time, but note that you should book them at least 10 minutes in advance, as you won't always find a taxi waiting for passengers in certain areas of the city.

Lecco

Sitting opposite of Como at the bottom of Lake Como's eastern branch is the petite city of Lecco, where you'll still find that classic Lake Como charm without as many summer tourists. The city is situated at the foot of the Bergamo Alps, where the mountains meet the most southeastern part of the lake. Due to its strategic location, Lecco serves as a great starting point for several biking and walking paths leading to other towns either on the lake or throughout the mountains.

While the shoreline is flat, the town grows more hilly the farther away you head from the waters. If you want to spend a day in a less crowded but still large lake town, Lecco is your place.

ORIENTATION

Lecco is rather compact, with the majority of bars, restaurants, shops, and sights concentrated within just a few blocks on a few main roads. The train station sits on the eastern side of the center of town, so stick between the train station and the lake's shore (which is about a seven-minute walk between the two) to get a good taste of Lecco. To walk along the shore, follow the Lungolario Isonzo road, which hugs the waterfront. If you grow weary, you can rest on one of the several benches that dot the road. Consider Via Parini as the northern border of the center of town, and Via Constituzione as the southern border. Via Roma, which runs north to

south parallel of Lungolario Isonzo, is the main shopping road in town, and intersects with most of the major piazzas, restaurants, and other roads in the city center. The Adda River flows south of the southwestern part of the town, with the village of Malgrate sitting just opposite of Lecco on the other side of the river, also on the southern shore of the Lecco branch of Lake Como.

SIGHTS

For those familiar with the 1827 novel *The Betrothed* by Italian author Alessandro Manzoni, you'll recognize that Lecco is the town in which the story takes place. Thus, many of Lecco's main sights connect to this piece of literature, including the Manzoni Art Museum. You'll also find plenty of historic churches as well as a neo-medieval palace.

BASILICA OF SAN NICOLÒ

Via S. Nicolò, 1; 034/128-2403; 9am-12pm, 2:30-6:30pm Mon.-Fri., 9am-12pm Sat.; free
With original construction dating back to the 11th century, this minor Roman Catholic basilica is the most prominent church in Lecco, named after the city's patron saint St. Nicholas (the patron saint of sailors and boatmen). Today's current structure was built on the site of ancient 13th-century city walls, although even this structure has undergone subsequent renovations up to this day. The

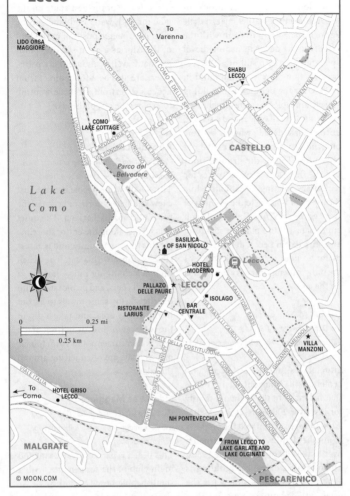

Lecco

Lake
Como

To
Varenna

SHABU
LECCO

LIDO ORSA
MAGGIORE

COMO
LAKE COTTAGE

CASTELLO

Parco del
Belvedere

BASILICA
OF SAN NICOLO

HOTEL
MODERNO

Lecco

PALLAZO
DELLE PAURE

LECCO

ISOLAGO

RISTORANTE
LARIUS

BAR
CENTRALE

0   0.25 mi

0   0.25 km

VILLA
MANZONI

To
Como

HOTEL GRISO
LECCO

NH PONTEVECCHIA

MALGRATE

FROM LECCO TO
LAKE GARLATE AND
LAKE OLGINATE

© MOON.COM

PESCARENICO

interior reveals Baroque elements and a number of beautiful frescos. At the entrance you'll find a double staircase and a 96-meter (315-foot) bell tower that looms over the rest of the city. Although located in the town center, it sits tucked away in a corner and manages to stay peaceful and quiet, despite its size and frequent visits by locals. The high ceilings and golden hues illuminating the interior enchant and entice you into staying a little longer in this refuge from the busy streets of town.

PALLAZO DELLE PAURE

Piazza XX Settembre, 22; 034/128-6729; 9:30am-6:00pm Tues.-Fri., 9:30am-6pm, 9pm-11pm Thurs., 10am-6pm Sat. and Sun.; €6

This palace, overlooking the waterfront, dominates Lecco's historic center. Architecturally, the Palazzo delle Paure doesn't seem to fit in with the rest of the city due to its neo-medieval appearance—the result of a 1916 reconstruction after its initial build in 1905. Over the decades, the building served multiple purposes, including as the site of civil offices and a school, until the last decade when it became one the city's more impressive art museums. Today, the ground floor and the first floor serve as spaces for temporary, rotating art exhibits, while the top floor is home to the Municipal Contemporary Art Gallery. If you appreciate art and plan on spending an entire day in Lecco, definitely stop by for an hour or two to view one of the only contemporary art collections on the lake.

VILLA MANZONI

Via Don Guanella, 1; 034/148-1247; 9:30am-6pm Tues.-Fri., 10am-6pm Sat. and Sun.; €6

Situated just outside of Lecco's city center is Villa Manzoni, a large house that belonged to the Manzoni family for just over 200 years. Italian writer Alessandro Manzoni sold the property to another family, who then turned it over to the city of Lecco in the 1960s. Today, this neoclassical building is a home-turned-museum, with the ground floor serving to memorialize Alessandro Manzoni's life and work and the floor above it serving as a civic art museum. Writers from every corner of the world can tour the home to get a better understanding of Italian literature and the importance of this famous Italian author, including his influence in the region.

RECREATION

Lecco is one of the best spots on the lake for both water and land sports, with its strategic position at the foot of the Alps as a main starting point for many cycling and trekking paths. There are also boat tours direct from Lecco's waterfront for those wanting to explore the rest of the lake.

BEACHES

Abbadia Lariana

Via Lungolago, 23A, Abbadia Lariana; www. lakecomo.is/free-beaches-lecco; free

This small, white pebble beach is just a few kilometers north of Lecco in the town of Abbadia Lariana. The quiet beach runs along the entire shoreline for this tiny community, and is accessible by those with a car. The beach includes changing huts, showers, a volleyball court, and picnic tables with benches. Bring some towels to lay out in the grassy area, and take a dip in the cool waters directly in front of the beach. Remember not to swim too far out, as boats are often jetting around the lake.

Lido Orsa Maggiore

Via Lungo Lario Piave, 5; 034/136-3405; www.orsamaggiorediscoclub.it; 10am-7pm daily Apr.-Sept.; free

This beach is part of a restaurant and night club of the same name, with a small pebble beach including deckchairs, sun beds, and umbrellas. Paddleboards and canoes are also available for rent for around €5 per hour. This place gets quite busy in July and August, so arrive when it first opens to snag a spot. You can rent a sun bed with an umbrella and shower service for €6 per person on week days, €10 per person on Saturdays and Sundays.

CYCLING

Lecco to Cassana d'Adda along the Adda River

Start from any point along the Adda river heading out of Lecco; free

The cycling route starting from the Adda River in Lecco takes you to Cassana d'Adda, a small, charming village just over 49 kilometers (30.4 miles) southeast of Lecco. This cycle route along the dirt and asphalt path is fairly easy, and the path is open to pedestrians as well, so take care to share the path as you cycle. You can find the trail by heading to the Adda River on the southwestern side of the city, then following the pedestrian trail along the river. While it starts hilly, the path flattens out more as you head farther south. Mixed in with a few industrial and hydro plants, there are also views of mountains and small, residential villages, giving you a true look at daily life in this area. Stop by the river for a rest once you reach the charming village of Cassana d'Adda, or grab a drink from a local bar before cycling your way back to Lecco. The round-trip takes about 5-6 hours, so block out an entire afternoon for this adventure.

Lecco to Lake Garlate and Lake Olginate

Azzone Visconti Bridge; free

Starting from the Azzone Visconti Bridge that crosses over the Adda River on the southwestern part of Lecco, this path is a loop around the Lecco area along Lakes Garlate and Olginate, two very small local lakes in Lecco just south of the much larger Lake Como. The path is primarily asphalt with some dirt areas and is 20 kilometers (12.4 miles). Cycling experts have designated the difficulty level of this path as easy, generally taking around three hours to complete the entire loop. Enjoy views of the mountains in the distance, while getting close-up views of the waters of these smaller lakes.

Rush Riders

Via Alessandro Volta, 32, Malgrate; 0341/184-0274; www.rushriders.cc; 9:30am-7:30pm Mon., Tues., Thurs.-Sat., 2:30pm-7:30pm Wed.; €35-50 daily

If you're wanting to rent a bike to hit the trails in the Lecco area, head to Malgrate, where you can stop by this cozy yet extremely professional bike shop to rent mountain bikes, road bikes, and electric bikes on a daily basis. The staff is incredibly friendly and knowledgeable about trails in the area, so soak in as much info as you can from them. They are also really proud of their bike collection, so they'll fit you for the perfect bike during your time on the lake. All rentals include pedals and helmets. Bikes can be rented via email through the website, or via walk-in; however, advance reservations are recommended.

BOAT TOUR

MANZONIAN BOAT TOUR BY TAXI BOAT LECCO

Via delle Foibe, 23900; 349/229-0952; www.taxiboatlecco.com; 8:30am-1pm and 2pm-5:30pm Mon.-Fri.; €10

Taxi Boat Lecco offers quick, 45-minute boat tours around the shores of Lecco and the surrounding area, up to the top of the Lecco branch near Bellagio. The tour focuses on the history and culture of Lecco, and the local guides take pride in showing you the beauty and uniqueness of their town. Tour guides discuss the significance of Lecco's patron saint and native author Alessandro Manzoni. Tours should be booked online in advance, but you can stop by the contact point in Lecco to

Local water taxi boats offer quick, private boat tours related to Lecco's history and culture

request a tour as well. While the contact point for the company is the address listed here, you will often find a stand on the shore in the middle of town near the local boat dock from which the boats depart. Group tours can include up to 10 people, but the company has boats that accommodate up to 40 people if you make arrangements in advance.

SHOPPING
Via Roma
From Piazza Manzoni and up Via Roma to the intersection of Via Conte di Cavour

Via Roma is home to some of the best chain stores on Lake Como. Start from the green square in Piazza Manzoni and head north on Via Roma until you reach Via Conte di Cavour. Along the way, you'll find shops such as O bag, Intimissimi, H&M, Kiko, and more. Most shops are open 7:30am-8:30pm daily.

Isolago
Via Cavour; www.isolago.it; 9am-7:30pm daily

For a mini American-style shopping mall experience with local cafés, bars, restaurants, and plenty of fashion and shoe shopping, head to Isolago on Via Cavour. The mall features international stores such as Flying Tiger as well as local fashion boutiques selling Italian leather purses and more. The mall is open every day.

FOOD

Lecco offers plenty of restaurants, bars, and cafés. You'll find just as many diverse options here as in any other small European city, from local cuisine to Japanese fusion. Dinner reservations are recommended but not required for most places; lunch reservations are generally not necessary.

ITALIAN AND PIZZA
Antica Osteria Casa di Lucia
Via Lucia, 27; 034/149-4594; www. osteriacasadilucia.com; €15-25

Tucked into a quiet corner of Lecco is this traditional Italian restaurant with a one-page menu, serving only a few options for each course. The dining room is warm and inviting, with old glass bottles perched on top of a piano, but the real treat is eating in the local garden full of draping flowers, greenery, and stringed lights. For a taste of local cuisine, try one of the full fish plates. Book in advance during high season if you want to dine here in the evenings.

Ristorante Larius
Via Nazario Sauro, 2; 034/136-3558; www.ristorantelarius.it; 12pm-2:30pm, 7:30pm-10:30pm Wed.-Mon.; €20-40 average

Ristorante Larius in the center of Lecco is dressed to impress, with the elegant dining room featuring high, decorated ceilings, polished glass, green plants, and plenty of space. The desserts of the day are on display upon walking in, enticing you to make it through your meal and to order one at the end. Here, you'll find plenty of traditional Italian courses, including meat and cheese boards, fish, wood-oven pizzas, and more. Reservations are recommended here, and outdoor seating is available during warmer months.

INTERNATIONAL
Shabu Lecco
Via Gorizia, 5; 0341/081-031; http://shabulecco.com; 12pm-2:30pm, 6pm-12am daily; €20-26

As one of the most popular Japanese fusion restaurants in the area, Shabu stays pretty busy. The menu is all-you-can-eat, where you pay a fixed price (not including drinks or cover charges) and order as much as you want as long as you finish most of each plate. The menu includes handmade dumplings, noodles, rices, meat and vegetable dishes, soups, and a variety of fusion sushi rolls. While you won't need reservations for lunch, it's better to book a table for dinner, especially on the weekends, as this is a hot spot for locals.

BAR AND CAFÉ
Bar Centrale
Via Roma, 43; 0341/283-330; 7am-8pm Tues.-Sun.; €2-10

Located on one of the main shopping roads in Lecco is Bar Centrale, a pastry shop and classic bar with a full range of Italian coffees and options for the *aperitivo* hour. Stop by for a croissant, hot chocolate, espresso, or glass of wine at any hour of the day. The real treats, however, are the traditional bite-size cream-, fruit-, and chocolate-filled pastries for about €1 each.

ACCOMMODATIONS

Accommodations in Lecco range from modest and affordable to classic Lake Como luxury, with plenty of options in each category. Make sure to book as far in advance as possible if you're coming in high season. Due to the accessibility of the town, hotels here often fill up quickly in the spring and summer.

€80-150
Hotel Moderno
Piazza Armando Diaz, 5; 034/128-6519; www.leccohotelmoderno.com; €80

This affordable and modern hotel is located close to the shore of Lecco, and just a quick walk away from the train station. Guest rooms are simply yet fully furnished with modern, neutral-colored furniture. Each room includes a view of the mountains, air conditioning, WiFi, and private bathroom. A full continental breakfast, available each morning, is included.

Lecco's Hotel Moderno is just a minute walk downhill from the train station

Como Lake Cottage
Via Grado, 6; 034/136-0957 http://bbcomolakecottage.com; €90

This little lake cottage is simple and comfortable, with a garden view in each guest room and daily homemade breakfast included. WiFi is available throughout the small property; private parking and airport shuttle service are available upon request for an additional fee. Each room includes air conditioning, WiFi, private bathroom, and cooling fan.

✪ NH Pontevecchia

Via Visconti Azzone, 84; 034/123-8000; www.nh-hotels.com/hotel/nh-lecco-pontevecchio; €120

The modern and spacious NH Pontevecchia is one of the best accommodation options in Lecco, with each guest room giving you a view of the Adda River or the lake. The shore is just a short 100 meters (109 yards) away from the property, with the city center just five minutes away by foot, and the train station a 10-minute walk away. There are family rooms as well as standard and superior double rooms available, with each room including air conditioning, WiFi, and private bathroom. The hotel also includes gym access and free parking for guests. A full breakfast is included.

€150-250
Hotel Griso Lecco

Via Provinciale, 51, Malgrate; 034/123-9811; www.griso.info; €160

Located in Malgrate just outside of Lecco is this luxury hotel, offering a peaceful place to get away from the throngs of visitors along the lake. The hotel is a 15-minute walk away from Lecco's city center and the shoreline, and includes a panoramic lounge, a rooftop hot tub, and terrace, and an Italian restaurant serving breakfast, lunch, and dinner on the property. Each room includes either a mountain or lake view as well as air conditioning, WiFi, and private bathroom. Breakfast and guest parking are included.

INFORMATION AND SERVICES

For information about Lecco and its offerings, head to the Infopoint Lecco (Piazza XX Settembre, 23; 0341/295-720; www.provincia.lecco.it/turismo; 9am-6pm daily). The English-speaking staff is very friendly and helpful, and there is a plethora of maps and reading material available to help you figure out how to spend your time in the area.

While there are a handful of police stations on Lecco, one of the most prominent ones is next to the train station in the town center (Via Salvatore Sassi, 18; 0341/481-343). The station is open 24 hours a day, and there is usually someone that speaks English available.

For medical help, head to the Ospedale di Lecco (Via Dell'Eremo 9; 0341/489-111), which offers emergency medical services 24 hours a day. Remember that if you need emergency assistance, you should call 112.

GETTING THERE AND AROUND

After Como, Lecco is the second most popular transportation hub on Lake Como. Lecco is served by train from Milan, Switzerland, and the city of Como. It's also easy to reach by car using the Italian highway system, and there are a handful of boat companies offering journeys to and from Lecco. Keep in mind that most of the center is a pedestrian-only zone, so you will need to explore the town on foot.

BY TRAIN

Trains to Lecco can be taken from both Milan's Central Station and Porta Garibaldi station approximately every hour from around 6am-9pm daily. Tickets are €4.80 per passenger each way and the trip takes around an hour. You can also take a direct train from Varenna to to Lecco, which runs from 6:20am-10:20pm daily, departing every half hour to an hour. The train ride lasts between 20-40 minutes and cost €2.90 each way. All tickets can be purchased online in advance at www. trenitalia.com.

BY CAR

From Milan, take the SS36 northeast out of the city toward Sesto San Giovanni, all the while following the signs to Lecco. You'll continue on the SS36 straight to Lecco for 55 kilometers (34 miles); the trip takes about an hour, depending on traffic.

From Como, take the SS342 about 35 minutes over 31 kilometers (19 miles) east, following the signs pointing to Lecco along the way. If you're coming from Varenna, you need to follow the SS36 south straight to Lecco, which is about a 25-minute drive spanning 21 kilometers (13 miles).

The center of Lecco has banned motor vehicles, so you cannot park in the center of town. If you're staying in Lecco, check to see if your accommodation offers free parking and if you need a special pass to drive your car on certain streets before arrival.

BY BOAT

You can take the official public boat service run by Navigazione Lago di Como (www.navigazionelaghi.it/lago-como), with Lecco's ferry station located in the middle town. You can arrive at the ferry station in Lecco from most other villages, including Bellagio (1h 30min) and Varenna (1h 10min). Ferries generally run from 7:30am-8pm or so. Tickets can be purchased directly at the ferry station or online; timetables are posted at the stations or online as well at www.navigazionelaghi.it.

BY BUS

Linee Lecco (www.lineelecco.it) runs a bus between Bellagio to Lecco a few times each day 7:30am-7:15pm. You can grab the bus from the center of Bellagio, with one-way tickets running at €2.80.

BY TAXI

Taxis in Lecco are available from many car hire operations, including Radio Taxi Lecco (www.taxilecco.net, 034/11-916). Taxis can be booked by phone or text message at least 5 minutes in advance. Note that while you may find taxis waiting for passengers near Lecco's train station, it isn't guaranteed, so booking is your best option.

LAKE MAGGIORE

Italy's second largest lake, span-
ning 212 square kilometers (82 square miles), is
one of the best kept secrets around Milan and a
favorite destination among international visitors.
Although not as large and prominent as Lake
Garda, nor as frequented by celebrities as Lake
Como, Lake Maggiore sits quietly and beautifully
an hour northwest of Milan. The mountainous
region seems to push the shoreline towns directly
into the deep, dark blue waters of the lake.

The towns and mountain villages encompassing the lake offer plenty of history, culture, and

HIGHLIGHTS

✪ **MOTTARONE CABLE CAR:** For aerial views of Lake Maggiore and the town of Stresa, take a ride in the cable car to the summit of the Mottarone mountain, where you'll find a unique botanical garden and the thrilling Alpyland Alpine Coaster (page 185).

✪ **PALAZZA BORROMEO AND GARDENS OF ISOLA BELLA:** Known for its lavish gardens and a grand baroque palace, the lush, symmetrical gardens of Palazza Borromeo on Isola Bella were influenced by Italian renaissance gardens, which in turn influenced much of the French and English gardening styles (page 193).

✪ **PALAZZO BORROMEO AND GARDENS OF ISOLA MADRE:** The 18th-century English-style gardens on Isola Madre highlight the beautiful wisteria outside the Palazzo Borromeo, offering a perfect visual balance against this 16th-century palace built on the ruins of an old island church (page 194).

✪ **ISOLA DEI PESCATORI:** This tiny island, so different in vibe from the other Borromean islands, steals the hearts of visitors with its quaint colorful buildings stacked next to one another (page 195).

✪ **VILLA TARANTO:** The 19th-century Villa Taranto, surrounded by botanical gardens, sits just near the waters of Lake Maggiore in Verbania. Known as one of the most relaxing, beautiful gardens in Italy, the 16 hectares (2.5 acres) boast more than 20,000 different plant types on the property, mostly from semi-tropical climates (page 198).

opportunities to enjoy the outdoors. However, Lake Maggiore's real draw are the Borromean Islands. These three islands dotting the lake's surface, with their lush gardens, extravagant villas, and slow island time transport you to another period and place.

For something completely different than an Italian city experience, visit Lake Maggiore for its natural beauty, timelessness, and truly unparalleled Alpine experience. The higher in altitude you go, the more the shoreline towns will evoke that classic Alpine feel. On the lake itself, however, especially on the Borromean Islands, you'll enjoy a more Mediterranean feel. To make the most of a trip here, visit in the spring when the gardens are freshly bloomed and the summer crowds have yet to arrive.

ORIENTATION

Lake Maggiore sits in the northern part of Italy, with the southern three-quarters of the lake falling in Italy, and the northern quarter falling in Switzerland. In Italy, the lake is almost evenly divided between the regions of Lombardy to the east and Piedmont to the west. In total, the lake spans 64.37 kilometers (40 miles) in length and 10 kilometers (6.2 miles) in width, so it is much longer than it is wide.

The lake's two main towns, **Stresa** and **Verbania,** sit in the center of the western shore. Stresa is the southern town between the two, while Verbania

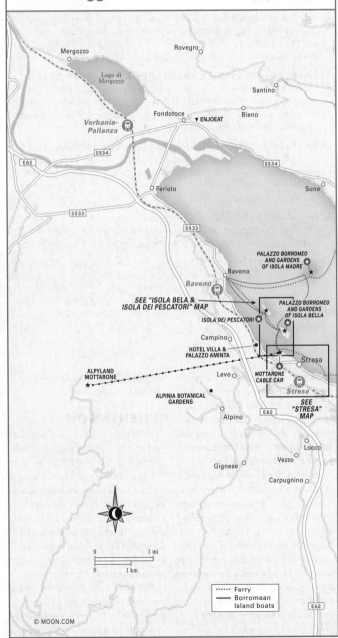

Lake Maggiore

Mergozzo

Rovegro

Lago di Mergozzo

Santino

Fondotoce   ▼ENJOEAT   Bieno

Verbania-Pallanza

SS34

SS34

E62

Feriolo

Suna

SS533

SS533

PALAZZO BORROMEO
AND GARDENS
OF ISOLA MADRE

Baveno

Baveno

*SEE "ISOLA BELA &
ISOLA DEI PESCATORI" MAP*

PALAZZO BORROMEO
AND GARDENS
OF ISOLA BELLA

ISOLA DEI PESCATORI

Campino

HOTEL VILLA &
PALAZZO AMINTA

Stresa

ALPYLAND
MOTTARONE

Levo

MOTTARONE
CABLE CAR

Stresa

ALPINIA BOTANICAL
GARDENS

SEE
"STRESA"
MAP

Alpino

E62

Locco

Gignese

Vezzo

Carpugnino

0   1 mi

0   1 km

······· Ferry
——— Borromean
        Island boats

E62

© MOON.COM

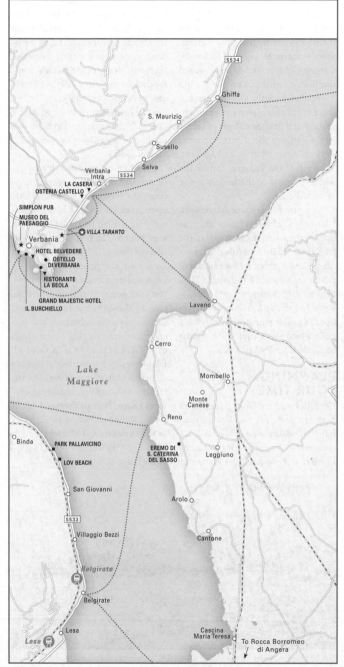

S. Maurizio

Susello

Selva

Ghiffa

SS34

Verbania
Intra   SS34

LA CASERA
OSTERIA CASTELLO

SIMPLON PUB
MUSEO DEL
PAESAGGIO

Verbania

VILLA TARANTO

HOTEL BELVEDERE
OSTELLO
DI VERBANIA

RISTORANTE
LA BEOLA

GRAND MAJESTIC HOTEL
IL BURCHIELLO

Laveno

Cerro

Mombello

Monte
Canese

*Lake
Maggiore*

Reno

Binda   PARK PALLAVICINO

LOV BEACH

EREMO DI
S. CATERINA
DEL SASSO

Leggiuno

San Giovanni

SS533

Arolo

Villaggio Bezzi

Belgirate

Cantone

Belgirate

Lesa

Lesa

Cascina
Maria Teresa
To Rocca Borromeo
↓ di Angera

sits roughly 14 kilometers (8.7 miles) north of Stresa. South of Stresa, follow the SS33 road hugging the western shore to reach the towns of La Sacca, Carcioni, Meina, and Arona. Toward the bottom of the lake, the Ticino River flows south. On the eastern shore of Lake Maggiore, from north to south, you'll find the villages of Luino, Porta Valtravaglio, Castelveccana, Laveno, Arolo, Ranco, and Angera. To reach these villages, follow the SP69 for most of the length of the eastern shore.

As a group, the three Borromean Islands in the lake sit closer to Stresa than Verbania on the west side of the lake. Isola Madre is the northernmost island, and is about a 25-minute boat ride from Stresa. To the south, Isola dei Pescatori is the smallest of the islands and visible from Stresa's shoreline. The southernmost island is Isola Bella, which is just a quick five-minute boat ride from Stresa.

PLANNING YOUR TIME

Considering that Lake Maggiore's primary draw are the Borromean Islands, which are fairly small, it's quite easy to get a good feel for the lake in a day or two, especially if you stay close to the center of the lake, where the islands are. Stresa is a great option for a home base on the lake, as the islands are a quick boat ride away, and there are plenty of food and accommodations options available. Stresa also has some lovely sights and activities of its own, from historic villas and churches to a cable car that takes you up into the mountains for a stunning view of the lake.

As with most areas of Italy that rely on tourism as the main source of income, the Borromean Islands are only open from the end of March until early November (exact dates vary per year, but you can find them on www.isoleborromee.it). Because the lake is known for its diverse and colorful foliage, and its islands for their gardens, consider going in spring, when the trees and flowers are in full bloom and the weather is not unbearably hot—average temperatures range from a high of 22°C (72°F) to a low of 18°C (64°F). Businesses and accommodations are open this time of year as well. For the remaining tourist seasons, temperatures range from an average high of 28°C (82°F) to a low of 18°C (64°F) in the summer, and an average high of 15°C (59°F) to a low of 9°C (48°F) in the fall.

The Borromean Islands of Lake Maggiore sitting in front of the Itailan Alps

Itinerary Ideas

Spend your weekend at Lake Maggiore exploring its verdant spaces, from the world-famous Borromean Islands to the various gardens and parks.

LAKE MAGGIORE ON DAY 1

1 Start your day bright and early with breakfast at your hotel in **Stresa** before purchasing a ticket from the ferry station on the lakefront for all three of the Borromean Islands (about €15 per person).

2 Head to **Isola Madre** first and spend the morning wandering through the botanical gardens surrounding the **Palazzo Borromeo**.

3 Take a boat to **Isola dei Pescatori** and grab a lunch of traditional northern Italian food at **Albergo Ristorante Belvedere**.

4 Take a quick stroll around the small, charming fishing island, and don't forget to stick your head into the historic **Church of San Vittore**.

5 Catch a boat to the final island, **Isola Bella,** where you can spend the rest of your afternoon exploring the grand, elegant **Palazzo Borromeo** and the lush, multilevel **Borromean gardens**.

6 Once you've had your fill of islands and gardens, head back to Stresa for the evening and unwind with a nice, relaxing dinner at **La Botte**.

LAKE MAGGIORE ON DAY 2

1 Start your day with a cappuccino and a sweet pastry at one of the cafés lining the waterfront, such as **L'Idrovolante Cafè** in Piazzale Lido.

2 Take the **Mottarone cable car** from Via Lido up to the **Alpinia Botanical Gardens** for a different garden experience from the previous day.

3 If you've had your fill of calm and quiet gardens, head on up to **Alpyland** for a thrilling downhill ride on an alpine coaster.

4 Take the cable car back down to Stresa's historic center for a cozy, casual meal at **Osteria degli Amici,** where you'll find a variety of Italian dishes ranging from vegetarian-friendly options to heavier meat and pasta dishes.

5 Walk off lunch with a leisurely stroll through **Parco Pallavicino** where you'll find several tree variations such as maples and sequoias. If you feel so inclined, you can stop to feed the deer, sheep, and birds. Find a bench under the shade to just sit and admire the gorgeous views of the lake.

Lake Maggiore Itinerary Ideas

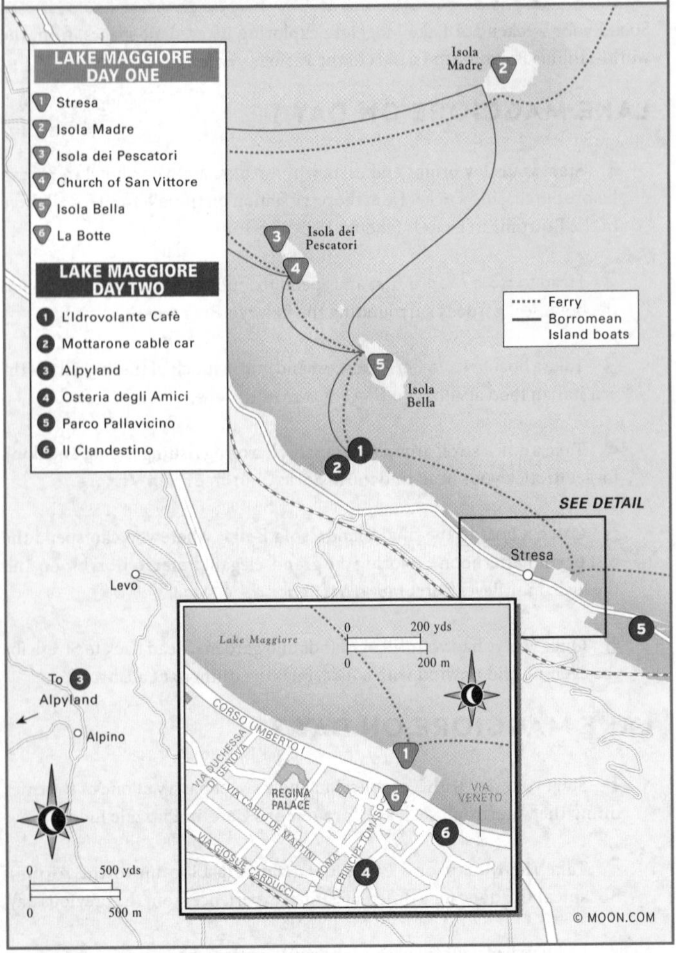

**LAKE MAGGIORE
DAY ONE**

1 Stresa
2 Isola Madre
3 Isola dei Pescatori
4 Church of San Vittore
5 Isola Bella
6 La Botte

**LAKE MAGGIORE
DAY TWO**

1 L'Idrovolante Cafè
2 Mottarone cable car
3 Alpyland
4 Osteria degli Amici
5 Parco Pallavicino
6 Il Clandestino

Isola Madre
Isola dei Pescatori
Isola Bella

...... Ferry
—— Borromean
Island boats

SEE DETAIL

Stresa

Levo

To 3
Alpyland

Alpino

Lake Maggiore

0   200 yds
0   200 m

CORSO UMBERTO I

VIA DUCHESSA DI GENOVA

VIA CARLO DE MARTINI

REGINA PALACE

VIA PRINCIPE TOMASO

VIA ROMA

VIA GIOSUE CARDUCCI

VIA VENETO

0   500 yds
0   500 m

© MOON.COM

6 For dinner, indulge your taste buds at the Michelin-star restaurant Il Clandestino. Be sure to book at least a few days in advance, as this place can get quite packed.

Stresa

The picturesque resort town of Stresa, sitting on Lake Maggiore's western shore just south of Verbania, is the most visited town on the lake each year, and rightfully so. The small mountainside town has plenty to offer, from historic churches and villas to botanical gardens and thrilling mountaintop alpine coasters. Even better, Stresa is the closest town to the beautiful Borromean Islands. They are prominently visible, as well as easily and directly accessible from Stresa's shoreline.

SIGHTS
PARK PALLAVICINO
Via Sempione Sud, 8, Stresa; 0323/933-478; www.parcopallavicino.it; 9am-7pm daily, mid-Mar.-early Nov.; adults €9.50, children €6.50

For more than 60 years, Parco Pallavicino, named after the family who still owns the villa today, has opened its magnificent gardens surrounding the villa to the public. The most outstanding feature of the park are the huge, looming trees in all shapes and types: palm, cypress, and magnolia. Meander along the paths lined with flowers in every color and magnolias that smell so strong and sweet that you won't want to leave.

The park also has as a small zoo for deer, sheep, birds, and other well-loved animals that you can not only view, but feed as well. Each wildlife group is fenced in its own habitat. The

Park Pallavicino is full of colorful gardens and wildlife interactions

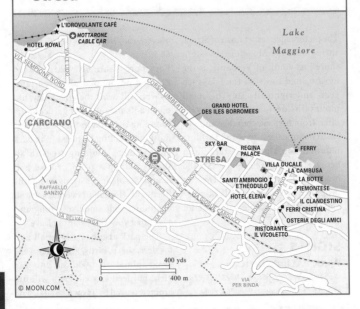

Stresa

L'IDROVOLANTE CAFÉ
MOTTARONE CABLE CAR
HOTEL ROYAL
VIA SEMPIONE NORD
VIALE LIDO
CORSO UMBERTO I
VIA PRINCIPE DI PIEMONTE
CARCIANO
VIA FRATELLI OMARINI
Stresa
VIA BAVENO
VIA GIUSEPPE VERDI
STRESA
GRAND HOTEL DES ILES BORROMEES
SKY BAR
REGINA PALACE
FERRY
VILLA DUCALE
LA CAMBUSA
SANTI AMBROGIO E THEODULO
LA BOTTE
PIEMONTESE
VIA TRIONTAGLIA
VIALE VIRGILIO
VIALE SIEMENS
VIA DUCHESSA DI GENOVA
VIA GIUSEPPE MAZZINI
VIA PRINCIPESSA MARGHERITA
VIA ROMA
HOTEL ELENA
IL CLANDESTINO
FERRI CRISTINA
OSTERIA DEGLI AMICI
VIA RAFFAELLO SANZIO
VIA SELVALUNGA
VIA CARDUCCI
RISTORANTE IL VICOLETTO
Lake Maggiore

0   400 yds
0   400 m

VIA PER BINDA

© MOON.COM

sanctuary fee is included in the entrance price to the park. Give yourself at least 90 minutes to take a leisurely walk around the place, and don't forget to look up from the flowers and animals to catch some gorgeous views of the lake across the way.

VILLA DUCALE

Corso Umberto I 15, Stresa; 0323/30-091; www.illagomaggiore.com; 9am-11:45am, 3pm-5:45pm Mon.-Fri.; free

Located directly on Stresa's waterfront just outside the historic center, Villa Ducale is the oldest known villa in town, dating back to the late 1700s. The most prominent external feature is the broad staircase made of pink granite steps and wrought iron handrails, making you feel like you're entering a royal palace rather than a lakeside villa. Inside, you'll find plenty of frescoes depicting mythical creatures as well as mosaic floors. Today, the villa is home to the International Center for Rosminian Studies, an order of the Roman Catholic church, with a library of more than 100,000 books spanning multiple rooms. More than anything, this villa allows you to take a step back in time and feel the historic roots that surround Lake Maggiore, giving you a deeper understanding of the lake's culture and history beyond the gardens and islands. Among locals, the villa is known to have been one of the Duchess of Genoa's preferred vacation spots in the mid-1800s.

PARROCCHIA ARCIPRETURALE DEI SANTI AMBROGIO E THEODULO

Via Principessa Margherita, 1, Stresa; 0323/30-475; www.parrocchiadistresa.it; 10am-6pm daily; free

Perched directly on Stresa's waterfront

is this locally beloved church, built in 1790 in a neoclassical style on a Greek cross plan, where there is one central part of a church with four arms of equal size and length. Two angel musicians grace the front, and inside the church, you'll find **three altars** beautifully decorated with frescoes, one of which depicts the Crucifixion. As the official parish church, it has seen many important local figures and events over its history, including the 1912 funeral of the Duchess of Genoa, who had lived in Stresa for several decades. The church itself is rather large with plenty of skylights, giving it an even airier feel. The natural sunlight streaming in washes over you as you enter the church, giving you a sense of peace.

❂ MOTTARONE CABLE CAR

*Via Lido 8, Stresa; 0323/30-295; www.
stresa-mottarone.it; 9:30am-6pm daily
Mar.-early Nov.; adult €11.50 one-way, €19
round-trip; child €9 one-way, €12 round-trip*
Departing every 20 minutes during opening times directly from the *lido* (waterfront) in Stresa, this cable car is one of the best ways to get unparalleled aerial views of the lake. The cable car has two stops: The first one takes you to the **Alpinia Botanical**

Mottarone cable car

Gardens, and the second takes you to **Mottarone,** one of the Stresa mountains. From the foot of the mountain to the peak, the trip is about 20 minutes in a closed-top cable car with windows on all sides.

From the second stop, it's roughly a 10-15 minute walk uphill to the summit on a mildly steep, stone-step path, which offers 360-degree views of the area; you can see seven different regional lakes, including Lake Maggiore, Orta, and Mergozzo. The second stop also serves the **Alpyland Alpine Coaster,** which is just a quick, painless, two-minute walk from the cable car station.

ALPINIA BOTANICAL GARDENS
(Giardino Botanico Alpinia)

*Via Alpinia, 22, Alpino, Stresa; 0323/927-173;
http://giardinobotanicoalpinia.altervista.org;
9:30am-6pm daily, early Apr.-early Oct.;
adults €4, children €3.50*
For one of Italy's more unique garden experiences, head up into higher altitude to reach Stresa's Giardino Botanico Alpinia. The gardens offer more than a thousand types of plant species, mostly coming from the surrounding Alps and foothills. Explore the many peaceful trails while enjoying the iridescent flora and panoramic views of the lake. A refreshing and relaxing experience tucked away in the mountains of the Lake Maggiore area, the botanical gardens offer a different experience for those wanting some time away from the waterfront.

You can drive to the botanical gardens, but I recommend taking the **Mottarone cable car** so you can admire the views of the lake on your way up. The gardens are about a 10-minute walk away from the cable car station, away from other attractions, and there is no café on the property, so do bring a bottle of water and some snacks.

SPORTS AND RECREATION

BEACHES AND WATERSPORTS
Lov Beach
Via Sempione Sud 3, Stresa; 335/608-3834; www.lov-stresa.it; 10am-8pm Sun.-Sat., 10am-10pm Sat.; €6 per person

This waterfront beach and mini golf course is a family-friendly place to spend an afternoon. The venue includes a nine-hole putt-putt course, a music and cocktail bar, and a beach and solarium with sunbeds and umbrellas. The wooden signs pointing to the beach, food, and other various parts of the property, as well as the mismatched outdoor lounge furniture, give this place a casual, local, and homey touch, so you don't feel like you're at yet another lake resort. Come at opening time in the summer to grab a sunbed before they run out, and remember that the beach is rocky, so bring water shoes if you want to take a dip in the lake.

AMUSEMENT PARK
Alpyland Alpine Coaster
Località Mottarone, Stresa; 0323/199-1007; www.alpyland.com; 10am-6pm daily Apr.-Oct., 10am-6pm Sat. and Sun. Nov.-Mar.; adults €5, children €4

Alpyland, the amusement park that sits on the top of Mottarone, is home to the exciting Alpine Coaster, which gives you a thrill of experiencing a ride on a luge combined with beautiful views of the Alps and Lake Maggiore on your way down. Feel the warm breeze whipping through your hair (definitely go in the warmer months) and take in all of the greens and blues at every angle, as you can nearly see the entire lake from the top of the coaster. You'll zip through 1,200 meters (1,312 yards) of track that goes down a decline of around 100 meters (109 yards) total, with the speed determined by a braking system within each one- or two-person car. I recommend paying for two rides; it's worth the small additional fee to catch the views a second time around. You'll find a much smaller crowd during the weekdays in the summer; expect to wait around 10-20 minutes on the weekends.

BARS
Sky Bar
Via Umberto Primo 33, Stresa; 0323/32-401; www.hlapalma.it/hotel/sky-bar; 12:30pm-12am daily; €5-15

After a long day on the lake, head up to the rooftop terrace at the Hotel La Palma for a cocktail and *aperitivo* at the Sky Bar, open until midnight daily serving a variety of cocktails and finger foods. With music buzzing in the background and busy waiters shuffling between tables, this chic yet casual place includes a large cocktail bar and a small infinity pool (for viewing pleasure only) overlooking the lake.

SHOPPING
La Cambusa
Via Cavour, Stresa; 0323/31-938; www.enotecalacambusastresa.com; 10am-10pm daily

The shelves and baskets at this tiny wine and food shop seem to overflow into the street, with bottles and bags coming at you in every direction, so you're bound to walk away from this shop with a delicious souvenir. The family that owns and runs the store is extremely knowledgeable about each product in the shop, from oils and vinegars to the large collection of local and Italian wine. The shop stocks goods in a range of prices, so there's something for every budget.

Ferri Cristina
Via A.M. Bolongaro 27, Stresa; 0323/30-603
This small and colorful shop in the center of Stresa owned by Christina Ferri and her welcoming family is beloved by hundreds of travelers and just as many locals. The shop specializes in handmade, authentic Venetian glass jewelry, ceramics, beads, pendants, and other trinkets. Cash and credit cards are accepted here, and Christina also provides paperwork for duty-free refunds.

FOOD
L'Idrovolante Cafè
Piazzale Lido, 6, Stresa; 0323/934-475;
www.lidrovolante.com; 8am-12am daily;
€2-5 for breakfast, €10-15 for lunch and
dinner
This casual and cozy restaurant right on the water is open all day and serves breakfast, lunch, and dinner. It sits in Piazza Lido near Stresa's shore and offers diners terrace views of the lake. If you're an early riser, stop in for some sweet treats and coffee. Or, swing by for a quick midday snack or late meal. In addition to smaller bites, you'll also find some traditional Italian plates, such as pizzas, grilled meats, pastas with seafood, and more. The restaurant is really informal, so swing by any time of day. No reservations are needed.

✪ Osteria degli Amici
Via Anna Maria Bolongaro, 31, Stresa;
0323/30-453; 12pm-3pm, 6:30pm-11:30pm
daily; €15-25
Situated in a quiet, shady corner of the town center is Osteria degli Amici, a friendly Italian restaurant with lovely patio seating under green vines, serving large plates of local risottos, seafood, and traditional pizzas. The ingredients here are both colorful and fresh, with plenty of vegetarian-friendly options on the menu along with heartier dishes like huge bowls of mussels with toasted bread and sauce, grilled steak cuts with rosemary, and tempting tiramisu for a sweet finish. The atmosphere is casual and friendly, but you should book a table in the evenings during high season if you're wanting to ensure a table under the vines.

Ristorante il Vicoletto
Vicolo del Pocivo, 3, Stresa; 032/932-102;
12pm-2pm, 6:30pm-10pm Fri.-Wed.; €15-30
Known for its high-quality and flavorful dishes, come here if you're wanting juicy, tender plates of meat and seafood, fresh pasta, and fine wine. Portions here are small but make an impact. Each dish is prepared with great attention to flavor and presentation. Dishes here include gazpacho, beef tartare, scallops, seafood pasta, lamb, and chicken. Both indoor and covered outdoor seating is available, and you shouldn't have trouble finding a table for lunch on weekdays. You may have a small wait on weekend evenings if you do not book a table in advance.

La Botte
Via Mazzini, 6, Stresa; 0323/30-462;
12pm-2:30pm, 7pm-10pm Thurs.-Tues.;
€15-35
Walking into La Botte almost feels like walking into the dining room of an old friend, with its cozy atmosphere accented by wooden furniture and enlivened by inviting chatter. You'll find some heavier dishes here, with a selection of grilled and roasted

meats and potatoes as well as polenta with mushrooms, and cold cuts and cheeses. Come here for the comfort food, and stay a while. Service here is rather quick and friendly, and you get a decent amount of food for the price.

Piemontese

Via Mazzini, 25, Stresa; 0323/30-235; www.ristorantepiemontese.com; 12pm-3pm, 7pm-10pm Tues.-Sun.; €25-45

Reserve a table for dinner in the garden patio of Piemontese, a highly regarded restaurant serving mostly local dishes, such as gazpacho with burrata, lake perch, and wine. Each dish is flavorful, and portions are larger than what you would receive in most fine-dining establishments. Take your time here, ordering a starter and working your way through each course, ending with one of the popular desserts such as the in-house crème brûlée with lavender or cooked pear with salted butter caramel and gelato. While you should be able to snag a table at lunch without booking ahead, reservations are recommended for evenings in the spring and summer.

❂ Il Clandestino

Via Antonio Rosmini, 5, Stresa; 0323/30-399; www.ristoranteilclandestino.com; 7pm-10pm Wed.-Mon.; €20-45

A Michelin-star restaurant on the waterfront in Stresa, Il Clandestino has a reputation locally as one of the most excellent dining options on Lake Maggiore. While the small door to enter the restaurant on a street corner doesn't look like much, the small plates here are known for their amazing flavors and beautiful presentation. The simple, unpretentious dining room gives off a much more casual vibe than most other Michelin-star restaurants, and prices aren't as high

either, but the food here is unparalleled, as you'll find some of the best seafood, pastas, and risottos in Stresa here. Start with a fresh selection of raw oysters before moving to a seasonal risotto or another meat dish. A section of their menu is dedicated to strictly local dishes, such as lake perch and stuffed ravioli. Reservations here are strongly recommended, as it's only open in the evenings.

ACCOMMODATIONS

€80-150
Hotel Elena

Piazza Cadorna, 15, Stresa; 0323/31-043; www.hotelelena.com; €92

This quiet, quaint family-operated hotel is just a short walk from the waters of Lake Maggiore, with some rooms overlooking Stresa's Piazza Cardorna. The hotel is small and cozy, with an unpretentious style that makes guests feel welcome and at home. Each guest room comes equipped with WiFi and private bathroom. A continental-style breakfast and guest parking are included in the price of each room, and there is also a small bar on the property serving wines, cocktails, and Italian coffee.

Hotel Royal

Viale Lido, 1, Stresa; 0323/32-777; www.hotelroyalstresa.com; €125

Despite being on the lakefront, staying at the Hotel Royal feels like a quiet, secluded getaway, with stunning views of both the lake and the surrounding Alps, a beautifully peaceful garden, an outdoor pool with a hot tub, and a restaurant with patio seating. Every guest room is bright and modern, and uniquely decorated with cozy furniture. Each room includes air conditioning, WiFi, private bathroom, and balcony overlooking either the hotel's garden or the lake. Parking and a continental breakfast are included.

€150-250
✪ Hotel Regina Palace
Corso Umberto I, 29, Stresa; 0323/936-936;
www.reginapalace.it; €170

The beautiful and large property of the Hotel Regina Palace sits directly on Stresa's main strip on the waterfront, near the ferry station in an art-nouveau building. Staying here really makes you feel like royalty, as each guest room features period pieces from various eras, as well as standards such as air conditioning, WiFi, and private bathroom. The hotel includes a modern indoor pool that is designed to make you feel as though you're swimming in the waters of an underground cave. A wellness center, with a Turkish bath, sauna, and gym, garden, tennis court, and terrace for enjoying drinks are also on the property.

the five-star Grand Hotel des Iles Borromees

bathrooms equipped with spa baths available in each guest room. The hotel is on the lake and includes an indoor and outdoor pool, as well as a wellness center with hot tubs and saunas offering massages and other services. Each room has either a private, garden, or lake view, and includes air conditioning, private bathroom with slippers, bathrobes, a marble tub, and WiFi. You'll also find a fine-dining restaurant and bar on the property; guest parking is included in the price of the room.

OVER €250
Hotel Villa e Palazzo Aminta
Via Sempione Nord, 123, Stresa;
0323/933-818; www.villa-aminta.it; €346

A stay at the five-star Hotel Villa e Palazzo Aminta feels nothing less than extravagant. All the guest rooms and common areas are luxurious and modern, yet adorned with antique decorations for a historic feel. The hotel offers a private dock, a heated outdoor pool overlooking the Borromean Islands, a wellness center featuring a Turkish bath, and a gourmet restaurant. Each bright and uniquely decorated room is soundproofed and includes a private balcony with a view of the hotel's gardens or the lake, a marble bathroom with Jacuzzi tub, minifridge,

Regina Palace Hotel in Stresa

Grand Hotel des Iles Borromees
Corso Umberto I, 67, Stresa; 0323/938-938;
www.borromees.com; €230

Everything about the Grand Hotel des Iles Borromees drips elegance, from its art-nouveau exterior to its chandelier-decorated dining room, to the marble

air conditioning, and WiFi. A substantial, made-to-order breakfast and guest parking are included in the price of each room.

GETTING THERE

Stresa is easily the most accessible town on Lake Maggiore, with plenty of trains and ferries stopping by every day, as well as roads from major highways leading down to the lakeside and a handful of local buses stopping in the center. Once you reach Stresa, the town is small enough to get most places on foot.

BY CAR
From Milan

Getting to Stresa is fairly simple from Milan, with most of the route supported by major highways up until you get to the lake itself. From Milan, take the A8 highway toward Laghi-Sesto Calende-Varese, then merge on to the A26 highway toward Gravellona Toce and stay on that until you reach the Carpugnino exit. From there, follow the signs to Stresa. Note that the road to Stresa is narrow and winding, and will continue as such until you reach the city center. Traffic moves both ways on this road, so pay close attention when taking the curves and prepare to brake often. The journey from Milan to the center of Stresa is roughly 90 kilometers (56 miles), or 1 hour and 20 minutes.

From the Lakes

From Lake Orta, follow the SP229 north up the eastern shore of the lake until you reach a roundabout near Gravellona Toce, then take the SS33 east, following the signs to Stresa. From Orta San Giulio to Stresa, it's about a half-hour drive spanning 26 kilometers (16 miles).

If you're traveling from Lake Como from the Como city area, take the A9 down to A36, then travel east for about 16 kilometers (10 miles) until you reach E62. Stay on this road, following the signs to Stresa, for about 75 kilometers (46.6 miles). The journey from the southwestern part of Lake Como to Stresa is about 87 kilometers (54 miles) and takes about 1.5 hours.

From the southern end of Lake Garda, head west on the A4/E64 highway towards Milan and Bergamo. Follow the A4 through Bergamo and Monza and the northern part of Milan, until you reach the A8 exit. From there, follow the instructions for reaching Lake Maggiore from Milan. The whole journey from Lake Garda to Stresa is about 202 kilometers (125.5 miles) and takes about 2.5 hours.

The easiest place to park a car in Stresa is at the large parking lot at the main Stresa train station, although you will find a few public parking spots and lots near the waterfront as well. Parking is generally €1.50-2.50 per hour in the public parking lots.

BY BOAT

The national **Navigazione Laghi** ferry service around Lake Maggiore stops

Private boat companies often transport travelers directly from Stresa's shore to and between the Borromean Islands.

at the **Stresa Ferry Terminal,** in the middle of town along the waterfront, near Piazza Marconi. Ferries from Verbania to Stresa cost €3.40 each way, and boats depart every 30 minutes to an hour or so 6:50am-7:10pm daily. The one-way trip from Stresa to Verbania takes about one hour. After departing Stresa, the ferry stops at each of the Borromean Islands, starting with Isola Bella (10 min.), Isola dei Peschatori (15 min.), and Isola Madre (35 min.). For more information on timetables and official prices for the public ferries, go to www.navigazionelaghi.it.

BY TRAIN
From Milan

Twenty-one trains run from Milan to Stresa between 6am-9pm daily. You can take one of the regional trains from Central Station or Porta Garibaldi for €5, and the ride is about 1 hour and 15 minutes, or you can take an international fast train, which cuts travel time down to 55 minutes, for €14.

From the Lakes

If you're traveling from one of the other the lakes in the region, the least complicated option is to head back to Milan's Central Station first and take a train from there to Stresa, including if you're traveling by train between Lake Maggiore and Lake Orta. The train station in Stresa is perched up on a hill directly in the middle of town, so you can simply arrive, walk out of the station, and follow the signs down to the lake for a quick 5-10 minute walk.

BY BUS

Buses from Verbania, Milan, and Lake Orta arrive at the **Stresa bus station** in Piazza Marconi. The **SAF** bus service (www.safduemila.com) uses the Milan-Arona-Stresa-Verbania line (6am-7:10pm daily). You can catch its blue bus from Verbania Pallanza or Verbania Intra for €2.70 per person each way, which is about a 20-minute ride.

There are two departures daily from Milan's Lampugnano bus station: at 8:15am and at 6:15pm. Each trip to Stresa takes approximately 1.5 hours and costs €9.20 each way.

During high season (June-mid-September), you can catch a blue SAF bus from Orta San Giulio on Lake Orta to Stresa. The bus runs only three times daily to Stresa, 9am-5pm. Tickets can be purchased on board, and children ride free. Tickets are €3.55 one-way, with a trip taking about 50 minutes each way.

Check the website for official timetables and prices for all these routes.

AROUND STRESA

If you're staying for longer than one or two days at Lake Maggiore, there are a couple sights of note in the villages around Stresa that are well worth a side trip.

EREMO DI SANTA CATERINA DEL SASSO (Hermitage of Santa Caterina del Sasso)

Via Santa Caterina, 13, Leggiuno; 0332/647-172; www.santacaterinadelsasso. com; 9am-12pm, 2pm-6pm daily, closes at 5pm Nov.-Mar.; free

The three buildings that comprise the monastery of Santa Caterina del Sasso are perched atop a rocky ledge in the village of Leggiuno on the lake's eastern shore and overlook Stresa and Lake Maggiore. They are considered an engineering feat, with the central building serving as the main church and the other two serving as convents.

The monastery complex first broke ground in 1170 and underwent centuries of construction before it was completed in the mid-19th century. The neutral-colored stone monastery almost blends into the white rocky cliff on which it sits, but the chapel inside offers a burst of color and light with its beautiful, well-preserved frescoes. Streams of natural light flood through the arched walkways, to bring the monastery to life.

You can reach Leggiuno from Stresa using Lake Maggiore's standard ferry services. Once you arrive at the small ferry station in the village, follow the signs to the monastery along Via Santa Caterina. You can then get to the monastery via a long, winding stairway from the center of Leggiuno from Via Santa Caterina, where the staircase starts in the church's parking lot. If you are arriving by car via the SS629 or from elsewhere around the lake, be prepared to drive around the southern half of the lake, which is roughly 60 kilometers (37 miles), first. This will take you about an hour, so hop on the ferry for a quicker trip.

Regardless of whether you arrive via ferry or car, either way, you'll have to hike your way up the 80 steps to the monastery and then back down again. But it's worth the sweat to gaze upon the frescoes and to lose yourself to monastery's serene surroundings.

ROCCA BORROMEO DI ANGERA

Via Rocca Castello, 2, Angera;
0331/931-300; www.isoleborromee.
it/angera.html; 9am-5:30pm daily
mid-Mar.-Oct.; adults €9, children €6

As Lake Maggiore's most famous and important castle, Rocca Borromeo di Angera, or Rocca d'Angera (also called the Borromeo Castle), is perched on one of the highest points in the village of Angera, overlooking the lake. Originally built to monitor the lake's activities and trade routes, it belonged to the famous Visconti family, one of the noble dynasties of the Middle Ages that dominated the history of northern Italy in the 14th and 15th centuries. It was eventually purchased by the Borromeos, an important aristocratic family that became extremely wealthy through banking in the region.

Today, you can visit five different structures of the castle, including the Torre Castellana and Giovanni Visconti towers, as well as the Scaligera, Borromeo, and Viscontea wings. Each of the towers gives you aerial views of the complex from different angles. If you are looking to save time, head straight to the Torre Castellana tower for a beautiful view of the castle with the lake in the distance.

In the Sala di Giustizia (Hall of Justice), you'll find an original fresco from the late 13th century depicting the then-Bishop of Milan during the Battle of Desio. The Sala delle Maioliche (Hall of Mythology) displays a beautiful art collection of 300 pieces, with most of them coming from Europe. Additionally, you'll find the Museum of Dolls and Toys (Museo della Bambola e del Giocattolo), founded by the Princess Bona Borromeo Arese in the late 1980s. With more than 1,000 pieces of dolls and toys on display, it is the largest museum of its kind in Europe. You'll also find the castle's quiet Medieval Garden (Il Giardino Medievale), a small natural plot of land featuring manicured lawns and colorful plants, similar to the gardens that you'll find on Isola Bella and Isola Madre.

To get here from Stresa or Verbania,

you'll need to follow E62 highway south until you reach the Castelletto Ticino exit, then follow Via Sempione/SS33 up to Angera. Once you arrive in the village, you'll find plenty of roadsigns directing you to the castle. From Stresa, the entire trip is 45 minutes over 46 kilometers (28.5 miles). Alternatively, you can take a ferry from Stresa or Verbania to Angera.

The Borromean Islands

The three beautiful Borromean Islands, known for their lovely gardens, elegant palaces, and small fishing villages, sit near the western shore of Lake Maggiore. The islands take their name from the historic, aristocratic, and wealthy Borromean family who took ownership of the islands in the 16th and 17th centuries. Isola Bella and Isola Madre are known for their Palazzo Borromeo palaces full of antique decorations and historic halls, and their palace gardens—the most well-known and extravagant in Italy. Isola dei Peschatori, on the other hand, is known for its charming, quaint fishing villages, with its local families living in a rainbow of houses stacked right up against each other.

SIGHTS

ISOLA BELLA

Isola Bella enchants visitors year after year with its Baroque palace and terraced, blooming gardens. The island is nothing short of extravagant, transformed over centuries from a rocky spot in the middle of the lake to a vibrant, lush corner of paradise. While the main attraction is the palace and its gardens, you'll also find a handful of restaurants and souvenir shops in the quiet village. The island is only 320 meters (350 yards) long and 400 meters (437 yards) wide, with most of the space taken up by the palace and the gardens.

✪ Palazzo Borromeo and Gardens of Isola Bella

Isola Bella; 0323/30-556; www.isoleborromee.it; 9am-5:30pm daily mid-Mar.-Oct.; adults €16, children €8.50

Along with its gardens, Palazzo Borromeo is Isola Bella's main attraction. Built in the mid-1600s, this baroque, historic House of Borromeo is dedicated to the wife of Carlo III,

Borromean Islands

CHURCH OF SAN VITTORE

Lake Maggiore

CONCRETA — ALBERGO RISTORANTE BELVEDERE

ALBERGO VERBANO

ISOLA DEI PESCATORI

Scoglio della Malghera

PALAZZO BORROMEO

ELVEZIA
IN FORNELLO

VICOLO DEL FORNELLO

0   200 yds
0   200 m

Isola Bella

VIA SEMPIONE NORD

MOTTARONE CABLE CAR

© MOON.COM   Stresa

The Palace of Borromeo is Isola Bella's main attraction

Isabella d'Adda, after whom the island is named. Over the years, the family used the house for luxurious parties and theatrical events for European nobility. Today, you can roam through parts of the elegant palace, including its fully furnished bedrooms, salons, and ballrooms, all of which are full of original artwork. Don't miss the underground halls of the palace, embellished with shells and mirrors of black marble from centuries ago. Simply walking the halls of this place makes you feel like royalty, even before you reach the multitiered, elaborately designed gardens. Take it slow here, as this is the island's most prized gem, and every turn of a corner leads to more eye-catching, finely detailed beauty.

A lot of travelers wonder if Palazzo Borromeo and the palace's gardens are really worth the price of a ferry as well as the entrance fee for yet another historic Italian house and garden experience. The answer, plain and simple, is without-a-doubt yes. There's a reason the Borromean gardens of Isola Bella are talked about all over the world: they are simply unparalleled in terms of uniqueness and beauty. In fact, when they were completed in the late 1600s, the multilevel, Italian-style gardens went on to influence later English and French gardens.

Full of lush, vibrant green grass and plenty of tree species, the manicured gardens exude a sense of elegance and grandeur. You'll see white peacocks wandering around amongst visitors, giving you a sense that you're almost in an entirely different time and space. The most notable feature of the gardens is the multilevel amphitheater, complete with statues, fountains, and draping greenery in the middle of the island. Trek up and down each staircase of the amphitheater to enjoy it from every angle and catch beautiful views of the lake and the town of Stresa. The amphitheater's most prominent feature is the unicorn statue, which is also a representation of the House of Borromeo's coat of arms.

ISOLA MADRE

At 220 meters (240.5 yards) wide and 330 meters (361 yards) long, Isola Madre is the largest of the Borromean islands and the farthest from Stresa. Despite being the largest island, it is nearly taken up by the Palazzo Borromeo and the palace's beautiful botanical gardens, so don't expect to find many places to grab a bite to eat or shop. You can easily see all of Isola Madre in a single morning or afternoon.

✪ Palazzo Borromeo and Gardens of Isola Madre

*Isola Madre; 0323/31-261; www.
isoleborromee.it; 9am-5:30pm daily
mid-Mar.-Oct.; adults €13, children €6.50*

This 16th-century palace was built on the old remains of an ancient church, cemetery, and possibly the castle of San Vittore. In addition to being surrounded by a prominent display of wisterias, this villa is also enveloped by strikingly impressive botanical gardens featuring azaleas, camellias, huge

The renowned gardens of Isola Bella are some of the most famous Italian gardens in the world.

cypresses, and fragrant lemon and lime trees. Garden paths wind in every which direction, leading you to secluded, magical corners of the island. Everywhere you turn, you'll encounter one eye-catching flower after another. You'll also come upon a habitat for the island's birds and a family chapel. A stroll through the house is worth some time as well, with its fancy, furnished rooms dedicated to dolls, puppet theater, and more. The multilevel villa includes a large balcony overlooking the gardens, hallways filled with antique furniture, Italian art, and unique pieces of ancient armor lining the walls. Your time, however, might be best spent exploring the enchanting gardens.

☙ ISOLA DEI PESCATORI
(Island of the Fishermen)

While Isola Bella and Isola Madre are home to lush, baroque-style palaces and gardens, the smallest Borromean Island, Isola dei Pescatori, may be the most endearing, with its colorful buildings stacked upon each other in such a small space and the island's inhabitants welcoming you to their unique homes as if you're old friends. The English translation of the island's name is Island of the Fishermen, an appropriate name for this tiny piece of

land and the 60 or so residents that call it home. As the only Lake Maggiore island that is inhabited year-round, it stays alive with a warm glow of life during the winter but buzzes with visitors during the summer. At only 375 meters (410 yards) long and 100 meters (109 yards) wide, you'll find here a handful of hotels and restaurants, as well as souvenir shops.

Church of San Vittore

Isola dei Pescatori; 0323/924-698; 8am-5pm daily; free

With such a historic and prominent presence near the ferry pier on such a small island, a stop at the Church of San Vittore is all but inevitable when on Isola dei Pescatori. The pointed spire reaches above the red rooftops of the island, so it's easy to find, serving as a guiding point to everything surrounding it. The baroque church serves as a peaceful, nearly silent spot on an island that is already fairly calm. Pop inside for a few minutes of solitude, which seems possible to achieve no matter how many other visitors or residents are in the church with you, and admire the well-maintained frescoes covering the walls and ceilings.

SHOPPING
ISOLA BELLA
Vicolo del Fornello

Via del Fornello, Stresa; www.isoleborromee. it/news-vicolo.html

Isola Bella's main shopping street (although it's more of a short, narrow path) is Vicilo del Fronella, which winds through the old fishermen houses and remains open most days, as well as most hours of the days, in March-October. While some shops may close around the lunch hour (1pm-3pm), you'll find that most shops

Small stands selling souvenirs and refreshments line the shores of the island in high season

are open during the late morning and late afternoon hours while the island remains open for visitors. The local shops lining the path focus on Italian-made brands, so don't expect to find any big-name department stores here. For Italian gastronomy such as meats, cheeses, and wines, step into I Capricci or Il Fornello, Bottega Con Cucina, which is also a restaurant. For clothes, accessories, and handbags, peek into Il Vicilo, which sells everything from local perfumes to scarves and silk pajamas. Visit Italia Independent for fine jewels.

ISOLA DEI PESCATORI
Concreta
Isola Superiore dei Pescatori, 28049 Stresa VB; 0323/30-354; 9am-5pm Tues.-Sun.
This tiny shop is owned by local Wanda Patrucco, who has been making her own beautiful, Japanese-style pottery for over three decades. The shop has been around for just as long and remains one of the most authentic roots of the village. Step inside to hear her talk proudly about her pieces, which include everything from bowls and serving dishes to pots and vases. While she creates many pieces that reflect the surrounding color of the blue waters, you'll also find more neutral-colored pieces. As far as souvenirs go,

a creation from Wanda is one of the best ones you can take home with you.

FOOD AND ACCOMMODATIONS
ISOLA BELLA
Elvezia
Via Lungo Lago Vittorio Emanuele, 18, Isola Bella; 0323/30-043; www.elvezia.it; 1pm-4pm daily; €15-30
Sitting directly on the island's shore is this charming Italian restaurant, which is part of the hotel of the same name. Regardless of whether you choose to sit up on the balcony overlooking the lake or directly on the shore-level patio seating, you'll be accompanied by stunning, relaxing views of the water. Dishes of fresh pasta, fish, and beautifully plated desserts full of chocolates, creams, and fruits. Despite the prime location and tasty dishes, you surprisingly won't break the bank to eat here, but definitely try to book a table in advance if you know in which area you want to sit, as this place is only open for lunch.

In Fornello
Via Lungo Lake Vittorio Emanuele, 18, Isola Bella; 338/794-5408; 9:45am-6:15pm daily; €15-45
Open daily during daylight hours, swing by this cozy restaurant for a late breakfast, lunch, or *aperitivo* before heading back to the mainland. The outdoor seating at this place is nothing less that intimate and snug, with cushioned patio furniture and string lights. Order a bottle of wine along with a selection of cold cuts, then sit back and enjoy a quiet corner of the island. If you're coming during lunch, order some of the freshly made pasta, fish, or cuts of meat, with vegetarian dishes as well. This place gets pretty packed during the regular

lunch hour, especially during high season and on weekends, so try to come for an early or late lunch for your best shot at scoring a table in the romantic patio setting.

ISOLA DEI PESCATORI
Albergo Verbano

Via Ugo Ara, 2, Isola dei Pescatori; 0323/30-408; www.hotelverbano.it; €110 d

Housed in a 19th-century villa at the end of the island, Albergo Verbano is a cozy hotel with a warm, homey feel. Situated on the island's shore, this place feels secluded from the rest of the world, nearly silent in the evenings—a perfect getaway for those looking for an escape from the daily noise and chaos. Each guest room includes a private balcony with views of the surrounding waters as well as air conditioning, WiFi, a private bathroom with toiletries, and a wardrobe. A breakfast buffet with sweet and savory options is included in the price of each room.

Albergo Ristorante Belvedere

Via di Mezzo, Isola dei Pescatori; 0323/32-292; http://belvedere-isolapescatori.it; €120 d

This clean, crisp, and classic hotel provides complete tranquility during your stay, with beautiful views of Isola Madre and the blue waters surrounding the island. Many guest rooms come with a small, romantic balcony, so you can wake up and enjoy shoreline views in a private, intimate setting. There's also a well-rated **restaurant** on the property serving local wines and freshly caught lake fish each day, open from 12pm-2:45pm and 7pm-9pm daily from March through November. Each room includes a television, air conditioning, a private bathroom with toiletries, WiFi, parquet or wooden floors, and

a wardrobe, with breakfast included in the price of each room.

GETTING THERE AND AROUND

The only way to reach the Borromean Islands, and to travel among them, is by boat. The islands are so small that you don't need a car, so if you're traveling by motor vehicle, park it in Stresa for the day.

PUBLIC FERRIES

To catch the public ferries traveling to and around the Borromean Islands, head to the ferry station located on the waterfront in Stresa, where you can purchase a ticket for €16.90 per adult and €8.50 per child for circulation between all three Borromean Islands.

The public ferries depart from Stresa every half hour between 7am-7:30pm daily March-October. The trip from Stresa to Isola Bella is just 5 minutes, the trip to Isola dei Pescatori is roughly 15 minutes, and the trip to Isola Madre is about 20-25 minutes. There are no intermediate stops between each of the islands, so you'll be taken from Stresa to Isola Madre, Isola dei Pescatori, then Isola Bella. You can purchase a round-trip ticket for €16.90 per adult and €8.50 per child for free circulation between all three Borromean Islands at the ferry station, meaning you can visit each island one time in any order that you like. Alternatively, you can purchase a ticket to and from only Isola Bella for roughly €3.50 each way. However, for trips to just Isola Madre or Isola dei Pescatori, you'll always have intermediate stops on your way back to Stresa, so you might as well visit the other islands. For more information on timetables and official prices for the public ferries, go to www.navigazionelaghi.it.

PRIVATE BOAT COMPANIES AND TOURS

You'll also find private boat companies, such as **LakeTours** (www.laketours.it), offering trips to and from the islands for similar prices, with roughly the same timetable as the public ferries, although they may stagger their departure times slightly to differ from the official public ferry service. Tickets for the private boat companies can be purchased directly on the Stresa lakeshore, right by where you would purchase tickets for the public ferries, while some offer the option to book ahead online. While there is no real advantage in terms of experience between taking a private boat company versus the public ferry, the ferries may get crowded in the high-season months, so booking a private tour ahead of time may save you time during your trip.

Companies such as **Viator** (www.viator.com) and **GetYourGuide** (www.getyourguide.com) also offer private tours of the islands with the price of boat tickets included in the trip. These packages can include private walking tours with a professional guide on each lake, entrance into the gardens and palaces, lunch, and transportation between each of the islands and Stresa, although you can also purchase packages that have only transportation and entrance fees for the palaces. Packages from both companies range between €15-200 per person.

Verbania

Lying just off the center of Lake Maggiore's western shore on the Borromean gulf is the town of Verbania. Despite being the lake's largest town in terms of geography and population, most tourists opt to visit Stresa to the south and the Borromean Islands, so Verbania is often overlooked by international tourists, giving it a more authentic, quiet feel for those wanting a more local experience. Verbania is a great home base if you're staying for a night or two on Lake Maggiore, as you'll find plenty of hotels, restaurants, and frequent transportation options.

SIGHTS
✪ VILLA TARANTO
Via Vittorio Veneto, 111, Verbania;
0323/556-667; www.villataranto.it;
8:30am-6:30pm daily Mar.-Oct.; adults €10, children €5.50

The grounds of the 19th-century Villa Taranto hold one of the most soothing and resplendent botanical gardens in Italy. The 16 hectares (39.5 acres) of land boast more than 20,000 different plant species, mostly from a semi-tropical climate. Multiple paths, which span a total of 7 kilometers (4.3 miles), send you winding through the colorful space, and plenty of benches offer shady spots to sit and relax. Visiting the gardens is a nice option even during the hot summer months. Give yourself at least an hour to stroll through the garden, two if you can. When you're finished, head to the café at the entrance of the gardens for a refreshing glass of wine or a quick bite to eat. The villa building is not open

Verbania's Villa Taranto offers some of Northern Italy's most famous botanical gardens

to visitors, as it is used for government functions.

MUSEO DEL PAESAGGIO

Via Ruga, 44, Verbania; 0323/557-116; www. museodelpaesaggio.it; 10am-7pm Tues.-Sun.; adults €5, children €3

For art enthusiasts, take a peek into the Museo Del Paesaggio, a collection of sculptures by artist Paolo Troubetzkey. Housed in a 17th-century building in one of the smaller, more tranquil streets of Verbania, this place tends to fly under the radar, so it's a great option for those looking for a quiet, cool way to spend an hour or two. Troubetzkey is one of the most celebrated 20th-century sculptors, known for likenesses of famous historical figures such as George Bernard Shaw and Tolstoy.

BARS
Simplon Pub

Viale delle Magnolie 4, Verbania; 0323/506-084; 11am-2am daily; drinks €3-10

Known locally for their friendly, professional service as well as a large selection of beers, wines, and original cocktails, Simplon Pub sits just off the main piazza in Verbania's center. In the warmer months, sit outside on the front patio to catch an evening breeze coming off of the lake and ask your waiter to recommend one of the many European grappas (grape-based brandy) available, or simply grab a leisurely coffee before heading back to your accommodations for the evening.

SHOPPING
EnjoEat

Via 42 Martiri, 110, Verbania; 340/079-2501; www.enjoeat.eu; 9am-6pm daily

This bright, cozy grocery market is one of Verbania's best shopping options, selling high-quality Italian gastronomy products from producers whom the shop owners have met and trust. You'll find a wide selection of Italian wines, salamis, cheeses, breads, pastas, olive oils, honeys, chocolates, marmalade, sauces, and more. The owners are extremely friendly and knowledgeable about their products, so feel free to ask them for suggestions, and stay for a plate of fresh, tasty products right in the store.

SPORTS AND RECREATION
Rent Boat Lago Maggiore
Via Carlo Alberto dalla Chiesa, 6 Verbania (VB) 28921; 0323/40-4544; www.rentboatlagomaggiore.com; 9am-6pm daily; €110+

If you're wanting to rent a private boat to jet around Lake Maggiore in style, Rent Boat Lago Maggiore offers a handful of private boats for rent, both with or without a boating license. Depending on how many people are in your group, you can rent a boat for up to 10 people. Boats can be rented for mornings, afternoons, entire days, multiple days, or weeks, starting at around €110 for the smallest boat (for 2-4 people) for a morning, with prices going up from there. Please note that due to local law, these private boats cannot be parked on the Borromean Islands, but can be parked at all lakeside towns and villages. You can rent a boat directly online, as well as see all official price tables, at www.rentboatlagomaggiore.com.

FOOD
La Casera
Piazza Daniele Ranzoni 19, Verbania; 0323/581-123; www.formaggidieros.it; 8am-10pm Tues.-Sun., closes 7pm Wed.; €8-20

Stop into this casual place for one of the best, most robust *aperitivo* hours on Lake Maggiore. Grab a glass of wine with huge plates of cold cuts and cheeses served with bread and honey. The menu comprises a simple list of meats and cheeses from which you can

Verbania is full of quiet streets full of boutiques, local restaurants, cafés and more

pick and choose to create your perfect plate. If you can't decide, you can't go wrong with one of their pre-selected cheese tasting plates featuring some of the best-known local cheeses. Stop by during lunch or dinner for a filling meal that goes easy on your wallet. Plates here are large enough to share between two to four people, depending on your appetite.

Il Burchiello
Corso Zanitello, 3, Verbania; 0323/504-503; 12:30pm-2:30pm and 7pm-10pm Wed.-Mon.; €15-30

This intimate, local eatery serves large plates of good old-fashioned Italian comfort food with a modern twist. The modern yet rustic atmosphere includes winding staircases, arched brick ceilings, and rooftop dining with calming views of the lake. You'll find everything here from seafood pasta to beef tartar to shrimp salads, topped off with house-made tiramisu for dessert. During spring and summer, book a table on the balcony to catch a spectacular sunset sky over the lake.

Osteria Castello
Piazza Castello, 9, Intra of Verbania; 0323/516-579; www.osteriacastello.com; €20-40

Everything about this little *osteria* screams cozy and local, with framed black and white photos covering the walls, and floor to ceiling wooden shelves displaying both local and national wines. You'll find homestyle food here, such as local lake fish, hearty pasta dishes, roasted potatoes, and more. For a casual, relaxing experience, grab a table on the patio, where you can dine wreathed in green vines.

✪ Ristorante La Beola

Via Vittorio Veneto, 32, Verbania;
0323/509-711; www.grandhotelmajestic.it;
€25-40

Housed in Verbania's Grand Hotel Majestic, this elegant fine-dining restaurant is known in the Lake Maggiore-region as serving some of the most delicious plates accompanied by high-level, professional service. The well-rated chefs focus on seasonal dishes, but you'll almost always find regional staples on the menu such as local pasta, lake perch, and pig cheek. Swing by in spring for a flavorful asparagus risotto with fresh strawberries for dessert. You shouldn't have any trouble finding a table for lunch but definitely book a table here for dinner during high season.

ACCOMMODATIONS

Ostello di Verbania

Via delle Rose, 7, Verbania VB;
0323/501-648; www.ostelloverbania.com;
€38 dorm bed, €50 private room

Located in Verbania's city center close to the lake, this hostel offers clean dorms as well as private double rooms with private bathrooms and WiFi for travelers wanting to stick to a budget. The staff is friendly, and the property includes a common dining area with vending machines, a computer lab, and an outdoor recreation area including a swimming pool. Beds in dorms can be reserved, with both gender-separated and mixed dorms available.

Hotel Belvedere

Viale delle Magnolie, 6, Verbania;
0323/503-202; http://pallanzahotels.com;
€95

Guest rooms at the Hotel Belvedere are homey and welcoming, with gentle color palettes and large, comfortable beds in each room. The property sits directly on the waterfront, with traditional hotel decor in the common areas. Each room includes air conditioning, private bathroom, and WiFi. Parking is included in the price of the room.

✪ Grand Majestic Hotel

Via Vittorio Veneto, 32, Verbania;
0323/509-711; www.grandhotelmajestic.
it; €140

The Grand Majestic Hotel has a dominating presence on Verbania's shoreline, taking up every level of the beautiful and prominent 19th-century villa that it calls home. The hotel includes an elegant restaurant on the property, a private beach for guests on the lake (included in the room price), and free access to the hotel's wellness

The Grand Hotel Majestic is one of many incredibly elegant accommodation options

center and tennis court. Each guest room includes air conditioning, a private bathroom with toiletries, safe, television, and WiFi. A breakfast buffet is included in the price of each room, as is parking.

GETTING THERE AND AROUND
CAR
From Milan
A trip from Milan to Verbania by car is roughly 1.5 hours over a span of 103 kilometers (64 miles), following the same route to Verbania that you would take to Stresa. From Milan, take the A8 highway northwest toward Laghi-Sesto Calende-Varese, then merge on to the A26 highway north toward Gravellona Toce and stay on that until you reach the Carpugnino exit. From there, follow the signs to Stresa, then on to Verbania. Note that once you exit off of the major highway and you start to follow the road to Stresa, you'll be winding your way down a narrow road until you reach the center of the town.

Once you're in the center of Stresa, Verbania is about a 20-minute drive from there along the S34 road, which hugs the western shore of Lake Maggiore, although that time may increase slightly in the summer months with traffic. You'll find a handful of public parking lots available in the center of the village, although they fill up rather quickly during high season, so find a parking spot early in the morning if you plan on parking for the day.

From the Lakes
From Lake Orta, follow the SP229 north up the eastern shore of the lake until you reach a roundabout near Gravellona Toce, then take the SS33 northeast until you reach the SS34 in Fondotoce. From there, you'll follow the SS34 east until you reach Verbania. From Orta San Giulio to Verbania, it's about a half-hour drive spanning 28 kilometers (17 miles).

If you're traveling from Lake Como from the Como city area, take the A9 down to A36, then travel east for roughly 16 kilometers (10 miles) until you reach E62. Follow this road east for about 75 kilometers (47 miles) until you reach Stresa, following the signs pointing toward Verbania and Stresa along the way. The journey from the southwestern part of Lake Como to Verbania is about 99 kilometers (61.5 miles) and takes about 1.5 hours.

From the southern end of Lake Garda, head west on the A4/E64 highway towards Milan and Bergamo. Follow the A4 through Bergamo and Monza and the northern part of Milan, until you reach the A8 exit. From there, you should follow the outlined instructions for reaching Lake Maggiore from Milan. The whole journey from Lake Garda to Verbania is about 213 kilometers (132 miles) and takes about two hours.

Once you're in Verbania, the easiest way to travel if you don't plan on spending most of your time near the water is by car. The SS34 cuts through the center part of town from west to east, while Viale Azari is an important road running through the center of town from north to south.

BUS
If you plan to arrive to Verbania by bus, your best bet to head to Stresa first (if you're traveling via public transportation, stick to the train for this leg of the journey), then hop on a bus from Stresa to Verbania. The blue **SAF** (www.safduemila.com) bus runs 6am-7:10pm daily. You can catch the

blue bus from Stresa's Piazza Marconi for €2.70 per person each way, which is about a 20-minute ride.

Alternatively, you can take a bus from Milan's Lampugnano bus station twice a day, once in the morning and once in the evening, which is about 1 hour and 45 minutes to Verbania costing around €10 each way. For official timetables and prices, you can go to www.safduemila.com.

TRAIN

There are frequent regional trains running between Milan's Central Station or Porta Garibaldi station and Verbania's Verbania-Pallanza station. Trains depart from Milan roughly every hour, and each ride is about 1.5 hours to Verbania. All tickets are €9.20 per person, with trains departing from either station in Milan from around 6am-9pm daily.

Keep in mind that the Verbania-Pallanza train station is quite a ways from the actual town of Verbania, so you'll want to catch a bus to the center of Verbania once you arrive. The bus is on the Omegna-Verbania route operated by the VCO Trasporti bus system. Buses depart roughly every half hour from the station to various areas of Verbania (the center stop being the Intra stop), from about

5:30am-10:30pm. Tickets between the station and the center of town run around €1.50 per trip each way. Official timetables and fares can be found at www.vcotrasporti.it.

BOAT

The national Navigazione Laghi boat service runs a daily ferry service to and from Verbania around Lake Maggiore. For those wanting a car-ferry, you can find one running between the ferry station in Verbania's Intra district and Laveno-Mombello on the eastern shore of the lake. The line runs 5am-12am daily, departing roughly every half hour in both directions for a price of €6-16, depending on the type of motor vehicle that you're wanting to take on the ferry.

All tickets can be purchased directly at the ferry station in the center of Verbania, with the most popular tickets being the hop-on-hop-off ticket between Verbania, Stresa, and the islands at around €15 per person, or tickets to Cannobio running at €6.80 for one way or €12-60 for a roundtrip. Services generally run from around 8am-6pm or 7pm daily from the end of March through mid-October. For more information on timetables and official prices for the public ferries, go to www.navigazionelaghi.it.

LUGANO

Straddling the border of south-

ern Switzerland and northern Italy is the beautiful blue glacial lake, Lake Lugano, so named for the Swiss city in which the majority of the lake lies. Given its proximity to Italy, most of the area's residents speak Italian. Although its geography is mostly Swiss, its culture is mostly Italian with influences of Swiss high society and Mediterranean cordiality.

More than any other Italian lake, Lake Lugano offers a balanced mix of recreational and cultural activities. Surrounded by the Swiss and Italian

HIGHLIGHTS

✪ **PARCO CIVICO-CIANI:** This park right on the waterfront in Lugano is full of meticulously manicured lawns, beautiful and colorful flower beds, and several different types of trees (page 211).

✪ **SANTA MARIA DEGLI ANGIOLI:** This lakeside church is home to Switzerland's most famous Renaissance fresco, *Passion and Crucifixion*, by Italian artist Bernardino Luini (page 211).

✪ **FUNICULAR MONTE BRÈ:** For more than 100 years, the funicular train has run between the Lugano suburb of Cassarate up to the peak of the beautiful Monte Brè, one of Lake Lugano's most beloved natural sights, where you can catch breathtaking views of the lake (page 212).

✪ **MORCOTE:** If you're cruising around Lake Lugano via motor vehicle or private boat, don't miss this small village composed of narrow alleyways connecting patrician homes and relaxing, colorful gardens. The village is a perfect example of a Swiss backdrop with Italian cultural influences (page 213).

Alps, the lake is a popular destination for nature enthusiasts. You can spend the day hiking in the mountains or sunning yourself on the beaches. For a dose of culture and history, you can wander through its world-class art museum or one of its charming lakeside villages. If you want to shop, there are plenty of shops to browse, and if you're looking to satisfy a culinary craving, Lake Lugano's restaurants will not disappoint. From hotel resorts and spas ideal for rest and relaxation to casinos, bars, and lounges perfect for a night on the town, there truly is something for everyone here—and it's all enjoyed against the backdrop of pristine glacial waters and the majestic Alps.

ORIENTATION

Lake Lugano takes the shape of the letter U with two branches stemming from the eastern side of the lake—one branches from the top of the U and the other from the bottom. Sixty-three percent of the lake falls on the Swiss side of Swiss-Italian border, and the remaining 37 percent falls on the Italian side, where it then flows into two separate provinces: Como to the west and Varese to the east.

The Swiss city of Lugano sits in the north-central part of the lake and is divided into a grid, with the shore of the lake making up the southern border of the city. The Lugano train station is located on the western side of the city and perched high on a hill, so you'll need to take the funicular running between the station and the city center to access the rest of the city. The Cassarate river runs from north to south directly through the middle of Lugano, flowing into the lake. Running parallel to the to the river is one of the city's main streets, Viale Cassarate. Another popular street that you can walk or drive along is Viale Castagnola, which runs along the shoreline and starts just east

Lake Lugano

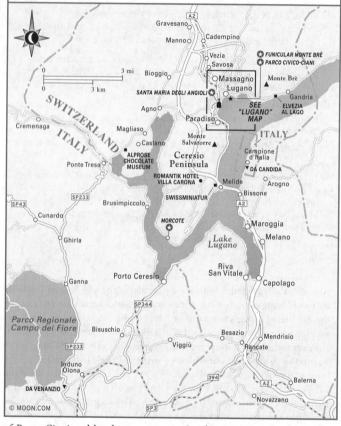

of Parco Ciani and heads east outside of the city to the small town of Castegnola, which is about five kilometers (three miles) east of Lugano.

To the northeast of the city sits the beautiful and beloved **Monte Brè,** to which you can take a funicular train from the Cassarate station near the eastern part of Lugano's shoreline. Nearby, just south of the mountain, you'll find the San Domenica bus stop, from where you can begin a leisurely walk on the **Olive Grove trail** heading east toward the nearby village of **Gandria,** only a few kilometers away.

On the opposite side of Lugano, to the southwest, you'll find the suburb of **Paradiso,** which is one of the larger and more residential suburbs of the city. Just south of that sits **Monte San Salvatore,** yet another beautiful mountain known for its outdoor recreational activities. Even farther south of the mountain are the towns of Carona and **Melide,** the latter being the home of the **Swissminiatur** (Miniature Switzerland), as well as the western-most point of the **Melide Causeway—** the bridge that passes over the lake's eastern branch. All of these villages

Lake Lugano is one of the trickier lakes to navigate due to its location on the Italian-Swiss border and its unique U-shape, where villages located on opposite sides of the same branch of the lake actually fall in different countries. Have your passport handy when traveling between villages on any mode of transportation, and keep these things in mind to avoid any confusion at the border:

- **Most prominent border control locations:** Chiasso (Switzerland), Ponte Tresa (Switzerland), and Gaggiolo (Italy)

- **What you need to bring with you:** A valid passport and any other travel documentation

- **Crossing by car:** Have your passport ready to present at the border checkpoints situated in a few of the villages. Border control agents generally move through the queue of cars quickly, so you shouldn't have to wait more than 10 minutes at a checkpoint.

- **Crossing by train:** All trains crossing the Italian-Swiss border are patrolled by train inspectors checking for your passport and validated train ticket, so have them both handy for the duration of your trip, especially as your train nears Chiasso.

- **Crossing by bus:** Buses are required to stop in dedicated coach lanes at the Italian-Swiss border, where border agents usually enter the bus to inspect all passports. This process can take 10-40 minutes, depending the number of passengers on the bus.

- **Crossing by ferry or water taxi:** Most of the time, you will need to present your passport and validated ticket upon boarding a public boat. Although you aren't required to show your passport to private water taxis, many companies do have their skippers check for passports before launching.

- **Currency exchange:** You can exchange euros for Swiss francs (CHF), or vice versa, at Lugano's main train station as well as in Chiasso, Como, and Milan. However, keep in mind that currency exchange rates are usually high, so it's best to use a credit or debit card and alert your bank of your travels ahead of time.

- **Using your phone:** Keep in mind that the country codes for phone calls change once you cross the border, so you will need to dial the +44 country code to make calls in Switzerland. Phone services change as well, so make sure you've checked ahead with your service provider for your international options before hopping the border in order to avoid excessive roaming charges.

sit on what is known locally as the **Ceresio Peninsula,** the land mass making up the middle of the lake's U shape. The Swiss village of **Campione d'Italian** sits off the eastern point of the Melide Causeway. Toward the center of the lake's U, at the southern end of the Swiss side, sits the charming village of **Morcate.** It is approximately 14 kilometers (8.6 miles) south of Lugano, or a roughly 20-minute drive.

On the westernmost branch of the lake sits Caslano, which is about a 20-minute drive southwest of the city of Lugano.

PLANNING YOUR TIME

Because the **Italian-Swiss border** divides the Lake Lugano region into two different countries, with the majority of it falling in Switzerland, it can be challenging to navigate. Regardless of your mode of travel, always have your **passport** handy, and remember that the currency changes depending on which side of the border you're on. If you plan to pay with cash during the better part of your trip, plan ahead to avoid having to pay exchange fees multiple times; also, make sure your credit card will work on both sides of the border.

To make the most of your time on Lake Lugano, give yourself at least a full weekend. Many of the best activities—whether cultural or recreational—are worth taking up an entire morning or afternoon for, including hiking the mountain trails, visiting the **LAC Lugano Arte e Cultura**, or exploring some of the smaller villages dotting the lake. If you prefer to stick to one place, the city of **Lugano** is your best bet, as it offers a good mix of cultural sights, hiking trails, beaches, shopping, and nightlife.

Lugano is easily accessible via train or bus, with direct lines from Milan as well as most other major Swiss cities. The climate in this area is similar to that of Milan's, albeit a bit cooler due to the altitude and more northern position. However, you'll still find warm summers, with average highs of 28°C (82°F) and lows of 18°C (64°F), and colder winters, with average highs of 7°C (44°F) and lows of 2°C (35°F).

Itinerary Ideas

LAKE LUGANO ON DAY 1

To make the most of your first day on Lake Lugano, head straight to the city of Lugano itself for a combination of history, Swiss culture, and nature all near the waterfront.

1 Start your morning with a hearty breakfast at your hotel, then set off for a leisurely walk along the **Olive Grove trail** from the San Domenico bus stop to the village of Gandria. This trails runs roughly 3.4 kilometers (2 miles) along the olive farms dotting the lake's shoreline.

2 Catch a bus or a private water taxi back to Lugano, and head for a bite to eat at **Agua Lugano,** a modern restaurant where you can order everything from fresh seafood to burgers to pasta.

3 After lunch, spend a couple hours visiting **LAC Lugano Arte & Cultura,** a prominent culture center dedicated to visual, musical, and performing arts.

4 Finish your evening with a cozy, homestyle meal at **Al Portone,** a local restaurant owned and operated by a husband-and-wife team, serving everything from tender steaks to homemade pastas.

Lugano Itinerary Ideas

CASSARATE

BESSO

LUGANO

Parco Civico
Villa Ciani

Parco del
Tassino

RIVA VINCENZO VELA

Lake Lugano

FUNICULAR
MONTE BRÈ

LAKE LUGANO DAY ONE	LAKE LUGANO DAY TWO
1 Olive Grove trail	1 Parco Civico-Ciani
2 Agua Lugano	2 Santa Maria degli Angioli
3 LAC Lugano Arts & Culture	3 La Cucina di Alice
4 Al Portone	4 Monte Brè
	5 La Tinera

0   0.5 mi
0   500 m

© MOON.COM

LAKE LUGANO ON DAY 2

1 Grab breakfast at your hotel, then start your morning with a relaxed nature walk near the lake through the peaceful and impeccably manicured grounds of **Parco Civico-Ciani.**

2 Continue your stroll through the center of Lugano, and stop to explore the beautiful **Santa Maria degli Angioli,** home to one of Switzerland's most famous frescoes.

3 Stop by the quaint yet modern **La Cucina di Alice** for an Italian lunch with a twist—its unique flavor combinations are sure to satisfy your palate.

4 Spend your afternoon on **Monte Brè**; you can either hike or grab the local funicular to the summit, where you can relax with a bottle of wine and admire the stunning views of the lake and city below.

5 End your evening with some authentic local cuisine at **La Tinera.** Its cozy atmosphere, low lighting, and wood-beamed ceiling will make you feel right at home.

Lugano

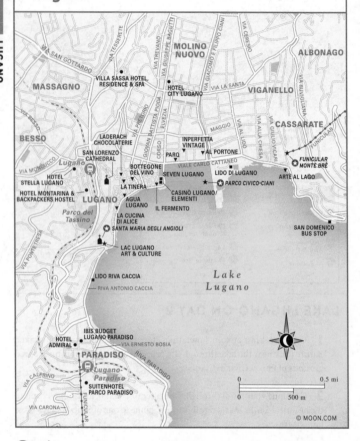

Sights

LUGANO
SAN LORENZO CATHEDRAL

Via Borghetto 1, Lugano, Switzerland;
+41 91/921-49-45; 7:15am-5pm Mon.-Fri.,
10am-8pm Sun.; free

Originally built in the Middle Ages and later reconstructed in the 15th century, this Roman Catholic cathedral dominates the center of Lugano. Its earliest known history traces back to 818, starting as just a local parish church before eventually growing into an important regional cathedral. The exterior is made of white stone and Carrara marble, with a bell tower in the back corner designed partly in Romanesque style and partly in Baroque style. The interior is stunningly detailed, with every corner from floor to ceiling catching your

Lugano's Parco Civico-Ciani is a colorful, tranquil lakeside park known as the city's green pearl

eye. The church was closed for several years as it underwent extensive renovations; be sure to take advantage of the opportunity to view the well-preserved frescoes and stained-glass windows.

✪ PARCO CIVICO-CIANI

Lugano, Switzerland; +41 58/866-66-00; www.lugano-tourism.ch; 6am-11pm daily; free

This park occupies more than 63,000 square meters (more than 15.5 acres) of land along the shores of Lake Lugano. Come here to feast your eyes on the verdant fields, redolent flower beds, and lush groves of oak, lime, maple, and more. Inside the park, you'll find a children's playground, and a regional library. There are also two sights within the park that are worth exploring. The first is the **Natural History Museum** (Museo cantonale di storia naturale di Lugano; www4.

ti.ch; 9am-12pm, 2pm-5pm Tues.-Sun.; free), which features information about the regional flora and other natural features of this unique area and can be covered with a quick walk. The other is **Villa Ciani** (www.ticino.ch), which is home to a number of rotating temporary art exhibitions—check the villa's website in advance of your trip to see what might be on view.

✪ SANTA MARIA DEGLI ANGIOLI

Piazza Bernardino Luini 6, Lugano, Switzerland; 8:30am-6:30pm daily; free

Located in a lakeside square in Lugano is Switzerland's most famous Renaissance fresco, the *Passion and Crucifixion* by Italian artist Bernardino Luini. The painting is undeniably beautiful, and it dominates the small church, so it's hard to take your eyes off of it once you enter the chapel. The fresco covers the entire wall of the nave, with more than 150 faces and characters in the

Santa Maria degli Angioli

painting. Despite the painting's large and vibrant presence, just spending a few minutes inside of the church is a humbling experience. Religious beliefs aside, it's impossible not to admire the beauty and detail of the fresco from the moment you step inside.

LAC LUGANO ARTE E CULTURA

Piazza Bernardino Luini 6, Lugano, Switzerland; +41 58/866-42-30; www. masilugano.ch; 10am-6pm Tues.-Wed., Fri.-Sun., 10am-8pm Thurs., ; adults 15CHF, age 16 and under free

The LAC Lugano Arte e Cultura arts center and museum is not only one of the most prestigious and visually stunning museums in Lugano, but in the entire southern part of Switzerland. The slate gray building, featuring a sharp point jutting towards the lake, is a dominating, yet not overwhelming, presence on Lugano's shoreline. This arts center hosts a number of exhibitions, concerts, performances, and other cultural activities every year.

The permanent collection known as the Art Museum of Italian Switzerland (Museo d'arte della Svizzera italiana Lugano) calls LAC home, with three levels of art installations. The impressive permanent collection features works from the 15th through 20th centuries that promote the regional culture. In contrast, the temporary installations are usually modern art exhibits that combine art with contemporary artistic research. For art lovers, the LAC is a must-see, and you should definitely carve out two or three hours to explore the property in its entirety.

If you happen to be in town on the first Thursday of the month, you're in luck, because you can visit the museum for free 5pm-8pm. Free guided tours in Italian and English are available at 1pm every Sunday, while guided group tours in English (from 200CHF) can be arranged ahead of time through the website.

TOP EXPERIENCE

✪ FUNICULAR MONTE BRÈ

Piazza Cioccaro, Lugano, Switzerland; +41 091/971-31-71; www.montebre.ch; 9am-11pm daily Jun.-Oct., 9am-6pm daily Nov.-May; 16 CHF, 25 CHF roundtrip

For over 100 years, this funicular train has been a staple in Lugano, shepherding people from the Lugano suburb of Cassarate up to the summit of beautiful Monte Brè, one of Lake Lugano's most beloved natural sights. At the

Grab the funicular up to higher ground for hiking trails and beautiful views of Lake Lugano

Monte Bre has a number of hiking trails, making for an ideal afternoon activity

top of the mountain, you are treated to a breathtaking view of the city of Lugano and the lake below—a sight that is worth the price of the funicular alone. But should you be looking for more to do at the top, there are several hiking paths, including the steep, roughly 1-kilometer (0.6-mile) stone path to the charming, rural village of Brè. In Brè, stop by the small Church of San Fedele for a moment of quiet reflection and to admire the surrounding frescoes. If you'd like to save money, take the funicular up the mountain, then have a leisurely walk down, but keep in mind that the path is not paved in its entirety, and it's rather steep.

There are two restaurants at the top of the funicular. The lower restaurant is more expensive but offers slightly better views of the mountain.

OUTSIDE LUGANO
☀ MORCOTE
Morcote, Switzerland

If you're cruising around Lake Lugano by car or boat, don't miss the charming Swiss village of Morcote, situated near the middle of the inner-bend of the lake's U-shape. In the village, small alleyways connect patrician homes and vibrant gardens—think of the beautiful little lakeside villages dotting Lake Como, but with a Swiss twist, and you have Morcote.

It's easy to spend a quiet afternoon getting lost in the beauty of this quiet little corner of the world. Visit the unique grounds of the Church of Santa Maria del Sasso (9am-8pm daily; free), with its complex of buildings, towers, and terraces of trees and bushes surrounding the old brick church. Step inside to admire the peaceful interior and frescoes. On the lakefront, wander through the sumptuous gardens of Parco Scherrer (10am-6pm daily; free), full of subtropical plants, statues, fountains, and gazebos.

The small village of Morcote is a must-see on Lake Lugano

and 1,500 trees surrounding the mini models to make up 14,000 square meters (more than 15,000 square feet) of space. You can easily spend an entire morning in this park: Grab a bite to eat on the terrace of the park's restaurant and purchase a unique and memorable Swiss-themed souvenir from the gift shop on your way out.

ALPROSE CHOCOLATE MUSEUM

Via Rompada 36, Caslano, Switzerland; +41 91/611-88-56; www.alprose.ch/museum; 9am-5pm daily; 3 CHF

Catch a local train from Lugano station or take a short drive a few kilometers outside of the city to the small town of Caslano, home of Alprose, the largest chocolate manufacturer in Switzerland. This Swiss chocolate factory houses the small Alprose Chocolate Museum, where visitors can enjoy an entertaining guided tour of the factory that teaches them all about the chocolate manufacturing process and the efforts that go into shipping this beloved chocolate worldwide. By the time you're finished with the tour, the whole time enticed by the aromas of chocolate wafting through the factory, you'll be ready to run to the shop to buy some chocolate of your own.

SWISSMINIATUR

Melide, Switzerland; +41 91/640-10-60; www.swissminiatur.ch; 9am-6pm daily mid-Mar.-early Nov.; adults 17.10 CHF, ages 6-12 12 CHF, 5 and under free

The Swissminiatur park, or mini Switzerland, is literally Swizterland in miniature. The 120 miniature models replicate the houses, castles, and other landmarks that you'll find throughout the country, such as Burgdorf Castle, the parliament building of Bern, and Heidi Village in Maienfeld. Beyond this, the park itself is lovely, with its more than 15,000 colorful flowers

Sports and Recreation

Lake Lugano's outdoor recreational activities vary in rigor. Hiking in the Swiss Alps near the city of Lugano ranges from easy to challenging. Depending on which mountain you choose to hike, you may be able to break up that hike with a funicular ride up the mountain. The hike down is typically slightly less strenuous. If you prefer a less-active occupation, enjoy one of the lakefront beaches either in the city or nearby. Most beaches have services on the premises that offer sun beds with umbrellas, and if you do not favor a dip in the lake, you can try the swimming pools instead. Most also have restaurants and bars on site.

PARKS AND BEACHES
LUGANO
Parco Civico-Ciani

Lugano, Switzerland; +41 58/866-66-00; www.lugano-tourism.ch; 6am-11pm daily; free

Often referred to as Lugano's "green pearl," this park offers a welcome respite from the occasionally bustling city. You can easily pass an hour or two of your day breathing in the fragrant flora, slowly strolling around the winding paths, picnicking on the lawns overlooking the lake, or simply sitting on a shady bench to watch the people go by.

Lido di Lugano

Via Lido, Lugano, Switzerland; +41 58/866-68-80; 9am-7:30pm daily May-Sept.; 11 CHF per entry

As one of the only sandy beach spots in the Ticino region, Lido di Lugano seems to have it all: a safe swimming zone, sun beds and umbrellas for rent, a bar and restaurant on the property, and a high dive into the lake. It's easy to enjoy an entire day here, grab a burger or other snacks at the restaurant for lunch, take a few laps in the Olympic-size swimming pool, or take the kids to the water play zone. Lifeguards are always on duty, and you'll find a diverse mix of people of all ages here on any given day.

To ensure you can rent one of the free sun loungers and umbrellas (5 CHF per day), make sure you arrive early on the weekends because the cleanliness and relaxation of this place tends to draw a crowd. To save some money, pack a lunch and snacks to bring into the beach, and bring your own towels to avoid the rental fee and deposit (5 CHF plus 20 CHF deposit) Bring cash here, as you'll need it if you're wanting to rent any equipment.

Lido Riva Caccia

Riva Antonio Caccia, Lugano, Switzerland; +41 91/921-04-28; 9am-8pm daily; 6 CHF per entry, plus 5 CHF per sun bed rental

A little off the touristy path, the Lido Riva Caccia is one of the preferred beaches of Lugano locals, with a clean, large deck and relaxing cocktail bar. The property includes a reserved swimming area of the lake, changing rooms and bathrooms, and a lifeguard on duty. The restaurant and bar offer several courses, including salads, focaccia, hamburgers, bratwursts, desserts, and a full range of beverages. Situated in front of Lugano's Museo d'Arte, the beach area is just a short walk away from the center of Lugano. You can rent a sun lounger with an umbrella for 5 CHF for an entire day, but get here within the first hour of opening in July and August to make sure you grab a spot.

HIKING
LUGANO
Olive Grove Trail

Start at the San Domenica bus stop; www.myswitzerland.com/en/olive-trail-lugano.html; free

The Olive Grove Trail is one of Lugano's more romantic, gentle walks. The 3.4-kilometer (about 2-mile) trail, which is mostly paved, winds through olive groves and offers plenty of opportunities to stop and admire the sublime lake and mountain views. The trail is just as informative as it is beautiful, as there are a number of educational posts along the way describing the history and olive culture of the region. The olive groves lining the trail are full of ancient trees from groves of a time passed, when olive oil was more popular in the region. (Although not as popular today, some local farmers have begun reintroducing the olive trees.) The hike takes 45 minutes-2 hours, depending on your pace.

From the San Domenico bus stop near Lugano train station, follow the Olive Grove Trail signs, which are marked with an olive on them, until you reach Gandria. Keep in mind that despite being one of the region's easier hikes, some spots are still steep, so bring plenty of water if you're going during the warmer months, and remember that the path is only shaded in some areas. You'll also find a few cafés and restrooms along the way, with a handful of benches and other natural spots to rest.

Once you're in Gandria, you can catch a bus back to Lugano using the line 490 bus from Gandria (Paese or Strada stops; once an hour; 7am-6:30pm daily; 10 CHF one-way) to Lugano, where it stops at Palazzo Saudi and the San Antonio area. You can also do the hike in reverse by first taking a bus to Gandria, and walking the trail back to the San Domenico area.

Paradiso to Monte San Salvatore

Start near the Lugano-Paradiso train station, Switzerland; +41 91/985-28-28; www.montesansalvatore.ch; free

To burn more than a few calories all while taking in panoramic views of the lake, hike the trail from Paradiso to the peak of Monte San Salvatore, the unique hump-shaped mountain near the city of Lugano. The trail starts just a stone's throw away from the Lugano Paradiso train station, in the parking lot of the mountain's funicular service; just follow the signs directing you up to the top of Monte San Salvatore, which takes on average 2.5-3 hours for the 3.2-kilometer (2-mile) journey. Of this total hike, approximately half a kilometer of it runs continuously uphill. The path is partially paved, while some of it is dirt and gravel. The entire trail is marked with signs in both directions, and there are plenty of stopping points, including benches and other natural sitting areas, with panoramic views of Lake Lugano and the surrounding Alps, some of the best views in the area. Congratulate yourself once you make it to the top by grabbing a glass of wine from the restaurant on the summit or pack a lunch and have a scenic picnic at the few tables overlooking the lake.

If you want the same beautiful views with a much easier experience, consider taking the **funicular** (www.montesansalvatore.ch, every half-hour, 9am-11pm Mar.-Nov., 9am-6pm Dec.-Feb., 23 CHF one-way, 30 CHF round-trip) up to the top of the mountain, then walking the trail back down.

Nightlife and Entertainment

Most nightlife and entertainment options around the lake are concentrated in the city of Lugano itself. Here, you'll find an eclectic and slightly upscale mix of bars, lounges, and nightclubs as well as art centers, cinemas, and theaters.

the city of Lugano, with plenty of bars, restaurants, and a handful of nightclubs

Casinò Lugano

Via Stauffacher 1, Lugano, Switzerland;
+41 91/973-7111; www.casinolugano.ch;
12pm-4am daily

This sizeable and architecturally innovative casino in the heart of Lugano has a long history—the casino was the first game room to open in the city in 1804 and it has since expanded to include fruit slots, major games, and boules (similar to roulette). It is the premiere gaming venue in the area. The casino is much like other casinos you'll find around the world: dimly lit, save for the glow emanating from the neon gaming signs. The casino comprises three levels: Level 0 hosts slot machines and poker tables; Level 1 hosts a smoking room, slot machines, bar, and terrace restaurant **Elementi**; and Level 2 hosts the poker room. You can gamble with either euros or Swiss francs. (Note that the minimum to play blackjack is 10 CHF.)

Il Fermento

Via Guglielmo Marconi 2, Lugano,
Switzerland; +41 91/923-4545; www.
ilfermento.ch; 11am-1am Mon.-Fri., 2pm-1am
Sat., 2pm-10pm Sun.; drinks 3-11 CHF

Open for lunch, dinner, and any meal that you may want in between, this local feel-good bar is a hot spot for Lugano residents. The casual ambience combined with the house craft beer, cocktails, *tagliere* plates, salads, focaccia bread, and homemade desserts (don't skip the tiramisu) and a number of other dishes makes this place a well-rounded option for any hour of the day. There are plenty of cozy tables inside but sit outside on the lively patio seating for lakeside views when the weather's nice. The bar gets pretty busy during *aperitivo* hour, so service may not exactly be prompt.

Seven Lugano

Via Stauffacher 1, Lugano, Switzerland; +41
91/290-7777; www.seven.ch/the-club-seven-

217

lugano; 12am-5am Fri. and Sat.; cover 20 CHF, drinks 12-20 CHF

Seven Lugano, located in the same building of the restaurant and casino of the same name, is one of Lugano's more lively and popular nightclubs. The resident DJ plays a mix of the latest pop and dance music, and the atmosphere is upscale without seeming overly elegant. The bar offers a selection of premium, housemade cocktails mixed with fresh ingredients. The combination of the atmosphere and bar selection means the club grows progressively packed as the night goes on. You can book a table to enjoy some nibbles and cocktails or wine, and entry is free if you arrive before 1am. The crowd here is between early 20s-early 30s. Be sure to arrive with a full wallet if you're looking to leave with a good buzz.

Shopping

Much like nearby Milan, shopping is part of the cultural fabric of Lugano. Most stores open 9am-7pm, give or take an hour or two in either direction. While you'll find such popular retail fashion chains such as H&M and Zara here, there is no shortage of designer stores either. You'll also find a bounty of local boutiques, food and gourmet shops, markets, and superstores.

Via Nassa

Via Nassa, Lugano, Switzerland

For the best shopping experience in Lugano, head to Via Nassa, one of the city's more historic and charming streets lined with a vast array of retailers selling everything from fashion to gourmet food and wine, antiques, jewelry, and more. You can also find some high-end brands, including Hermes, Gucci, Versace, Cartier, and Rolex.

Läderach Chocolaterie

Via Pessina 17, Lugano, Switzerland;
+41 91/923-19-00; www.laederach.ch;
9am-6:30pm Mon.-Sat., 9am-9pm Thurs.

Stop by this Swiss chocolate shop for decadent delicacies that you can't find anywhere else. Located in the heart of Lugano is this beloved little corner of paradise, with aromas so enticing that it's almost impossible to walk out empty-handed. The handcrafted, bite-size chocolate treats lining the display case every day are just as high-quality and delicious as they are visually beautiful. While you can grab prepackaged boxes and chocolate barks right off the shelf, be sure to make the most out of your experience here by creating your own hand-selected box of chocolates.

The center of Lugano is the best area to shop around Lake Lugano

Inperfetta Vintage

Via Luigi Lavizzari 9, Lugano, Switzerland;
+41 79/583-52-82; http://inperfetta.
blogspot.com; 10am-6pm Tues.-Sat.

For vintage fashion lovers, a stop into the Inperfetta Vintage shop near the center of Lugano is a must. This little showroom-shop is lined with racks of handpicked items, meticulously selected by the owner himself. Known as one of the best eclectic and vintage corners of the city, you'll find everything from colorful bow ties and scarves to antique costume jewelry to patterned sport coats. The place is alive with color, so even if you don't want to buy anything, stop by for a little window shopping and to admire the well-merchandised mannequins.

Food

Due to the unique location of the region of Ticino, with proximity to both Italy and France, you'll find a lot of Italian and French cuisine around Lake Lugano. The widest range and largest selection of dining options will be concentrated in Lugano itself, where you can find a well-balanced mix of classic Italian family restaurants, upscale and fine dining, international cuisine, and pizza-to-go places as well as more modern fusion restaurants. Elsewhere around the lake, you'll find mostly small trattorias, osterias, bars, and cafés focusing on Italian cuisine, although some of the more popular restaurants will also mix in some French fare as well.

LUGANO
ITALIAN
Artè al Lago

Piazza Emilio Bossi 7, Lugano, Switzerland;
+41 91/973-48-00; www.villacastagnola.
com; 12pm-2pm, 7pm-10pm Tues.-Sat.;
30-80 CHF

Artè al Lago is one of the most elegant spots in Lugano, with a Michelin-star chef creating plates so beautiful that you almost feel guilty touching them. Although the restaurant is actually part of the Villa Castagnola hotel, it sits across the street from the hotel, connected to a local art gallery. The head chef here focuses on local lake fish as well as other seafood plates that are simply spectacular, such as red risotto with salmon, gnocchetti pasta, or shellfish reduction with cumin. The upscale atmosphere calls for you to dress up, and you should reserve a table as far in advance as possible, as this place gets and stays busy.

La Tinera

Via dei Gorini 2, Lugano, Switzerland; +41
91/923-52-19; https://m.facebook.com/
laTineralugano; 11am-3pm, 5:30pm-11pm
Mon.-Sat.; 23-40 CHF

This little hole-in-the-wall is warm and intimate, with the wood-beamed ceilings matching the antique wooden tables and chairs. The name derives from the region in which it sits, Ticino, therefore you'll find local dishes and wines here, such as polenta and game, tartare, and risottos served with Delea and Zanini wines. The small room sits in a cellar, with just over 50 seats total in the intimate space, so book a table in advance.

Bottegone del Vino

Via Massimiliano Magatti 3, Lugano,
Switzerland; +41 91/922-76-89;
11:30am-12am Mon.-Sat.; 28-48 CHF

The Bottegone del Vino is known for its ever-changing seasonal menu, with the daily specials paired with an excellent local or European wine selection. Although located in the center of Lugano, this restaurant is tucked away in a corner so can be hard to find (it's on the corner of Via Massimiliano Magatti and Via Canova); and local wine lovers frequent this restaurant as it's said to have one of the best wine lists in the city. You can ask the knowledgeable and attentive waitstaff to help you find the best wine pairing for each dish, which includes such entrées as beef tartare and stuffed ravioli. You'll also see on the menu a variety of dessert pastries. Be sure to make a reservation, as the place usually stays busy.

✪ La Cucina di Alice

Riva Vela 4, Lugano, Switzerland; +41
91/922-01-03; www.lacucinadialice.ch;
12pm-2:45pm, 7pm-10pm daily; 40-57 CHF

This local restaurant breaks the status quo by taking classic Italian recipes and slightly modifying them, resulting in an innovative fusion of flavors, for example, veal chop with cherries (rather than a traditional veal cutlet) or robust, colorful salads that expand beyond the typical Italian dinner salad of lettuce and tomatoes. Situated right on the lake, the menu is seasonal and ever-changing, so you're not likely to have the same experience twice here. Locals have learned to love this place, so it stays busy for both lunch and dinner, therefore reservations are encouraged here. Whatever you do, don't leave without grabbing a Swiss chocolate-related dessert, whether it be a cake or fondant.

✪ Al Portone

Viale Cassarate 3, Lugano, Switzerland; +41
78/722-93-24; www.ristorante-alportone.ch;
6:30pm-10pm Tues.-Sat.; 51-91 CHF

This family-run establishment doesn't wow in terms of appearances; its decor is simple and classic, a few tables covered in white linen and mostly bare white walls. The wow factor here is the exceptional service and high-quality gastronomy. Husband-and-wife team Patricia and Chef Francis are what make this place as memorable as it is, offering both a tasting menu as well as an à la carte menu. They're known for their foie gras, handmade pasta, and second courses that include scallops with eggplant, tender rib eye, and wild sea bass with ratatouille. You'll find a backbone of French cuisine with Italian and other European influences. Book early at this intimate place and ask Patricia for wine and dessert suggestions to make the most of your experience.

INTERNATIONAL
Elementi

Via Stauffacher 1, Lugano, Switzerland;
+41 91/973-72-72; http://casinolugano.ch;
7pm-1am daily; 11-40 CHF

Located in the Casinò Lugano, this modern Mediterranean kitchen specializes in fusing unique flavors together—from octopus bites with pea mousse to steaks and tartare for meat lovers to savory veggie dishes for those wanting to stay on the lighter side. The urban-designed kitchen is open, so you can see your food being prepared. Note that you have to enter the restaurant through the casino, meaning that you must show an official ID, as this is an adults-only place.

Switzerland has always been a unique European country in that it is one of only a handful of countries that doesn't have its own language. You'll find that many Swiss citizens are multilingual, with German, French and Italian spoken throughout the country. Lugano is no exception to this, as the Italian language and culture are huge influences on the city's culture. In fact, some go as far as to ask if the residents of Lugano are Swiss Italians, or Italian Swiss?

The food, the language, religion, and many other aspects of the culture in Swiss Lugano are identical to its neighbor to the south. You'll also find French cuisine in Lugano due to the proximity to France. Despite these influences, in many ways the city is still distinctly Swiss, as evidenced by the surrounding snow-capped mountains, the high-end boutiques and cultural centers, and the crisp, clean streets. You can take in this unique meeting of cultures on a walk along the cobblestone streets with a gelato or as you tuck yourself into a family-run pizzeria.

✪ Parq

Via Pasquale Lucchini 1, Lugano, Switzerland;
+41 91/922-84-22; 11:30am-3pm, 7pm-11pm
Mon.-Sat.; 34-70 CHF

Parq is a very modern, chic sushi spot in Lugano's center, known for its special sushi rolls and high-quality ingredients. The fresh rolls are beautifully prepared and presented, with a refreshing mix of classic rolls and original rolls incorporating beef, fruits, housemade sauces, and more. If you're looking for something a little heavier, they also have hot dishes such as duck, steaks, soups, and tempura. While you shouldn't have trouble finding a table during the week, book ahead on the weekends, as this is a hot spot among locals.

Agua Lugano

Piazza della Reform 1, Lugano, Switzerland;
+41 91/923-80-80; 8am-1am daily; 40-57
CHF

Opening early and closing late every day, this restaurant focuses as much on the atmosphere as it does on the food. Sitting in the heart of Lugano, this spacious and modern place feels chic without being pretentious—giving off a vibe of not needing to "dress to impress." The menu is quite diverse, serving everything from fresh seafood and avocado to gourmet burgers and fries to classic Italian desserts. Unlike most places that close between traditional lunch and dinner hours, you can stop by here for a coffee in the morning or a glass of wine paired with a light plate in the late afternoon.

LIGHT BITES
Gabbani

Via Pessina 12, Lugano, Switzerland;
+41 91/911-30-90; www.gabbani.com;
8am-6:30pm Mon.-Sat.; 5-27 CHF

This deli, which is part of a larger complex that includes a hotel and restaurant, is a great place to pick up staples for picnics or cheap lunches to eat around town, such as at the park or on a hike. While you can sit down for coffee, risotto, or housemade pasta, you can also pick up and take away fresh breads, cheeses, cold cuts, olives, pickled vegetables, or pasta salads. Swing by for some local goodies, souvenirs, or a quick lunch without breaking the bank.

OUTSIDE LUGANO
EUROPEAN
Da Candida

Viale Marco 4, Campione d'Italia,
Switzerland; +41 91/649-75-41; www.

dacandida.net; 12pm-2pm, 7pm-11pm
Wed.-Sun., 7pm-11pm Tues.; 46-91 CHF

Just a short drive outside of the city of Lugano, this small eatery blending Italian and French cuisines has won the hearts of visitors again and again, as well as earned itself many repeat customers—for these loyal patrons, Da Candida makes sure that the food and dining experience improves with each trip. The dining room envelops you in lamp-lit warmth and welcomes you with its decorated fireplace surrounded by wine-filled shelves. Start with the European mixed-cheese plate accompanied by honeys and jams and ask the waiter to recommend a perfect wine pairing. Then move on to a course of either fresh pasta, fish, or meat. Try to save room for a grand finish, as the desserts here are to die for, from the white coffee parfait with salted caramel and cocoa to the classic fresh ricotta and pears.

Accommodations

Lake Lugano has a nice mix of accommodations, with everything from youth hostels to resorts with world-class wellness centers. If you're traveling without a car, your best bet is to stay in the city of Lugano, which offers the most options all within walking distance or reachable by public transportation. If you're getting around with a car, many of the small villages tucked into the mountains or dotting the lake's shoreline offer quiet, cozy getaways.

LUGANO

€80-150
Hotel Montarina & Backpackers Hostel

Via Montarina 1, Lugano, Switzerland; +41 91/966-72-72; www.montarina.ch; 92 CHF

For a historic, charming experience on a budget, try this hotel and hostel near Lugano's train station. The hotel sits in a beautiful pink villa, originally built in the 1800s. You can book a double room with a private bathroom, or a bunk in a dormitory with a shared bathroom. Double rooms include air conditioning, a refrigerator, and key access. The hotel has a small, well-maintained park on the property that includes an outdoor pool. WiFi in common areas and guest rooms and guest parking is included in the price of each stay. Breakfast can be added for an additional price.

Hotel Admiral

Via Geretta 15, Lugano, Switzerland; +41 91/986-38-38; www.luganohoteladmiral. com; 132 CHF

If you're wanting to stay on the outskirts of Lugano, preferring to stay nearby some of the outdoor recreation that the lake region offers, try Hotel Admiral, which is just a short walk away from the Monte San Salvatore funicular station and on Lake Lugano's waterfront. This clean, modern hotel is minimalist in style. It maintains a seasonal outdoor pool (available in the warmer months), and a year-round indoor pool and fitness center, all of which are included in the room price. Guests who are interested can add the cost of breakfast as well for 19.5 CHF per room. Each room includes air conditioning and private bathroom.

hotels on Lake Lugano in Switzerland

Hotel Stella Lugano

Via Francesco Borromini 5, Lugano, Switzerland; +41 91/966-33-70; www. albergostella.ch; 157 CHF

This simple, clean hotel is surrounded by a garden with a seasonal outdoor pool. It sits just 100 meters (109 yards) away from the Lugano train station, with guest parking and breakfast available at an additional price per room. Each room includes air conditioning, WiFi, and private bathroom. The hotel is a great option for those looking for a simple, quiet stay in the locale without all of the frills and the costs.

Suitenhotel Parco Paradiso

Via Carona 27, Lugano, Switzerland; +41 91/993-11-11; www.parco-paradiso.com; 172 CHF

Sitting near the bottom of Monte San Salvatore is this modern, suave place seems like more than just a hotel. Start your morning off with a huge breakfast buffet (waffles and prosecco, included) on the terrace overlooking the lake, which is included. Each room includes air conditioning, WiFi, and private bathroom with a bathtub. Also on the property are an indoor swimming pool, fitness center, parking, and a Cuban bar, complete with cocktails, Cuban music, and Havana cigars.

Ibis Budget Lugano Paradiso

Via Geretta 10, Paradiso, Switzerland; +41 91/986-19-29; www.ibis.com; 101 CHF

As one of the many Ibis budget hotels sprinkled through Europe, this Lugano hotel is simple, getting the job done for those on a budget and wanting a satisfactory, comfortable short stay. The hotel is just a few minutes by foot from the lake, and about 1.5 kilometers (less than a mile) from the Lugano city center. Each guest room includes air conditioning, WiFi, and private bathroom. Breakfast can be added to your stay for an additional price.

€150-250
✪ Hotel City Lugano

Via Giuseppe Bagutti 4, Lugano, Switzerland;
+41 91/222-09-00; http://hotelcitylugano.
ch; 275 CHF

This modern hotel located near Lugano's city center is a kilometer or so away from the waterfront. It leans on the swanky side, with LED lights illuminating the white and gray furniture and walls of the lobby. The sleek interior and chill ambiance of the inviting common rooms make you feel like you're living a lush life. The wide terrace serves as a nice spot for drinks or snacks. Guest rooms are WiFi equipped and have air conditioning and private bathroom. Guest parking and breakfast are available at an additional cost per room. The main train station is 1.5 kilometers (less than a mile) away, with the Piazza Molino Nuovo bus station just a short walk away.

Villa Sassa Hotel, Residence & Spa

Via Tesserete 10, Lugano, Switzerland; +41
91/911-41-11; http://villasassa.ch; 275 CHF

Just far enough outside of Lugano's city center (about at 15-minute walk) is the Villa Sassa Hotel, surrounded by a quiet park with views of the lake and the surrounding mountains—stay here if you want some seclusion from the city and indulge in its luxurious onsite wellness center. The spa includes an indoor pool as well as an outdoor infinity pool overlooking the lake, a hot tub, sauna, Turkish bath, and relaxation lounge and a gym. In addition to air conditioning, WiFi, and private bathroom with a tub, every room has a beautiful view of the surrounding gardens, mountains, or lake. An Italian and Swiss restaurant and bar are also on the property.

✪ Elvezia Al Lago

Sentiero di Gandria 21, Castagnola,
Switzerland; +41 91/971-44-51; www.
elvezialago.ch; 209 CHF

For a peaceful getaway where the guest rooms have private balconies overlooking the lake, head to Elvezia Al Lago, a traditional Ticinese villa with a private dock and bright rooms full of antique furniture, making this place feel like a true home away from home. Each room is equipped with WiFi and private bathroom. A breakfast buffet is included in the price of each room, as well as guest parking. Guests can also enjoy a private beach on the lake. From the property, it's not more than a 15-minute walk to the village of **Castagnola** or **Gandria**, and a 20-minute walk to the San Domenica bus stop that takes you to Lugano's city center.

OUTSIDE LUGANO
€150-250
Romantik Hotel Villa Carona

Via Principale 53, Carona-Lugano,
Switzerland; +41 91/649-70-55; www.
villacarona.ch; 209 CHF

This beautiful, period hotel is nothing short of charming, with the mountain-style wood-beamed ceilings combined with antique furniture and beautifully gleaming chandeliers making an elegant yet comfortable experience for guests. Rooms are decorated on an individual basis, with no two rooms the same. Each room includes WiFi and private bathroom; some rooms also include a living area with a sofa. Breakfast is included in the price of each room, and the villa itself has a ping pong table, garden and sun area, children's pool, pergola, and restaurant on the property.

Getting There

FROM MILAN

BY CAR

From Milan, take the A2 highway in the direction of Chiasso, Como, and Switzerland (when you're still in the Milan area, this portion of the A2 highway is combined with the A8 and A9 highways). You'll stay on A8, which is a toll road, until you reach the E35/A9 exit toward Como and Chiasso. Take the exit and stay on the A9 for approximately 36 kilometers (22 miles) before continuing onto the A2 highway, which will take you over the Melide causeway that runs across a portion of Lake Lugano. Take exit 50 to reach Lugano Sud (Lugano South), which will take you to the city of Lugano. Remember to bring your passports, as you will have to go through border control once you reach Chiasso, Switzerland. The entire trip from Milan to Lugano takes about 1.5 hours, including going through border control.

BY TRAIN

Alternatively, you can take a train from Milan's Central Station to the city of Lugano throughout the day. Direct trains depart every hour from Milan approximately 7am-7:25pm daily. You can take a Eurocity train (similar to the Italian *freccia* trains), which allows you to select a seat in either first or second class, with tickets running between €24-33 one-way. Tickets can be purchased directly at the station or online in advance at www.trenitalia.com.

Alternatively, you can take a regional TILO train, which does not sell out because seats are not assigned,

1:10pm-9:10pm daily. Tickets range from €24-40 per person, and can be bought directly at the station of departure or online at https://tilo.ch. These trains get pretty full, so get to the station early and have your ticket already validated, so you can jump on and grab a seat as soon as the train arrives.

FROM THE OTHER LAKES

BY CAR

You can get to Lugano directly from Como on Lake Como using only the A2 highway. Take the A2 toward Switzerland, up the southern part of Lake Lugano's eastern shore, across the Melide causeway and north to Lugano. The trip takes about 35-40 minutes and is roughly 30 kilometers (19 miles).

To reach Lake Lugano from the western side of Maggiore (Stresa or Verbania), head southeast on the E62 highway for roughly seven kilometers (just over four miles). Near the town of Gallarate, take the exit for the A8 to Tangenziale Nord Est di Varese. Stay on the A8 through the Varese region, about 62 kilometers (38.5 miles), then follow the signs for the A2 route north to Lugano and Paradiso. Once on the A2, you'll cross the Swiss border in Gaggiolo before reaching Lugano. (Note that this route has tolls €3-6 for the trip.) The entire drive from Stresa to Lugano takes about 1 hour and 20 minutes, including going through border control.

From Lake Garda, you will first need to head back toward Milan from the southern shore following the A4. Once you're on the A4, follow the tollway west past Brescia, Bergamo, and Milan, heading toward Chiasso, Como, and Switzerland, then follow the directions for getting to Lugano from Milan.

BY TRAIN

The same Tilo train that departs from Milano Centrale toward Lugano also stops at the Como San Giovanni train station most hours of the day as well, and you'll also find regional trains with a duration of around 30-45 minutes running between Como San Giovanni and Lugano. Direct trains between the two stations depart about once an hour from 7:45am until 11:45pm daily, costing between €15-20 per trip. Official timetables and fares can be viewed at www.trenitalia. com. However, because this train crosses an international border, you must purchase tickets directly at the train station.

From Lake Maggiore or Lake Garda, there is no quick way to travel to Lake Lugano by train. Take a train back to Central Station from Stresa on Lake Maggiore, or from Desenzano del Garda or Peschiera del Garda on Lake Garda, before heading to Lugano.

Getting Around

Due to its position right on the Italian-Swiss border, transportation may be a little trickier on Lake Lugano than on other lakes. It's best to plan your time carefully if you want to avoid going through border control repeatedly. Any time you're traveling from one village to another, it's safest to keep your passport on you, as many public transportation routes around the lake also cross the border.

Note that if you're wanting to stay in or around the city of Lugano, the area is quite walkable, with funicular trains and buses for areas that may be steep. Many of the streets in the city center are pedestrian only, so you should be able to see most sights by foot. If you're wanting to travel around the lake, your best bet is by car, as not all villages are accessible via ferry, bus, or train.

BY TRAIN

The main train station of Lake Lugano is in Lugano itself, and is perched on a hill above the main part of town, so you can either walk down the hill to the center, which is about a 15-20 minute walk, or take the station's funicular line, which is a great option for those that may be traveling with luggage. The funicular runs daily 5am-12am, departing roughly every five minutes from the station, and costs 1.30 CHF per person each way. It will drop you off in Piazza Cioccaro.

You can also take the train from the Lugano main rail station to the Lugano-Paradiso train station, which only takes two minutes. The trains depart roughly every half hour 6am-11:30pm, with tickets costing 2.10 CHF each. All Swiss train timetables and fares, along with online

STRETCH YOUR LEGS AT THE SACRO MONTE OF VARESE

If you're driving from Lake Maggiore to Lugano, you can take a break to see the **Sacro Monte of Varese** (Sacred Mount of Varese, www.sacromonte.it). This mountain is a UNESCO World Heritage site known for its "Holy Road" with 14 chapels along the trail from the foot of the mountain to the peak. Nestled into the Campo dei Fiori park, the small Sacred Mount is located just a few kilometers away from the town of Varese and about 17 kilometers (10 miles) southwest of the southern part of Lake Lugano.

HOLY ROAD
The walking path, which is fairly steep and mostly paved with cobblestones, starts at the Prima Cappella on Via Sacra at the foot of the mountain in Varese. At roughly 2 kilometers (1.2 miles) long, the trip can take anywhere between 1.5-3 hours, depending on how long you want to spend in each chapel. Along the way, you can follow the pebbled paths that branch off from the main trail and lead to each chapel, and take a peek inside each one. The small chapels aren't as grand as churches in larger surrounding towns, but together they paint a picture of the various mysteries of the life of Jesus Christ. You can also take a quick stroll through the medieval village of **Santa Maria del Monte,** which is at the top of the mountain near the peak, where sits the final cluster of chapels. At the very top is the **Sanctuary of the Virgin Mary,** which is technically the 15th chapel of the mountain. If you want to skip the walk, you can take the **Vellone-Sacro Monte funicular** (www.avtvarese.it), right by the parking lot of the Prima Cappella chapel at the foot of the mountain.

FOOD
At the top, you'll find a few restaurants and bars, should you need a refreshment after your walk. However, if you want to explore the Italian side of Lake Lugano even more, stop by **Da Venanzio** (Via Olona, 38, Induno Olona, Italy; +39 0332/200-333; www. davenanzio.com; 12pm-3pm, 7pm-11pm Tues.-Sun.; €35-60). This quaint restaurant, tucked among the mountains in the Italian village of Induno Olona, has been around for nearly 100 years. Its traditional Italian menu includes handmade pastas, homemade soups, classic lasagna, and Mediterranean fish with pastries and coffee to finish the meal.

ticket purchasing, can be found at www.sbb.ch.

BY BOAT
Lake Lugano has a daily ferry service, operated by Società Navigazione del Lago di Lugano (SNL), that runs from the city of Lugano to the village of Ponte Tresa, with stops along the way in several smaller villages including Gandira, Porlezza, Morcote, and Porto Ceresio, among others. A trip from Lugano to Gandria is about 20 minutes, while a trip from Lugano to Morcote is about 50 minutes.

Because ferries stop in both Swiss and Italian villages, you may be asked to show your passport either upon boarding or while exiting the ferry, so have it handy during your travels. The service generally runs about 8:30am-9:30pm from Lugano, and 8am-6pm for ferries returning from Ponte Tresa to Lugano. Timetables vary depending on your point of departure, but you can find updated timetables at www.lake-lugano.ch. The price of your ticket depends on your starting point and final destination, with prices ranging 8-26 CHF, or you can buy a day pass running at 49 CHF.

BY WATER TAXI

Water taxis should be booked in advance, either by calling ahead or by contacting the company online. Most companies, such as Boatcenter Palace (www.boatcenterpalace.com), offer a few boats that can seat up to 10-12 passengers at a time. Some companies also offer cocktails and other services on board for an additional price. Expect to pay anywhere from 30 to 100 CHF for a private water taxi.

BY BUS

The city of Lugano and the nearby villages are well-served by a local bus system, the Trasporti Pubblici Luganesi SA (TPL SA, www.tplsa.ch), which is easy to navigate and recognize, as buses are blue and gray. Most lines run between the Lugano train station and the downtown area. Buses generally run 6:30am-12am daily, with most of the 13 lines running a handful of times each hour. Bus line 2 will be particularly useful to you, as it runs between the train station, the Lugano town center, Paradiso, Cassarate, and Castagnola, meaning that you can easily access San Salvatore, Monte Brè, and the path to Gandria from the San Domenico stop using this bus.

From Paradiso to Lugano center, the trip is about 10 minutes by bus. From the city center to Cassarate, it's about a 5-minute drive, and then another 15 minutes or so to Gandria. Single tickets cost between 3.60-5.70 CHF per trip, depending on your starting and finishing points. Tickets can be purchased at most tobacco shops in town or at train stations, but make sure you validate the ticket upon boarding the bus.

Likewise, the Società Navigazione del Lago di Lugano (SNL) provides bus routes to Campione and Gandria using the 490 bus line, which can be taken from the Lugano train station or the San Domenico bus stop. Tickets can usually be purchased directly at bus stops using the ticket machines (which are available in English), although note that some machines only accept coins, while others accept banknotes and credit cards. Tickets range from 2.50 CHF for a short distance single ride to 7.50 CHF for a day pass. Buses run approximately 7am-10:30pm daily, roughly once every hour.

BY CAR

The city of Lugano can be easily accessed via the A2 highway from Milan or other larger cities and lakes. Since a large part of the city center is pedestrian-only, there are just a few paid parking garages and lots available during the day. You'll find that street parking tends to be a little bit cheaper than garages.

If you're wanting to reach some of the smaller villages along the lake, navigating by car will be your most convenient and cheapest option, but remember to bring your passports with you, depending on your destination. You should use an updated GPS system to navigate the lake's region, especially as you distance yourself farther from Lugano.

From the city, you can take the SS340 northeast, hugging the shore, to towns such as Gandria. Running south from Lugano is the Highway 2 (not the same as the A2 tollway), which runs right along the shore toward Carrabia, Melide (across the

Melide Causeway), Bissone, and down the southeastern shore, connecting to the A2 tollway, which can lead you down to Chiasso or Varese.

BY TAXI

Taxis in Lugano need to be called in advance by 10 minutes or so to ensure that a car is available. While there are several different companies around the area, Swiss Taxi Lugano (+41 091/967-70-70, www.swisstax-ilugano.ch) is a reliable service with positive reviews. Taxis usually have a minimum fare of 15 CHF, charging 4 CHF per kilometer.

LAKE ORTA

Located in the Novara province

just west of Lake Maggiore, Lake Orta is often called the secret little sister of the three major northern Italian lakes. Although it has largely remained out of the international spotlight, it is no less worthy of attention. The glistening deep blue waters of the lake are calm and quiet, which set the tone for the quaint villages dotting its shores. Although it sits on the southern edge of the Italian Alps, the surrounding area isn't nearly as mountainous as the areas around Lakes Maggiore,

HIGHLIGHTS

✪ **ISOLA SAN GIULIO:** Named after the patron saint of Lake Orta, Saint Julius, the lake's only island is a charming mix of history, spirituality, and ancient architecture (page 233).

✪ **PIAZZA MOTTA:** Wander around this romantic waterside square, the heart and soul of Orta San Giulio. The medieval buildings come in a rainbow of colors and are full of local restaurants, gelaterias, boutiques, and more (page 235).

✪ **HIKING SACRO MONTE DI ORTA:** Trek your way up to the top of Orta's sacred mountain, full of small but beautiful chapels from foot to peak (page 235).

Como, or Garda, with more rolling hills and rural villages.

Orta San Giulio, the main village on the lake, is composed of narrow cobblestone alleys, ancient churches, local eateries, and a bustling, picturesque piazza on the waterfront. From here, take a quick boat ride to the beloved Isola San Giulio, a colorful and charming little island floating on the lake. If you're looking to spend a relaxing day on the lake and get a full dose of Italian history and culture away from the hordes of international tourists, Lake Orta is your place.

ORIENTATION

Lake Orta is located roughly 24 kilometers (15 miles) east of Lake Maggiore, with the largest nearby cities being Varese to the east (on the other side of Lake Maggiore and Lake Varese), Domodossola to the north by 48 kilometers (30 miles), and Novara 52 kilometers (32 miles) to the south. The lake's main village, the medieval Orta San Giulio, is located in the center of the eastern shore, on a peninsula jutting into the lake. The lake's famous island, Isola San Giulio, is just over a kilometer west of the peninsula.

On the lake's eastern shore, you'll find the villages (from north to south) of Omegna, Crabbia, Pettanasco, Orta San Giulio, Vacciago, Corconio, and Buccione, with the town of Gozzano just below the lake. The western shore (from north to south) includes the villages of Prà della Marta, Oira, Ronco, Pella (including San Filiberto), Lagna, and San Maurizio d'Opaglio. The historic Sacro Monte d'Orta is located in the village of Orta San Giulio, almost directly in the center of the peninsula, off the lake by a couple kilometers.

PLANNING YOUR TIME

Given that Lake Orta is fairly small in comparison to Lakes Como, Maggiore, and Garda, it's possible to get the full experience of the lake in a day trip. For the best experience on the lake, head straight to Orta San Giulio, the most easily accessible area of the lake. It's an excellent base from which to take a ferry to Isola San Giulio, or hike Sacro Monte di Orta. It offers the most dining, accommodation, and shopping options, so it's your best choice if you're looking to stay on the

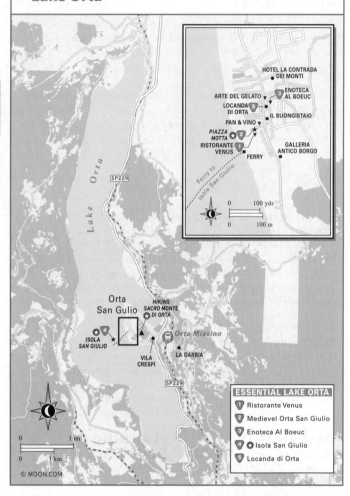

Lake Orta

ESSENTIAL LAKE ORTA
1. Ristorante Venus
2. Medievel Orta San Giulio
3. Enoteca Al Boeuc
4. Isola San Giulio
5. Locanda di Orta

© MOON.COM

lake. Public transportation is limited on Lake Orta, so traveling to, and around, the lake is best done by car.

The weather, like much of northern Italy, is humid subtropical. You'll find an average high of 28°C (82°F) and average low of 15°C (59°F) in the summer months, and an average high of 7°C (44°F) and average low of -4°C (25°F) in the winter months. Given that the lake generally stays under the radar, you shouldn't have to worry about dodging crowds of tourists. With that said, from a weather perspective, your best time to go is late spring in May or late summer in September.

Itinerary Ideas

ESSENTIAL LAKE ORTA

Spend a relaxing day at Lake Orta wandering through the charming Piazza Motta and Isola San Giulio.

1 Grab a coffee and a pastry at **Ristorante Venus** in Piazza Motta and enjoy your breakfast while sitting by the lake.

2 Spend your morning walking around the medieval village of **Orta San Giulio,** wandering the narrow alleys that branch off from **Piazza Motta.** You'll find plenty of shops and art galleries to browse through, and a few bars as well, should you want a mid-morning refreshment.

3 Enjoy a local lunch of *tagliere* plates and *bruschette* at the intimate **Enoteca Al Boeuc,** and wash it all down with a glass from one of the largest and finest wine selections on the lake.

4 Take a boat from Piazza Motta to **Isola San Giulio,** and step into the historic **Basilica di San Giulio** to admire the frescoes and paintings inside before wandering leisurely through the charming, colorful little island.

5 Catch the boat back to Orta San Giulio, then head to **Locanda di Orta** for dinner (book ahead!) for a Michelin-star experience.

Sights

✪ ISOLA SAN GIULIO

Isola San Giulio; 0322/911-972; www.comune. ortasangiulio.no.it; free

This petite island—measuring at just 275 meters (300 yards) by 140 meters (153 yards)—floats with picturesque charm atop Lake Orta. So small is this island that its buildings are stacked right up against each other. The island exudes a spiritual ambiance accented by classic Italian lakeside lure. The island was named after Lake Orta's patron saint, Saint Julius, who lived and died here in the late 4th century; he was later buried on the island where his body supposedly still remains in a crypt under the main alter of the basilica. The entire island can be easily seen in a single morning or afternoon, but to fully soak in its allure and quiet, take your time strolling around the waterfront and through the narrow passageways. Take notice of the slow way of life here, with locals sitting out on their patios watching the tourists walk by.

The island can be reached by the frequently running public ferry from Piazza Motta in Orta San Giulio. Each ride is just 10 minutes long, as the

The medieval town of Orta San Giulio is the most prominent and visited town on Lake Orta

island is only 400 meters (437 yards) away from Piazza Motta. During high season, you can purchase a round-trip ticket for €3.15, with ferries departing 10am-7pm daily from Orta San Giulio to the island and 9am-7pm daily from the island back to Orta San Guilio.

Basilica di San Giulio

Isola San Giulio; 0322/90-358; www.orta. net/ita1/ambone.htm; 9:30am-6:45pm daily; free

At the heart of Isola San Giulio is this minor basilica, which was founded in 390 CE by Saint Julius, who is said to have miraculously arrived to the island with his brother by riding his cape. He then saved the island by defeating dragons and serpents before founding the church. A few hundred years later, a new, larger church was built on the same grounds, and multiple modifications have been made to it over subsequent centuries. The

Romanesque exterior can be seen from the central shores of the lake, as well as from Piazza Matta—the heart of Orta San Giulio.

Once you step inside the church you are immediately awash with a sense of calm and wonder; every corner drips with astonishing history and art. Take your time to explore the interior, stopping to admire the frescoes and paintings along the walls that depict biblical scenes and religious figures. The most notable piece of art is the 12th-century Amon in Oira Serpentine figure prominently displayed and held up by four columns and dedicated to the four evangelists in the Christian tradition—Mark, Matthew, Luke, and John. Stay a while here; take the time to read the informational placards (written in Italian and English) to better understand the historical importance of the church for both the island and the lake.

❂ PIAZZA MOTTA

Piazza Motta, Orta San Giulio; 0322/90-101; www.comune.ortasangiulio.no.it; free

Lake Orta's liveliest, most beloved lakeside piazza is in the town of Orta San Giulio. While you'll inevitably pass it on your way to town, rather than walk through it, linger for a while. Soak in the atmosphere of the square, perhaps while resting on one of the shady benches near the water with a gelato or granita (slushy) from one of the cafés or gelaterias in hand. The piazza epitomizes everything that comes to mind when you think of life in Italy: locals occupying the bar and restaurant patios for hours, friendly shop clerks flaunting their homemade goods, colorful buildings—some with faded frescoes adorning the exteriors—intimately linked. The piazza is the beating heart of the town, and from here stairways to various pedestrian streets and alleyways branch out into the rest of the town.

Sports and Recreation

HIKING
❂ Sacro Monte di Orta

Atop one of Northern Italy's nine sacred mountains is the small chapel complex of Sacro Monte di Orta. Listed as a UNESCO World Heritage site, the complex comprises a total of 20 chapels scattered around the mountain. Construction began in 1783 and finished in 1788. By far this sight is one of the most beautiful and unique experiences on Lake Orta.

The spiraling hiking trail that leads you to the complex begins at the foot of the mountain near the village of Orta San Giulio—you'll see the signs for it near the parking lot at the foot of the mountain. The walk up the mountain gets steep in some places, but the path is mostly gravel; on hot days, make sure to pack a water bottle. On your way up, you'll pass some stunning green landscape; be sure to stop at each of the chapels, all of which are dedicated to Saint Francis of Assisi, to admire the beautiful frescoes and sculptures depicting his life. Once you reach the summit, you will be rewarded with a spectacular and peaceful view over the lake and Isola San Giulio. The total hike is just 4 kilometers (2.4 miles) long. If you plan to stop briefly at every chapel, the hike will take you about two hours to complete.

If you prefer to skip the hike, you can drive the small road that starts in the parking lot at the foot of the mountain to near the top of the mountain. From there, you'll enjoy a stunning view of Isola San Giulio.

BEACHES AND WATERSPORTS
Miami Beach (Spiaggia Miami)

Via Novara 69, Reg. Valle Orta San Giulio; 348/451-7462; www.spiaggiamiami.com; 9am-7pm daily May-Sept.; €7 pp

This small, private beach and popular swimming area lies just south of Orta San Giulio. Although the water temperature remains chilly all year round, swimming in the clear, clean water of Lake Orta is a relaxing way to beat the heat in the summer, and the shallow descent from beach to water makes that easy to do. The private beach includes a restaurant and bar serving snacks and meals, including grilled vegetables, pastas, fruit, and traditional *aperitivo* drinks and finger foods. Umbrellas with a pair of sun beds can be rented for €24 a set for the entire day. During busy months, you can book your umbrella in advance

through the Miami Beach website or by calling ahead.

You can also rent paddleboats and canoes directly from the beach for an entire day. A four-person paddleboat can be rented for €15 per hour, a single-person canoe for €6 an hour, and a tandem canoe for €12 an hour. If you want to rent for the entire day, call ahead. Life jackets are included for each person in every rental.

Shopping

Il Buongustaio

Via Olina, 8, Orta San Giulio;
0322/905-626; www.ortafood.it

This Italian gastronomic market is known by locals not only for its selection of high-quality products, but also for its vibrant staff (you have to meet Giovanni!) who proudly show off their greatest passion throughout the store. Stop in for a fresh sandwich or to purchase one of the hand-selected bottles of oils and vinegars, mushrooms, honeys, spices, or beloved truffle products. Ask the lively owner for suggestions, as he knows everything about every product in his store.

Galleria Antico Borgo

Piazza Motta, 10, Orta San Giulio;
0322/905-151; www.galleriarotaross.com;
10:30am-12:30pm and 4:30pm-7:30pm
Tues.-Sat.

In the heart of Piazza Motta is this beautiful, cozy, bright, and multilevel modern art gallery displaying paintings, sculptures, and drawings by

select Italian artists. Art style ranges from portrait to landscape to still life to abstract. The knowledgeable gallery owner is discerning about where to hang the art within the gallery, taking care to create an artistic experience for visitors the moment they step into the quiet space. While not all works of displayed art are for sale, the ones that are make for a unique and authentic souvenir.

Galleria Antico Borgo in Piazza Motta sells paintings and other artwork from Italian artists

Villa Crespi

Via Fava, 18, Orta San Giulio; 0322/91-1902; www.villacrespi.it; €350

Everything about this five-star hotel, housed in a lavish 19th-century building, screams maximum luxury and comfort. Every corner is extravagantly detailed with historic, antique elements, and a night here makes you feel like royalty. The hotel itself is off of the lake, but you can get to the waterfront by a short 10-minute walk or an even shorter drive. It's surrounded by colorful, manicured private gardens and includes a renowned Italian restaurant, a wellness center, and an elegant bar.

Villa Crespi

Each antique room includes a private balcony, WiFi, air conditioning, and private bathroom with bathtub.

Ristorante Venus in Piazza Motta offers dining right on the waters of Lake Orta

Getting There

Lake Orta is smaller than the three major Italian lakes and slightly farther away, so there is no direct way to reach it via public transportation from Milan or the other lakes, other than from Lake Maggiore. Therefore, your best bet is to drive.

FROM MILAN

BY CAR

From Milan, take the **A8** northwest, heading out of the city's metro area. Stay on the A8 until you reach the **A26** exit toward Gravellona Toce. After about five kilometers (three miles) on this road, take the exit toward Arona and the ramp to Borgomanero. From there, take the **SP142** until you reach SP229. Follow **SP229** north until it becomes **Via Panoramica,** which hugs the lake and takes you directly to Orta San Giulio. The whole trip is roughly 80 kilometers (50 miles) from Milan to

Orta San Giulio, and it generally takes about an hour and 15 minutes.

BY TRAIN

There are no direct trains from Milan to any towns on Lake Orta. From Milan's Central Station, take a regional train to **Novara,** a city south of Lake Orta, from Milan's Central Station. The trip to Novara is about 40 minutes and costs €5.50 each way. The trains from Central Station to Novara run roughly every half hour around 6am-10:30pm, with the last train from Novara back to Milan departing at 11:18pm daily.

From Novara, catch the **Novara-Domodossola** train, which stops at the Orta-Miasino, Pettenasco, and Omegna stations along Lake Orta. The journey from Novara to Orta-Miasino, the station for Orta San Giulio, takes around 40-55 minutes and costs €4.40 each way. The Novara-Domodossola

Food

ITALIAN AND PIZZA

✪ Ristorante Venus

Piazza Motta, 50, Orta San Giulio; 0322/90-362; www.venusorta.it; 8am-12am Tues.-Sun.; €10-40

Dine under peeling frescoes on the patio of Venus for some of the best views of the island and the water right at your feet. Choose from cold cuts and cheeses, large plates of risottos and fresh pastas, grilled meats, fish and vegetables, and plenty of wines during lunch or dinner. You can also grab a coffee and a sweet pastry for breakfast on the water. The atmosphere here stays fairly casual throughout the day, and the service is friendly and attentive. You should be able to walk in without reservations at any time of the day, but if you're dead set on eating here for dinner during high season, calling ahead wouldn't hurt.

Locanda di Orta

Via Olina, 18, Orta San Giulio; 0322/905-188; www.locandaorta.com; 12:30pm-2pm and 7:30pm-9:00pm Wed.-Mon.; €40-70

This Michelin-star, fine-dining restaurant is one of Lake Orta's most beloved and best-known, with every aspect of the dining experience consistently receiving gold stars across the board—from its elegant yet relaxed ambience to its attentive service to its top-quality entrées that burst with flavor. Don't expect heaping portions of pasta or pizza. Rather, prepare for small plates that have been prepared with the utmost attention and care. First you'll start with fresh bread and a small selection of appetizers—complimentary of the chef. Next, you'll order one of the several dishes that incorporate one or more of the following: roasted meats, handmade pastas, creams, sauces, eggs, fresh vegetables, and more. Considering this is one of the best spots to eat in this area, book well ahead to reserve a table, as the restaurant has only about 20 seats.

BAR AND LIGHT BITES

✪ Enoteca Al Boeuc

Via Bersani 28, Orta San Giulio; 339/584-0039; 11am-3:30pm and 6:30pm-1am Wed.-Mon.; €3-15

This intimate stone cavern dating back to the 16th century is well liked by both locals and tourists and is known for its large selection of fine wines and *aperitivo* plates, including *tagliere* dishes and *bruschette*. The atmosphere is casual and inviting, with a friendly staff and a small but tasteful food menu. Wines and food focus on local culture, so grab a bottle of the regional wine and ask your waiter about a local dish to pair it with for an authentic local Northern Italian experience. The place is small, so you can book a table if you're dead set on eating here, but walk-ins are welcomed as well.

Pan & Vino

Piazza Motta, 37, Orta San Giulio; 393/858-3293; www.panevino-orta.it; 10am-10pm Thurs.-Tues.; €10-20

This small shop not only sells one of the lake's best selections of Italian wines, cold cuts, and cheeses, but you'll also find a few welcoming tables inside, inviting you to take a seat and grab an *aperitivo* to escape the summer heat or cool winter breeze coming off the lake. The menu is composed of various *tagliere* plate options, all with a diverse selection of meats, cheeses,

Pan & Vino is a delicious option for wine and *tagliere* plates in a bustling environment

pickled vegetables, and honeys. Below each option, you'll find a suggested wine pairing. If you want the best, most-flavorful experience, trust the experts here and follow their guidance. However, they welcome you to go off the beaten path, so don't be afraid to ask for suggestions based on your preferences. In the warmer months, stop by for a late lunch or early dinner outside to take in the bustling atmosphere of Piazza Motta along with the beautiful blue waters of the lake.

GELATO

Arte del Gelato

Via Olina, 30, Orta San Giulio; 335/832-9298; www.gelateriaartedelgelato. it; 9am-10pm daily; €2-10

This tiny hole-in-the-wall gelateria is just off of Piazza Motta in Orta San Giulio, with no seating but a case full of colorful ice creams of many flavors. The friendly staff produces some of the lake's best and freshest gelato each day, with plenty of fruity, chocolatey, and creamy flavors to choose from. They also offer sorbet popsicles and frozen cakes, if you're looking to skip the gelato for another tasty dessert.

Accommodations

€80-150

Locanda di Orta

Via Olina, 18, Orta San Giulio; 0322/905-188; www.locandaorta.com; €90

Just 50 meters (55 yards) from the waterfront in Orta San Giulio, this beautifully rustic hotel sits just off of a quiet alley in the center of town, making you feel like you've found a magical hidden corner while remaining close to the heart of Lake Orta. Guest rooms here are modernly decorated, but the stone walls give them an air of a time long ago that enchants you to sleep at night. Rooms vary greatly here, with some overlooking the quiet internal courtyard, and others including a romantic jacuzzi bath. There's also an Italian restaurant on the property, with a large breakfast served daily. Each room includes air conditioning, WiFi, a private entrance, and a private bathroom.

✪ Hotel La Contrada dei Monti

Via dei Monti, 10, Orta San Giulio; 0322/905-114; www.lacontradadeimonti. it; €112

Just a quick walk from Lake Orta's waterfront and Piazza Motta in Orta San Giulio, this affordable and classic Italian hotel sits in a quiet alleyway in the center of town. Guest rooms overlook the internal courtyard with its beautifully exposed stone walls and patio seating, where you can sit and sip on wine in the evenings. Some rooms also feature wood-beamed ceilings. Each room includes WiFi and private bathroom, and breakfast is included.

Hotel La Contrada is just one of many small, charming hotels in Orta San Giulio

OVER €150

La Darbia

Via Covini, Vacciago, Ameno; 389/311-3813; www.ladarbia.com; €240

If you're traveling in a group of two or more and you're wanting a private luxury experience, look into the intimate, secluded La Darbia vacation apartments. Just three kilometers (under two miles) outside of the town of Orta San Giulio, the apartments are modern yet rustic, giving you the feel of a home-away-from-home while providing you with that classic Italian charm. Each apartment is right on the lake, with a communal outdoor pool and a beautiful stone terrace with plenty of patio seating. Each apartment includes a full kitchen and living area, WiFi, air conditioning, and a queen-size bed. The apartment complex is surrounded by quiet gardens and vineyards leading you down to a peaceful area of the waterfront, making it a perfect place for a romantic getaway.

trains from Novara run only a handful of times each day 6:45am-7:15pm daily. The last train from Orta-Miasino back to Novara departs at 7:52pm daily. You can purchase tickets online in advance and check full timetables for trains in both directions on www.trenitalia.com.

The main train station for the town of Orta San Giulio, Orta-Miasino, is roughly three kilometers (under two miles) away from the main part of the town along the lake. During daylight hours in the high season, you can catch the Trenino di Orta train that runs between the train station and the town for €3.50 each way. Trains run about every hour 9am-6pm daily. You can find the official timetable on www.treninodiorta.it.

However, luggage isn't allowed on the train, so if you are coming to Orta with luggage, you'll need to call a taxi from Orta-Miasino to get you to the main town. If the bar at the train station is open, the staff are always friendly and can help you call a taxi. Otherwise, you can go to www.taxilagodorta.it and book a taxi in advance for when you arrive, as it's rare to find one waiting outside of the station. Taxis to the center of town from the train station usually cost around €10-15, and the trip is only a few minutes.

FROM THE OTHER LAKES

BY CAR
From Lake Maggiore, it's a quick drive from the western side of the lake to Lake Orta. From Stresa, follow the SS33 until you get to Feriolo, then follow the signs to continue onto SS33 until you reach SP229 at a roundabout near Gravellona Toce. Follow SP229 road south, which will take you down to Orta San Giulio on the eastern shore of Lake Orta.

From the town of Como on Lake Como, head south on the A9 highway toward Milan until you reach the A36 tollway heading west just north of Saronno. From there, drive a few kilometers west before taking the E62/A8 exit and follow the signs toward Varese. Stay on the A8 until you reach the A26 exit toward Gravellona Toce. After about five kilometers (three miles) on this road, take the exit towards Arona and the ramp to Borgomanero. From there, take the SP142 until you reach SP229. Follow SP229 north until it becomes Via Panoramica, which takes you to Orta San Giulio. The whole trip is roughly 110 kilometers (68 miles) from the Como area to Orta San Giulio, and it generally takes about two hours.

From Lake Garda, you simply need to head back to Milan using the A4 highway. You'll continue driving over the northern part of the city on the A4 highway until you reach the Rho Fiera district, where you'll use the right two lanes to take the A8 exit toward Varese, then follow the outlined steps from Milan to Lake Orta.

BY TRAIN
From Lake Maggiore, you can catch a train from Stresa to Cuzzago (in between Lakes Maggiore and Orta), then from there to Orta-Miasino for a total of €4.40. The two train trips take around two hours one way, so you may be better off catching a bus or a taxi if you're wanting to save time. The train from Stresa to Cuzzago starts running around 6:15am each morning, with the last running at 6:20pm each evening, and only a handful of trips in between every day. All tickets can be purchased directly at each station, or online in

advance (where you'll also find a full timetable) at www.trenitalia.com.

From **Lake Como or Lake Garda,** your best bet is to travel back to Milan's Central Station first before taking the train from Milan to Novara, and then from Novara to Lake Orta. This would mean you're taking at least three trains from your starting point to your final destination, so you will need to set aside most of a day for travel or consider renting a car. From Como, grab a morning train (which starts running around 6am) from the Como San Giovanni station to Milan's Central Station for €4.80, before starting your trip to Lake Orta.

If you're coming from the southern end of Lake Garda, take the regional or *freccia* train from Peschiera del Garda or Desenzando del Garda in the morning, with trains running roughly every half hour to Milan's Central Station starting around 6am. All tickets can be purchased online in advance, and full timetables can be viewed at www.trenitalia.com.

BY BUS

During the high season (June-mid-September), you can catch a blue **SAF** bus from Stresa on Lake Maggiore to the villages of Omegna and Orta San Giulio. The bus runs only three times a day from Stresa, at 9am, 2pm, and 5pm from the Stresa train station, costing €11.00 for a one-way trip. Tickets can be purchased on board, and children ride free. Tickets are €3.55 from Stresa to Orta San Giulia, with the trip taking about 50 minutes. Official timetables can be found at www.safduemila.com.

BY TAXI

A handful of local taxi companies can arrange rides between Lake Maggiore and Lake Orta for around €50-70 each way. In addition to regular taxi trips between the two lakes, **Davide's BlueTaxi** in Stresa also offers guided taxi tours or private minivan tours that can accommodate small groups, so you're able to split the cost between your group, if needed. You can book taxis by calling ahead (338/179-2093) or by contacting them through the website (https://sites.google.com/site/bluetaxistresaorta).

Getting Around

BY TRAIN

The **Novara-Domodossola regional train line** stops at Orta-Miasino, Pettenasco, and Omegna with the trains running in either direction several times a day 6:45am-7:15pm daily. Tickets are €2-4, and the trips between the villages are usually around 10 minutes each. Official timetables and fares can be found at www.trenitalia.com.

BY BOAT

The public boat system runs frequently around Lake Orta each day during the high season (June-mid-September), so it's a great option for getting directly from one point to another on the lake. Most visitors want to see Isola San Giulio, and you can catch one of the many boats running between the island and Piazza Motta in Orta San Giulio daily. The ride is

The lake's public boat system offers quick trips from Piazza Motta to Isola San Giulio several times a day

just 10 minutes each way, and a round-trip ticket costs €3.15 in the peak season. Ferries run from Orta San Giulio to the island 10am-7pm daily.

You'll also find ferries running between the various lakeside villages such as Omegna, Pella, San Filiberto, Lagna, and Gozzano. You can find official timetables and fares for your journey at www.navigazionelago-dorta.it.

BY BUS

The Comazzi bus service runs a Novara-Domodossola line that stops in a few villages dotting the eastern shore of Lake Orta, including Omegna, Orta San Giulio, and Gozzano. This line only runs a handful of times each day, so it may not be the quickest or easiest way to travel between the villages, considering that the lake's official boat services run to each village and more frequently. Buses run about 5:30am-2:30pm roughly every hour, with a trip between each of the lake villages taking about 5-10 minutes

each. A journey between villages costs between €1-4, depending on the destination and starting point. You can find the official timetables and fares at www.comazzibus.com.

BY CAR

Traveling by car is the easiest and quickest way to get around Lake Orta. To access the villages along the eastern shore of the lake, including Orta San Giulio, take SP229, also known as Via Panoramica, which gives you beautiful views of the lake. On the western side of the lake, you can follow SP46 from the southern end to the northern end, although the road is not directly on the lake.

BY TAXI

While traveling by ferry is the most convenient way to village-hop on Lake Orta, you can splurge for a taxi around the lake if you're wanting a more private mode of transportation, or if you're traveling with a lot of luggage. Companies such as Davide's BlueTaxi (https://sites.google.com/site/bluetax-istresaorta) or Taxi d'Orta (www.taxi-lagodorta.it) offer taxi services between the villages around the entire lake, as well as to and from the Malpensa Airport, Lake Maggiore, and other areas in the region. Trips between villages can cost anywhere between €20-70, so it's not the most budget-friendly option. However, both companies offer customized taxi tours around the lake, and taxis can be booked ahead online through each website's contact form or by calling in advance.

LAKE GARDA

As Italy's largest lake, Garda is known by all as the "king" of Italian lakes, spanning a total area of 370 square kilometers (143 square miles). Sitting halfway between the cities of Brescia and Verona, the lake dominates a fairly large portion of north central Italy and serves as one of the most popular holiday destinations for Europeans year after year.

The southern end of Garda feels like a piece of Mediterranean paradise at the foot of the Italian Alps, with palm trees and little villages of colorful buildings stacked up against one another. As

HIGHLIGHTS

✪ **ROCCA SCALIGERA, SIRMIONE:** This medieval fortress lies directly in the blue waters of Lake Garda. Climb to the top of the towers for an aerial view of the entire castle as well as the surrounding village of Sirmione along the turquoise backdrop of the lake (page 254).

✪ **ISOLA DEL GARDA, SIRMIONE:** This privately owned island with a gorgeous villa is a true example of luxury and elegance with classic Northern Italian style. From March to October, grab a guided boat tour and discover the many charms (and uses) of Lake Garda's largest island over the years (page 254).

✪ **GARDALAND RESORT AND AMUSEMENT PARK, PESCHIERA DEL GARDA:** This family-friendly amusement park is one of the best-known theme parks in Italy, with thousands of locals as well as Europeans visiting every year for a full day of roller coasters, thrill rides, themed events, and more (page 263).

✪ **PUNTA SAN VIGILIO, BARDOLINO:** Lying just six kilometers (3.7 miles) north of Bardolino, this small peninsula is one of the most naturally beautiful spots on Lake Garda. Visit here for a peaceful outdoor experience (page 274).

✪ **MONTE BALDO, MALCESINE:** This towering mountain range serves as the backdrop of Lake Garda's northeastern shore, and is most easily accessible by a high-tech cable car from the village of Malcesine. Once at the top, catch picturesque aerial views of the northern part of the lake, paraglide from the top, or hike one of the many trails near the summit (page 281).

✪ **CASCATA DEL VARONE, RIVA DEL GARDA:** The beautiful waterfalls in Varone near Riva del Garda make for one of the most unique experiences in the region. Here you can walk through natural caves to view the falls from the very bottom up and feel the clear water pooling at your feet as you do. Likewise, you can view the falls from high above, looking down to experience the full length of the falls (page 288).

✪ **WATERSPORTS ON LAKE LEDRO:** Hop in a canoe, kayak, or paddleboard for an hour or two to enjoy the still water—free of noisy motorized boats and crowds of tourists (page 302).

you head north on the lake, you'll see towering mountains that are so dominating in their presence, they seem to push the relaxing villages right up against the water.

Lake Garda offers a little of everything, from water sports to amusement parks to historic villas and ancient Roman ruins. The towns dotting its shores are nothing short of vibrant and charming, with plenty of things to do and see—both indoors and outdoors. More than any other lake, Garda is family-friendly in nature, with plenty

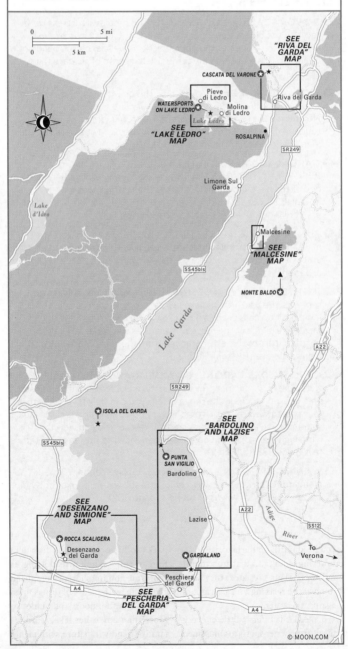

Lake Garda

0 — 5 mi
0 — 5 km

SEE "RIVA DEL GARDA" MAP

CASCATA DEL VARONE

Riva del Garda

WATERSPORTS ON LAKE LEDRO

Pieve di Ledro

Molina di Ledro

Lake Ledro

SEE "LAKE LEDRO" MAP

ROSALPINA

SR249

Lake d'Idro

Limone Sul Garda

Malcesine

SEE "MALCESINE" MAP

SS45bis

Lake Garda

MONTE BALDO

A22

SR249

ISOLA DEL GARDA

SEE "BARDOLINO AND LAZISE" MAP

SS45bis

PUNTA SAN VIGILIO

Bardolino

SEE "DESENZANO AND SIMIONE" MAP

Lazise

A22

Adige River

SS12

To Verona

ROCCA SCALIGERA

Desenzano del Garda

GARDALAND

Peschiera del Garda

SEE "PESCHERIA DEL GARDA" MAP

A4

A4

© MOON.COM

of events and activities for children. No matter how long you spend on Lake Garda, you'll never get bored.

ORIENTATION

As Italy's largest lake, Garda takes up a large chunk of the country's northern central area. It sits halfway between the cities of Brescia and Verona, and is divided between three provinces: Brescia (to the west), Verona (to the southeast) and Trentino (to the north). If you're starting at the southern end of the lake and working counter-clockwise, the towns are ordered as following: Desenzano del Garda, Sirmione, Peschiera del Garda, Lazise, Bardolino, Malcesine, Riva del Garda, and Limone Sul Garda.

Desenzano del Garda, on the southwestern shore of the lake, is one of the biggest towns on Lake Garda. In between Peschiera and Desenzano at the two southern corners, you'll find the peninsula of **Sirmione,** a historic medieval village sitting nearly directly in the center of Lake Garda's southern shore.

On the lake's eastern shore, from south to north, you have **Peschiera del Garda, Lazise, Bardolino,** and **Malecesine.** The first three towns make up the popular southeastern shore of the lake, with Peschiera sitting at the southeastern corner. There are only a few kilometers between each of these towns, so it's a short drive to get from one to the other. Malcesine sits along the northeastern shore, closer to Riva del Garda and **Monte Baldo,** the area's famous mountain range.

Riva del Garda is the northernmost town on the lake and is one of only two lake towns (Nago-Torbole is the other) in the Trentino province. On the western side of the shore, which

The walkable waterfront of Limone sul Garda is much smaller than that of other lakeside villages, but is still full of just as much charm and beauty.

isn't nearly as crowded with tourists as Lake Garda's eastern shore, is Limone sul Garda, which is a roughly 15-minute drive south of Riva Del Garda in the northern part of the lake. Despite being so close to Riva, it actually lies in the province of Brescia, not Trentino.

About 14 kilometers (9 miles) southeast of Riva del Garda sits Lake Ledro, a much smaller lake that can serve as an escape from the crowds on Garda. For a quiet day of vegging out on the beach with a picnic lunch or peaceful paddling uninterrupted by the din of motor boats, this is your spot.

PLANNING YOUR TIME

The best way to plan your time on Lake Garda is to understand what is easily accessible to you based on your primary mode of transportation.

If you're traveling by train, stick to Desenzano or Peschiera, which are two of the larger towns on the lake, and the only two served directly by train. Peschiera is also close to a number of interesting and family-friendly attractions, such as Gardaland and other smaller amusement parks, and there are shuttles to and from the train station to the parks, so a car isn't necessary.

If you're traveling by car, you have the luxury of all of the lake's towns at your fingertips. You could stay in one of the smaller towns on the southeastern side of the lake and hop between them. Each town offers its own charms, and with plenty of dining and accommodation options in each, so you shouldn't have trouble finding a place to stay with plenty of food, shopping, and lake activities around you.

Alternatively, you can spend a weekend in Riva del Garda and nearby Limone sul Garda if you're traveling by car, which has plenty of historic sights and watersports, all with a gorgeous backdrop of the surrounding Dolomites. Or you can opt to spend a day at peaceful Lake Ledro: At just 3.5 kilometers (2 miles) long and 1.5 kilometers (1 mile) wide, this tiny lake is perfect for spending a day canoeing, kayaking, paddle boating, or stand-up paddle boarding in calmer surroundings than the more popular Garda.

Give yourself at least two days on the lake if you plan on hopping between towns, but you can easily fill an entire week here based on the diverse range of things to do and see.

Lake Garda is one of Europe's most popular vacation destinations in the summer, so book your hotels as early as possible if you plan on staying here during the months of July and August.

Lake Garda has a slightly cooler climate than other regional lakes, with average temperatures hovering around 22°C (72°F) in the summer and lowering to 5°C (41°F) in the winter. The best months to visit for the highest water temperatures for swimming and water sports are June and July.

- **If you want family-friendly fun:** Head to Peschiera del Garda and spend a thrilling day at Gardaland or the underwater wonder of the Sealife Aquarium. Or, head to Lazise, where you'll find a smaller Hollywood-themed amusement park that includes a large waterpark.

- **If you want to avoid the crowds:** Stick to Bardolino in the spring or late summer, where you'll find a quieter, local vibe. Just north of the village, you'll find the beautiful, nature-oriented Punta San Vigilio peninsula.

- **If you enjoy outdoor recreation:** Spend a day on the water in Riva del Garda, where you can rent kayaks, stand-up paddleboards, sailboats, and more. Alternatively, head to higher altitude by trekking around one of the several hiking trails in this mountainous area.

- **If you want an easy trip from Milan:** Visit Desenzano del Garda, where you can shop your heart out and visit the historic peninsula of Sirmione, or to Peschiera del Garda for a walk around the shore.

- **If you want a good mix of history and nature:** Malcesine is your spot, with a medieval castle overlooking the lake as well as a huge, locally famous mountain from which you can paraglide or take a cable car up to the top.

Itinerary Ideas

LAKE GARDA ON DAY 1

For your first day on Lake Garda, start on the southern part of Lake Garda in **Desenzano del Garda.**

1 Start your morning with a hearty breakfast at your hotel, then head to the ferry station to grab a boat to **Sirmione.** Spend your morning exploring the **Rocca Scaligera castle.**

2 Head to the Roman ruins of **Grotte di Catullo** before grabbing a boat back to Desenzano.

3 Have lunch at **La Cambusa,** a small, cozy restaurant off of the lakefront known for its robust *tagliere* plates.

4 Walk off lunch by exploring the ruins of **Villa Romana.**

5 Wander the streets of Desenzano, popping into a few local stores. For a break, head to the **waterfront** and grab a seat and a gelato at one of the handful of gelaterias lining the shore.

6 Have dinner at **Molin22,** one of the highest-rated restaurants in Desenzano, serving quality Italian food near the waters of Lake Garda.

7 If you still have energy after a long day of exploring, head to Coco Beach for a night of dancing and drinks.

LAKE GARDA ON DAY 2

If you have a second day, explore the northern part of the lake in the beautiful town of Malcesine.

1 Grab breakfast at your hotel, then head straight to the center of town to grab the cable car up to the peak of Monte Baldo.

2 Once on Monte Baldo, spend your morning in the sun doing one of the several recreational activities on the mountain, such as paragliding or hiking the Peace Trail.

3 Head back down near the water for a casual, filling lunch of meat and other roasted treats at Speck & Stube.

4 In the afternoon, catch some rays right on the water at the free, public Lido Paina beach. The nearby bar offers drinks, snacks, and gelato.

5 From the beach, walk a little farther to the prominent Castello Scaligero, looming over the lake, for a more in-depth look into the village's history.

6 For dinner, try the locally beloved Ristorante Vecchia Malcesine for a full tasting menu of local flavors.

Desenzano del Garda and Sirmione

The town of Desenzano del Garda sits on the southwest corner of Lake Garda. Since the 1st century, it has been one of the preferred vacation spots for wealthy Veronese and has since grown as a favorite spot for many tourists from Germany, Austria, and Switzerland.

The colorful town has quite the breadth of things to do and see: Roman ruins and castles at your fingertips, relaxing beaches, fine dining and casual restaurants, plenty of nightclubs, and bars that stay open late. If you plan to spend a night or two here, you can select from the more than 25 major hotels and dozens of other accommodation options. Despite it being Lake Garda's most bustling town, it is no less charming or beautiful than its smaller sibling villages.

The village of Sirmione, located on a narrow peninsula of the same name that juts up from the southern, is just 10 kilometers (6 miles) northwest of Desenzano. The historic village is

Lake Garda Itinerary Ideas

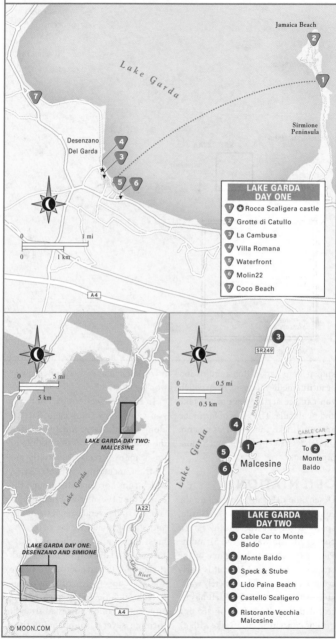

Jamaica Beach

Lake Garda

Sirmione
Peninsula

Desenzano
Del Garda

LAKE GARDA DAY ONE

1 ⊕ Rocca Scaligera castle
2 Grotte di Catullo
3 La Cambusa
4 Villa Romana
5 Waterfront
6 Molin22
7 Coco Beach

0 — 1 mi
0 — 1 km

A4

LAKE GARDA DAY TWO: MALCESINE

0 — 5 mi
0 — 5 km

LAKE GARDA DAY ONE: DESENZANO AND SIMIONE

Lake Garda

A22

Adige River

A4

© MOON.COM

SR249

VIA PANZANO

CABLE CAR

To 2
Monte
Baldo

Malcesine

LAKE GARDA DAY TWO

1 Cable Car to Monte Baldo
2 Monte Baldo
3 Speck & Stube
4 Lido Paina Beach
5 Castello Scaligero
6 Ristorante Vecchia Malcesine

251

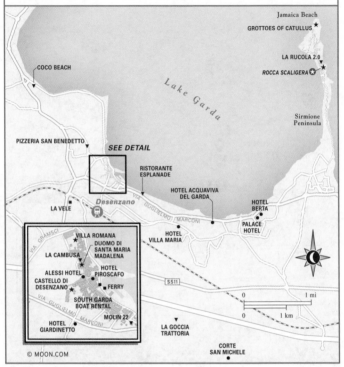

Desenzano and Sirmione

Jamaica Beach
GROTTOES OF CATULLUS ★
LA RUCOLA 2.0 ■
ROCCA SCALIGERA ●★
Sirmione
Peninsula

Lake Garda

COCO BEACH ▷

PIZZERIA SAN BENEDETTO

SEE DETAIL

RISTORANTE
ESPLANADE

Desenzano

HOTEL ACQUAVIVA
DEL GARDA

HOTEL
BERTA
PALACE
HOTEL

LA VELE ■

VIA GUGLIELMO MARCONI

HOTEL
VILLA MARIA

VILLA ROMANA ★
DUOMO DI
SANTA MARIA
MADALENA
LA CAMBUSA ★
HOTEL
PIROSCAFO
ALESSI HOTEL ■
CASTELLO DI
DESENZANO ★
■ FERRY
SOUTH GARDA
BOAT RENTAL
MOLIN 22
HOTEL ●
GIARDINETTO

VIA GRAMSCI

VIA GUGLIELMO MARCONI

S511

LA GOCCIA
TRATTORIA

0   1 mi
0   1 km

CORTE
SAN MICHELE ●

© MOON.COM

known for its park of Roman ruins and beautiful medieval castle, from which you can see aerial views of the lake and peninsula. The vibes of Sirmione are much like those of Desenzano, though its deep history is much more prominent.

ORIENTATION

Desenzano del Garda, located on the southwestern shore of Lake Garda, spans from the far southwestern corner all the way to the Sirmione Peninsula. Despite being one of the largest towns on the lake, it is fairly compact and mostly completely walkable. Although the town itself has no real structure (it is not organized by a grid or concentric circles like Milan),

if you stick to a few main streets, you won't get lost.

In the northwestern part of town, you can follow Lungolago Battisti along the lakeshore until you reach the Roman Villa. In the middle of town, many streets are strictly pedestrian, including Via Santa Maria, which runs horizontally through the core of the city center, and along which you will find several bars, restaurants, and shops, including La Vele. The most important churches and piazzas are found directly off of this road. If you want to drive across town, use Via Marconi, which runs horizontally through the southern part of the city center. Follow this road straight through several roundabouts then eastward, and you will see signs pointing toward the Sirmione Peninsula, on which the town of Sirmione sits 10 kilometers (6 miles) northeast of Desenzano.

If you want to visit Coco Beach, a popular nightspot in Lonato del Garda, follow Lungolago Battisti north until it turns into Via Vo'. The town in which the club is located is only a few kilometers north of the main part of Desenzano.

SIGHTS

DESENZANO DEL GARDA
Cathedral of Saint Mary Magdalene (Duomo Di Santa Maria Maddalena)

Via Roma, 5, Desenzano del Garda; 030/991-4164; www.duomodesenzano.it; 8:30am-6:30pm daily; free

Sitting in the center of Desenzano is the Duomo Di Santa Maria Maddalena, the town's main cathedral and religious heart. The facade features Baroque-style details, and the inside is full of paintings depicting the life cycle of Mary Magdalene. Inside you'll also notice these immense arched columns and darkly frescoed ceilings, illuminated by the natural lighting streaming through the grid-like patterned windows. As this church holds frequent mass services, it's best to remain quiet during your visit so as to not disturb the worshippers.

Villa Romana

Via Crocefisso, 22, Desenzano del Garda; 030/914-3547; www.comune.desenzano. brescia.it/italian/villa.php; 8:30am-7pm Tues.-Sun.; adults €4, 18 and under free

Although the Roman ruins that laid for centuries under Desenzano's city center were not discovered until the 1920s, their origins date back to a villa built in the 1st century BCE—a villa that represents one of the most significant pieces of history in this region. At that time, the villa with its piers and moorings overlooked the lake. Since its discovery, the space has been fenced in and gated, and is now surrounded by residential buildings in a tranquil corner of the center of town. Today, you can walk around the covered ruins, which are perfectly outlined in the villa's blueprint, in less than an hour. You can also read about the history of the villa in English and Italian.

Desenzano's Villa Romana is full of ancient Roman ruins visible from the streets surrounding the old villa structure.

Castello di Desenzano

Via Castello, Desenzano del Garda; 030/374-8726; www.comune.desenzano. brescia.it/italian/castello.php; 10am-12:30pm and 3pm-6pm Tues.-Sun.; adults €3, under 18 or over 65 €1

Castello di Desenzano, the historic castle overlooking Lake Garda and the town of Desenzano, houses a small museum outlining the history of the 11th-century fortress and its four angular towers. The castle takes on an irregular rectangular plan, with the grey sonte walls slightly crumbling, showing the age of the fortress. Today, you can climb up to the highest tower to reach the panoramic observatory, from which you can catch an aerial view of the surrounding town and the southern shore of Lake Garda. You can also walk along the outer walls and towers, and down to the lower level of the castle for a peek at an ancient collection of old military arms. This is a great option if you can not or do not want to make your way to the castle in Sirmione.

from the towers of Rocca Scaligera castle in Sirmione

SIRMIONE

✪ Rocca Scaligera

Piazza Castello, 34, Sirmione; 030/2896-5218; www.polomuseale. lombardia.beniculturali.it/index.php/ castello-scaligero; 8:30am-7:30pm Tues.-Sun.; adults €6, 18 and under and over 65 €3

Rocca Scaligera, also known as the Scaligera Castle of Sirmione, originally served as a battle fortress during the Scaligeri era in the 13th and 14th centuries. The white stone castle, surrounded by the calm, gorgeous turquoise waters of Lake Garda, is one of the most visited and beautiful sights in the area. The castle's sturdy walls were built into the lake, along with its three giant towers. Heading up to the towers for the views is a must-do, as is visiting the boat dock near the water for a better understanding of how the castle functioned when it was in use.

Inside the castle, you'll find an exhibit outlining the history and importance of the castle during Roman and medieval times; descriptive placards are available in several languages, including English. Do not leave without climbing the wooden staircase up to the tower keep for an awesome panoramic view of the castle, village, and the surrounding lake—definitely one of the most breathtaking views you

will experience. The elevated walkways that connect the walls and towers also offer an experience that no other castle offers.

Grottoes of Catullus

Piazza Orti Manara, 4, Sirmione; 030/916-157; www.grottedicatullo. beniculturali.it; 8:30am-7:30pm Tues.-Sat., 9:30am-6:30pm Sun.; adults €6, 18 and under free, free first Sunday of the month

These Roman ruins at the tip of the Sirmione Peninsula were originally part of a 1st-century Roman villa that overlooked the southern shore of Lake Garda, and today they are part of a large park dedicated to the villa's remains. The park leads you through various levels and sections of the former villa, with signs (in Italian and English) identifying the room you're standing in and its purpose. It's easy to feel the historical impact of this place, how somber and peaceful it is as you gaze out at the waters of the lake. The best time to visit is in the morning on weekends or on a weekday, when you'll likely have the place mostly to yourself to wander about at your leisure.

✪ Isola del Garda

San Felice del Benaco; 328/612-6943; www. isoladelgarda.com; daily tours Mar.-Oct., €31-38

Isola del Garda is Lake Garda's largest island and has been used in various ways over the centuries, including as a pirate's retreat, Roman burial site, Franciscan monastery, and fortification. Today, this still beautiful, but now private, island owned by the Cavazza family is home to **Villa Borghese Cavazza**—a villa surrounded by Italian and English gardens and the quintessential example of Northern Italian luxury and elegance. The Cavazza family opens their private island to visitors March-October each year. From Sirmione (at the main docking area along the peninsula), you can grab a private boat once a day to and from the island on Tuesdays and Thursdays. Each ride is about a half an hour each way.

Upon arrival to the island you'll be welcomed with a glass of wine. The engaging tour (approx. two hours) will teach you a great deal about the historical and cultural significance of the island, as well as throughout the villa, including the private rooms

Isola del Garda is the largest island on Lake Garda, with a stunning and luxurious private villa that offers guided tours in the summer

where much of the elegant and antique furniture are prominently displayed. You'll also be taken throughout the magnificent gardens, where you'll find groomed hedges and a plethora of fruit trees including grapefruit, lemons, pears, pomegranates, and capers.

In addition to arriving from Sirmione, guests can also board from other villages along Lake Garda's shores, including Lazise, Bardolino, Manerba, and San Felice del Benaco. An official timetable with prices is available on the island's website.

SPORTS AND RECREATION
BEACHES AND WATERSPORTS
Jamaica Beach
Lago di Garda, Sirmione; 24 hours daily; free
If you're looking for a local hangout that is totally free, hit Jamaica Beach for a few hours or for a full day of sun and swimming. No frills here; the public spot sits just next to the Grottoes of Catullus in Sirmione, where you'll see locals grab their beach gear and set up camp on the flat rocks near the shallow waters for a full day of fun. Pack a lunch, grab some towels, and set up early here, as this free spot fills up fast in the summer. Simply follow the walking path down from Grottoes of Catullus, where you'll find the flat rocky area as well as beach bar selling drinks, gelato, and traditional *aperitivo* food, including olives, potato chips, peanuts, finger sandwiches, and cold cuts.

South Garda Boats Rental
Piazza Ulisse Papa, 5, Desenzano Del Garda; 333/534-7687; www.gardaboatrent.com; 9am-6pm daily; €70+
Whether you want to rent a private boat or jump on a guided boat tour

around the southern end of Lake Garda, South Garda Boats Rental has you covered. Boats can be rented hourly or up to a week at a time, starting from €70 per hour. Boats can be rented with or without a boating license, with smaller boats with a capacity of up to eight people available for those without a license. Insurance and a full tank are included in the price of each hour or day, although other petrol fill-ups come out of your pocket. If you're not wanting to rent a boat but still wanting an experience on the water, the company offers several private and group boat tours, ranging from romantic sunset cruises with wine and *aperitivo* included to quick, fun tours showing you the shoreline of each southern Garda village. Tours can last anywhere from a couple hours to entire days and accommodate up to 28 people per tour. Prices range from €90-450 per boat, but official quotes are given based on the number of people and tour selected. The company's website also outlines recommended self-tours for boat rentals, which can be pre-rented directly from the website or by calling ahead. With more than 30 boats, there are several options, but book far ahead if you plan on renting during July or August.

WALKS
From Desenzano to Sirmione
Lungolago shoreline in the middle of Desenzano

While the southern shore of Lake Garda isn't as known for hiking as is the northern part of the lake, you'll still find a handful of nice, flat trails on which to spend a few hours of your day. The trail from the center of Desenzano to the village of Sirmione on the Sirmione Peninsula is one of them. Start your journey on the

waterfront in the center of town, then continue east along the shore, following the water's edge for nearly 10 kilometers (6 miles) over a course of a couple of hours. Along the way, you'll encounter plenty of bars, restaurants, and benches to stop for a break or simply admire the water at your feet. Once you're in Sirmione, you can turn back and walk the same way that you came, or you can take a ferry back to Desenzano.

NIGHTLIFE
Coco Beach
Via Catullo, 5, Lonato del Garda; 392/172-1659; www.cocobeachclub.com; 8pm-4am; €15-20

Coco Beach is one of Lake Garda's most popular disco clubs. On the weekends, this place gets flooded by young locals, mostly between the ages of 20-30 years old, coming for a night of popular new music spun by DJs, drinking, and dancing. On Friday and Saturday evenings, starting at 9:30pm, you can reserve a dinner table for your group. On Sundays you'll find a happy hour buffet starting at 6pm, but the club doesn't come to life until midnight. In the summer, you'll find an interesting mix of locals and international tourists filling the multiple dance floors and beach-style lounge furniture. The first drink is included in the entrance price, with all subsequent drinks costing around €10 each. There is also a restaurant and beach that you can enjoy during the day.

SHOPPING
La Vele
Via Guglielmo Marconi, 1, Localitá Viadotto, Desenzano del Garda; 030/912-0435; http://levele.info; 9am-8pm daily

The small shopping complex on La Vele features a handful of shops selling anything from clothing, footwear, gastronomy products, home goods, sports gear, accessories, books, and more. The small mall has a nice balance of department chains such as Geox and H&M, and local shops selling local products. The complex also has a few Italian bars and restaurants where you can grab a quick bite between stores. Located just outside the main part of Desenzano, the two-story mall also offers a free parking garage for shoppers and is a great spot for those wanting to get out of the town center for a while.

FOOD
CASUAL DINING
Pizzeria San Benedetto

Via S. Benedetto, 151, Desenzano del Garda; 030/999-1976; 6pm-11pm daily; €7-15

For a classic Italian dinner that doesn't break the bank, head to Pizzeria San Benedetto in the center of Desenzano for a traditional pizza and beer combo. The atmosphere is casual, and you can see your pizzas being put into the large brick oven as soon as it's made. Pizzas range from simple margaritas to those with plenty of toppings, such as sausages, pepperoni, potatoes, zucchini, and more. Tables can be booked, which isn't a bad idea on weekends, and pizzas can also be called in and taken to go.

✪ La Cambusa

Via Canonica 12, Desenzano Del Garda; 342/762-7535; 10:30am-2am Mon., Tues., Thurs.-Sat., 10:30am-12am Sun., 3:30pm-1am Wed.; €15-25

This tiny, hole-in-the-wall restaurant sits back from the lake, in a quiet corner in the center of Desenzano, and is known mostly for its robust *tagliere* plates of local meats, cheeses, honeys, and jams. You really can't have a complete meal here without starting with a

La Cambusa in Desenzano is known for their robust and delicious *tagliere* plates full of local meats, cheeses, and honey.

tagliere. From there, you'll find a small menu of Italian classics such as lasagna and spaghetti. The cozy and unpretentious atmosphere is accented by mismatched decorations, plates, and mugs. At the front of the restaurant where you pay your bill, you'll find a selection of local products available for purchase. Book ahead here in the evenings, as the tables are limited and can fill up.

FINE DINING
La Goccia Trattoria

Location Montonale Basso, 13, Desenzano del Garda; 030/910-3194; www. lagocciatrattoria.it; 12pm-2:30pm and 7:30pm-11:00pm Thurs.-Tues.; €20-45

This Pugliese restaurant located on the lake offers a comfortable yet refined atmosphere and a large menu of housemade pastas and lake fish. You'll find seafood platters brimming over with oysters and shrimp, handmade stuffed ravioli, crab legs, and plenty of vegetable side dishes. Sit inside for a white-tablecloth experience under the exposed wood-beamed ceilings and brick-and-stone walls, or outside on the patio surrounded by colorful flowers and greenery. Save room for a dessert prepared right at your table, including seasonal fruits, chocolates, creams, and more. Book ahead, especially in the evenings.

Molin22

Via Tommaso dal Molin, 22, Desenzano del Garda; 030/991-4437; www.molin22.it; 12pm-10pm Tues.-Fri., 10am-11pm Sat. and Sun.; €25-50

Dining on the terrace at Molin22 with a sensational cocktail in hand is one of the hidden treats of Desenzano. The large patio seating overlooks the blue waters of Lake Garda, and customers come back for the innovative and well-balanced cocktails time and time again. Dishes are classic Italian with a modern twist, so you'll see traditional local ingredients such as Garda olive oil, tomatoes, pastas, and risottos mixed with fresh cheeses and asparagus, or paired with black sepia chips or colorful flowers. If you want to stay away from the lunch crowd, stop by in the late afternoon for a cocktail at happy hour.

❂ La Rucola 2.0

Strentelle Pass, 7, Sirmione; 030/916-326; www.ristorantelarucola.it; 12pm-10pm daily; €30-70

La Rucola 2.0 is a Michelin-star restaurant known for its innovative and modern cuisine that is so beautifully plated that it looks like art that you shouldn't touch. The flavors of each dish, from the risotto with roasted rabbit to the octopus and tuna, are strong and perfectly balanced, composed of the highest-quality ingredients. The atmosphere is modern and upscale without feeling pretentious, and the

staff is knowledgeable and attentive. You can opt for the daily fixed menu or an à la carte menu. Book ahead, regardless of when you're coming, as this place really is a treat and stays busy.

Ristorante Esplanade

Via Lario 3, Desenzano del Garda; 030/914-3361; www.ristorante-esplanade. com; 12:30pm-1:45pm and 8-10pm daily; €30-70

Ristorante Esplanade is a great fine-dining spot and offers one of the best views of Lake Garda. Food here is high quality and beautifully presented, with plates including raw seafood, fresh cheeses, homemade pastas, and sensational desserts full of chocolates and fruits. Customers consistently rave about the exceptional, attentive, and friendly service here, with staff well prepared to help you make the best of your experience from start to finish. The ambience leans toward elegant, so dress accordingly and book ahead, specifically requesting a table on the terrace for lulling views of the water.

ACCOMMODATIONS

UNDER €80

Hotel Giardinetto

Via Guglielmo Marconi, 33, Desenzano del Garda; 030/914-1228; www. hotel-giardinetto.com/reservation.html; €77

Located in the center of Desenzano is this classic, simple, family-run hotel with free parking and a breakfast buffet included in each room. The exterior is surrounded by colorful plants, and the area is full of plenty of restaurants, bars, and shopping. Each room includes a private bathroom with toiletries, air conditioning, safe, television, and WiFi. For those looking for a comfortable stay without any frills, Hotel Giardinetto is a great choice.

€80-150

✪ Corte San Michele

Località San Michele, 1, Desenzano
del Garda; 333/774-9532; www.
cortesanmichele.it; €80

This quaint and modern B&B features exposed stone walls and bright guest rooms with handmade quilts, exposed wood-beamed ceilings, and antique furniture. The homemade breakfast each morning is plentiful and delicious, and the property is near the lake and includes a peaceful outdoor swimming pool and a large garden. Each room includes air conditioning, WiFi, and a private bathroom. Parking is included.

Hotel Berta

Via Costantino il Grande, 7, Desenzano
del Garda; 030/911-9600; www.
hotelbertadesenzanodelgarda.it; €90

Just 100 meters (109 yards) from the shores of Lake Garda sits Hotel Berta, a simple hotel with modern rooms and classic furniture, creating a comfortable yet unpretentious stay for guests. The small outdoor pool is surrounded by lounge chairs, patio furniture, and plenty of greenery. Each room includes air conditioning, a private bathroom with toiletries, a television, WiFi, and a safe. A classic Italian breakfast is included in the price of each room, and an airport shuttle can be arranged upon request for an additional fee.

Alessi Hotel

Via Castello, 3, Desenzano del Garda;
030/914-1980; www.hotelalessi.com; €95

The modern, sleek guest rooms at Alessi Hotel are a nice option for those wanting an upscale feel without emptying their wallets. Located in the center of Desenzano and just a stone's throw away from the shore, the hotel includes an internal courtyard as well as two restaurants, a wine bar, a pizzeria, and a terrace. Each room includes a patio or balcony with a garden or city view, air conditioning, and a private bathroom. A large, diverse breakfast buffet and parking are included.

Hotel Piroscafo

Via Porto Vecchio, 11, Desenzano del Garda;
030/914-1128; www.hotelpiroscafo.it; €132

Located in the heart of Desenzano, the Hotel Piroscafo sits right on the shore of Lake Garda and is surrounded by tons of restaurants, bars, shopping, and entertainment, making it an optimal choice for those traveling without a car (although parking is included for guests). The interior is simple and bright, with hints of exposed stone walls to show the history of the building. Each guest room includes air conditioning, WiFi, and private bathroom with toiletries. A large breakfast buffet is included.

€150-250

Hotel Villa Maria

Via Michelangelo, 150, Desenzano del Garda;
030/990-1725; www.villamariadesenzano.
it; €156

This beautiful villa sits outside of Desenzano, so it's a great option for those traveling with a car and wanting some peace and quiet during their stay on the lake, which is only about a five-minute walk away from the property. The villa is surrounded by a large park with giant, ancient trees and includes an outdoor swimming pool, tennis court, and free access to the gardens. Each guest room includes air conditioning, WiFi, private bathroom, and sofa. The property also includes a restaurant onsite, and breakfast and parking are included.

Hotel Acquaviva del Garda

Viale Francesco Agello, 84, Desenzano del Garda; 030/990-1583; www. termedisirmione.com; €180

Hotel Acquaviva del Garda is about three kilometers (just under two miles) outside the main part of Desenzano del Garda, so it's a tranquil option for those with cars wanting a relaxing, upscale getaway near the lake. Apart from the modern building and interior, the hotel includes an outdoor pool and a private beach as well as a beautiful, colorful garden with views of the lake and Sirmione. The wellness center includes an indoor pool, a hot tub, sauna, and Turkish bath. Each room includes a balcony with a garden or lake view, air conditioning, WiFi, and a private bathroom. A large breakfast buffet is included in the price of each room, as is parking.

✪ Palace Hotel

Viale F. Agello, 114A, Desenzano del Garda; 030/990-2262; www.palacehoteldesenzano. it; €192

This bright and elegant hotel sits right on Lake Garda, and includes a huge pool overlooking the lake and surrounded by plenty of green plants and lounge chairs as well as a smaller, intimate infinity pool. The modern interior is classically furnished, with a wellness center that includes a sauna and Turkish bath as well as a selection of massage treatments. Each guest room includes a private patio with a garden view, air conditioning, a private bathroom with bathtub, and a small living area. A large, fresh breakfast and parking are included in the price of each room.

INFORMATION AND SERVICES

The official **tourist office** in Desenzano (Via Porto Vecchio, 34; 9am-12pm and 3pm-6pm Mon.-Sat.) is located in the center of town. From here, you can grab a free physical map of the city and learn more about the local attractions, dining, and accommodation options from the English-speaking staff.

In case of emergencies, you can find the local *questura* (police) office at Via Dante Alighieri, 17. You need to press the buzzer outside of the gate to enter the building at any time of day or night, and you can call 118 in case of emergencies. The **hospital** of Desenzano is found at Località Montecroce (030/91-451), and it is open 24 hours a day.

GETTING THERE
BY CAR

From **Milan,** or from any of the other lakes east of Garda except for Iseo, head east on the major A4 tollway until you reach the exit off of A4 for Desenzano del Garda. Follow the signs directing you to the city center. The whole trip from Milan is approximately 121 kilometers (75 miles) and will take about 1.5 hours to drive.

From **Lake Iseo,** you can drive down the SP510 highway that runs along the eastern shore of the lake until you reach the A4 tollway near Brescia, then follow the tollway east until you reach Desenzano. From the town of Iseo to Desenzano, it's a 40-minute trip of roughly 50 kilometers (31 miles).

From the northern part of the lake, such as from **Riva del Garda,** your quickest way to Desenzano is via the A22 highway on the eastern side of the lake. When you're heading south on A22, take the SR11 exit, then follow the SR11 west toward Desenzano. Once you're in the Desenzano area, after about 20 kilometers (12 miles), take the Desenzano center exit. From Riva del Garda to Desenzano, the entire trip is about 93 kilometers (60 miles), which is about a 1.25-hour drive. If you're coming from Lake Molveno, you'll also need to reach the A22 highway and head south following the same directions. From Lake Molveno, the trip is about 1.75 hours over 143 kilometers (89 miles).

BY TRAIN

Desenzano falls directly on the main rail line connecting Milan and Venice, which means that both *freccia* (fast) and regional trains running between the two cities stop in town. Trains departing Milan's Central Station run roughly every 30 minutes 6:25am-10:25pm, with one-way fast train tickets starting around €15 and one-way regional trains around €10. Travel duration from Milan on a *freccia* train is about 50 minutes to Desenzano and on a regional train it is about 70 minutes. Tickets can be purchased online in advance at https://trenitalia.com or directly at any train station.

GETTING AROUND

As with every town on Lake Garda, the center of the village is entirely walkable, unless you're wanting to get to more remote restaurants or accommodations.

BY CAR

To drive to the village of **Sirmione** from Desenzano, follow Via Marconi east, staying straight on the road (it eventually turns into Via Molin, then Viale Agello), until you reach Via Colombare, where you need to turn left to head north into the peninsula. From the center of Desenzano to the village of Sirmione, it's about a 25-minute drive spanning 10 kilometers (6.2 miles).

For those wanting to reach **Coco Beach,** you can do so by following Lungolago Battisti north until it turns into Via Vo'. The club is only a few kilometers north of the main part of town, which is about a 5-10 minute drive. While there are a handful of paid parking lots or street parking near the center of town, remember that these lots tend to fill up quickly during high season, so you're more likely to find a spot the earlier in the day you arrive.

BY BOAT

Traveling by boat is the quickest way to get between Desenzano and Sirmione, if you're without a car. From the Desenzano ferry station in the center of town, you can take a 20-minute ferry, which generally departs for Sirmione every hour 8am-10pm June-October. A one-way ticket costs around €3 per person. Official fares and timetables can be found at www.navigazionelaghi.it.

AROUND DESENZANO DEL GARDA

VITTORIALE D'ITALIA

Via Vittoriale, 12, Gardone Riviera; 0365/296-511; www.vittoriale.it; 9am-8pm Apr.-Oct., 9am-5pm rest of the year; adults €16, under 18 and over 65 €13

In the village of Gardone Riviera, roughly 25 kilometers (15.5 miles) north of Desenzano via route SP572, sits the villa named Vittoriale d'Italia, the former home of famous Italian writer Gabriele d'Annunzio. The historic and gorgeous property sits on a hillside overlooking the lake and includes several buildings and structures, including an amphitheater, the *prioria* (priory, d'Annunzio's former residence), and a mausoleum. As one of the most famous villas in Italy, the huge and historic property sees thousands of European visitors each year.

The villa originally belonged to a German art historian but was rented by d'Annunzio in the 1920s, who eventually renovated and owned it. Because the writer strongly disagreed with Italy's fascist government and alliance with Nazi Germany at the time, the Italian government was happy to keep the writer occupied near the lake and away from politics in Rome, offering him 10 million lire to expand and renovate the property. Over time, the estate was nicknamed a "fascist lunapark" because of its funding source and the visit Benito Mussolini made in 1925.

Today, you can visit the entire property, though only by guided tour, which takes a couple of hours, and read about its historic and cultural significance. You'll be guided through each room of the villa, all of which are filled with so much colorful detail that it can be almost overwhelming to soak in (just wait until you see the dining room). The interior is still full of antique furniture, and despite the historical ties to Fascism, the property is truly a work of art. Although you can only book guided Italian tours in advance, call ahead to see if you can arrange an English tour, and know that many of the signs you see around the property are also written in English.

From Desenzano, you can reach the complex by taking the SP572 northwest, then continue north along the western shore of Lake Garda. Once you get to the Campoverde area after about 23 kilometers (14 miles), take the roundabout exit to follow the SS45bis northeast for about five kilometers (three miles) until you reach Via Vittoriale. Turn onto this road and follow it until you reach the villa. The entire trip is about a half-hour drive spanning 26 kilometers (15.5 miles).

Peschiera del Garda

The colorful resort town of Peschiera del Garda sits on the southeastern corner of Lake Garda, roughly 15 kilometers (9 miles) east of Desenzano del Garda and 25 kilometers (15 miles) west of the city of Verona. The town is a wonderfully family-friendly place to visit, with resorts, beaches, and lakeside walkways. And next to Peschiera del Garda is the small village of Castelnuovo del Garda, which is home to Gardaland, one of the most popular amusement parks in Europe. Still, there is plenty of old-world charm to be had in Peschiera, as a stroll through the historic center full of rainbow-hued buildings, local boutiques, and restaurants will show.

Peschiera falls on the main rail line connecting Milan and Venice, so it is an ideal place to stay for those traveling without a car. And for those with a car, its proximity to Lazise and Bardolino, other charming villages on the eastern shores of Lake Garda, make Peschiera a nice basecamp for your visit to the region.

Peschiera del Garda

BRACCOBALDO BEACH

Lake Garda

To ★GARDALAND RESORT
AND AMUSEMENT PARK
and Gardaland
Sea Life Aquarium

VINO E DINTORNI

SR11

VIA MILANO

SR249

IL PENTAGONO
BOAT TOURS   FERRY

MARCO AND
DANIELA TIME   BAR AL PORTO

HOTEL
GARDEN

OSTERIA
RIVELIN

Peschiera
Del Garda

VIA VENCIONI

SR249

0   500 yds

0   500 m

SR11

A4

© MOON.COM

To Parc Hotel

SIGHTS

HISTORIC TOWN CENTER

Town Center, bounded by Via Mantova
(west), Via Nencioni (east), the SR11 (south),
and the shoreline (north)

To pass a pleasant hour or two in
Peschiera, simply wander around the
charming, historic center against the
backdrop of the sparkling lake waters and ancient Venetian city walls.
Enjoy the Mediterranean feel in the air
as you browse through clothing boutiques, leather goods shops, family-run
restaurants, bars with flower-draped
patio seating, and more. Hopping
from one establishment to another is a
treat in and of itself, as the owners are
friendly and welcome you in, inviting
you to stay for as long as you please.

Foodies and shoppers are sure to find
the perfect souvenir here.

⊕ GARDALAND RESORT AND AMUSEMENT PARK

Via Derna, 4, Castelnuovo del Garda;
045/644-9777; www.gardaland.it;
10am-6pm late Mar.-late Sept., 10am-11pm
Jul.-Sept.; adults €40.50, 10 and under and
age 60 and over €32.50

The Gardaland Resort and
Amusement Park is Peschiera del
Garda's main draw year after year,
drawing more than three million visitors since it first opened in 1975. Not
only is it Italy's most visited and most
beloved theme park spanning 26 hectares (64 acres) but it is one of Europe's
most popular parks as well. Sitting on
the eastern shore of Lake Garda, the

Gardaland Amusement Park is Italy's most popular theme park, full of roller coasters, thrill rides, themed areas, and more.

park actually faces away from the lake, and is divided into multiple-themed areas such as Camelot, Arabia, Rio Bravo, and Fantasy Kingdom.

The park also hosts a variety of rides including roller coasters, water rides, inside rides, thrill rides, and family rides. For roller coaster fans, don't miss the giant Blue Tornado with its double inline twist ending, or the Shaman with its double loop and double corkscrew. You'll also find plenty of bars and food stalls selling everything from chocolate-covered waffles to American food in the park, as well as an Italian cafeteria. The place is packed on the weekends and on the special theme nights (especially at Halloween), so visit during the weekdays and in the mornings if you want to avoid long queues; waits can get up to an hour long during peak season.

To make a holiday out of it, you can stay at one of the resorts near the park to receive discounts on park entrances and other package deals: The Gardaland Hotel (www.gardalandhotel.it, €132 per night) or the Gardaland Adventure Hotel (www.gardalandadventurehotel.it, €147 per night). In addition to its regular opening season,

the park is open during certain times in October, November, December, and January for special themed events. Official timetables can be found on the website. I recommend purchasing tickets online, as you will get a discount (€36 per adult). Kids under one meter (3 feet, 3 inches) are always granted free admission.

To get from the center of Peschiera del Garda to Gardaland, take the SR249 northeast, following the signs to the aquarium along the way. It's about a 10-minute drive over 4 kilometers (2.5 miles).

GARDALAND SEA LIFE AQUARIUM

Via Derna, 4, Castelnuovo del Garda;
045/644-9777; www.gardalandsealife.it;
10am-6pm daily Apr.-Oct.; €10.50-16

Like many sea life aquariums around the world, the aquarium in Peschiera is a family-friendly, interactive space with both fresh and saltwater creatures from all over the world. For most visitors, the top attraction is walking through the transparent ocean tunnel, completely surrounded by blue waters and hundreds of fish, including sharks. Visitors can also witness daily shark feedings and watch a quick film on marine life. Small pools scattered throughout the aquarium invite children to interact with the marine life. There's also a decent restaurant on the property serving quick snacks and drinks. You can purchase an individual aquarium ticket, or buy one in combination with a ticket to Gardaland for €43.50. The aquarium is generally closed during the winter months of November-March, but there are a few days in that period when it is open. Official timetables can be found directly on the website.

To get from the center of Peschiera

del Garda to the aquarium by car, take the SR249 northeast, following the signs to the aquarium along the way. It's about a 10-minute drive over 4 kilometers (2.5 miles). Alternatively, you can catch the free shuttle bus between the Peschiera del Garda train station during the park's opening hours. The shuttle departs from both the park and the station every half hour, and the journey takes 5-10 minutes each way.

SPORTS AND RECREATION

BOAT TOURS
Il Pentagono Boat Tours

Central Harbor Peschiera del Garda, Riviera Carducci, 1, Peschiera del Garda; 340/905-8331; www.pentagonorent.com; 9am-6:30pm daily Mar.-Oct.; deposit €150, €30 per hour

For a little lake fun off of the shore, rent a boat from the Il Pentagono boat company, a local group of boatmen that are incredibly friendly and knowledgeable about Lake Garda. Not only do they offer boat rentals, they also give you the best advice for your tour around the lake. Boats can be rented by the hour or the day, starting at €30 without gas or €50 with gas. During high season, I strongly recommended renting a boat for less than four hours

the sun setting over Peschiera Del Garda's main port full of local fishing boats

with fuel included, so you can avoid the long lines for gas. You can always book a boat by calling in advance. Personalized quotes are available if you're wanting to rent a boat for multiple days. To rent a boat, a deposit is required along with a valid identification card and phone number.

BEACHES
Braccobaldo Beach

Locality Fornaci, Peschiera del Garda; 342/125-4336; www.pentagonorent.com; 9:30am-6:30pm daily; €6-18

The Il Pentagono boat company also offers private beach access for those wanting to relax on the shores of Lake Garda. Braccobaldo Beach is one of the more unique beaches on the lake because it is dog-friendly. One sun bed for one person and one sun bed for one dog is included in the entry price. Each deck chair comes with an umbrella. During the summer, it's best to book a few days of chairs in advance, as there is a limited capacity (total 60 people). Nearby, you'll find a bar serving drinks and snacks as well as parking and restrooms.

WALKS
Walk along the Mincio River to Borghetto sul Mincio

Start at the Mincio River in the middle of Peschiera del Garda

To get a taste of the Veronese countryside and the little towns just south of Lake Garda, follow the flow of the Mincio River straight out of the Peschiera and down to the charming riverside village of Borghetto sul Mincio, nationally known for their delicate handmade tortellini. To make a day out of this, start walking in the morning, make your way to the village by lunch, then fuel up on tortellini and wine before walking back to

Peschiera. The paved pedestrian and bike path, which is fairly flat the entire way, follows the river and simply guides you to this little piece of paradise, which is complete with a quiet village church, a water wheel, cobblestone pathways full of restaurants, and local boutiques. The entire walk from Peschiera to Borghetto is roughly 12 kilometers (7.5 miles), which takes a couple hours each way. Along the way, you'll walk parallel to the SR249 and eventually onto the SP74 down to the village.

NIGHTLIFE
Bar Al Porto
Riviera Carducci, 5; 339/211-5643; 10am-3am daily; €10-20

Bar Al Porto is a small and modern bar overlooking Lake Garda and beloved by locals. It stays open late into the night and serves traditional *aperitivo* treats like Spritz, chips, olives, and finger foods. This place stays pretty busy in the summertime, and if you swing by just after dinner, you'll observe the bartenders talking to old friends and diners and drinkers mingling amongst one another well past midnight. Despite its late-night hours, this is not a club. Rather, it's a cozy local place ideal for slowing down and enjoying the night breeze coming off the lake.

SHOPPING
Vino e Dintorni
Via Bell'Italia, 39; 045/640-2358; www. vinoedintorni.biz; 8:30am-12:30pm and 2:30pm-6:30pm Mon.-Sat.

For an extensive wine selection focusing on regional wine from Veneto, stop into Vino e Dintorni. The owner and small staff are extremely knowledgeable and friendly, so feel encouraged to tell them your preferred tastes and they'll help you find the best choice.

Additionally, you'll find champagnes, French wines, and labels from elsewhere in Italy, but stick to the local wines for a real treat, as the shop's merchants partner with local vineyards to ensure they feature the region's best lugana (dry white wine), whites, reds, and chiaretti (dry rosé). You'll also find a small selection of food items to pair with your wines, such as oils and olives.

FOOD
Marco and Daniela Time—Peschiera del Garda
Via Risorgimento, 1; 045/755-3582; www. marcoedanielatime.it; 12pm-3pm and 6pm-10pm Fri.-Wed.; €5-12

Beloved by locals and highly rated by travelers, this cozy, casual spot serves Italian comfort food for cheap prices, all with a buzzing atmosphere and great flavors. Whether you're ordering a freshly made Italian meat sandwich, a mixed salad, the pasta of the day, bruschetta, or tiramisu, everything is house-made and with great care. Stay for a while to soak in the cool vibes. Study the local foodstuffs stocked on the wall-to-wall wooden shelves; enjoy a local beer from the tap. No need for reservations, but know that this place fills up quickly for lunches and dinners, especially during high season, so come right when it opens.

Osteria Rivelin
Via Milano, 1; 045/252-6048; 7pm-10:30pm Mon., Wed.-Fri., 12pm-2pm Sat. and Sun.; €10-20

This cozy, local joint makes you feel like home the moment you walk in the door, with the low lighting and wooden shelves full of regional wines. The arched brick walls lead to a domed ceiling, evoking an intimate and relaxed atmosphere. The menu includes local pasta dishes as well as beef filets with truffle, livers, tartares, chicken lasagna, and other baked pasta dishes. Start your meal off with a large plate of cold cults, cheeses, honeys, and jams paired with a local wine, like a Bardolino red wine. Book ahead, regardless of when you plan on coming, as this place stays full during opening hours.

ACCOMMODATIONS

Hotel Garden

Viale Stazione, 18; 045/755 3644; www. hotel-garden.it; €64

Located conveniently next to the Peschiera train station, the Hotel Garden is a nice option for those wanting to stay a little bit away from the lake and close to transportation options. The hotel itself is simple yet modern, with a classic American hotel feel. The property includes a bar with patio seating, and the hotel partners with a nearby Italian restaurant to offer meals at discounted rates. Each guest room includes air conditioning, WiFi, and private bathroom. Continental breakfast and parking are included in the price of each room.

Parc Hotel

Via Paradiso di Sopra; 045/6405-2011; www. parchotelpeschiera.it; €150

Peschiera's Parc Hotel is a family-friendly, modern and bright hotel that is beloved by tourists visiting the resort town year after year. The huge complex includes both an indoor and outdoor pool, a wellness center, a restaurant, playground, and many sports areas, including a golf course. Each guest room includes air conditioning and private bathroom with a tub. Some rooms also include a balcony overlooking the recreation areas below. A huge buffet breakfast

and parking is included in the price of each room.

GETTING THERE

BY CAR

If you're coming from Milan or from one of the other lakes east of Garda, you'll need to start by heading east on the major A4 tollway until you reach the Peschiera del Garda exit (136 kilometers/84.5 miles, 1.75 hours from Milan). Signs clearly direct you to the city center. However, your best bet at finding paid public parking near the city center is at the train station. Once you park, walk about 10 minutes to the lake.

To reach Peschiera from Desenzano, you simply need to follow the SR11 state road directly east for 15 kilometers (9 miles) straight; the total drive is 15 minutes. From the northern part of the lake, like Riva del Garda, your quickest way to Peschiera is via the A22 highway on the eastern side of the lake. When you're heading south on A22, take the SR11 exit, then follow the SR11 southwest to Peschiera. The SR11 will take you straight to Peschiera after about 7 kilometers (4.3 miles). From Riva del Garda to Peschiera, the entire trip is about 79 kilometers (49 miles), which is about an hour drive. If you're coming from Lake Molveno, you'll also need to reach the A22 highway and head south following the same directions. From Lake Molveno, the trip is about an hour and 35 minutes over a distance of 129 kilometers (80 miles).

BY TRAIN

Peschiera del Garda, like Desenzano, also falls directly on the main rail line connecting Milan and Venice, so *freccia* (fast) and regional trains stop here. Trains departing Milan's Central

Station run roughly every 30 minutes 6:25am-10:25pm daily, with fast train one-way tickets starting around €15 and one-way regional trains around €10. Traveling from Milan on a *freccia* train takes about a little over an hour to Peschiera and a regional train takes about 1 hour and 35 minutes. Tickets can be purchased online in advance at https://trenitalia.com or directly at any train station.

BY BOAT

Infrequent ferry trips to Peschiera del Garda are available from Sirmione, Lazise, Bardolino, and Riva del Garda, with fares running from €3-10 one-way per person. Trips are quite long and slow, with a three-hour trip from Riva del Garda and a 3.5-hour trip from Sirmione. The ferries stop at the main port in the center of Peschiera del Garda. Official fares and timetables can be found at www.navigazionelaghi.it.

GETTING AROUND

The center of Peschiera is entirely walkable, unless you're wanting to get to more remote restaurants or accommodations, or to Gardaland. To get from the center of Peschiera del Garda to Gardaland, take the SR249 northeast, following the signs to the aquarium along the way. It's about a 10-minute drive over 4 kilometers (2.5 miles). If you don't want to drive, you can catch the **free shuttle bus** between the Peschiera del Garda train station during the park's opening hours. The shuttle departs from both the park and the station every half hour, and the journey takes 5-10 minutes each way.

Lazise

The colorfully charming lakeside town of Lazise offers everything you could want in a little Italian village: a historic medieval castle, cobblestone streets full of local boutiques, peaceful olive groves, and of course, a long waterfront to stroll up and down. Lazise is positioned between Peschiera del Garda and Bardolino on Lake Garda's southeastern shore, about 10 kilometers (6 miles) north of Peschiera and 5 kilometers (3 miles) south of Bardolino on SR249. If you want to stay away from the resort crowd of Peschiera, but still have easy access to the family-friendly attractions and theme parks in the area, Lazise is a good place to stay.

SIGHTS
SCALIGER CASTLE

Via Castello, 13; 366/422-3017; www.tourism.verona.it/en/enjoy/history-heritage/castles-and-fortresses/castle-of-lazise

Although privately owned and now only open for special occasions, the Scaliger Castle's dominating presence in Lazise is unavoidable, as you'll more than likely have to walk through a gate in one of the walls to enter the center of town along the lake. The earliest known date of the castle goes back to 983 CE, but because several dates are inscribed on the castle's walls, history shows that it was reconstructed several times and changed hands over the centuries. In the latter half of the 19th century, the current owner built

Lazise and Bardolino

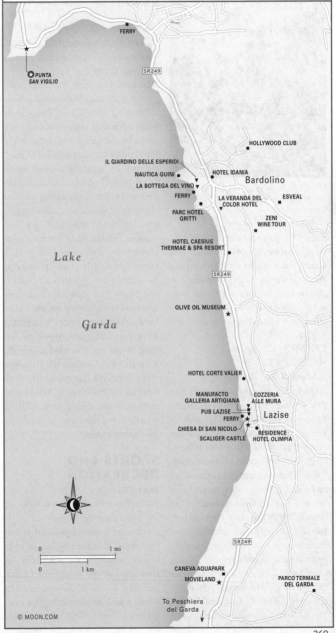

FERRY

PUNTA SAN VIGILIO

SR249

HOLLYWOOD CLUB

IL GIARDINO DELLE ESPERIDI
NAUTICA GUINI
LA BOTTEGA DEL VINO
FERRY
PARC HOTEL GRITTI

HOTEL IDANIA
Bardolino
LA VERANDA DEL COLOR HOTEL
ESVEAL
ZENI WINE TOUR

HOTEL CAESIUS THERMAE & SPA RESORT

Lake

SR249

OLIVE OIL MUSEUM

Garda

HOTEL CORTE VALIER

MANUFACTO GALLERIA ARTIGIANA
PUB LAZISE
FERRY
CHIESA DI SAN NICOLO
SCALIGER CASTLE

COZZERIA ALLE MURA
Lazise
RESIDENCE HOTEL OLIMPIA

| 0 | | 1 mi |
| 0 | 1 km | |

SR249

CANEVA AQUAPARK
MOVIELAND

PARCO TERMALE DEL GARDA

To Peschiera del Garda

© MOON.COM

The medieval roots of Lazise make it one of the most historic villages on Lake Garda

a beautiful green park around the castle to combine his love of nature and history, so you can walk around the public gardens area on warm summer afternoons. The stone walls and towers evoke a medieval feel, so stop by for a quick walk around the exterior.

CHURCH OF SAINT NICHOLAS
(Chiesa di San Nicolo)

Via Fontana, 5; 8:30am-6:30pm; free

The prominent yet gentle, beautiful Chiesa di San Nicolo sits lakeside in Lazise, surrounded by local fishing boats floating in turquoise waters. Originally built in the 12th century, the old stone exterior gives off ancient and rustic vibes. An earthquake from the same century destroyed part of the church shortly thereafter. The **tall bell tower** sticks out on the shoreline, and the interior is much more austere than your average, centuries-old Italian church, with only a handful of pews and frescoes scattered across the walls. However, it's worth a step inside for a unique Italian church experience, as it isn't full of golden alters and frescoes on every inch of the walls, showing the true story of the church's history.

MOVIELAND

Via Fossalta, 58, Fossalta; 045/696-9900; www.movieland.it; 10am-7pm daily, Apr.-Sept.; €22-28

Perched between Peschiera del Garda and Lazise is the small but entertaining Movieland amusement park. Although somewhat overshadowed by the larger and more popular Gardaland, Movieland still holds its own by offering a small world filled with Hollywood-themed rides and attractions, including its own Hollywood mountain. Rides include the Hollywood tower falling rollercoaster, the House of Horrors, river rapid rides, and more. The park is extremely family-friendly, offering something for children and adults of all ages, and there are restaurants and food stalls serving mainly Italian foods like pizzas, pastas, and gelato. This is a great option if you're traveling by car and you want to skip the long lines at Gardaland. However, you can catch a free round-trip shuttle from the Peschiera del Garda train station to the theme park. Official shuttle timetables can be found on Movieland's website.

SPORTS AND RECREATION
WALKS
Waterfront Walk to Bardolino

Shoreline in the center of Lazise

If you want to enjoy a peaceful, stress-free stroll along the waters of Lake Garda, wander your way from the shoreline in the middle of Lazise, heading north to Bardolino. The stroll, which is only about five kilometers (three miles), takes around

The stone walkways comprising Lazise's center against Lake Garda are small and full of historic charm

an hour each way, so you can easily fit the walk into a single morning or afternoon, stopping along the way for a glass of wine or lunch at one of the many bars and restaurants lining the walk, which is completely paved and flat the entire way, making it easy for families to complete the journey.

WATER PARK
Caneva Aquapark
Via Fossalta, 56, Fossalta; 045/696-9900; www.canevaworld.it; 10am-7pm daily; €20-26

This Caribbean-themed aquapark is one of Lazise's biggest summer hits, complete with thrilling water slides, diving boards, a lazy river, an adults-only pool, and restaurants and bars to keep you fueled and hydrated all day. With multiple pools and areas to lounge, it's easy to pass an entire fun-filled day beating the heat here. For a thrill, take a ride down either the new **SuperSplash** or **Stukas Boom** waterslides, or relax for a while floating along the **Windy Lagoon** or **Lazy River.** For those with children, keep in mind that the park gets pretty crowded as the day continues, so come early, grab some lounge chairs, and hang out before the swarm of people arrive to cool down.

If you're not traveling by car, you can catch the free shuttle bus to the Caneva park from the Peschiera del Garda train station. The shuttle runs during the park's opening hours, departing every 30 minutes or so in both directions. Official shuttle timetables can be found on the water park's website.

WELLNESS CENTERS
Parco Termale del Garda
Via Madonna, 23, Colá; 045/759-0988; www.villadeicedri.it; 9:30am-11pm daily; €17-26

This public wellness center located at a local villa is one of Lake Garda's most relaxing places to spend an afternoon. The warm thermal pools are sourced by local spring, with the average water temperature between 33-34°C (91-93°F). The park has two small lake bodies, and within each lake you'll find Jacuzzis, jets, waterfalls, geysers, and other hydromassages. The first lake dates back to the 18th century, with the additional lake and the rest of the water features slowly added on over time. In the villa and around the property, you'll also find a gym, bar, restaurant, and cafeteria, as well as medical spas offering massages and other wellness treatments. When the sun sets and most families go home for the evening, the crowd thins out and the place gets a little more intimate, with lights illuminating the water in the dark.

The best way to reach the wellness center is by car. Follow the SP5 east outside of the center of Lazise for a few kilometers until you reach the Verona Lago Hotel, then turn right following the signs pointing you to the villa and wellness center. Once you reach the small village of Cola, turn right on Via Madonna, and continue straight until you reach the parking area for the center. From Lazise, it's about a 10-minute drive spanning seven kilometers (four miles).

NIGHTLIFE
Enjoy Pub Lazise
Calle Prima, 8; 045/647-0502; 10am-1:30am daily; €3-10 per drink

Although Lazise is a little quieter in the evenings and less nightlife-oriented than some other towns like Desenzano or Bardolino, the Enjoy Pub Lazise is a nice low-key place where you can grab a table and a Guinness and relax with friends for a few hours. The wooden furniture and dim lighting inside create a warm, cozy atmosphere that invites you to stay as long as you'd like. Traditional Italian bar snacks can be brought to you with your drinks upon request. Don't expect a lively, buzzing crowd here, but it is one of the few places in town that stays open late, so you'll have plenty of time to sit around and catch up with friends.

SHOPPING
Manufacto Galleria Artigiana
Vicolo Gafforini, 16/18; 347/319-3177; www.manufacto.it; 10am-12:30pm and 3:30pm-7pm Tues.-Sun.

Whether or not you plan to shop during your time on Lake Garda, if you're in Lazise, stop inside this little treasure of a shop. The entire store is filled with handmade creations from a local goldsmith; here you'll find everything from intricate jewelry to unique interior design pieces. You won't find price tags all over the room, as the establishment is just as much a gallery as it is a shop. But if you're looking for a one-of-a-kind souvenir or gift to bring back from Lake Garda, you're sure to find something here.

The lakeside promenade in Lazise is full of local restaurants and boutiques

FOOD
Cozzeria Alle Mura
Via Cansignorio, 16; 045/647-0644; www. cozzeria.com; 12pm-2pm, 6pm-10:30pm Tues.-Sun.; €12-30

Come as you are to this casual, laid back seafood restaurant in the heart of Lazise. The place is beloved by both locals and tourists, with the huge plates of mussels in a tomato broth being the main draw. While you'll find a handful of non-seafood items, it's almost a sin to come here and not get a fish-related dish. You'll find grilled and fried seafood options, as well as pizzas and other options for children that may not be fond of branching out. The place gets fairly packed in the evenings, especially on the weekends, so book ahead if possible.

ACCOMMODATIONS
Residence Hotel Olimpia
Piazzale Marra, 4; 045/758-0123; €130

This simple yet fulfilling hotel is continuously garnering positive reviews for its service and high-quality staff. The hotel is housed in an old, expanded villa, with classically and minimally furnished rooms and a beautiful outdoor pool in the back surrounded by lawn chairs and palm trees, making an afternoon here feel like you've escaped to a quiet, private corner of paradise. Each guest room includes air conditioning and private bathroom. Parking and breakfast are included in the price of each room, and lake access is just outside the property.

Hotel Corte Valier

Via della Pergolana, 9; 045/647-1210; www. cortevalier.com; €320

This modern, luxurious hotel is one of the largest properties in Lazise, complete with a lakeside pool, bar with a terrace overlooking the lake, fine-dining restaurant, and a highly rated spa area that includes an indoor pool, Finnish sauna, Turkish bath, and a selection of massage treatments. The hotel sits just outside the center of Lazise, so you're far enough away from the noise of tourist crowds but close enough to walk into town for the day without needing to move your car (free parking is available for guests). Each modern and sleekly decorated room is air conditioned and equipped with a balcony and private bathroom. A large continental breakfast is included.

GETTING THERE AND AROUND

BY CAR

To get to Lazise from **Milan**, and from the other lakes east of Garda, head east on the major A4 tollway until you reach the southern shore of the lake, then take the exit for Peschiera del Garda. From there follow the signs for SR249 and head north to Lazise. The entire trip from Milan is about 140 kilometers (87 miles) and takes

1.75 hours. A handful of paid parking lots are available near the center of town, although they fill up very quickly in the summer, so arrive early to find parking or consider finding an accommodation that offers free parking for guests.

From **Desenzano,** follow the SR11 for about 20 kilometers (12 miles) east until you reach the SR450, then head north on the SR450 for 6 kilometers (just under 4 miles). Once you reach the SP5, take a left to head west toward Lazise for a few kilometers. Between the two villages, the drive is about 31 kilometers (19 miles), which is about a half-hour trip. From **Riva del Garda,** your quickest way to Lazise is via the A22 highway on the eastern side of the lake. When you're heading south on A22, take the SP31/A exit, then follow the SP31 southwest to Lazise. From Riva del Garda to Lazise, the entire trip is about 67 kilometers (41 miles), which is about a 50-minute drive.

BY TRAIN AND BUS

From Milan, take a fast or regional train to the **Verona Porta Nuova** station, located directly along the main rail line between Milan and Venice. Trains start between 6:30am-10:30pm daily, departing every half hour from Milan's Central Station. *Freccia* (fast train) tickets are around €20 each way, with the trip lasting 1.25 hours. A regional train ticket costs €12 each way, with the trip lasting just under two hours. From Verona's Porta Nuova train station, grab the 163, 164, or 185 **ATV bus** from Verona's Porta Nuova train station to the center of Lazise. Buses usually depart once an hour 7:13am-7:20pm daily. Tickets can be purchased at the public transit office in the train station, and generally run between €3-10 one-way. Official timetables and fares can be found at www.atv.verona.it/Linee_e_orari_autobus.

BY BOAT
Infrequent public ferries run from Bardolino and Peschiera del Garda to Lazise 8:30am-6:30pm. The trip from Peschiera is about 30 minutes, and from Bardolino it's about 20 minutes, with fares running from €3-10 one-way per person. The ferry station can be found in the center of the village lakefront. Official fares and timetables can be found at www.navigazionelaghi.it.

Bardolino

The little wine village of Bardolino is known nationally in Italy for its delicious red wine and high-quality olive oil pressed from locally grown olives. Sitting about five kilometers (three miles) north of Lazise on SR249, the small town dates back to at least the early Middle Ages, although human traces from the prehistoric era were once found here.

While walking around town, you'll experience a nice balance of Italy's modern lake life, with the town's rainbow-colored residences, local shops, and restaurants complementing the historical architecture, including its 12th-century city walls and gates guiding you around the city as well as its numerous ancient churches. All of Bardolino can be easily seen in a day, and because there's plenty to do all along Lake Garda's eastern shore, it can serve as a great home base.

SIGHTS
OLIVE OIL MUSEUM
(Museo dell'Olio)
Via Peschiera, 54, Cisano; 045/622-9047; www.museum.it; 9am-12:30pm and 2:30pm-7pm daily; free
Owned and operated by a local family, the Olive Oil Museum in Bardolino was opened in 1987 and is the first museum in the world focused on the process of making olive oil. The completely free museum allows visitors to take a look at the step-by-step process of turning olives into oil, including a view of the giant stone mill used to smash the olives. The guides do a great job outlining the importance of olive oil for their region, as well as how the process has changed over the last hundreds of years. Video guides are available in English, German, French, Dutch, and Italian. At the end of your path through the museum, visit the shop full of olive-related products and purchase a bottle of local extra virgin olive oil or other organic foods.

✪ PUNTA SAN VIGILIO
Via S. Vigilio, 17, Garda; 349/939-5748; www.punta-sanvigilio.it; 9:30am-8pm daily, late May-Oct.; €3-12
Punta San Vigilio, which is actually about 6 kilometers (3.7 miles) north of Bardolino, is a quiet, green peninsula jutting out into the eastern side of Lake Garda, full of cypress trees and olive groves over three kilometers (less than two miles), give or take, of natural space. While locals enjoy spending time here year-round for its tranquility and beauty, it can get particularly busy during summer. The peninsula

Punta San Vigilio offers a natural park, two luxury villas, and a quiet shoreline

includes a 16th-century villa that now houses a luxury hotel, a peaceful park with a beach, a swimming pool, and another elegant accommodation option. Regardless of your reason for visiting, you'll enjoy the feeling of being lost on a secluded piece of quiet paradise here. While parking directly on the peninsula is limited, there is an hourly paid parking lot nearby, just off the SR249. From the parking lot, it's about a 5-10 minute walk down a gravel path to the shore.

If you're wanting to spend a few hours at the point, start by taking a walk along the shore of the peninsula to the small port, from which you can see the lake, tall dark trees, and the tumbling mountains in the distance. Bring a towel with you and park yourself near the water for an hour or so under a shady tree with a drink in hand, as you'll find a handful of bars and inns along this walk.

WINERIES
Zeni Wine Tour

Via Costabella, 9, 37011 Bardolino; 045/721-0022; www.zeni.it; €5-20; tours on request

For a truly local experience that will enlighten you on the significance of Bardolino wine culture, book a tour and tasting at the Zeni winery in Bardolino. Call ahead to book your tour, which can be arranged in Italian or English, for up to 10 people. The tour includes a walk through the on-site wine museum, which gives you a detailed history of regional wines and of the winery itself. It also includes a quick walk through the vineyards and other production areas of the site. You'll end the tour with a wine tasting of a Bardolino Zeni bottle of your choice, hence why tour prices may change, depending on your tasting selection. The staff is incredibly affable and convincingly in love with what they do, making it a worthwhile way to spend two or three hours of your day. The winery itself is located a few kilometers away from the lake; walk from the center of town steadily up the hill to the winery, or book a taxi (try Taxi Bardolino, www.bardolinotaxi.it).

SPORTS AND RECREATION

WALKS

Waterfront Walk to Punta San Vigilio

Start in the center of Bardolino along the paved walkway on the shore

For a beautiful and relaxing family-friendly stroll, try this waterfront trail. Note that the paved pathway has a very minor incline. From Bardolino, the 6-kilometer (3.7-mile) walk will take about 1.25 hours. The walkway is easy to follow, as you just need to walk north the whole way until you reach the peninsula, which is marked by signs. You'll also recognize its noticeable jut out toward the lake. Along the way, you'll find shady areas, benches for resting, bars

Bardolino's shores are full flowers, making for a pleasant walk in the spring and summer

and restaurants in case you want to stop for a quick bite to eat or refreshment, local shops, and more. No need to try to arrange transportation back to Bardolino, as the walk is short enough to make a round-trip in a full morning or afternoon.

BOAT RENTAL

Nautica Guini

Punta Cornicello Bardolino; 346/288-6677; www.nauticaguini.it; 9am-7pm daily; €40+

Local fishing boats float in the center of Bardolino

For a private boat experience for up to eight people, this experienced local company rents boats to those with and without licenses. By renting your own boat, you can easily avoid the road traffic and get to other towns, such as Sirmione or Punta San Vigilio, on the lake much more swiftly. The friendly and professional staff prepares you before departure with all of the information and equipment that you'll need. Boats can be rented with or without gas by the hour or day. Each boat includes a GPS system, a sun deck, awning, bathroom, safety equipment, and life jackets (also available in children's sizes). To rent a boat, you'll need a valid identification card as well as a €250 cash deposit. You can book a boat in advance directly on the website.

NIGHTLIFE
Hollywood Club

Via Montavoletta 11, Bardolino;
045/721-0580; www.hollywood.it;
8:30pm-4am; €20-25

Hollywood is one of Lake Garda's most popular night clubs; it is definitely the hottest weekend spot for young locals. The multilevel space has low neon lighting, several dance floors, and lounges. The outdoor space is modern and upscale, with small pools and comfortable patio furniture for those wanting to enjoy the night air and chat. You'll often find DJs and live music sets here, with popular pop and house music playing. It also offers a selection of dinner menus for those wanting to come early, grab a table, and enjoy a full night here. Tables for dinner or for the club can be booked by calling the establishment or via the WhatsApp instant messenger.

SHOPPING
Esveal

Contrada Ceola, 19, Bardolino;
370/724-1618; www.esveal.it;
10:30am-12:30pm and 2pm-6:30pm daily

This small but professional shop sells strictly high-quality organic products sourced from local farms on Lake Garda, including certified organic olive oil that can be bought by the bottle, regular olive oil, or oil infused with garlic, orange, lemon, or chili peppers. They also sell traditional limoncello made from lemons grown on local farms; other similar types of liqueurs are sold here as well. The store promotes well-being and healthy quality of life through their products, so items like essential oils are sold here as well. The owners firmly believe in the mission of their store and helping guests find what they need. You will find them to be very helpful, approachable, and fluent in Italian, English, German, and French.

FOOD
ITALIAN
Il Giardino delle Esperidi

Via Mameli, 1, Bardolino; 045/621-0477;
5pm-11:30pm daily, 11am-3pm Sat. and Sun.;
€20-50

Diners at Il Giardino delle Esperidi are always raving about the flavors here: from baked parmesan and truffles, to local meats and fresh lake fish, to the stuffed pastas, suckling pig, and to-die-for chocolate cake. What's more unique about this place: it's run entirely by women, with a female chef, waitstaff, and hostess. The low lighting illuminates the large wooden cabinets filled with local and national wines. This spot is perfect for a cozy date, but also amenable to families. For the best experience, ask your server for the best local wine to pair with your meal, and don't leave without grabbing dessert. Booking a table in advance is recommended.

La Veranda del Color Hotel

Via Santa Cristina 5, Bardolino;
045/621-0857; www.
ristorantelaverandabardolino.it;
7pm-9:30pm daily; €20-60

This Michelin-star restaurant epitomizes everything that is fine dining: exquisite flavors, high-quality ingredients, beautifully plated dishes, attentive and friendly staff beaming with pride about their establishment, and elegant, reserved atmosphere. Yet, despite its reputation as one of the finest dining establishments on Lake Garda, it doesn't feel unapproachable. Try the beef tartare, handmade stuffed pastas, fresh fish, scallops, and more. The dress attire is a little more formal than other restaurants in the area, so bear this in mind if you choose to dine here. If you do, you should definitely book a table a couple days in advance, especially during high season.

WINE BARS
La Bottega del Vino
Piazza S. Nicolò, 46, Bardolino;
328/701-0914; 10am-2am daily; €5-15
This cozy wine bar in the middle of Bardolino is a hot spot for locals and tourists alike, with a huge selection of both wines and beers and beautiful *tagliere* plates served from open to close. Select from one of a handful of plates including a cheese tasting board, locally sourced cold cuts, *caprese,* and more, all served with a large basket of freshly made bread and crackers. Of course, if you're in Bardolino, you can't miss the opportunity to try the well-known Bardolino red wine. The bar also has a vibrant, buzzing happy hour and a small selection of sandwiches for those wanting an official meal. Considering how busy this place gets during the normal *aperitivo* hour before dinner, come here in the early afternoon for a late lunch if you want to miss the crowds.

ACCOMMODATIONS
Parc Hotel Gritti
Via Gabriele D'Annunzio, 1, Bardolino;
045/621-5011; www.parchotelgrittibardolino.
it; €120
Situated right on the shore of Lake Garda, the Parc Hotel Gritti is one of the more refined, luxurious accommodations in Bardolino, complete with two pools (one indoor and one outdoor), three Italian restaurants and bars, a gym, sauna, Turkish bath, and a selection of beauty treatments from the wellness center. The space is bright and covered in beautiful green trees and vines, with rooms that reflect a balanced mix of antique furniture and modern details. Each guest room is equipped with air conditioning, WiFi, and private bathroom. A substantial buffet breakfast and parking is included in the price of each room.

Hotel Idania
Via Marconi, 18, Bardolino; 045/621-0122;
www.hotelidania.com; €140
Situated in the heart of Bardolino, roughly a five-minute walk away from Lake Garda's shores, is this comfortable, classic hotel with an outdoor pool. The hotel is beautifully decorated with classic hotel furniture, and the inviting outdoor areas are bursting with colorful plants, giving the place a more at-home feel than other hotels. Each guest room includes air conditioning, WiFi, and a private bathroom. A continental breakfast and parking are included in the price of each room.

Hotel Caesius Thermae & Spa Resort
Via Peschiera, 3, Bardolino; 045/721-9100;
www.hotelcaesiusterme.com; €255
The beautiful and luxurious Hotel Caesius Thermae & Spa Resort is so relaxing that it's tempting to spend your entire Garda holiday on the property. If you're looking for an upscale wellness center situated right on the lake, this is your place. You'll find a gorgeous outdoor swimming pool overlooking the waters of Lake Garda, a cool and relaxing indoor swimming pool, multiple saunas and Turkish baths, a gym, a tea room, an onsite wine cellar, three Italian restaurants and bars, and various relaxing lounge spaces. Each room includes air conditioning, WiFi, and private bathroom.

A large buffet breakfast and parking are included in the price of each room.

GETTING THERE AND AROUND

BY CAR

If you're traveling to Bardolino by car, head east on the major A4 tollway until you reach the the the southern shore of the lake, then take the exit for Peschiera del Garda. From there follow the signs to SR249 north to Bardolino. From Milan, the entire trip is about 145 kilometers (91 miles) and just under two hours. A handful of paid parking lots are available near the center of town, although they fill up very quickly in the summer, so arrive early to find parking or consider finding an accommodation that offers free parking for guests.

From Desenzano, follow the SR11 for about 20 kilometers (12 miles) east until you reach the SR450, then head north on the SR450 for 6 kilometers (3.7 miles). Once you reach the SP31, follow it north straight to Bardolino. Between the two villages, the drive is about 36 kilometers (22 miles), which is about a 35-minute trip. From Riva del Garda, your quickest way to Bardolino is via the A22 highway on the eastern side of the lake. When you're heading south on A22, take the Affi-Lago di Garda Sud exit, then follow the SP31 southwest to Lazise. From Riva del Garda to Bardolino, the entire trip is about 67 kilometers (41 miles), which is about a 50-minute drive.

BY TRAIN AND BUS

From Milan, take a fast or regional train to the Verona Porta Nuova station, which falls directly along the main rail line between Milan and Venice. Trains run 6:30am-10:30pm daily, departing every half hour from Milan's Central Station. *Freccia* (fast train) tickets are around €20 each way, with the trip lasting 1.25 hours. A regional train ticket is €12 each way, with the trip lasting a little under two hours. From Verona's Porta Nuova train station, grab the 163, 164, or 185 ATV bus from Verona's Porta Nuova train station to the center of Bardolino. Buses usually depart once an hour 7:13am-7:20pm daily. Tickets can be purchased at the public transit office in the train station, and generally run between €3-10 one-way. Official timetables and fares are posted at www.atv. verona.it/Linee_e_orari_autobus.

BY BOAT

Infrequent public ferries run from Lazise and Peschiera del Garda to Bardolino 8:30am-6:30pm. The trip from Peschiera is about 45 minutes, and from Lazise it's about 20 minutes, with fares running from €3-10 one-way per person. The ferry station can be found in the center of the village lakefront. Official fares and timetables are posted at www.navigazionelaghi.it.

Malcesine

This beautiful and historic lakeside town is the perfect mix of history and natural beauty. The 13th-century Castello Scaligero, with its stone exterior and tower, presides over the rest of the bustling town, teeming with colorful residential buildings, small shops, and local restaurants. The town's backdrop is the giant Monte Baldo, arguably the most well-known and important mountain range in the province of Verona, and accessible by cable car from the town. For those looking to enjoy the outdoors—whether down by the lake or up in mountains—Malcesine is a great spot to visit.

Malcesine sits on the northeastern shore of Lake Garda, about 18 kilometers (11 miles) south of Riva del Garda and 30 kilometers (18.6 miles) north of Bardolino.

SIGHTS

SCALIGER CASTLE
(Castello Scaligero)

Via Castello, Malcesine; 045/657-0333;
www.comunemalcesine.it; 9:30am-7pm
daily; adults €6, children €3

It's impossible to spend a day in Malcesine, or simply drive through it, without admiring the medieval Castello Scaligero, perched up on a rocky cliff overlooking Lake Garda and the town of Malcesine below. The **stone guard tower** looms over the rest of the area, serving as an undeniable symbol of the rich history of the Garda region.

The castle is presumed to date back to the Lombard Period (starting from 568 AD), but it was destroyed by the Franks in 590 and later rebuilt into its current structure. Although the fortress traded hands many times over the centuries, it was most notably the home of Alberto della Scala of the important Scaliger family, as well as the Milanese Visconti family.

Today, you can enter through the quiet courtyard and into the castle, now home to a Natural History Museum (same hours and included in the entrance price to the castle), which gives a multisensory experience of the regional landscape and wildlife. A tour of the castle takes you through several antique-filled rooms, small gardens and courtyards, and a beautiful balcony overlooking the waters of the lake. End your tour by going up to the tower for gorgeous views overlooking the entire town of Malcesine and the serene lake below you.

ANTICA PIEVE DI
SANTO STEFANO

Via Parrocchia, 14, Malcesine;
045/740-0065; free

This 8th-century church sits on a hilltop overlooking Malcesine, home to what was once a pagan temple and later turned into a Catholic church. Easily reachable by a marked, sloped foot path (or a parallel-running sloped road) from the central waterfront promenade, the church is easily seen over the trees and buildings in town. Inside, the church's white walls are intermittently adorned with framed fresco paintings, with an intricately detailed arched ceiling directing the eyes to a larger colorful fresco found above the altar. Considering that the church is located off of the lake, many visitors tend to skip it. But it is well worth a few minutes of your

Malcesine

EUROPA SURF & SAIL

Lake Garda

SPECK & STUBE

SR249

SUN HOTELS
MAJESTIC PALACE

LIDO PAINA   HOTEL
                 VILLA LARA
CASTELLO
SCALIGERO
CASANOVA   CABLE CAR
FERRY   TO MONTE BALDO
                 ⊙ MONTE BALDO
ANTICA PIEVE DI Malcesine
SANTO STEFANO   RISTORANTE
                 VECCHIA MALCESINE

PANZANO

SR249

            0   0.5 mi
HOTEL
MAXIMILIAN 0   0.5 km

© MOON.COM

time. Consider it a quiet escape from the crowds. Daily mass occurs here, so make sure to remain quiet as you enter.

☉ MONTE BALDO

The Monte Baldo mountain range is arguably the most well-known and most beloved amongst the Veronese, spanning a total of 40 kilometers (25 miles) between the provinces of Trento and Verona along the northeastern border of Lake Garda. The mountains, primarily made of calcareous rocks, peak to 2,218 meters (7,277 feet) at its highest. Near the foot of the range, you'll find such Mediterranean flora as olive trees, chestnut trees, and rosemary bushes. Near the top, the earth is very rocky, so you'll mostly find wild

herbs. Monte Baldo is full of outdoor recreation options, such as hiking and paragliding. There's also the cable car to Monte Baldo, which offers visual rewards and is less physically taxing.

Cable Car to Monte Baldo (Funivie di Malcesine e del Monte Baldo)

Via Navene Vecchia, 12, Malcesine; 045/740-0206; https://funiviedelbaldo.it; 8am-7pm daily late Mar.-early Nov.; €6-22

For truly unforgettable and unmatched panoramic views of Lake Garda, the rest of the mountain range, and the towns below, grab the cable car to the top of Monte Baldo from the center of Malcesine. The cable car system itself is one of the most modern and high-tech in the world. Each car is surrounded by windows on all sides, so you don't miss a single angle. This trip gives you the best aerial views of anywhere on Lake Garda and gets busy quickly in high season. To avoid long lines, arrive first thing in the morning. The cable car runs every half hour, with each ascent and descent lasting just a few minutes. Once you get to the top, you'll find a small station with a flat, natural viewing area.

SPORTS AND RECREATION

BEACH
Lido Paina

Localitá Paina, 49, Malcesine; open 24 hours; free

This public pebble beach is just north of the Scaliger Castle and a quick walk from the center of town. The small public park area includes a swimming raft out on the lake, beach volleyball courts, a small skateboard park, and a separate recreation area where you'll usually find little kids kicking around a soccer ball while taking a break from

The medieval castle in Malcesine sits on a rocky cliff directly on the shores of Lake Garda

the water. Along the shore, you'll find several bars and restaurants up until the ferry dock, where the beach ends. A large parking lot is located directly next to the beach. Because the beach is public and free, it fills up quickly in the summer, so come stake your spot early in the morning or later in the afternoon to grab a place near the water.

HIKING

Monte Baldo is a good place to hike in the Malcesine area.

San Zeno di Montagna

Via Canevoi, San Zeno di Montagna

For an easy walking trail that avoids the crowds around the cable car on Monte Baldo, start on Via Canevoi in the small village of San Zeno di Montagna (reachable by driving about 20 kilometers south of Malcesine on the SR249) and follow its entire length of 10 kilometers (6.2 miles) until it circles back around to the starting point. The path takes you through the Sperane pinewood to the small historic mountain village of Lumini, then to the summit of Mount Belpo in the Monte Baldo range. From there, you'll pass a small adventure park, pass through Dosso Croce (cross on Via Dosso Croce) and wind up back where you started. The entire trip climbs to around 300 meters (984 feet), and usually takes about 2.5 hours to complete. Because it's a fairly easy path, mostly paved or guided by tarmac with minor elevation changes, it's suitable for beginners as well as families with young children. It is open every day of the year without any entrance fee.

Peace Trail
(Sentiero della Pace CAI Path)

Peak of Monte Baldo, near the cable car station

Near the peak of Monte Baldo, you'll find the Peace Trail, part of a significant and historic long-distance trekking trail that follows a former World War I military trail. Although the

Peace Trail is just a small fraction of the famous E5 long-distance trail that starts in Brittany, France, and passes through Italy, you can hike as much of it as you want, then simply turn back around in the direction from which you came. The dirt path makes for an easy, stress-free trek. To find the trail, exit the cable car and look for posted signs directing you to the Sentiero della Pace CAI path. The trail isn't very steep in this area, but bring water and take general safety precautions when hiking it.

PARAGLIDING

If you are an adventure lover and want a completely unparalleled experience during your stay on Lake Garda, try tandem paragliding off the summit of Monte Baldo and land near the village of Malcesine. Seasoned paragliding professionals in the area have years of experience with this jump and make the entire time both fun and thrilling. The 20-40 minute glide down to the foot of the mountain gives you amazing aerial views of Lake Garda and Malcesine below.

Fly2Fun

Via Navene Vecchia, 12, Malcesine; 334/946-9757; www.tandemparagliding. eu; €150

Fly2Fun organizes Monte Baldo paragliding trips. You'll start your day at the cable car station in Malcesine before catching a car (included) up to the summit of Monte Baldo. You'll meet your paragliding pilot at the jumping-off point near the top of the mountain, gear up (wear comfortable clothes and tennis shoes), learn more about the safety and overall experience, then tandem jump your way off

the mountain top. Group flights and flight videos can be arranged. Book your advance tickets directly from the website.

WATER SPORTS
Europa Surf & Sail

Via Gardesana 205, Malcesine; 338/605-3096; www.europasurfandsail.com; 9am-6pm daily Apr.-mid-Oct.; €10-300

From this locally run surf and sailing center on the banks of Malcesine, you can rent stand-up paddleboards, catamarans, wind sails, dinghies, kayaks, and bikes. For beginners, the onsite sailing school offers hourly lessons for windsurfers, dinghies, catamarans, and stand-up paddle boarding from friendly professional, certified instructors that are fluent in English, Italian, and German. All equipment can be rented either hourly or daily, and various clothing and protection equipment can be rented as well. The sailing center includes nearby parking, a restaurant and bar, changing rooms, and showers. Equipment can be booked in advance by calling or contacting the center through the form on their website.

SHOPPING
Casanova

Vicolo Cieco di Mezzo 13, Malcesine; 045/740-0728; 9:30am-12:30pm and 3pm-6pm daily

This beloved and authentic linens shop in Malcesine is owned and operated by Antonella, a local woman, who infuses all her linen creations with her own personality and style. Stop in to admire the fabric piled in every which direction and her workstation with simple sewing machine in the center of the store. Browse her impressive handmade collection of quilts, pillowcases, kitchen linens, and other goodies that make nice souvenirs.

FOOD
Speck & Stube
Via Navene Vecchia, 139, Malcesine;
045/740-1177; http://www.speckstube.com;
12:00-11:45pm daily; €15-25

For a casual, quick bite with giant, filling portions, head to the cafeteria-style Speck & Stube. The German-inspired restaurant serves up plenty of roasted meats, from ribs to rotisserie chickens to hamburgers and sausages, with sides like french fries, pickles, fresh bread, and prosciutto crudo. The idea is simple: grab a tray and fill it with as much food as you want from the various stations, top it off with a pint of one of the many varieties of beer, pay for your meal at the cash register, then head out to the covered patio for a casual meal in the garden.

Ristorante Vecchia Malcesine
Via Pisort, 6, Malcesine; 045/740-0469;
www.vecchiamalcesine.com; 12pm-2pm and
7pm-10pm Thurs.-Tues.; €30-80

This upscale local restaurant, popular among locals and tourists, has put itself on the Michelin map for its original and delicious tasting menu. After earning its first star, it continues to receive fabulous reviews for the breathtaking setting overlooking Lake Garda, the attentive service, and the seven-course tasting menu complete with perfect wine pairings. While a la carte dishes for both first and second courses are available (such as pastas, risottos, and lake fish dishes), stick to the daily tasting menu (which is about €140 per person, including your choice of paired wine) for a real treat. Dishes from this menu may include

beautifully plated shrimp and scampi cocktail, asparagus risotto, perfectly cooked steak and fish, biscotti, and more. Book at least a few days in advance for lunch or dinner, and note that the dress is more formal than casual.

ACCOMMODATIONS
Hotel Villa Lara
Via Gardesana, 108, Malcesine;
045/740-0411; www.villalaramalcesine.
it; €40

Just a short walk outside Malcesine, this small hotel is similar to a B&B and is run by the Benamati family. It features a few simple furnished guest rooms surrounded by a small garden with olive trees and other green plants, giving it a private, cozy feel. Each room comes with either a mountain or lake view from the balcony, as well as a private bathroom and free Wifi. Upon booking, specify if you want meals included during your stay. Breakfast is included in the price of the room, but you can also add dinners in the evening for €10-15 extra per room per evening. There is also an outdoor pool and jacuzzi available for guests in the warmer months, as well as parking.

Sun Hotels Majestic Palace
Via Navene Vecchia, 96, Malcesine;
045/740-0383; www.sunhotels.it; €200

This beautiful hotel feels like a little corner of paradise. The property is huge and host to several outdoor swimming pools and gardens. You'll find it a kilometer (0.6 mile) away from the lake and two kilometers (about a mile) away from the center of town, giving you plenty of privacy away from the crowds. The hotel also has an Italian restaurant and bar, indoor pool, and gym. The guest rooms are spacious and classically decorated.

Each is equipped with air conditioning, WiFi, and private bathroom. A large breakfast buffet is included in the price of each room, as is parking.

Hotel Maximilian

Via Val di Sogno 6, Malcesine;
045/740-0317; www.hotelmaximilian.com;
€260

This sleek, modern, and upscale hotel sits right on Lake Garda, with a large outdoor infinity pool and an intimate hot tub surrounded by bright green gardens that open up to beautiful views of the water. Directly below the hotel sits a quiet pebble beach; the hotel has its own sun loungers and lawn area near the lake as well. Each room is modernly decorated and includes a balcony with either a garden or lake view, air conditioning, WiFi, and private bathroom. Breakfast each morning and parking are included in the price of the room.

GETTING THERE AND AROUND

BY CAR

If you're traveling to Malcesine, head east on the major A4 tollway until you reach the southern shore of the lake, then take the exit for Peschiera del Garda. From there follow the signs for SR249 and head north to Malcesine. From **Milan,** the entire trip is about 180 kilometers (112 miles) or 2.5 hours. A handful of paid parking lots are available near the center of town, although they fill up very quickly in the summer, so arrive early to find parking or consider finding an accommodation that offers free parking for guests.

To get to Malcesine from **Riva del Garda,** you simply need to follow the SS240 southeast along the shore of the lake. Once you reach Torbole,

continue south through each roundabout, as the road eventually turns into SS249, which will lead you directly to Malcesine. Between the two towns, it's about 25 kilometers (15.5 miles) and takes 50 minutes.

From **Desenzano,** follow the SR11 for about 20 kilometers (12 miles) east until you reach the SR450, then head north on the SR450 for 6 kilometers (3.7 miles). Once you reach the SP31, follow it north to Bardolino. Once you reach Bardolino, follow the SS249 north directly along the eastern shore of the lake until you reach Malcesine. Between Desenzano and Malcesine, the drive is 74 kilometers (46 miles) and takes about 1.75 hours.

BY TRAIN AND BUS

If you're traveling by public transportation, you can take a fast or regional train to the Peschiera del Garda station, which falls directly in the main rail line between Milan and Venice. Trains departing Milan's Central Station run roughly every 30 minutes 6:25am-10:25pm daily, with one-way fast train tickets starting around €15 and one-way regional trains around €10. Travel from Milan on a *freccia* train takes a little over an hour to Peschiera and a regional train takes a little over 1.5 hours. Tickets can be purchased online in advance at https://trenitalia.com or from any train station.

From the Peschiera del Garda station, grab one the **ATV buses** running from the train station. Lines 483 and 484 run between Peschiera del Garda, Malcesine, and Riva del Garda. Buses depart generally 6:30am-8:30pm daily, but you can find official timetables and prices at https://atv.verona.it. Tickets, which cost from €2.80-4 one-way, can be purchased in the bars

ferries running between Malcesine, Limone sul Garda, and Riva del Garda

or tobacco shops at the Peschiera del Garda train station. You can also ask the staff there for a physical timetable for the buses to carry around with you. Each 1.25-hour trip departs hourly 8:22am-6:52pm daily.

BY BOAT

Infrequent public ferries run from Limone Sul Garda and Riva del Garda to Malcesine 8:30am-6:30pm. The trip from Limone is about 45 minutes, and from Riva it's about an hour, with fares running from €3-10 one-way per person. The ferry station can be found in the center of the village lakefront.

There is also a direct car ferry service between Limone sul Garda and Malcesine daily 9:10am-6:10pm, departing every hour, with a one-way trip lasting about 20 minutes. Tickets range between €9.50-20.10 each way, depending on the type and size of the motor vehicle. Official fares and timetables can be found at www.navigazionelaghi.it.

Riva del Garda

Sitting at the very top of Lake Garda, Riva del Garda is arguably the most beautiful town on the lake. The resort town is a perfect mix of gorgeous natural views, relaxation, recreation, and history, providing enough of each to fill a full, long weekend here. With the giant Italian Dolomites serving as the backdrop, the colorful squares hug the shoreline and bring life to the northern tip of the lake. Riva is unique in that, due to its more northern position, you see a true blend of Mediterranean and German cultural influences, especially in terms of architecture (you'll

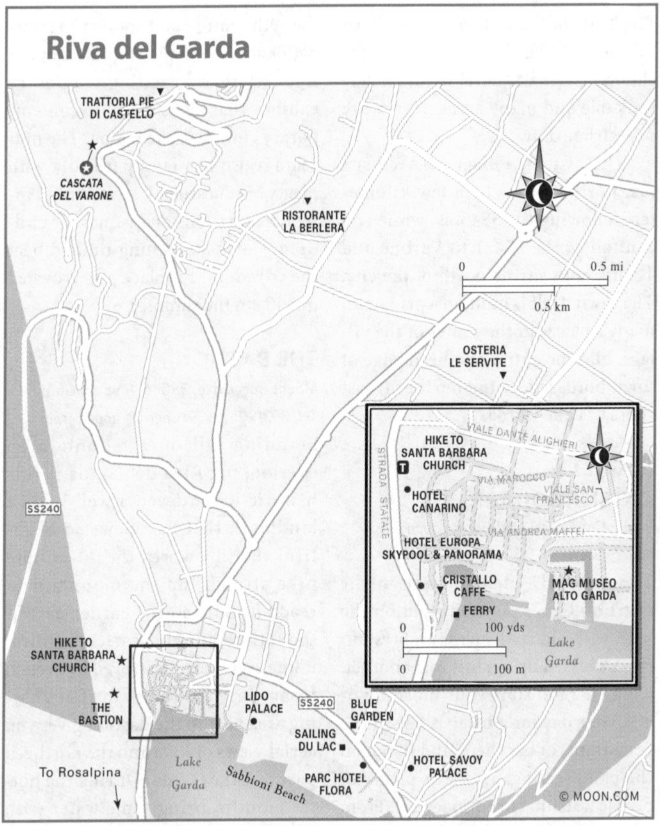
Riva del Garda
TRATTORIA PIE DI CASTELLO
CASCATA DEL VARONE
RISTORANTE LA BERLERA
0
0.5 mi
0
0.5 km
OSTERIA LE SERVITE
SS240
HIKE TO SANTA BARBARA CHURCH
THE BASTION
To Rosalpina
Lake Garda
Sabbioni Beach
LIDO PALACE
SS240
BLUE GARDEN
SAILING DU LAC
PARC HOTEL FLORA
HOTEL SAVOY PALACE
VIALE DANTE ALIGHIERI
STRADA STATALE
HIKE TO SANTA BARBARA CHURCH
VIA MAROCCO
VIALE SAN FRANCESCO
HOTEL CANARINO
VIA ANDREA MAFFEI
HOTEL EUROPA SKYPOOL & PANORAMA
CRISTALLO CAFFE
MAG MUSEO ALTO GARDA
FERRY
0
100 yds
0
100 m
Lake Garda
© MOON.COM

see more wood-beamed ceilings and cozy inns) and food.

The neighboring village of **Arco** is just north of Riva del Garda, and although it is not on the lakeshore, it is just as beautiful and historic. The two towns are often seen together by tourists and both get equally flooded during the summer months. Northern European travelers especially find this area alluring, as you can get a taste of the Mediterranean lifestyle without having to drive to the sea.

Riva del Garda, often just called Riva, is the farthest Lake Garda town from Milan, at about 170 kilometers (105 miles) away. Other than neighboring Limone Sul Garda to the southeast and Torbole to the southwest, there are few other resort towns in the area, and Riva is much more isolated than the other resort towns on the southern end of the lake.

ORIENTATION

Riva del Garda sits on the northwestern corner of Lake Garda, and is the lake's northernmost village. The SS240 runs directly through the center of town horizontally, cutting the town almost in half, while the SS45bis runs from north to south along the western edge of town, connecting Riva to Limone sul Garda and Arco.

The heart of Riva sits on the western side of town. The **historic center** (including Catena Square) is completely walkable and many areas nearby are pedestrian-only.

The historic village of Arco sits just north of Riva by a few kilometers following the SS45bis, while you can follow the SS421 to Varone and Tenno, both sitting north of the city. The town itself is built on a grid, with many squares in the center of the village, and the entire southern edge of town bordered by the northernmost shore of Lake Garda.

SIGHTS
CATENA SQUARE
Piazza Catena Riva del Garda; open 24 hours; free

The colorful Catena Square in the heart of Riva is perched right on the lake, with old apartments and restaurants pressed up against one another. Come here to start your morning or end your day for a meal at one of the restaurants or bars here, and sit out on the patio seating, as there's plenty of people watching to be done here. From here, you can also catch a boat to other towns on the lake or head down one of the narrow paths branching off the square for some local shopping.

MAG MUSEO ALTO GARDA
Piazza Cesare Battisti, 3 / A, Riva del Garda; 0464/573-869; www.museoaltogarda.it; 10am-6pm daily; adults €5, students and seniors €2.50

Located in a small medieval castle right on Lake Garda, the Mueso Alta Garda is part of the MAG network of museums focused on combining art and history in the Trentino region. The museum is home to a handful of permanent exhibits, including one dedicated to landscape paintings from the 19th century and another to international archeology from the Copper Age. There are rotating temporary exhibits that focus on more contemporary culture of the region. The museum is also very family-friendly, with plenty of educational, creative, and interactive stations and games for children. Come at opening time to beat the crowd, as this place gets crowded quickly in the summer.

THE BASTION
Mount Rocchetta, 38066, Riva del Garda TN; 393/905-0379; open 24 hours; free

Standing tall on a mountaintop overlooking Riva del Garda is this historic watchtower, a well-known landmark that has views so beautiful that it's worth the 20-minute hike straight up the mountain to reach it. Built in the earlier part of the 16th century to protect the town, it was eventually destroyed by French troops in 1703. Today, the flat viewing area next to the Bastion gives you aerial views of Riva and the northern part of Lake Garda. During the hotter months, bring some water with you and take your time getting up to the landing, as the hike can be tiring. To start your trek, follow the signs for the 404 trail on Via Monte Oro. The trail is mostly gravel and dirt, with steep elevation in some parts, so dress accordingly.

✪ CASCATA DEL VARONE
Cascata del Varone; 0464/521-421; www.cascata-varone.com; 9am-5pm daily; €6

One of the most attractive natural sights near Riva is the gorgeous waterfall of Varene coming from the Magnone River. With two different observation points, you can see the

SPORTS AND RECREATION

HIKING

Hike to Santa Barbara Church

Start from Via Monte Oro in Riva del Garda

If you want stunning panoramic views of Riva and the northern part of Lake Garda while dodging the crowds at the Bastion, hike up to Santa Barbara Church, which was built by miners in 1925 while the town's hydroelectric power plant was also being constructed. The hike can be quite a challenge if you're not used to trekking uphill, as it's on an incline the entire way and often takes at least an hour to get there from the town of Riva, but the views are worth it. Start the hike by following the signs for the 404 dirt trail on Via Monte Oro to the Bastion, and once you're there, continue past it and follow the signs up to the church, which is 620 meters (2,034 feet) above town. Along the way, you'll find two small cafés where you can stop to grab a refreshing drink and take a breather before continuing on the path.

Low Loop 1: From Riva del Garda to Arco

Start from Via Monte Oro in Riva del Garda

The Low Loop 1 that starts in Riva del Garda and ends at the castle in Arco is one of the area's most popular trekking trails, as it hits major landmarks and offers gorgeous views of the towns below. Start by following the trail 404 signs from Via Monte Ora in Riva. Along the way, you'll walk along the dirt path past the Bastion, the Romanesque church of San Lorenzo in Trenno, and Monte Baone before reaching the Arco Castle. The trail is clearly marked with "GardaTrek Low Loop" signs, but the website listed here also provides turn-by-turn directions. This 13.8-kilometer (8.6-mile) trail is

Cascate del Varone

waterfall from the bottom and from higher up. The waterfall is part of a cave, so to get there you have to walk through the cool and tall walls of the cave, along a railed walkway over a clear, calm pool of water. You'll arrive in the lower cave first, which gives you a view from the bottom of the waterfall looking up, before you start the fairly easy climb up the stairs to the upper cave, and you can see the waterfall's full length and admire the full beauty of the area. Wear comfortable walking shoes with good traction here, as the waterfall sprays can make the paths slippery.

The waterfall is roughly three kilometers (less than two miles) outside of the city, so you'll need to drive to it from Riva by following the SS421. Parking is available near the entrance of the park. If you're up for it, you can also walk to the waterfall from Riva using the main driving road (pay attention to traffic), with a slight incline the entire 2.7 kilometers (1.5 miles). The walk takes about 40 minutes from the center of town.

moderately difficult as you will gain about 400 meters (1,312 feet) in elevation, and it usually takes around a full six hours to complete.

To get back to Riva after you've completed the hike, you can walk an hour from the castle along the SS45bis from Arco to Riva, or take the Trentino Transporti B861 bus from the Arco bus station (Arco-Autostaz., 38062 Arco) back to Riva, which is about a 20-minute trip. Buses depart from 7:23am-8:23pm, with tickets costing around €2 each way.

BEACHES AND WATERSPORTS
Sabbioni Beach
Via Filzi, 2, 38066 Riva del Garda TN; 347/688-7085; open 24 hours; free
This public piece of well-manicured natural space in the center of Riva del Garda is a family-friendly jack-of-all-outdoor-trades. Here you'll find a pebbled and grassy beach where you can lay out your towels, a basketball court, playground with sandboxes and

Rent a paddleboat, catamaran, sailboat, kayak, or paddleboard from various sailing schools and boat rental companies directly on the shore

trampolines, and floating platform with a slide inside the large, netted swimming zone in the lake. There are plenty of shaded areas in the park, but come early if you're wanting to make a day out of this beach, as the shady spots are claimed quickly. The beach is free and public and known for its clear, clean waters. There is a lifeguard on duty during the daylight hours in the summer months, and showers are available as well. Because the pebbles on the beach become hot, bring water shoes to get in and out of the lake. Pack a lunch or snacks if you're wanting to save money, but there is a snack bar serving sandwiches, drinks, and more just next to the park.

Fraglio Vela Riva Sailing School
Via Giancarlo Maroni 2, Riva del Garda; 0464/552-460; www.fragliavelariva.it; 9am-5pm daily, €50-300
Two widely popular watersport activities is in the northern area of Lake Garda are sailing and windsurfing. On any given summer day, you'll see dozens and dozens of sailboats gliding across the lake. The Fraglio Vel Riva Sailing School owns several of those boats, giving groups of visitors sailing lessons through their official sailing school. The school is divided into two groups: children ages 7-13 and teens ages 14 and older. You can sign up for a daily, weekend, or week-long course. There are also family packages available. The instructors are local sailors that have been teaching the sport for years. You can book a sailing lesson directly on their website in advance.

Sailing School at Du Lac Grand Resort
Du Lac et Du Parc Grand Resort, Viale Rovereto, 44; 0464/562-274; www.

sailingdulac.com; 8:30am-6pm daily late Apr.-mid Oct.; €13-90

If sailing isn't your thing, no worries. The sailing school at the Du Lac Grand Resort offers hourly or daily rentals of both single and double kayaks as well as stand-up paddleboards. Kayaks can either be rented for one, two, or four hours, or for an entire day. A life jacket for each kayaker is included in the price. Additionally, you can rent a wet suit for only a few euros more. For a change of pace, you can also rent a stand-up paddleboard hourly, or for two to four hours. For beginners, the school offers two-hour courses daily starting from €35, with the price including a board, wetsuit, life jacket, and a certificate of attendance all while learning from a certified SUP trainer. The school also offers rentals for yachts, bikes, kites, sailboats for leisure or wind surfing, and more. You can book in advance directly by the email form on their website or by calling ahead.

FESTIVALS
Nights of Fairytales (Notte di Fiaba)

Various locations, Riva del Garda; 0464/554-444; www.nottedifiaba.it; last weekend of August annually; free

One of Lake Garda's most family-oriented and diverse experiences is the annual Notte di Fiaba, known as the "Nights of Fairytales." This event takes place during the last weekend of August each year. Over the course of just a few days, the town transforms—even shops and restaurants participate. Each year focuses on a different theme and can range from Disney classics such as the Little Mermaid or Aladdin, to longtime childhood favorites such as Sherlock. Parades and different games are incorporated into each day,

as well as storytelling activities and a number of theater performances. The weekend always ends with a giant fireworks show over the waters of Lake Garda. Get there a couple hours early with plenty of water and some gelato to hold you over while you save your seat for an awesome, up-close view of the show.

SHOPPING
Blue Garden

Viale Rovereto, Riva del Garda; 0464/522-064; http://blue-garden.it; 9am-8:30pm daily

The Blue Garden shopping mall is one of the more popular shopping venues in Riva del Garda, parked on the main strip of road that hugs the lake's northern shoreline. Inside, you'll find plenty of small shops selling books, clothes, accessories, gadgets, and more as well as a number of restaurants ranging from classic Italian to sushi to Indian cuisine. As far as clothing shops, you'll find international department stores including Tally Weijl and Piazza Italia, as well as a supermarket and a cozy bookstore selling both Italian and English titles.

FOOD
TRENTINO CUISINE
Trattoria Pié di Castello

Via al Cingol Ros 38, 38060 Tenno TN; 0464/52-1065; www.piedicastello.it; 12pm-2:30pm Wed.-Mon., 6:45pm-10pm Fri.-Sun.; €10-25

Red meat lovers can't miss this place tucked back into the mountains near Lake Tenno, away from the crowds that gather in Riva in the summertime. Founded at the end of the 19th century, this quiet, family-run restaurant focuses on one main dish: boiled carne salada (cuts of beef). In fact, the meat is usually served family style along with a heaping amount of bread, baked beans, and pickled vegetables. While there are other options such as homemade gnocchi and *canederli* in broth, you shouldn't skip the opportunity for this deliciously unique take on the *carne salada*. To reach Tenno from Riva, follow the Via Molini north until it becomes SS421, then follow the curvy mountain road for about eight kilometers (five miles) until you reach the village.

ITALIAN
Osteria Le Servite
Via Passirone 68, 38062, Arco TN;
0464/557-411; www.leservite.com;
5pm-11:30pm Tues.-Sun., Apr.-Sept.; €15-35

Eating under the stringed twinkle-lights on the patio next to a local vineyard at this osteria evokes the quintessential feeling of having an authentic homemade Italian meal at an old friend's house. The atmosphere is relaxed and casual, with a friendly staff welcoming you to sit back and enjoy the dining experience. Dishes include tagliatelle with ragu, grilled fish and beef, risottos, and creamy desserts. This is a place loved by both frequent visitors and locals, so book ahead, as it is only open in the evenings.

Ristorante La Berlera
Località Ceole, 8/B, Riva del Garda;
0464/521-149; www.laberlera.it; 7pm-10pm
Tues.-Sun., 12pm-2pm Fri.-Sun.; €20-50

A meal at Ristorante La Berlera is worth the higher prices for the setting alone: The restaurant is built into a mountainside. Dishes include homemade stuffed ravioli, roasted octopus, beef stew, and a selection of gelatos and sorbets to finish. The food is plated like artwork, and portions focus on quality over quantity. The

attire runs on the formal side. Book at least one day ahead here, especially during high season, and note that the restaurant is roughly a kilometer outside of the town center.

GELATO
Cristallo Caffé
Piazza Catena, 17, Riva del Garda;
0464/553-844; www.cristallogelateria.com;
7am-1am daily; €2-10

With plenty of indoor and outdoor seating, this café and gelateria is a hot spot for tourists to cool down during the summer months. It stays open late, so ideal for those that want a place to sit and hang with friends late into the night. Gelato flavors range from chocolates to creams to fruity sorbets, and they come in cups, cones, on top of waffles, and inside crepes. A full-service bar is also available, so stop by during opening hours for coffees and pastries in the morning or an *aperitivo* in the afternoon.

ACCOMMODATIONS
€80-150
Rosalpina
Località Pregasina, 106, Riva del Garda;
0464/554-293; www.hotelrosalpina.it; €99

Sitting up in the mountains away from the lake, the Rosalpina hotel is a simple, affordable option for those wanting a little peace and quiet away from the summer crowds without the frills of fancy resorts. The family-run inn offers unpretentious rooms with classic hotel furniture, each with a balcony. The property includes a small playground and an outdoor pool as well as free parking. Each room includes a private bathroom and WiFi. The restaurant below serves breakfast as well as classic Italian dinners with local dishes.

The towering Italian Dolomites surround the entire lakeside village of Riva del Garda

Hotel Canarino

Via Monte Oro, 11, Riva del Garda;
0464/554-086; www.casacanarino.it; €110
This cozy, family-run hotel sits in the heart of Riva del Garda, close to several restaurants and shops as well as near the waterfront. The stone exterior may make the property look old, but the inside is completely renovated and modern, with a garden that includes an intimate hot tub, a large outdoor swimming pool, spa center, and a bar with a sun terrace. Each room has large windows with a garden or city view, air conditioning, WiFi, and a private bathroom. Parking is included.

Hotel Europa Skypool & Panorama

Piazza Catena, 13, Riva del Garda;
0464/555-433; www.hoteleuropariva.it;
€157
Located in the beautiful Catana Square in Riva is the beloved and elegant Hotel Europa, known for its rooftop pool and bar with a terrace lending to gorgeous panoramic views of the town and the lake. The restaurant in the hotel serves classic Italian dishes, and a continental breakfast each morning. Each room includes air conditioning, WiFi, and private bathroom with toiletries. Parking is included.

€150-250
Hotel Savoy Palace

Via Longa, 10, Riva del Garda;
0464/554-242; www.hotelsavoypalace-
lagodigarda.it; €173
In the center of Riva Del Garda is this lovely, bright, large family-friendly resort with a sizeable garden, an outdoor swimming pool, and a hot tub. During the day, children can hang out at the kids club, which includes activities and a play area. Each bright and simply furnished room includes air conditioning, WiFi, and private bathroom. A large breakfast buffet is included in the price of each room, as is guest parking.

Parc Hotel Flora

Viale Rovereto, 54, Riva del Garda;
0464/571-571; www.parchotelflora.it; €174

Located along the waterfront, the modern and relaxing Parc Hotel Flora is near the beach yet hidden by tall palm trees. The property includes a shaded, heated outdoor pool and a wellness center. Each room is elegantly yet simply furnished, with a cool color palette differentiating each room. Rooms include air conditioning, WiFi, and private bathroom. A huge breakfast buffet with fruits, eggs, bacon, and more is included.

OVER €250
Lido Palace

Viale Giosuá Carducci, 10, Riva del Garda;
0464/021-899; www.lido-palace.it; €450

For the ultimate luxurious getaway, book a room at the five-star Lido Palace, which has its own Michelin-star chef and one of the best wellness and spa centers in the region. Every corner of this place drips relaxation and modern elegance, with the property including a Mediterranean restaurant and a sophisticated bar. Each air-conditioned room includes WiFi, and private bathroom.

INFORMATION AND SERVICES

For assistance during your trip, visit the tourist information office (Largo Medaglie Oro al Valor Militare, 5, 0464/554-444, https://gardatrentino.it, 9am-7pm daily) in the center of Riva. The English-speaking staff can provide information on all of the attractions in and around Riva as well as give dining and accommodation suggestions. They also offer free maps of the area and other informational booklets.

There's a public hospital (Largo

Marconi, 2, 112 in case of emergency or 0464/582-629) and a local police station or *carabinieri* (Via Oleandri, 10, 118 in case of emergency, or 0464/576-300). Both places are open 24 hours, but note that you'll need to ring the buzzer to enter the *carabinieri* station. While you may run into some luck with English-speaking help, it isn't guaranteed.

GETTING THERE
BY CAR

From Milan or one of the other lakes east of Garda, head east on the A4 tollway until you reach Brescia and take the exit for Brescia Est. Then follow the SS45bis up to Salò, and drive along the western shore of Lake Garda. The entire trip from Milan is roughly 170 kilometers (105 miles) and 2.5 hours.

From Lake Iseo, take the SP510 down to Brescia, then follow the SP11 east toward Lake Garda. After about 16 kilometers (9.9 miles), take the Salò/Tenno Rampo to merge onto SS45bis north, which follows the western shore of Lake Garda in its entirety until you reach Riva del Garda. From Iseo to Riva, it's about a 1.5-hour trip of 100 kilometers (62 miles). From Lake Molveno, simply take the SS421 south through Ponte Arche and Tenno until you reach Riva. The drive is about an hour, spanning 49 kilometers (30 miles).

From Desanzano, take the SS11 to reach the A22 tollway heading north toward Bolzano. Take the exit toward Rovereto Sud/Lago di Garda Nord, then head east on the SS240, following the signs to Riva del Garda for roughly 18 kilometers (11 miles). The total time from Desenzano to Riva is about 1.25 hours, with a drive of 65 kilometers (40 miles). Keep in mind that this road is packed during peak season, so hit the road early to avoid major traffic delays.

There are several paid **parking lots** in Riva, but most of the lots near the lake will fill up quickly in the warmer months, so get here as early as you can or consider finding an accommodation that offers parking for guests.

BY TRAIN AND BUS

If you're traveling by public transportation, you can take a fast or regional train to the **Peschiera del Garda** station which falls directly along the main rail line between Milan and Venice. Trains departing Milan's Central Station run roughly every 30 minutes 6:25am-10:25pm daily, with one-way fast train tickets starting around €15 and one-way regional trains around €10. Travel from Milan on a *freccia* train takes a little more than an hour to Peschiera and a regional train takes a little more than 1.5 hours. Tickets can be purchased online in advance at https://trenitalia. com or directly at any train station.

From the Peschiera del Garda station, catch one of the **ATV buses** running from the train station. Lines 483 and 484 run between Peschiera del Garda, Malcesine, and Riva del Garda. Buses depart generally 6:30am-8:30pm daily, but you can find official timetables and prices at https://atv.verona. it. Tickets, which cost from €2.80-4 one-way, can be purchased in the bars

or tobacco shops at the Peschiera del Garda train stations. You can also ask the staff there for a physical timetable for the buses to carry around with you. Each bus trip is about 1.25 hours long and departs once an hour 8:22am-6:52pm daily.

BY BOAT

Infrequent public ferries run from Limone Sul Garda and Malcesine to Riva del Garda 8:30am-6:30pm. The trip from Limone is about 15 minutes and from Malcesine, it's about an hour, with fares running from €3-10 one-way per person. The ferry station can be found in the center of the village lakefront.

GETTING AROUND

Given that most of the historic center is pedestrian-only, and the town is rather compact, you should take advantage of the beautiful sites on every corner by walking around the village, as it generally takes no longer than 10-15 minutes on foot to get from one point to another. However, for those wanting to visit **Arco**, you can take the Trentino Transporti B861 bus between the Riva del Garda bus station (Riva del Garda Autostaz., 38066 Riva del Garda) to the Arco bus station (Arco-Autostaz., 38062 Arco), which is about a 20-minute trip each way. Buses depart 7:23am-8:23pm, with tickets costing around €2 each way.

Limone sul Garda

Despite being much smaller than its sister town Riva del Garda to the north, Limone has enough picturesque charm and character to hold its own as one of Lake Garda's most visited towns. Its name in English means "Lemon on the Garda," which comes from the town's long history of growing lemons and other citrus fruit. A simple walk through the quiet residential alleys in the center of the village near the lake reveals hints of this history, as you'll see tiles for house numbers painted with the famous lemon.

The waterfront walkway is full of lively local bars and restaurants, with friendly boutiques weaving in and out the different pathways throughout the town. You'll also encounter family-run lemon farms, which gives the place a more authentic feel than other resort towns on the lake. The town is situated about 11 kilometers (nearly 7 miles) south of Riva del Garda, which is about a 15-minute drive down the western shore of Lake Garda.

SIGHTS

LA LIMONAIA DEL CASTEL
Via Orti, 17, Limone sul Garda; 0365/954-008; 10am-10pm daily; €2

For a true understanding of the town's name and longstanding affair with the yellow fruit, swing by the La Limonaia del Castel to view the rustic gallery, museum, and lemon farm in the heart of Limone. The museum takes you through the history of the once-northernmost lemon farming community in the world and the trade business that put this little village on the map. Don't skip a stroll around the living gardens, with the enticing citrusy fragrance. Note that there are no elevators available here, and there are quite a few steps between the five different levels of the museum.

CHIESA DI SAN BENEDETTO
Via Monsignor Daniele Comboni, 52, Limone sul Garda; 0365/954-017; 8:30am-6:30pm daily; free

Visible from the waters of Lake Garda, the Chiesa di San Benedetto stands tall over the rest of the village. The church was built in the late 1600s, with its white walls surrounded by colorful residential buildings. The facade is shaped like a temple, with the most notable feature being a **tall bell tower** that points into the sky, noticeably higher than everything else around. On the inside, the single nave is decorated with several bays and columns, all with low lighting and Baroque features. During the summer when tourists tend to swarm into the village, a

Limone's Chiesa di San Benedetto

step inside the church serves as a little, quiet escape for a few minutes.

WATERSPORTS
Surfing Lino Limone
Spiaggia Foce fiume S. Giovanni, Limone Sul Garda; 338/409-7490; www.surfinglino. com; May-Sept.; €20-200

Windsurfing and sailing are two of northern Garda's most beloved sports, with several locals hitting the water each day during the warmer months. The Surfing Lino companies offers hourly or daily rental of equipment, as well as lessons for beginners in windsurfing, kitesurfing, and cat-sailing. You can either choose from one-hour private lessons, one-day, or three-day courses, starting from €50. One-person and two-person kayaks and stand-up paddleboards are also available for rent directly from the shore starting at €10 per hour.

Limone Rent Boat
Via Lungolago Marconi, Limone sul Garda; 333/761-6432; www.limonerentboat.com; 9am-7:30pm daily; €40-220

Travelers with or without a boating license can rent boats directly from the shore in the middle of Limone Sul Garda. The staff at Limone Rent Boat is not only extremely friendly, but very proud of their professional service. Each staff member is very welcoming and helpful, giving you a full briefing on how to use their equipment. Boats can hold one to eight people, depending on the size you rent. While you can always rent on a whim when walking along the lake, note that boats tend to be rented out rather quickly during high season, so call ahead to book a boat in advance.

SHOPPING
Fra Luca
Via IV Novembre, 29, Limone sul Garda; 0365/691-174; 9:30am-7pm daily

Fra Luca sells citrusy products and other local gastronomy goods such as limoncello, olive oil, regional wines, and more.

Fra Luca is one of a handful of shops selling local gastronomy products, with a whole wall dedicated to local and Italian wines, as well as limoncello made from the village's lemons and other citrus products made from local ingredients. The shop owner is friendly and helpful, so feel free to ask about the products overflowing the shelves and barrels. While you'll find olive oils, sauces, pastas, and more, don't walk out without grabbing a bag of the candies made from Limone Sul Garda lemons.

FOOD
Ristorante Al Tamas
Via A. Volta, 86, Tremosine; 0365/954-298; 12pm-2pm and 6pm-10pm Tues.-Sun.; €12-30

Tucked into the mountains overlooking Limone Sul Garda and the lake is this seafood lover's delight, with an intimate atmosphere and a wide-ranging menu that includes fish, pastas, pizzas, salads, roasted vegetables, lake fish, and more. Although the place is rather low-key and casual, it can easily turn into a nice date night spot for those wanting to get away from the summer crowds along the lakeshore. Portions here are rather large, so save room for tiramisu for dessert. From the center of Limone, it's just a quick five-minute drive to the restaurant heading south on the SP115.

La Cantina Del Baffo

Via Caldogno, 1; 0365/914-061; www.lacantinadelbaffo.it; 5pm-11pm daily; €15-45

Stop by this casual, comfort-food restaurant for classic Italian dishes without any frills or nonsense. Ask for a table on the patio that overlooks the lake from higher altitude, then enjoy heaping portions of pasta with ragu, grilled red meats with potatoes, lake fish, and more. While you can order from the à la carte menu, spring for the €45 tasting menu that includes gazpacho, veal, and a selection of handmade desserts. The place prides itself on using top-quality ingredients cooked to perfection, so come here for fine flavors. Reservations are recommended, especially during high season, as the place is only open for dinner.

ACCOMMODATIONS

Hotel Villa Margherita

Via Luigi Einaudi, 3, Limone sul Garda; 338/114-5591; www.villamargheritalimone.com; €80

If you're looking for a quiet, quick getaway spot without all of the frills of lake resorts, consider a stay at Hotel Villa Margherita. Just a few minutes from the beach, the property sits in the middle of a peaceful, family-run olive grove with beautiful views of the lake below. Rooms are simply yet elegantly furnished, and there's a **cozy bar** in the hotel for those wanting to hang around and take in the relaxing ambiance. Each room includes air conditioning and private bathroom.

Hotel San Pietro

Via Tamas, 20, Limone Sul Garda; 0365/958-111; www.hotelsanpietrolimone.it; €187

As one of Limone's most beloved hotels, the Hotel San Pietro is full of couples looking to get away, families looking for fun, and everyone in between. The property doesn't sit directly on the waters of Lake Garda, but you do get a nice view of the lake from the beautiful outdoor pool, which is surrounded by tropical trees and plants. Here, you're about a 20-minute walk from the center of Limone, so it's a good option for those traveling by car. Each room includes air conditioning, WiFi, and private bathroom. The property also includes free parking for guests, an Italian restaurant and bar. Breakfast is included.

GETTING THERE AND AROUND

BY CAR

From **Milan** or one of the other lakes, head east on the major A4 tollway until you reach the Brescia, take the exit for Brescia Est, then follow the SS45bis up to Salò, and then along the western shore of Lake Garda. The entire trip is roughly 160 kilometers (99 miles), which takes about 2.25 hours from Milan to Limone. From **Desenzano**, follow the SP572 north until you reach Salò, then follow the SS45bis straight up the western shore of the lake until you reach Limone. From Desenzano to Limone, it's about an hour drive of 54 kilometers (33.5 miles).

From **Riva del Garda**, simply follow the signs to Limone sul Garda via SS45bis south for roughly 10 kilometers (6 miles) for about 15 minutes.

There's only a handful of **parking** garages and lots at the top of Limone sul Garda, but most of the lots directly above the village center will fill up quickly in the warmer months, so get here as early as you can. The lakefront of Limone and most of the town is not directly accessible by car, meaning you'll need to follow the signs that lead you down to the main part of the village by foot.

BY BOAT
Infrequent public ferries run from Malcesine and Riva del Garda to Limone 8:30am-6:30pm. The trip from Malcesine is about 45 minutes, and from Riva it's about 15 minutes, with fares running from €3-10 one-way per person. The ferry station can be found in the center of the village lakefront.

A direct car ferry service between Malcesine and Limone departs every hour 9:10am-6:10pm daily; the one-way trip lasts about 20 minutes. Tickets range between €9.50-20.10, depending on the type and size of the motor vehicle. Official fares and timetables can be found at www.navigazionelaghi.it.

Lake Ledro

Like Lake Garda, Lake Ledro was created from the glacial melt of Garda Glacier. It is one of the many small, crystal clear lakes dotting the region of Trentino, and it remained inaccessible until the 19th century when a road between it and Lake Garda was finally built. The pristine blue waters of Lake Ledro are brighter than that of Lake Garda but not as turquoise as that of other Trentino lakes. Surrounded by heavily forested mountains, Lake Ledro draws visitors for its fairytale setting and for the ample opportunities to enjoy the outdoors, whether that's lounging on the beach, canoeing on the lake, or walking its circular path.

The two main villages on Lake Ledro are **Pieve di Ledro** on the western side and **Molina di Ledro** on the eastern side, with no more than 4 kilometers (2.5 miles) between the two. For dining and accommodation options, stick to the village of Pieve di Ledro, although any other restaurant or hotel near the lake will be within walking distance or a very short drive away.

SIGHTS
CHIESA DELL'ANNUNCIAZIONE DI MARIA
(Church of the Annunciation of Mary)
Via Vittoria, 3, Pieve di Ledro; 04/6459-1019; 8am-6pm daily; free
As soon as you step inside this long and narrow church with its plain rounded ceiling and white walls, you will feel a certain sense of serenity and spirituality wash over you, whether you're religious or not. The church dates back to at least 1235. The sunlight flooding through the windows, illuminating the old wooden pews and the small altar at the front, serves as the only source of significant light.

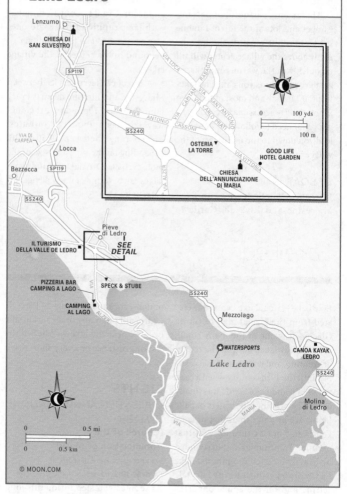

Lake Ledro

Lenzumo

CHIESA DI
SAN SILVESTRO

SP119

VIA DI
CARPEA

Locca

Bezzecca   SP119

SS240

VIA LUCA

VIA RABAGLIA

VIA PIER ANTONIO
CASSONI

VIA CAPITAN
VIA CARLO PRATI

VIA SANT'ANTONIO

SS240

VIA ALZER

OSTERIA
LA TORRE

VIA VITTORIA

GOOD LIFE
HOTEL GARDEN

CHIESA
DELL'ANNUNCIAZIONE
DI MARIA

0   100 yds
0   100 m

Pieve
di Ledro

IL TURISMO
DELLA VALLE DE LEDRO

SEE
DETAIL

PIZZERIA BAR
CAMPING A LAGO

VIA ALZER

SPECK & STUBE

SS240

CAMPING
AL LAGO

Mezzolago

WATERSPORTS

Lake Ledro

CANOA KAYAK
LEDRO

SS240

VIA
VAL
MARIA

Molina
di Ledro

0   0.5 mi
0   0.5 km

© MOON.COM

Walk slowly from the back to the front of the church to admire the various shrines and paintings of saints and angels on either side. On the outside, take note of the tall bell tower whose top is perforated with small openings that used to serve as observation decks. You'll also notice an old clock. You'll more than likely be just one of a few people inside, so respect and soak in the silence.

CHIESA DI SAN SILVESTRO (Church of Saint Sylvester)

Via Unità D'Italia, Lenzumo; 8am-6pm daily; free

This two-story church sits off of the lake and directly on the main road that passes through the small village

In the warmer months, you'll see several sail boats and other non-motorized boats drifting along the waters

of Lenzumo, which is a quick, four-kilometer drive north of Pieve di Ledro on SP119. It is worth making a pit stop here to admire the beauty within. The church's single, narrow nave features a traditional altar at the front, which is surrounded by colorful stuccos depicting scenes from the Bible. When facing the church from the outside, you'll notice its height is much greater than its width, so the tall windows on either side of the church allow so much natural light to stream in that it illuminates the white, intricately detailed ceiling. The bell tower behind the main building has a beautiful clock painted on each side. Because the church is somewhat off the beaten path, note that it may not always be open.

SPORTS AND RECREATION

BEACHES

No matter where you are on Lake Ledro you are never far from its shallow, relaxing shores on which you'll find plenty of grassy areas and pebbled beaches. Two official beach areas are in the main towns, Pieve di Ledro and Molina di Ledro, but you'll find some shadier, more secluded spots along the lakeside path between the two villages. Most of these are not official beach areas, but they do offer a little more intimacy away from the summer crowds. You won't find any services included at these spots, so pack everything you need, including food and drinks, if you head to one of these places.

Pieve di Ledro

The beach in Pieve di Ledro, often called the Mezzolago, is a public beach just a short walk north from the center of the village along the path hugging the lake. The pebbled shore is met by a large grassy area, great for lounging and equipped with picnic tables. The beach also includes a floating pontoon for diving just off of the shore, and parking is free in the lot next to the grassy area.

Molina di Ledro

The free, public beach along the shores of Molina di Ledro is located near the center of the village, with a large lawn for relaxing as well as a beach volleyball court, tennis courts, restrooms, a parking lot with an hourly fee, and a bar serving snacks and drinks. This beach often gets crowded in the summer, so get here early to claim your spot, and pack a picnic lunch.

✪ WATERSPORTS

The waters of Lake Ledro are eerily calm before 11am and after 5pm each day. For the most relaxing experience, get to the lake early in the morning for a paddle.

Canoa Kayak Ledro

Via Maffei, 127, Molina di Ledro; 348/772-0199; www.canoakayakledro.com; €8+ per hour

For a little fun atop the waters of Lake Ledro, rent a canoe, kayak, paddleboat, or stand-up paddleboard directly at the shore in Molina di Ledro, which is a 4-kilometer (2.5-mile) walk or very short drive from Pieve di Ledro. Canoes and kayaks can be rented by a single person or in pairs starting from €8 an hour. Rental equipment is available from May-September, as are beginner courses organized by the club.

Camping al Lago

Via Alzer, 7/9, Pieve di Ledro; 04/6459-1250; http://camping-al-lago.it; 9am-7pm Apr.-Sept.; €5-8 per hour

If you're in Pieve di Ledro, head to the waterfront to rent a single canoe, single kayak, or stand-up paddleboard for €5 per hour. Pairs can be rented for €8. Rental equipment for water sports is generally available from May-September, although some equipment may get rented out quickly in July, and August, so it's worth calling ahead to ask if there is equipment available in June, July and August.

Sailing on Lake Ledro

HIKING
Lake Ledro Loop
Molina di Ledro

Given the diminutive size of this beautiful little corner of Trentino, one of the best activities on Lake Ledro is simply walking along the shore, which has a clearly marked trail around the entire circumference. Start in the small village of Molina di Ledro near the quaint outdoor museum, which features these small huts that were once an important part of Ledro's culture and history. From there, walk down to the beach, then follow the signs that direct you to the start of the loop that circles the lake. Almost every point and turn of the trail opens up to panoramic views—the gorgeous waters with the backdrop of the mountains always reflected in them take on various shades as you walk.

The path is paved in most areas, but still mainly dirt at the foot of the mountains. Stop along the way at one of the many small beaches, docks, picnic tables, and benches for a rest if you need it, or just to enjoy the scenery. Bring water with you and pack a lunch or snacks so that you can stay hydrated and energized. The path is mostly flat and not terribly rigorous at any point. From start to finish the entire loop around the lake is about 10 kilometers (6.2 miles) with a very gentle slope of 35 meters (38 yards) gradually throughout the loop. The average time it takes to walk the whole the loop is 2.5 hours, including a couple of quick rest stops.

The loop around Lake Ledro is also bike-friendly. Bikes can be rented from Camping al Lago (Via Alzer, 7/9, Pieve di Ledro; 04/6459-1250; http://camping-al-lago.it; 9am-7pm Apr.-Sept.; €5-8 per hour) in Pieve di Ledro.

FOOD AND ACCOMMODATIONS
Ristorante Pizzeria Bar Camping Al Lago
Via Alzer, 7/9, Pieve di Ledro; 0464/591-250; http://camping-al-lago.it; 7:30am-10pm; €5-20

This family-friendly, casual establishment is a staple on Lake Ledro, offering many services along with an all-day bar, so you can swing by for any meal, midday snack, or drink. Sit out on the patio overlooking the lake in the morning with a pastry and a cappuccino or stop in for an afternoon strudel paired with a local wine. During mealtimes, you'll find a small selection of pastas and local dishes such as beef with arugula and shaved parmesan as well as a large menu of wood-fired pizzas. Although they take reservations, you should be fine to walk in without them.

Osteria La Torre
Via Vittoria, N.28, Pieve di Ledro; 0464/590-168; 10:30am-2pm and 5pm-12am Thurs.-Tues.; €10-30

Osteria La Torre offers an intimate and casual dining experience in a quiet corner of Pieve di Ledro village. The wooden tables and chairs surrounded by completely stone walls and ceilings, accented by the occasional brick column, create a rustic feel. The warm and friendly service is faster than at typical Italian restaurants, yet you're invited to stay for as long as you'd like. You'll find traditional Trentino dishes here, such as *canederli* (bread dumplings), potatoes, spätzle (soft egg noodles), *tagliere* plates (dishes of cold cuts and often cheeses) with speck, and a menu full of pizzas. In the summertime, you can enjoy the outdoor seating. While you should be able to snag a table without reservations for lunch, it's better to book a table in advance for dinner to be safe.

Good Life Hotel Garden

Via Vittoria, 6, Pieve di Ledro;
04/6459-1033; www.gardenledro.it; €70 d

Sitting in the middle of the Pieve di Ledro village and just a stone's throw away from the shores of Lake Ledro is the Good Life Hotel Garden, tucked among the Italian Dolomites and surrounded by a beautiful, natural park and gardens. The hotel creates a mountain lodge feel without breaking the bank, and its guest rooms are simple yet modern and stylish in decor. The hotel includes a large outdoor swimming pool and sun terrace as well as an Italian restaurant serving local cuisine. Each room includes WiFi and private bathroom. A hearty Italian and German-style breakfast buffet is included in the price of a double room, as is guest parking.

INFORMATION AND SERVICES

Il Turismo della Valle di Ledro

Via Nuova 7, Pieve di Ledro; 04/6459-1222;
www.valledeledro.com; 9:30am-1pm and
3-7pm daily

Lake Ledro's official tourism company has its office in the center of the Pieve di Ledro village, open daily and easily accessible, with a very friendly English-speaking staff ready to answer any questions you may have. Their website is extremely detailed, accurate, and always up-to-date with any information you may need regarding lake activities, surrounding activities, entertainment, sports and recreation, accommodations, or dining options. They can help you book hotels, tables at restaurants, and other tours or activities that may interest you.

GETTING THERE

FROM MILAN

The easiest and most direct way to get to Lake Ledro from Milan is to drive.

By Car

Head east out of Milan on the A4 tollway until you reach Brescia. Then, take the Brescia East exit in the direction of Madonna di Campiglio and Val Sabbia. Follow the SS45bis north until it turns into SS237 and continue north along the western shore of Lake Idro, following the signs for Valle di Ledro. The entire trip from Milan to Lake Ledro is about 180 kilometers (112 miles), and takes about 2.75 hours.

By Public Transit

If you aren't driving, you'll need to catch a train to Brescia from Milan's Central Station. These trains depart every 20 minutes or so depending on whether you take the regional (€7.30, 1 hour 5 minutes) or *freccia* (€10.80+, 45 minutes) trains. You'll then need to walk to the Brescia SAIA bus station that is just outside of the train station and grab the Slink 202m bus to Riva del Garda in Lake Garda. Tickets for around €5 each can be bought directly on board. Once in Riva del Garda, you'll need to catch a final bus to Pieve di Ledro. Take the 214 bus for about 30 minutes until you reach the lake. Official ticket prices and timetables for both busses can be found at www.gardatrentino.it.

FROM LAKE GARDA
By Car

From Lake Garda, you'll first need to get to Riva del Garda, then head east out of the city, following the signs for Valle di Ledro on SS240. The trip from

Riva to Lake Ledro takes about 20 minutes over 14 kilometers (8.6 miles).

By Public Transit

From Riva del Garda, take the 214 bus to Valle di Ledro, which is about a 30-minute trip. Buses generally run 6am-6pm daily, with a one-way ticket around €5 each. Official ticket prices and timetables can be found at www.gardatrentino.it.

GETTING AROUND

With Lake Ledro only being 3.5 kilometers (2 miles) in length and 1.5 kilometers (1 mile) in width, the best way to get around the lake is on foot or by canoe or kayak. The mostly paved trail that hugs the entire circumference of the lake makes for a beautiful way to get to each of the small villages located on either side of the lake. The paths are also bike-friendly, for those that bring their own bikes or want to rent one, although a bike isn't necessary for traveling around the lake.

If you're calling Pieve de Ledro home during your stay on Lake Ledro, note that most hotels here offer private guest parking, and you'll also find a grassy parking lot directly on the beach as well.

LAKE ISEO

With peaceful fishing villages

dotting its shores, Italy's fourth-largest lake is also one of the most naturally beautiful lakes in Europe. Although Lake Iseo was put on the international map in 2016 due to The Floating Piers installation, a work of art that allowed visitors to literally walk on the waters of the lake, it remains relatively untouched by hordes of tourists. Lake Iseo is also home to the largest habitable lake island in Europe, Monte Isola, a wooded abyss with a few fishing villages that make it seem the stuff of fairy tales.

HIGHLIGHTS

✪ **PIEVE DI SANT'ANDREA:** As one of Iseo's most beloved and ancient churches, this place is known for its well-maintained frescoes and bell tower. Step inside for a little moment of peace and serenity (page 310).

✪ **MONASTERO DI SAN PIETRO IN LAMOSA:** If you're traveling by car, take a side trip to this monastery, known today for its collection of frescoes and other art exhibitions. It's located in a quiet, historically rich corner of the region and on a beautiful, ancient piece of property (page 319).

✪ **CASTELLO DI BORNATO:** Visit this Renaissance castle for a better understanding of the history and culture of the Franciacorta wine region, and to admire the views of the rolling vineyards below (page 319).

✪ **FRANCIACORTA WINERIES:** You can (and should) indulge in a glass or two of this sparkling white wine during *aperitivo* hour at a lakeside restaurant, but for a deeper understanding of the importance of wine culture in the region, book a tour at one of the local wineries (page 320).

✪ **MONTE ISOLA:** Wander around the fishing villages, colorful waterfront, and winding pathways full of ancient churches on Europe's largest lake island. (page 322).

Lake Iseo sits just north of the cities of Brescia and Bergamo in northern Italy and about 100 kilometers (62 miles) northeast of Milan. Italians will tell you this is one of the best kept secrets of Northern Italy. With its quiet waters surrounded by quaint medieval villages, it is a popular destination for couples heading here for romantic weekends full of Franciacorta wine.

ORIENTATION

Although Lake Iseo is the fourth-largest lake in Italy, it is still much smaller than Lakes Como, Maggiore, or Garda. The town of Iseo, after which the lake is named, sits on the lake's southeastern corner. Working clockwise from Iseo toward the western shore of the lake, you will find Clusane right next to Iseo, Paratico and Sarnico on the southwestern corner, Predore just north of that, and Riva di Solto sitting in the northern part of the western shore. The main towns on the northern end of the lake are Lovere on the northwest and Pisogne on the northeast. On the eastern shore, you'll find Marone, then Sale Marasino and Sulzano just south of that. Sale Marasino and Sulzano are the towns closest to the beautiful Monte Isola, and direct ferries to the island can be found in both towns.

Just off the southern part of the lake, you'll find the heart of the Franciacorta wine region. Just a few kilometers south of the town of Iseo on SPXI is Provaglio d'Iseo, where you'll find a handful of well-known

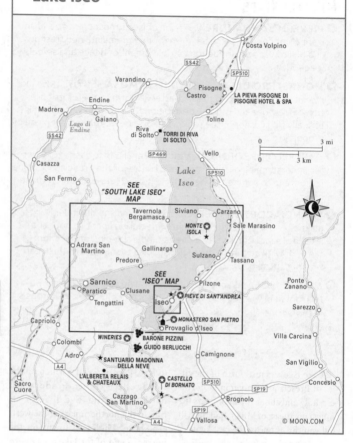

Lake Iseo

Costa Volpino

SS42 SP510

Varandino
Pisogne
Castro
LA PIEVA PISOGNE DI
PISOGNE HOTEL & SPA

Endine
Madrera
Gaiano
Toline

Lago di
Endine
Riva
di Solto
TORRI DI RIVA
DI SOLTO

SS42
Casazza
Vello

San Fermo
SP469
SP510

Lake
Iseo
SP510

SEE
"SOUTH LAKE ISEO"
MAP

Tavernola
Bergamasca
Siviano
Carzano

MONTE
ISOLA
Sale Marasino

Adrara San
Martino
Gallinarga
Sulzano

Predore
Tassano

SEE
"ISEO" MAP
Pilzone
Ponte
Zanano

Sarnico
PIEVE DI SANT'ANDREA
Paratico
Clusane
Iseo
Sarezzo

Tengattini
MONASTERO SAN PIETRO
Provaglio d'Iseo

Capriolo
WINERIES
BARONE PIZZINI
Villa Carcina

Colombi
GUIDO BERLUCCHI

Adro
Camignone
San Vigilio

A4
SANTUARIO MADONNA
DELLA NEVE

Sacro
Cuore
L'ALBERETA RELAIS
& CHATEAUX
CASTELLO
DI BORNATO
SP510
SP19
Concesio

Cazzago
San Martino
SP19

A4
Vallosa
Brognolo

0 _____ 3 mi
0 _____ 3 km

© MOON.COM

Franciacorta wineries, as well as the **Monastero di San Pietro in Lamosa**. Just south of Provaglio d'Iseo following SP71, you'll find the small villages of **Borgonato** and **Bornato** (the latter being part of the larger village of **Cazzago San Martino**). **Adro**, on the other hand, is more southwest of the lake and of Iseo by about 13 kilometers (8 miles), closer to the main E64 road connecting Brescia and Lake Iseo. The village of **Erbusco** is just a few kilometers below Adro following SPXII.

PLANNING YOUR TIME

It's fairly easy to get a good taste of the lake in a **weekend trip**, with the more popular destinations sitting at the southern end of the lake as well as on Monte Isola. You'll find the most sights, dining, and accommodation options in the southern towns of Iseo, Clusane, and Sarnico, or on the island. Don't leave this area without sipping on a glass of Franciacorta wine and trying the local lake fish, such as the salted sardines.

If you're traveling without a car, you can still see a lot of what Lake Iseo has to offer by sticking to the town Iseo, where you can also grab a ferry to Monte Isola or a train up the eastern shore of the lake. You'll find a similar climate as in Milan and the other lakes: hot summers and colder winters, with most businesses and attractions open or running more frequently in the summer months. Visit from May to September to take advantage of one of the several sports or recreation activities.

Itinerary Ideas

ESSENTIAL LAKE ISEO

To make the most of a single day on Lake Iseo, head straight to the town of Iseo to begin your day before hopping on a ferry to Monte Isola.

1 After breakfast at your hotel, start your day peacefully at the **Pieve di Sant'Andrea** in Iseo, taking in the frescoes and the quiet atmosphere.

2 Explore the town of Iseo on foot, stopping first at **Piazza Garibaldi** to catch a glimpse of local life.

3 Poke your head inside of some of the region's most historic churches, like the **Chiesa di Santa Maria del Mercato.**

4 Take the ferry to **Monte Isola,** where you can grab a bite to eat and a glass of Franciacorta wine on the waterfront at La Foresta in the quiet and charming fishing village.

5 Spend the afternoon exploring the largest lake island in Europe, starting at the **Church of San Michele** in Peschiera Maraglio and slowly making your way around the footpath on the island's edge.

6 Head back to Iseo for dinner at the intimate **I Due Roccoli** for fresh pasta or lake fish. Book your table in advance to make sure you don't miss this spot during the high season.

Iseo Itinerary Idea

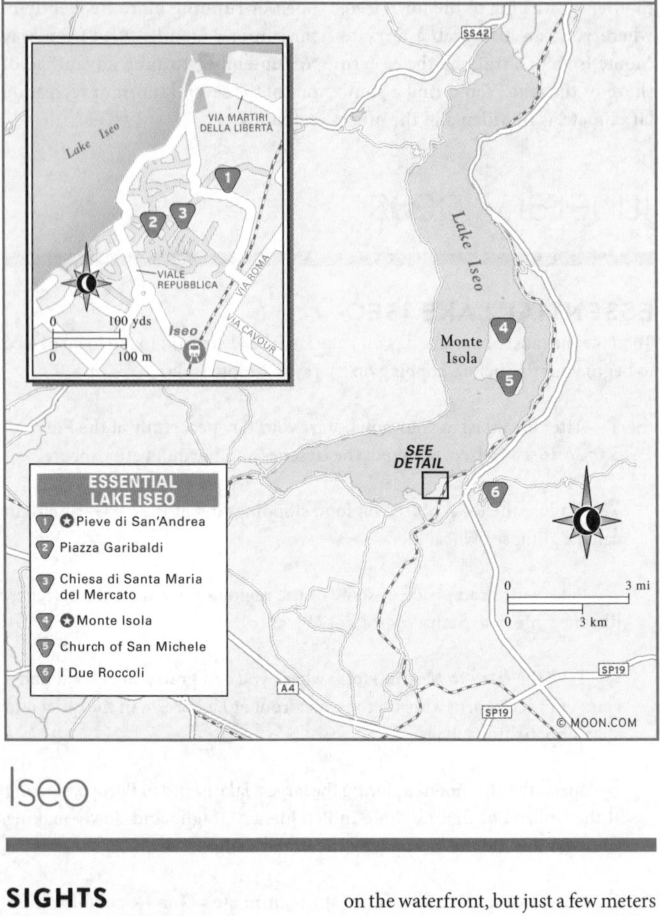

ESSENTIAL LAKE ISEO

1. ✪ Pieve di San'Andrea
2. Piazza Garibaldi
3. Chiesa di Santa Maria del Mercato
4. ✪ Monte Isola
5. Church of San Michele
6. I Due Roccoli

Iseo

SIGHTS

PIAZZA GARIBALDI

Iseo; free

This lively, colorful square serves as the heart of the historic center of Iseo, surrounded by bars, restaurants, churches, shops, and more. The center of the piazza is home to the statue of Guiseppe Garibaldi, who helped found the Kingdom of Italy, and the promenade serves as a popular meeting place by locals. Unlike many lakeside villages, this piazza isn't located directly on the waterfront, but just a few meters away. From here, most other sights in the town are generally a 5-10 minute walk away.

✪ PIEVE DI SANT'ANDREA (Church of Saint Andrew)

Piazza del Sagrato, 7, Iseo; 030/980-206; 9am-6pm daily; free

This historic church first broke ground on the current site in the 5th century, although it has been reconstructed several times in the centuries

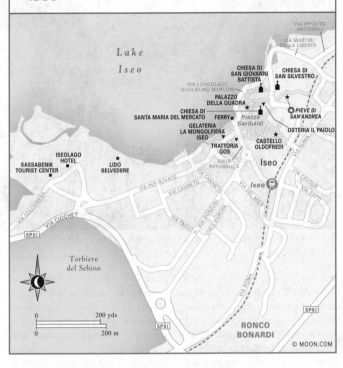

Iseo

since. Close to Iseo's center, the Pieve di Sant'Andrea may seem old and overlooked from the outside, but the frescoes on the inside are well-preserved and the atmosphere is very quiet and dimly lit. The peaceful, short walk away from the lake and Piazza Garibaldi will take you through narrow, ancient roads full of local homes and shops. The most important architectural feature of the church is the bell tower, which houses a small oratory.

CHIESA DI SAN SILVESTRO

Via Duomo, 27, Iseo; 030/980-577; 9am-6pm daily; free

This church was first built in the 13th century as a bishop's chapel but later

became the seat of the Discipline of the Holy Cross. A building was later added to its southern facade. Today, most of the original frescoes from anonymous artists have been covered, but you will still find traces of them on the wall. Stop by here if you're visiting the Pieve di Sant'Andrea, as it sits just across from it. Due to the degradation of the property in the past decades, locals have taken it upon themselves to restore this beloved church.

CASTELLO OLDOFREDI

Via Rampa Cappuccini, Iseo; 2pm-6:30pm Mon., 9am-12pm and 2pm-7pm Tues. and Fri., 2pm-6:30pm and 7:30pm-9pm Thurs., 9am-12pm and 2pm-6pm Sat., closed Wed. and Sun.; free

The Pieve di Sant'Andrea's frescoes, despite being centuries old, are still bright, clear, and well-preserved.

Just south of Iseo's historic center is Castello Oldofredi, once one of the most important castles of the Brescia region. The castle dates back to the later part of 9th century, and its name comes from the influential noble family of the same region; however, there is no official documentation claiming that the Oldofredi family actually owned the castle. Today, the old castle serves as a house for many municipal offices, including a local library and courtyard that are both open to visitors. Even if you skip the inside of the castle, the structure alone is a marvel to witness, as it stands as a reminder of how deeply the history of this region runs.

PALAZZO DELLA QUADRA

Between Piazza Giuseppe Garibaldi and Via Sombrico, Iseo; free

Palazzo delle Quadra, also known as Piazza Statuto in Iseo, was a very important spot for the city during the Middle Ages due to its prominent

location in the city center and was owned by the historically influential Oldofredi family. Today, it houses local government buildings. Most of the construction of the palace took place during the 13th-16th centuries. The interior features wooden ceilings and human figureheads. Although there are no formal visiting hours for the building itself, the internal courtyard is always open; wander through it for a momentary trip back through time and experience the local history.

CHIESA DI SAN GIOVANNI BATTISTA

Via Duomo, Iseo; 030/980-577; 8am-12pm and 2:30pm-5pm Tues.-Sun.; free

This 18th-century church now sits on the site of a destroyed medieval baptistery just across the Pieve di Sant'Andrea. Parts of the original building were preserved, such as three Romanesque tiles. Today, you'll notice a unique barrel roof and works by Andrea Fantoni on the walls. This building is one of the three churches within very close proximity of one another in the sacred area of San'Andrea, so don't miss an opportunity to stop in on your way to the main church.

CHIESA DI SANTA MARIA DEL MERCATO

Vicolo Chiuso, 3, Iseo; 8am-12pm and 3pm-6:30pm Tues.-Sun.; free

The Chiesa di Santa Maria del Mercato, known in English as the Church of Santa Maria, overlooks Piazza Garibaldi in Iseo, wedged into a little corner in the center of town. The 18th-century frescoes, which are partially peeled and on display on canvas while the rest remain on the church's walls, were painted by a village artist. Each represents the cycle of the Passion of the Christ. The church is shaped irregularly between different buildings in the piazza, which was built by the Oldofredi family in the 14th century. Due to its unique position and size, you may easily overlook this little church, but it's worth visiting for a few moments of silence.

The Chiesa di Santa Maria del Mercato is wedged into a small corner in the center of Iseo.

BEACHES
Lido Belvedere

Via Per Rovato 28, Iseo; 030/980-970; www. lidobelvedereiseo.it; 9am-8pm Mon.-Sat., 8am-12pm Sun. and Tues. mid-May-mid-Sept.; €5-12 per person

Lido Belvedere comprises a park with a beach on the lake located in the southern part of Iseo. It includes a swimming pool, waterslide, playground for kids, and a BBQ area with a grill and picnic tables. There is also a café on the premises serving sandwiches, burgers, beers, and cocktails. Private parking is available for visitors. A full day for an adult is €12, with reduced prices for children and those arriving later in the day. This place fills up quickly in the summer, so come in the morning for a chance at snagging a sunbed.

Sassabenik Tourist Center

Via Colombera 2, Iseo; 030/980-603; https://www.sassabanek.it; 9am-8pm daily May-Sept.; €8.50-13.50, children 5 and under free

For an all-inclusive day in the sun, head to the Sassabenik Tourist Center, which includes swimming pools, lakeside beach access, a playground, a marina, and tennis courts. This is a great option for families, as the swimming pools are all kid-friendly. If you didn't pack a lunch, there's an onsite restaurant and bar serving pastas, sandwiches, and more. Much like other beaches on this lake, this place fills up rather quickly in the summer months.

CYCLING
Lake Iseo Loop

Start and finish in the town of Iseo

Cycling the loop around the shores of Lake Iseo is one of the best ways to see the lake from all angles. The loop, a total of 65 kilometers (40 miles) all the way around, is free and open to the public year-round and suitable for all bicycle types and fitness levels. However, there are slightly hilly areas around the northern part of the lake that are more difficult, so keep that in mind if you're an inexperienced cyclist or traveling with kids. I recommend starting in Iseo and heading southwest, following the signs to Paratico, then on to Sarnico and Predore before heading north all the way to Lovere. Go around the northern tip to Pisogne, before you head down the eastern shore back to Iseo. The whole loop will take you about four hours to complete. The loop gets fairly busy in the summer time, and is shared with pedestrians and occasionally cars, so take caution and use general safety rules.

Iseo Bike
Via per Rovato, 26, Iseo; 340/396-2095; www.iseobike.com; 9:30am-12:15pm and 2:30pm-7pm daily Apr.-Oct.; €5-110

If you're looking to spend some time cycling around Lake Iseo, bikes can be rented for 1-5 hours (€3.50-15) or all day up to 10 consecutive days (€110) at Iseo Bike. Bikes can be picked up or delivered to a meeting point. Each rental includes a lock, a kit for punctures, and a map with the most popular routes of the Lake Iseo and Franciacorta area. The owners were born and raised in this region, so tell them exactly what you'd like to get out of your time in the region, and they will set you up perfectly. They also offer guided and unguided bike tours, including one of the Franciacorta wine region. You can book your rental bikes directly on the website or by phone.

FOOD
ITALIAN AND PIZZA
Trattoria Gos
Viale Repubblica, 6A, Iseo; 030/982-1818; www.trattoriagos.it; 11:30am-3pm and 6:30pm-11:30pm Mon., Wed., Fri.-Sun.; €15-25

For something a little heavier than fish, head to Trattoria Gos for plenty of meat options and handcrafted beer. The atmosphere is casual and cozy, with only a few tables (so reserve a spot to be safe). Start with a board of cold cuts or cheeses, then select from the variety of meat dishes: beef, donkey, ostrich, lamb, foal, and duck, just to name some. There's also a small selection of vegetable sides and pastas, for those wanting to stay on the lighter side.

Trattoria Gos serves craft beers and a unique selection of various kinds of meat.

Osteria il Paiolo
Piazza Mazzini, 9; 030/982-1074; 12pm-10:30pm daily; €15-35

This small and simple osteria is one of the tried-and-true restaurants of Lake Iseo, with a classic menu of pastas, fish, vegetables, and traditional Italian wines and desserts. If you're wanting an unpretentious, quiet dining experience with Italian comfort food, look no further. You shouldn't have a problem getting in at lunch or for an *aperitivo*, but it wouldn't hurt to book a table in advance for dinner.

GELATO
Gelateria La Mongolfiera Iseo
Via Campo, 26, Iseo; 035/449-1333;
9:30am-11pm daily; €3-10

For a sweet and cold treat during the hot summer months, swing by this gelateria for some handmade gelato, mini sweet treats and cakes, or granitas. While there isn't much seating, the taste makes up for it. You'll find a variety of gelato flavors, from passion fruit to salted caramel.

ACCOMMODATIONS
€80-150
Empire Resort Hotel
Via del Dossello, 30, Iseo; 030/989-8128;
www.hotelempireresort.it; €118

Located on top of a serene hill surrounded by nature, the Hotel Empire Resort is the peace and quiet you may be looking for. Guest rooms are cozy and accommodating, and the hotel includes a seasonal outdoor pool and private beach; a short 10-minute walk is all it takes to get to Lake Iseo. Each room includes air conditioning, WiFi, and private bathroom. Breakfast is included.

Araba Fenice Hotel
Via Fenice, 4, Iseo, 030/982-2004, www.
arabafenicehotel.it; €142

Located directly on Iseo's waterfront, the Araba Fenice features modern, neutral-colored guest rooms, some with a hot tub and terrace. Each room includes air conditioning, WiFi, and private bathroom. Breakfast is included.

Iseolago Hotel
Via Colombera, 2, Iseo; 030/98-891; www.
iseolagohotel.it; €150

The Iseolago Hotel is right on the lake, just a quick walk away from beaches and near the city center. The bright and modern hotel includes private beach access, an outdoor pool, hot tubs, a sauna, a gym, and a Turkish bath. Each room includes a balcony, WiFi, air conditioning, and private bathroom.

Southern Lake Iseo

SIGHTS
CASTELLO CARMAGNOLA
Via Porto, 3, Clusane; www.lagoiseo.it/
castello-carmagnola-a-clusane-diseo; free

Dominating a decent portion of Clusane's shoreline, this private castle was conquered by Venetians in the early 1400s, but later donated by the Venetians in exchange for military services. The loggia, unique to the castle, was recently restored along with several other smaller parts of the property. Today, you can book a guided tour to learn more about the castle's history and its importance to the village. Tours need to be booked in advance, but you don't need a tour to admire the beautiful exterior.

PINACOTECA GIANNI BELLINI
(Gianni Bellini Picture Gallery)
Via San Paolo, 8, Sarnico; 035/910-900;
10am-12pm and 3:30pm-6:30pm Sat. and
Sun. Mar.-Dec.; free

This picture gallery, located in the

Southern Lake Iseo

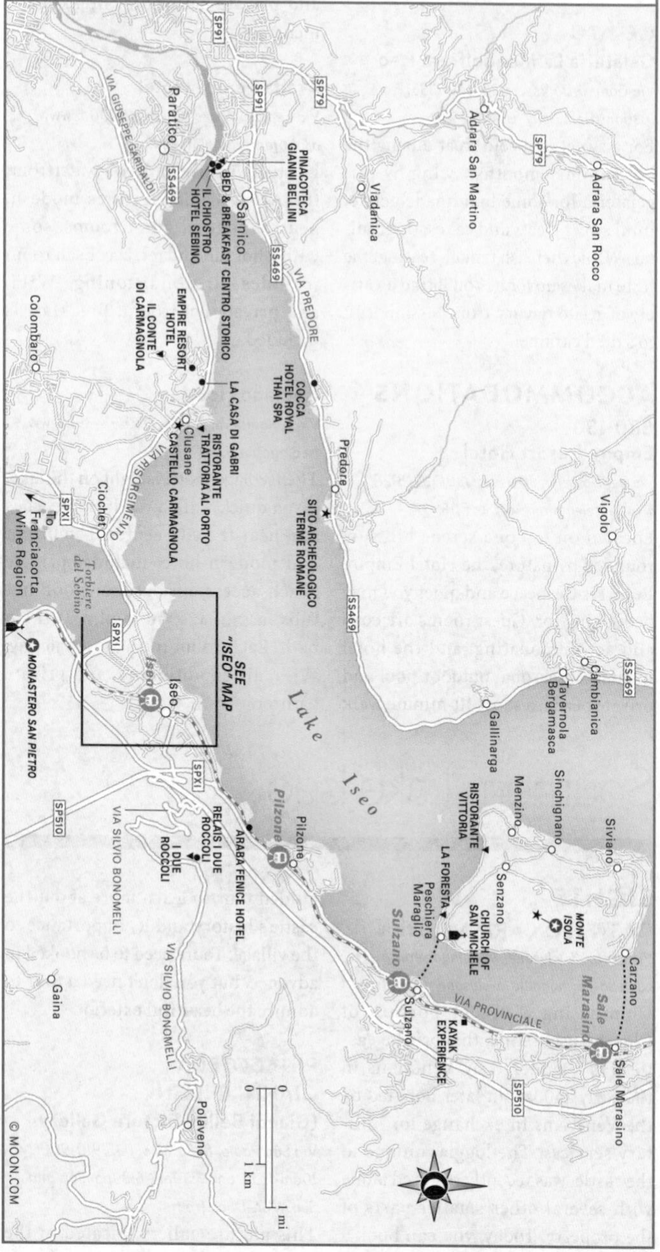

LAKE ISEO
SOUTHERN LAKE ISEO

© MOON.COM

15th-century Palazzo Gervasoni in Sarnico, is home to about 150 works, most of them paintings from 1500 to 1700. Most art was collected by art admirer don Gianna Bellini, after whom the gallery is named. Here you'll find work from Palma the Younger, Antonia Cifrondi, Francesco Cairo, and more. Today, you'll also find works from art students from Lombardy, Bergamo, Veneto, and parts of central Italy, with a special collection of still life and landscape paintings found on the top floor. The *pinacoteca* is arguably the most prestigious art gallery in the Iseo region.

SITO ARCHEOLOGICO TERME ROMANE

Piazza Antonio Lanza, Predore; 035/938-032; 6pm-10pm Thurs.-Sat., 9am-1pm Sun.; free

Located in the small village of Predore, these Roman baths housed in a 1st-century villa were previously a very important gathering place for locals to socialize while enjoying the natural hot springs. Some even claimed that these springs had healing properties back in the day. The archaeological site is rather large, so historians speculate that there could have been rooms for baths with different temperatures, a sauna, small theaters, and more. When you visit the baths today you feel like you have stepped back in time. It is one of the most unique and historical attractions in the region.

FOOD
SEAFOOD
Il Conte di Carmagnola

Via Mirabella, 34, Clusane; 030/989-8051; www.relaismirabella.it/menu.php; 12:30pm-2pm and 7:30pm-10pm daily; €30-70

Il Conte di Carmagnola at the Relais Mirabella in Clusane pairs fine dining with excellent views from the hilltop. You can see the lake near and far while sipping wine and eating some of the finest food on the lake, including local lake fish with polenta and fresh, handmade pastas. The chef takes great pride in perfecting the presentation and flavors of each dish. The wine list here is also extensive. Book in advance and request a table closest to the terrace's edge for the best view.

ITALIAN AND PIZZA
✪ I Due Roccoli

Via Silvio Bonomelli, 79, Iseo; 030/982-2977; www.idueroccoli.com; 12:30pm-4pm and 7:30pm-10pm daily; €30-50

I Due Roccoli is an intimate, romantic spot located in the hotel of the same name in Iseo, with fresh flowers, quiet music, a fireplace, and paintings on the wall. The large windows give diners panoramic views of the lake, and all dishes are beautifully plated. The restaurant offers dishes such as fresh pasta with seafood, risotto, lake fish, and classic appetizers and desserts. Reservations are recommended.

The secluded and peaceful I Due Roccoli gives guests hilltop views of the lake below.

Ristorante Trattoria Al Porto

Porto dei pescatori, 12, Clusane;
030/989-014; www.alportoclusane.it;
12pm-2pm and 7pm-10pm Thurs.-Tues.;
€15-30

Open for more than 150 years, this historic trattoria specializes in fish from Lake Iseo. Housed in a charming stone-front villa, this place feels like a romantic fine-dining establishment, but one that doesn't empty your wallet. The congenial staff is happy to explain the local dishes that you'll find on the menu. The atmosphere is warm and intimate, and reservations are recommended.

Il Chiostro

Piazza Oliva Besenzoni, 1, Sarnico;
035/911-190; www.hotelsebino.com/en/
restaurant-bar/restaurant-il-chiostro;
12pm-3pm and 6:30pm-12am Wed.-Mon.;
€20-35

This large restaurant is owned and operated by a local hotel and has a sizeable wine cellar. The menu includes pizzas, traditional Italian pasta dishes (served in large portions), a selection of classic appetizers, and various options for second courses and desserts. When the weather is nice, you can sit outside in the nearby piazza, on a covered terrace, or inside; no matter where you sit, you'll enjoy beautiful views of the lake. Book in advance for dinner during high season.

ACCOMMODATIONS

UNDER €80
Bed & Breakfast Centro Storico

Via Lantieri, 26, Sarnico; 035/066-7273;
www.centrostoricosarnico.it; €69

Situated in the historic center of the village of Sarnico is this simple and affordable B&B, about a 10-minute walk away from the shore of Lake Iseo. The stone entrance is picturesque, and

there's a small dining room for breakfast each morning. Each guest room includes air conditioning, WiFi, and private bathroom. There is free parking for guests, and breakfast (included in the price of the room) includes both gluten-free and vegan options on request.

€80-150
Cocca Hotel Royal Thai Spa

Via Predore, 75, Sarnico; 035/4261-361;
www.coccahotel.com; €127

Located on the shores of Sarnico is the Cocco Hotel Royal Thai Spa, with guest rooms ranging from simple and accommodating to luxurious and elegant. Each room includes a balcony with a view, air conditioning, WiFi, and private bathroom.

✪ Relais I Due Roccoli

Via Silvio Bonomelli, 79, Iseo; 030/982-2977;
www.idueroccoli.com; €130

For an intimate and quiet getaway, try the Relais I Due Roccoli, situated in an old villa just outside of Iseo. Guest rooms are full of antique furniture and have vaulted ceilings. The property is adorned with bright green plants sprouting everywhere, and there is also a beautiful restaurant with a terrace overlooking the lake. Each room includes a balcony, air conditioning, WiFi, and private bathroom with a tub. Parking is included.

OVER €150
✪ La Casa di Gabri

Via Traversa XIII, 2, Clusane sul Lago;
333/800-6056; www.lacasadigabri.com;
€180

La Casa di Gabri (Gabri's House) is a quiet, luxurious, and intimate house that combines modern features with complete relaxation and classic Italian hospitality. Select from one of the themed suites in the small house, then take a dive in the outdoor pool or soak in the hot tub surrounded by green gardens and stone pathways. Each guest room includes air conditioning, WiFi, and private bathroom. Book in advance for this little piece of heaven, as it fills up quickly.

Franciacorta Wine Region

SIGHTS

✪ MONASTERO DI SAN PIETRO IN LAMOSA

Via Monastero, 5, Provaglio d'Iseo; 030/982-3617; www.sanpietroinlamosa.it; 10am-12pm and 3pm-6pm Sat. and Sun.; free

The Monastero di San Pietro in Lamosa (Monastery of San Pietro in Lamosa) is one of the oldest recognized religious structures on Lake Iseo. The history of the monastery is very intriguing, as it was originally lived in by pagan and, later, Christian cults before being donated to Cluniac monks and transformed into an official monastery. Today, it is private property and has been expanded, renovated, and converted to residences. You can visit on the weekends to see a collection of frescoes about the life of Jesus Christ from an unknown 16th-century artist. The monastery's silence and tranquility complements the surrounding Franciacorta vineyards. It is best accessed by car, as the village is small and not served by train.

✪ CASTELLO DI BORNATO

Via Castello, 24, Bornato; 030/725-006; www.castellodibornato.com; 10am-12pm and 2:30pm-6pm Sun.; €12 per person

This Franciacorta castle is known

The Monastero di San Pietro in Lamosa is one of Lake Iseo's hidden treasures, known for its frescoes depicting the life of Jesus.

The Castello di Bornato is in the heart of Franciacorta wine country, looking over the surrounding vineyards.

just as much for its wine cellars as it is for its Renaissance fortress. From the castle, you can see the Alps as well as the Po Valley. Today, you can book a guided tour for an additional price (which varies based on what you want to see and taste) to see the fully furnished castle, the interior of which takes you to another place and time. The villa on the castle grounds provides excellent views of the vineyards below. Don't leave without a bottle of wine from the cellars, mostly full of local Franciacorta wine made near the property.

Sanctuary of the Madonna of the Snow (Santuario Madonna della Neve)

Via Carlo Cattaneo, Adro; 030/735-6623; https://madonnadellaneveadro.it; 6:30am-12pm and 3pm-7pm daily; free

This little Catholic church in the countryside, seemingly away from the rest of the world, was built in the 17th century on the day of the local Madonna della Neve festival. Built with just a single nave and two altars on either side of the church, it features a 15th-century fresco depicting baby Jesus and Mary. Step inside to enjoy a few quiet moments of peace.

TOP EXPERIENCE

✪ WINERIES
Barone Pizzini

Barone Pizzini Soc. Agr. Via San Carlo 14, Provaglio d'Iseo; 030/984-8311; www.baronepizzini.it; 9am-12:30pm and 2pm-6pm Mon.-Sat., 9am-12:30pm Sun.; tours €20-30

Priding itself as one of the first truly organic labels in the Franciacorta region, Barone Pizzini is one of the highest-quality wineries in Italy. Everything about this winery, from its vineyards to its cellars, from the grapes to the wine-making process itself, exudes integrity. You can book three different types of tours, each showcasing a different pairing of wines and locally produced nibbles. All tours take you through the steps of the wine production process from vine to bottle and end in the cellar and store, where you can purchase some of Franciacorta's finest wines, including the renowned Golf 1927 Franciacorta DOCG. All of the buildings open to visitors are modern and sleek, yet reflect the region's rustic and authentic feel. English-speaking tours must be booked online in advance.

Guido Berlucchi

Piazza Duranti, 4, Borgonato di Corte Franca; 030/984-381; www.berlucchi.it; tours €25-35

The drive up to this beautiful, massive property makes you feel like you're in a movie set in the Italian countryside. The rustic, stone building that greets you is welcoming as it is historic. The family-run establishment has been around since the beginning

the Franciacorta vineyards as seen from the Castello Bornato

If you were to ask the Milanese about their top regional wines, they wouldn't hesitate to tell you that many come from the Franciacorta wine area, which sits just next to Lake Iseo. The Franciacorta vineyards are well known by Italians, although they still remain relatively unknown outside of Italy due to the age (the area isn't centuries old, like most wine regions, but came into production in the 1950s) and location. Most would think of Tuscany or Veneto for some of the best Italian labels, but the **sparkling white wines** from here are highly regarded countrywide, especially in Lombardy.

The vineyards of Franciacorta, which are just about an hour east of Milan, start at the foot of the Alps and tumble right down to the lake. You'll be hard pressed to find a restaurant on or near the lake that won't serve multiple Franciacorta labels. The sparkling wine, made with chardonnay and pinot bianco grapes and a bit drier than prosecco, is especially well-known.

The best part of this region is that unlike highly popular areas like Tuscany that are flooded with wine tour buses, Franciacorta is refreshingly authentic and quiet. Vineyard owners still aren't used to flocks of tourists stomping around their farms. You'll find that local restaurants will proudly suggest a glass during *aperitivo* hour or lunch along with a plate of salted sardines from the lake.

For a true taste of Lombard wine culture, take a bike tour around the Franciacorta vineyards with **Iseobike** (340/396-2095; www.iseobike.com) or follow the brown road signs for the **Franciacorta Strada del vino** (wine road), which you'll find on the SPXI from Iseo, for a relaxing drive.

of the Franciacorta wine region in the 1950s, but a complete restructuring of the property in the past decade has made it one of the more beloved and most-visited wineries in northern Italy. There are three different tours available; each includes a quick look at the vineyards, a walk through the historic wine cellar and tunnel, and an intimate wine tasting paired with artisanal treats. The staff sommelier is also on hand to answer any questions. Don't leave the property without trying the Berlucchi '61 Nature 2011 or Berlucchi Palazzo Lana Extrême Reserve 2008. Tours should be booked online in advance, and be sure to specifically request an English-speaking tour, if you need one.

ACCOMMODATIONS
L'Albereta Relais & Chateaux

Via Vittorio Emanuele, 23, Erbusco;
030/776-0550; www.albereta.it; €260

L'Albereta Relais & Chateaux is a spacious and luxurious resort on Erbusco, located just south of Lake Iseo. This spot not only boasts a quiet, secluded location, but also features a great wellness center with a sauna, Turkish bath, hot tub, and large swimming pool. Each room includes a garden view, air conditioning, WiFi, and a private bathroom.

✪ Monte Isola

Monte Isola (www.visitmonteisola.it) is not only the largest island on Lake Iseo, but it is the largest lake island in Europe. There are a handful of small villages on the lake, Silviano being the main residential village, where you'll find a town hall as well as a few beautiful churches. Peschiera Maraglio is the main tourist village, and you'll find most ferries arriving and departing from here. Carzano is best known for the thousands of paper flowers that decorate the village every five years.

If you want to visit just one of the eleven towns on the island, stick with Peschiera Maraglio. As you wander along its steep and winding paths, you'll come across the Church of San Michele. As you amble through the town's narrow passageways, you'll notice the laundry hanging from the clotheslines above you, and the residents bustling to and fro around you; time here takes on a different quality. For an Italian-lakes version of an island getaway, this is the place for you. You'll also find plenty of local restaurants and accommodations. To get here, take one of the ferries from the various shore towns on Lake Iseo.

KAYAKING
Kayak Experience

Via Fotane 50, Sale Marasino;
345/253-2030; http://kayakexperience.it;
Apr.-Sept.; €40-60 per person

For a unique way to explore Lake Iseo, try a kayaking trip around Monte Isola. Along the way, you'll pass the three main villages as well as olive fields and the more natural, quiet corners of the island. The excursion lasts one full day, with prices starting at €60 per person for groups of two or €40 per person for groups of six. The instructors will guide you around the lake and give you basic kayaking lessons before departure. Food and drink are not included in the trip, so pack snacks for the day. Make reservations in advance through the website or by phone.

FOOD
SEAFOOD
Ristorante Vittoria

Loc. Sensole, 22, Monte Isola;
030/988-6222; 12pm-3:30pm and 7pm-9pm
daily; €12-35

To eat directly on the water on Monte Isola, try Ristorante Vittoria, with a handful of plates available for every course. The real prized plates here are the selection of fish, from grilled salmon and trout to a platter of mixed grilled catches from the lake. If you're wanting to keep cool during the summer, the indoor dining room also has air conditioning.

✪ La Foresta

Via Peschiera Maraglio, 174, Monte Isola; 030/988-6210; www.forestamontisola. it; 12pm-2pm and 7pm-9pm Thurs.-Tues.; €20-40

Located in a prime waterfront spot on

The intimate La Foresta restaurant sits in a garden-like atmosphere right on Monte Isola's shoreline

Monte Isola with beautiful lake views, the family-run La Foresta restaurant is known for its traditional menu of lake fish and local cuisine. The restaurant sits on a quiet strip just outside of the main core of Peschiera Maraglio, with both indoor and outdoor seating in a garden-like atmosphere. Reservations are recommended in high season.

GETTING THERE AND AROUND

The only way to reach the beautiful island of Monte Isola is via a private boat or the public ferry system run by **Navigazione Lago d'Iseo** (www.navi-gazionelagoiseo.it). Note that the permission to drive motor vehicles (other than motor scooters) is reserved for officially selected locals. Bicycles and motor scooters are permitted on the island, and you can bring them onboard the ferry for an additional €2.60 each way.

While several towns along the lake's shore offer ferries to Monte Isola, the only direct ferries run from **Sulzano** and **Sale Marasino,** with about a 10-minute ride from each village to the island. You can also take ferries that stop at other towns from Iseo, Pisogne, Clusane, Lovere, Tavernola, and Sarnico. You can find the official timetable for the ferries at each village's ferry station or online at www.navigazionelagoiseo.it. Timetables vary greatly depending on your point of departure and season, but the website always has the most reliable and updated information. Tickets run from €2-5 one-way, depending on the length of validation time per ticket, and they can be bought directly at the ferry station of each town.

Riva di Solto and Northern Lake Iseo

The small village of Riva di Solto on the shores of Lake Iseo is home to several medieval buildings and a handful of historic towers. The first tower on **Via Torre** was built in the 13th century and was part of one of the village's fortresses. Two more towers in close proximity to each other are found on private properties near the lake and were used as part of a defensive complex for the village.

Walking along **Via del Porto** on the waterfront, you'll encounter several medieval buildings from the 12th-14th centuries, some with vaulted entrances and others with old fortress towers. Here you'll also find the **church of San Rocco**. Time in this small village seems to crawl and the hustle and bustle of city life is essentially nonexistent for the people who live and visit here.

ACCOMMODATIONS

€80-150

Pisogne Hotel & Spa (La Pieve di Pisogne)

Village Don Giovanni Recaldini, 1, Pisogne; 0364/86-214; www.lapievedipisogne.it; €99

La Pieve di Pisogne Hotel & Spa is a relaxing place to stay year-round, as it's just as beautiful in the snow as it is during the warm summer months. The hotel is modern and focuses on relaxation, with a spa that includes a sauna, Turkish bath, and hot tub along with various massage options. Each guest room includes air conditioning, WiFi, and private bathroom. The hotel has free parking for guests, and there is an excellent restaurant and bar on the property, with breakfast included.

Getting to Lake Iseo

FROM MILAN

BY CAR

If you're traveling from Milan, take the A4 heading east to Bergamo. From here, your route depends on which part of the lake you're wanting to reach. To get to the northern part of the lake, take the SS42 directly to the town of Lovere. The trip from Milan to Lovere is about 95 kilometers (59 miles) and takes just under two hours.

To reach the southern part of the lake, continue on the A4 past Bergamo until you reach the Rovato exit, then follow the SPXI state road north toward the lake until you reach the town of Iseo, keeping an eye out for the signs leading you to the town. The trip from Milan to Iseo is about 96 kilometers (59 miles) and takes approximately 1.75 hours.

BY TRAIN

Lake Iseo is also easily accessible by train from Brescia. From Milan, take either a regional or fast (*freccia*) train from Central Station to the Brescia railway station. Trains depart from Milan to Brescia roughly every 20 minutes, either using the *freccia* (€19.90, 36 minutes) or regional trains (€7.50, 1 hour 5 minutes), and you can purchase tickets directly at the train station or online in advance at www. trenitalia.com.

Once at the Brescia station, take the regional **Brescia-Iseo-Edolo** line that runs up Lake Iseo's eastern shore and passes through the Franciacorta area. This line stops at Iseo, Sulzano, Sale Marasino, Marone, and Pisogne. The train departs from Brescia about every hour with departures starting around 7am. The last train from Iseo back to Brescia is around 9:30pm each evening. The journey between Brescia and Iseo is about 30 minutes by train, with tickets running at €3.30 each way. You can purchase tickets directly at each train station or online in advance at www.trenitalia.com.

FROM THE OTHER LAKES

BY CAR

Regardless of the lake from which you're traveling to reach Lake Iseo, you will more than likely have to get on the **A4** at one point or another. If you're traveling from Lakes Como, Maggiore, Orta, or Lugano, head back in the direction of Milan to reach the A4 highway, then follow the directions outlined in the previous section to get to Lake Iseo.

Likewise, if you're traveling from Lake Garda (or the nearby Lakes Ledro and Molveno), your best bet is to head back to the A4 highway, then take it west in the direction of Brescia. Once in Brescia, continue on A4, then take the **SP11** highway north toward Lake Iseo until you reach the **SP510** highway, which will continue to take you north until you reach the town of Iseo. From Brescia, the trip to Iseo is about 20 kilometers (12.5 miles), which is about a 20-minute drive.

Getting Around

Getting around Lake Iseo and the region is easiest and most comfortable to do by car, as many of the more popular sights are spread in various villages and towns around the lake. If you're traveling without a car, your most reliable mode of transportation will depend on which shore you're hoping to visit. For the eastern shore, stick with the train. For the western shore, you can get around by bus. All villages and towns are walkable, so don't be afraid to explore by foot, as it will give you the best sense of the culture and history of this quiet corner of Lombardy.

BY TRAIN

The regional **Brescia-Iseo-Edolo** train stops at Iseo, Sulzano, Sale Marasino, Marone, and Pisogne, with just a few minutes between each stop. The trip from the southern town of Iseo to the northern lake town of Pisogne is just half an hour at €2.90 each way. Tickets between each village run around €1.80-2.50, and trains run roughly every hour 6:30am-8:30pm.

You can purchase tickets either online at www.trenitalia.com or directly at the train stations in each town. Regional trains have no seat limit, so tickets will not run out, and you can use the ticket within three hours from the time you validate your ticket using the stamping machines on each platform.

BY BOAT

The frequently running ferries (www.navigazionelagoiseo.it) are an inexpensive and convenient way to hop around the various lake villages, with ferries stopping at all of the larger villages on the lake, including Iseo, Clusane, Sarnico, Sulzano, Pisogne, Lovere, and more. The ride is usually 20-30 minutes between each village, and one round-trip ride generally stops at several villages in the middle of the lake, although villages on the northern and southern ends of Lake Iseo only have ferry stops a few times each day. Tickets should be purchased directly at the ferry station in each village, and the cost is based on the length of time for which you want the ticket to be valid, for example, from €2 per hour to €13.50 per day. If you plan

on village-hopping using the ferries, grab a day ticket in order to avoid possible lines. Otherwise, a one-way ticket is fine for each trip.

BY BUS

You can access the western shore of Lake Iseo via the Line E buses that run from Bergamo's train station and stop in the towns of Sarnico, Predore and Tavernola. If you plan on traveling between these three villages, the bus is a great, affordable option. But if you're wanting to reach other villages, taking the ferry or driving is a better option. The buses run around 6am-7pm each day, about every hour. A full list of timetables can be found at https://bergamotrasporti.it. Tickets are around €2 per person and per journey and can be purchased directly from the bus driver. Remember that you must validate your ticket on the bus.

BY BIKE

With nearly 200 bike routes around the Lake Iseo area, you're bound to find something suitable for your cycling needs, from flat routes to hilly routes, to circular loops and paths winding through Franciacorta vineyards. However, most paths through the hills are for more experienced mountain bikers, as they can be quite hilly and variable in terrain.

The circular bike path (not completely paved) that spans 65 kilometers (40 miles) around the circumference of Lake Iseo gives you the opportunity to pedal from lakeside village to lakeside village. Keep in mind that bike paths are often shared with pedestrians or cars on regional roads, so follow general safety rules and common sense when biking in the area.

The only way to reach Lake Iseo's Monte Isola is by ferry or private boat.

BY CAR AND SCOOTER

A motor vehicle is definitely the easiest and most recommended way to get around this region, as many of the sights and restaurants aren't found directly on the lake, but in the Franciacorta hills surrounding the area. The two main roads are the **SP510,** which runs up and down the eastern shore of the lake, and the **SP469,** which runs on the western side from Sarnico to Lovere. The small regional roads winding through the little villages along the shore and stretching into the mountains are very well marked, so you can get nearly everywhere just by reading the road signs. Most major sights, churches, restaurants, and hotels are marked by road signs as well.

Pay **parking lots** are available in all villages, but keep in mind that they fill up quickly in the warmer months. It's best to park early, then village-hop via train or ferry. Parking lots are marked with blue P signs and cost around €1.50-2 per hour.

LAKE MOLVENO

Lake Molveno, with its emerald green waters, is one of the most romantic and naturally beautiful places in northern Italy. Although overshadowed by the larger Lake Garda that lies about 40 kilometers (25 miles) south, this smaller lake is one of the gems of the Trentino Alto Adige region. For a quiet and calming escape from the thousands of visitors that choose to summer on the larger lakes, opt for Lake Molveno.

The Lake Molveno area is also home to one of the most diverse and spectacular landscapes in northern Italy. For outdoor enthusiasts, the

HIGHLIGHTS

✪ **FUNIVIA MOLVENO-PRADEL-CROZ DELL'ALTISSIMO:** Take this cable car to higher altitudes for unparalleled views of the lake and the Dolomite mountains. At the top, you'll find a plethora of outdoor activities to fill your day (page 332).

✪ **CANOEING:** With no large motorized boats authorized on Lake Molveno, spend an hour or two calmly floating atop the turquoise waters at your own unhurried pace (page 333).

✪ **FOOD OF TRENTINO ALTO ADIGE:** Grab a bite to eat at a local restaurant by the lake for a taste of the regional cuisine, with Italian and German flavors blended together on one plate (page 336).

backdrop of the Italian Dolomites not only offers spectacular views, it also provides plenty of hiking and biking opportunities both down near the waters as well as higher in the mountains. And due to the lake's proximity to Austria, its culture is a unique blend of German, Austrian, and Italian influences, which is evident in everything from the spoken language to the cuisine.

ORIENTATION

Lake Molveno is one of the many small lakes in the Trentino Alto Adige region, sitting about an hour (47 kilometers/29 miles) directly north of Lake Garda. The town of **Molveno**, the largest village on Lake Molveno, sits on the northern tip, with the small village of Seghe just southwest of it. South of Lake Molveno, you'll find the village of San Lorenzo Dorsino, accessible via the SS421. This road also runs up the lake's eastern shore and directly through the town of Molveno, and up to Andolo, which sits about five minutes and a few kilometers north of Molveno. The nearby cable car, **Funivia Molveno-Pradel-Croz dell'Altissimo,** runs from the town

of Molveno up to the nearby mountain villages of Pradel and Croz dell' Altissimo.

PLANNING YOUR TIME

At only 4 kilometers (2.5 miles) in length and less than a kilometer in width, the entire lake can be seen and explored in a day or two. It's easy to get your fill of the lake itself in a day, as you can easily spend a morning soaking up the rays on the beach, canoeing around the waters, or hiking the circumference of the shore. However, given that it's further away and less accessible than the other larger lakes, note that you'll need at least one morning of travel in each direction. Spending a long weekend here is ideal, especially if you're wanting to split your time between lounging on the lake itself and engaging in the outdoors among the Italian Dolomites. There are a handful of accommodation and dining options scattered around the village of Molveno, so you won't have trouble finding a place to stay near the lake, but book in advance, especially in the summer, as they tend to fill up rather quickly.

Lake Molveno

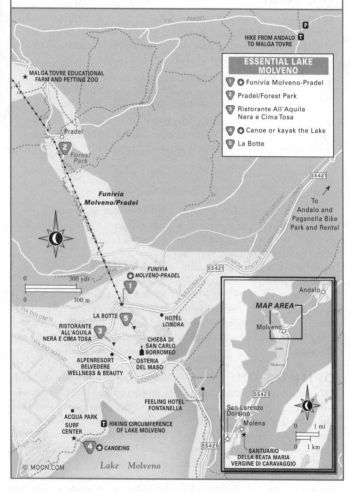

ESSENTIAL LAKE MOLVENO

1. ✪ Funivia Molveno-Pradel
2. Pradel/Forest Park
3. Ristorante All'Aquila Nera e Cima Tosa
4. ✪ Canoe or kayak the Lake
5. La Botte

© MOON.COM

Due to the altitude and more northern position of this lake compared to the other Italian lakes, the weather is slightly cooler in the warmer months, ranging from highs of 21°C (70°F) and lows of 14°C (55°F). Although it might be hot during the day, it cools down in the evenings, so bring a light jacket even in July or August. This area is quite cold in the wintertime, with highs of 5°C (40°F) and lows of 0°C (30°F), so bundle up to enjoy the snow!

Itinerary Ideas

ESSENTIAL LAKE MOLVENO

For a complete day on Lake Molveno, make the most of both the lake itself and the beautiful backdrop of the Italian Dolomites.

1 Start your day with breakfast at your hotel, then take the **Funivia Molveno-Pradel,** a cable car that will whisk you over a thousand meters (or more than three thousand feet) above sea level for absolutely breathtaking views of the lake below.

2 Get off the cable car at **Pradel,** and hit up **Forest Park** for ziplining and other outdoor activities that put your agility and balance to the test.

3 You'll have worked up a hearty appetite, so head back down to the lake for lunch at **Ristorante All'Aquila Nera e Cima Tosa.** Choose among the traditional Trentino dishes such as giant gnocchi, braised meats, speck, and more. Save room for homemade apple strudel made with regional apples for dessert.

4 Suit up for a relaxing afternoon at **the lake,** splitting your time between laying around the beach and **renting a canoe or kayak** to paddle your way along the lake top.

5 For dinner, head to **La Botte** for a regional or classic Italian pizza and a brew accompanied by a friendly, buzzing atmosphere, as this place stays open late each evening. Make yourself comfortable and mingle with the staff for a low-key, casual, and fun evening.

Sights

CHIESA DI SAN CARLO BORROMEO

Piazza S. Carlo, Molveno; 0461/586-904; www.parrocchiadimolveno.com; 7am-7pm daily; free

The small parish church of Chiesa di San Carlo Borromeo was reconstructed in the mid-1900s, so much of its original, historic charm from as early as the 1500s has been replaced with bright, clean, and plain walls.

Fortunately, a few of the church's original frescoes still remain to add color and interest to an otherwise unornamented structure. Of note, however, are the large, circular stained-glass skylights that hang directly over the altar. Bright lights stream through the glass and bounce off the chandelier below to create a sort of hanging halo effect at the front of the church, lending to its serene and ethereal air. The place is well-maintained by locals, as it's only one of a handful of churches near the lake—situated in the center of town and tucked away from the water. During the summer while most people are congregating on the shore, take a step away to enjoy a few moments of peace and quiet.

SANTUARIO DELLA BEATA MARIA VERGINE DI CARAVAGGIO

Deggia, San Lorenzo Dorsino; 9am-6pm daily; free

This little 1800s sanctuary with its two-pitched facade and tower and only 10 pews serves as a peaceful stop along the path around the small, unpopulated village of Deggia—so seemingly in the middle of nowhere. The church is one of the few remnants of a once-busy little village. Inside, you'll find frescoes and other paintings over the minor front altar, which has retained some of its brilliant colors, despite being centuries old. The natural light flooding through the few stained-glass windows makes this place appear as though it comes straight out of a storybook. The exterior is just as charming, as the building stands completely alone amongst the backdrop of the rolling hills and Italian Dolomites.

TOP EXPERIENCE

✪ FUNIVIA MOLVENO-PRADEL-CROZ DELL'ALTISSIMO
(Cable Car Molveno-Pradel-Croz dell'Altissimo)

Via Nazionale, 33, Molveno; 0461/587-008; www.molveno.it/it/funivia-and-impiant; 8:30am-12:45pm and 2pm-5:45pm daily late Apr.-Oct.; one-way €8, round-trip €12

Although it's enticing to stick to the turquoise waters of the lake during your whole visit, outdoor lovers will finds plenty of sports and other recreational opportunities among the high-altitude Dolomite mountains that surround the lake and offer unparalleled views. Take the cable car up to Pradel, which sits 1,350 meters (4,429 feet) above sea level. There you will find an intertwining network of mid-mountain hiking and biking trails. You'll also find the adventurous Forest Park, the Malga Tovre Educational Farm and Petting Zoo, and a number of observation areas for simply admiring the beauty around you. You can also continue the cable car journey up to Croz dell'Altissimo at 1,530 meters (5,020 feet) above sea level for even more biking and hiking trails. Even if you don't plan on hitting a trail or visiting Forest Park, a ride up for the views alone is worth the money.

MALGA TOVRE EDUCATIONAL FARM AND PETTING ZOO
(Agriturismo Malga Tovre)

Via Dolomiti, Molveno; 340/148-7467; www.molveno.it/it/la-fattoria-didattica; 9am-5pm daily; free

Whether you're traveling with children or not, this charming little family-run farm and petting zoo is one of the most authentic places that you can visit at Lake Molveno. Take the Molveno-Pradel cable car up to Pradel, where you'll be just a short walk away from this home of sheep, cows, pigs, donkeys, goats, hens, and more. While you can simply walk right up to this classic Trentino-style home without charge, stop for a bite to eat at one of the many wooden picnic tables outside and order a plate of traditional, local cold cuts and cheeses or a dessert of apple strudel or cake with berry marmalade. The route around the property is well-marked with descriptive placards of the region's history and culture. You can feed the animals or watch milking and cheese production demonstrations. Don't leave before heading to the small souvenir shop that sells local milk, honey, cheeses, flour, and more.

Sports and Recreation

BEACHES
Lido di Molveno
Lido di Molveno, Molveno

This free, public, pebble beach punctuated by grassy areas is one of the most relaxing options on the lake. Located in the village of Molveno, it spans nearly the entire width of the lake (so about a kilometer). There are no services on the beach itself, so you'll need to pack a picnic and bring any equipment you'd like for your time there. However, you can find a handful of restaurants and other services just a few minutes' walk from the beach. Swimming is permitted in the lake, although the water temperature stays fairly cold due to the region's cool climate, so visiting in July and August are your best bet if you're wanting to spend some time in the water.

TOP EXPERIENCE

✪ CANOEING
Because large motorized boats and sail boats on are prohibited on Lake Molveno, canoeing its crystal-clear

Lake Molveno, named most beautiful lake in Italy in 2015

333

waters is a relaxing activity. You can spend a few pleasant hours leisurely paddling the easy-to-navigate 4-kilometer (2.5-mile) canoe course around the tranquil lake.

Surf Center

Lido di Molveno, Molveno; 0461/586-086;
www.molveno.it; canoe rental €8 per hour

On the shore of the lake in Molveno sits a small office where you can rent canoes, kayaks, and paddleboards. Single and double canoes can be rented daily in the summer. For something more adventurous, try one of the stand-up paddleboarding lessons offered June-September.

HIKING

Lake Molveno Perimeter

Starts and ends at the Lido di Molveno

The hike around the circumference of the lake is short and easy, and you can follow the trail in either direction from the shoreline in the village of Molveno. It spans a total of 11 kilometers (6.8 miles) and is only mildly hilly in some areas, so it's a fairly easy option for those wanting some exercise without overtaxing themselves. The path allows you to see the crystal clear turquoise waters around the entire lake while passing other beautiful points such as bridges, waterfalls, and quiet and shallow banks. The majority of the trail is a dirt path shaded by trees and will take about 2.5-3 hours to complete. Bikes are allowed on the trail, so you can cycle it, if you'd rather.

Andalo to Malga Tovre

Start at Val Biole parking lot in Andalo

If you're feeling more energetic and active, skip the cable car up to Pradel and hike up the dirt path from Andalo, a small town just a few minutes north of Molveno, instead. You can get to the Val Biole parking lot in Andalo by car from Molveno on the SS421, or you can walk or bike there on the path that runs parallel to the road. From the parking lot, follow the signs marking the path toward Pradel up to Malga Tovre, one of the handful of Trentino-style farmhouses tucked into the mountains that also houses a petting zoo. The hike from Andalo to Pradel takes about 45 minutes to complete, and it is uphill most of the way. But throughout the hike you're rewarded the whole way with wonderful aerial views of the lake below. Once you're up in the mountains, you can continue hiking around to the other farmhouses in the area—you'll find several posted signs marking other paths to follow, with the distances marked (in meters or kilometers) for each path.

BIKING

Paganella Bike Park & Rental

Piazzale Paganella, 5, Andalo;
0461/585-298; www.dolomitipaganellabike.
com; 9am-12:30pm and 2:30pm-6pm
Mon.-Fri.; €15-35 per hour

Located at the intersection of multiple cycling routes in the surrounding Brenta Dolomite mountains, this bike park is full of trails for all levels, and also includes three downhill courses, a pump track, and a skills area for more experienced bikers. The expert cyclists that run the company are deeply knowledgeable about all the trails and can help you pick one based on your experience and fitness level. They also offer guided cycling tours (which can be booked online starting at €25), cycling holiday packages (starting at €107), and more.

You can also rent various types of leisure and professional bikes, from city bikes to mountain bikes. The staff can recommend which type of bike to rent, depending on your interests. Bikes can be rented directly online or by calling ahead, and you can arrange for delivery to your hotel.

PARKS
Forest Park
Forest Park, Pradel; 0461/586-412; www.molveno.it/forestpark; 10am-5:30pm Jun.-Sept.; €4-23

One of Lake Molveno's more adventurous options, this family-friendly park can entertain everyone for hours with plenty of outdoor activities both on the ground and in the trees. Each activity focuses on either balance, acrobatics, agility, or a combination thereof, and it's highly rated by both children and adults. Activities include obstacle courses, ziplining through the trees, tightrope walking, and tree climbing; there are also adventure-themed playgrounds for the kids. You can either pay per activity or per group of activities, which are categorized by difficulty level. To get to the park, take the cable car (*funivia*) from Molveno to Pradel. While helmets are provided, be sure to wear athletic shoes and comfortable clothing.

Acqua Park
Via Lungo Lago, 17, Molveno; 0461/586-015; www.molveno.it/en/acquapark; 9am-6pm daily; adults €8, children €5

Situated near the waterfront of Lake Molveno, this small waterpark includes an Olympic swimming pool as well as a family-friendly pool with a pair of slides, whirl jets, and other sorts of splash pads for smaller children. In the Olympic pool, you'll also find an aqua gym with various exercise activities. In the summer, the park fills up fast with families quickly claiming the handful of available sun beds in the grassy area fenced in alongside the swimming pools, so get here early if you plan on sticking around for a while. In July and August, swimming floats for both children and adults are offered for an additional price as well.

Food

La Botte
Via Cima Tosa, 4, Molveno; 0461/586-948; www.tavernalabotte.it; 6:30pm-2am daily; €10-20

This tavern is both a pizzeria and a local brewery, with a really welcoming, affable atmosphere that is so casual that you feel like you're dining amongst old friends. Here, you'll find a full menu of both traditional and regional pizzas, which may be topped with speck, mushrooms, or potatoes. If you're wanting something a little heavier, try their grilled meats, such as steaks with fried potatoes and other vegetable sides. The full beer menu includes local, national, and international brews, with the chatty bartenders and waitstaff ready to offer their suggestions based on your food selection. The tavern stays open late each evening, making it a lively, bustling place to hang out for the night.

Osteria del Maso
Via Lungo Lago, 7, Molveno; 0461/586-345; www.osteriadelmaso.it; 12pm-2:30pm and 7pm-9:30pm Wed.-Mon., 12pm-2:30pm Tues.; €20-35

This simple and rustic family-run

THE BLENDED CULTURE OF TRENTINO ALTO ADIGE

Thanks to its proximity to Austria, Italy's northernmost region of Trentino Alto Adige is a beautiful, balanced mix of Italian, Austrian, and German cultures. Both languages are used interchangeably here, so you'll see road signs, directions, restaurant names, and more written in both Italian and German. The region itself is composed of two provinces, with Trentino comprising the area from Trento to Bolzano, and Alto Adige comprising Bolzano and directly north to Austria. The region is one of only five autonomous Italian districts, meaning it has significantly more independence from the Italian government due to the population of minority groups and sub-cultures living here.

More than half of the people who call these provinces home are native German speakers. While they are also fluent in Italian, the accent is much different than the accent you'll hear in Verona, just a couple hours south or in Milan, which lies just west. In fact, to work in a public service or tourism job in the region, you have to pass a written exam proving your fluency in both languages. Trentino is arguably the most diverse and beautiful province in northern Italy, with gorgeous crystal emerald green lakes dotting the entire area, punctuated by the towering Italian Dolomites and valleys. It is an idyllic and peaceful place to spend a holiday. Because of this, you'll find just as much tourism here (mostly by central Europeans) as other parts of Italy. Most people working in restaurants, hotels, and other travel-industry-related jobs are trilingual with additional fluency in English.

✪ FOOD

The food here might be one of the most unique features of the region, as it perfectly exemplifies the blended culture. You'll find traditional Italian meals with a German twist, such as pizzas topped with speck or tagliatelle with rabbit or deer ragu. Additionally, *canederli,* a variation of German or Austrian dumplings with an Italian flavor with the addition of speck, is extremely popular in this area, as is homemade apple strudel made from the apple farms spread throughout the region.

osteria is one of the most frequented restaurants on Lake Molveno, serving strictly local dishes such as *tagliere* plates full of specks and Trentino cheeses, braised meats, mushroom and ragu pastas, dumplings, and ravioli. Given the German influence in this region, the checkered linens and wooden furniture here give the place a very German or Austrian vibe, and create a relaxed, cozy atmosphere. Portions are on the larger side of the scale, and while you shouldn't need a reservation for lunch, it's not a bad idea to make one for dinner during high season.

✪ Ristorante All'Aquila Nera e Cima Tosa

Via Nazionale, 6, Molveno; 0461/586-928; www.alexandermolveno.com; 12pm-2pm and 7pm-9pm daily; €30-50

With large portions of traditional Trentino dishes and balcony seating overlooking the turquoise waters of Molveno, this is one of the most beloved restaurants on the lake. Here, you'll find some of the heartier Italian dishes such as slow-roasted beef, tagliatelle with ragu, lake fish with potatoes, cheesy risottos topped with local apples, and more. Many dishes are served directly in the pan in which they were cooked, giving you the cozy sense of home. The restaurant gets rather packed in the summer, so book ahead in the evenings, especially if you want to grab an outdoor table. You really can't go wrong with any dish you get here, but you have to save room for the house-made apple strudel and cream, a beloved Trentino dish made from local farm-picked apples, for dessert.

Accommodations

UNDER €150

Feeling Hotel Fontanella

Via Bettega, 3, Molveno; 0461/586-955;
www.hfontanella.it; €110

The mountain lodge of Hotel
Fontanella is cozy and modern and
offers guests visiting Lake Molveno
an intimate and relaxed place to stay.
The property is a short five-minute
walk from the shore; it includes private guest parking, and there is a local
restaurant with a terrace overlooking
the lake on the premises. Each guest
room features exposed wood-beamed
ceilings, wooden furniture, a balcony
that offers either a mountain or lake
view, and a private bathroom.

✪ Alpenresort Belvedere Wellness & Beauty

Via Nazionale, 9, Molveno; 0461/586-933;
www.alpenresortbelvedere.it; €130

This large, gorgeous property sits
perched on a slight incline at the foot
of the mountains surrounded by the
waters of Lake Molveno, so each room
gives you beautiful, unobstructed
views of the lake. Despite being off of
the lake, it's just a short two-minute
walk down to the shore. The property includes a wellness center with
a relaxing indoor pool and an adults-
only spa that includes a hot tub, sauna,
and Turkish bath. You'll also find
a panoramic cocktail and wine bar
with a terrace facing the lake, as well
as a quiet, private garden and veranda.
Each guest room has a balcony with
either a mountain or lake view, WiFi,
and private bathroom. Parking and a
delicious homemade breakfast are included in the price of the room.

Hotel Londra

Via Nazionale 34, Molveno; 0461/586-943;
www.londramolveno.it; €140

The Hotel Londra is perched up on
a hill overlooking the waters of Lake
Molveno and housed in a cute pink
building with white balconies popping
out in each direction. Guest rooms
here are traditionally and simply decorated, while the common areas are
more elaborate, yet cozy, inviting you
to grab a book and stay for a while.
The property includes a restaurant
serving local cuisine with a terrace of
tables overlooking the lake. Each room
includes a balcony with either a lake
or mountain view, WiFi, and private
bathroom. Free parking is available
as well.

Information and Services

Lake Molveno is one of the smaller
lakes in the region, so you won't find
a lot of tourist services directly on the
lake. However, the Molvino Holiday
tourist company (www.molveno.it)
has a very informative, updated website with contact information for any
questions or help you may need before
or during your time on the lake.

Getting There

FROM MILAN

To get to Molveno from Milan via public transportation, you'll need to take two trains and a bus, so consider renting a car to save time and the headache of juggling several modes of public transit.

BY CAR

Follow the **A4 tollway** out of Milan and east toward Verona, passing the southern shore of Lake Garda, until you reach Peschiera del Garda. This leg of the trip will take about an hour and a half, and keep in mind that you'll pay a toll of around €9 once you take the Peschiera del Garda exit, then follow the **SR450** north until you reach **A22**, and follow this tollway north toward Brennero and Trento for roughly an hour. Take the exit for Rovereto Sud/ Lago di Garda Nord, then follow the **SS240** northwest to Lake Molveno, paying close attention to the signs at each roundabout and intersection that point you directly to Molveno. From Milan to the town of Molveno, it's nearly 250 kilometers (155 miles) and roughly a three-hour drive.

BY PUBLIC TRANSIT

From Milan's Central Station, grab a regional (€12.50, 2 hours) or *freccia* train (€21+, 1.25 hours) to **Verona Porta Nuova.** These trains depart roughly every 20 minutes. From there, you'll need to grab a regional train to the **Trento train station** (€7.85, 50 minutes). From there, take the **B611 bus** to Molveno (€2-4, 1 hour). Tickets can be purchased at the public transport ticket office at the train station or onboard. In the summer, the B611 bus runs anywhere from 10-20 times a day. Official timetables and ticket prices for the bus to Molveno can be found at www.ttesercizio.it.

FROM THE OTHER LAKES

BY CAR

If you're driving from other lakes to Lake Molveno, getting to the northern end of Lake Garda (Riva del Garda) first is the best way to go. From Lakes Como, Maggiore, Orta, and Lugano, it's easiest to head back toward Milan, then head east on the **A4** tollway until you reach the eastern shore of Lake Garda (Peschiera del Garda). From Lake Iseo, you can get the **A4** tollway east to Peschiera del Garda directly.

Once you're near Lake Garda, take the **A22** tollway north in the direction of Brennero and Trento until you reach the Rovereto Sud/Lago di Garda Nord, then follow the **SS240** northwest to Lake Molveno, paying close attention to the signs at each roundabout and intersection that point you directly to Molveno. If you're already in Riva del Garda, simply follow the **SS421** out of town and northwest to Molveno, driving through Ponte Arche.

BY PUBLIC TRANSIT

Reaching Lake Molveno via public transportation from most of the other lakes is trickier, so consider renting a car instead. Unless you're already at Riva del Garda on the northern end of Lake Garda, the best thing to do is to take a train to the **Verona Porta Nuova** train station (more than likely from Milan's Central Station), then grabbing a train to Trento (€7.85, 50 minutes).

From Riva del Garda, you can reach the train station in Trento by bus. From the Trento train station, take the **B611 bus to Molveno** (€2-4, 1 hour). Tickets can be purchased at the public transport ticket office at the train station or on-board. During peak season, the B611 bus runs anywhere from 10-20 times a day. Official timetables and prices can be found at www.ttesercizio.it.

Getting Around

Considering Lake Molveno is only 4 kilometers (2.5 miles) in length and narrow in width, the best way for you to get around the lake is by walking or biking your way around the edge of the lake. Motorized boats are not authorized on the lake, so you can rent a canoe or kayak to get from one end to the other if you don't want to walk the entire length.

You'll find a handful of pay-per-hour public parking lots scattered throughout the walkable Molveno center, with rates running between €1.50-3 per hour.

To get to Andalo from Molveno, take the SS421 road heading north by car for about 5 kilometers (3.1 miles), or by foot or bike using the pedestrian path running parallel to the road. To reach San Lorenzo Dorsino, you'll need to drive south on SS421 for about 7 kilometers (4.3 miles).

ESSENTIALS

Transportation

GETTING THERE
FROM THE UNITED STATES

Booking your air travel as far as possible in advance is recommended. Traveling directly from East Coast cities like **New York** or **Miami** is generally the most cost-efficient way to travel, with direct round-trip tickets from these cities to Milan's **Malpensa** airport ranging $300-500 for

an economy ticket. Look on websites such as https://skyscanner.net for the round-trip tickets from airlines like **American Airlines, Delta, Alitalia,** and **Emirates** that offer direct flights.

All airports have direct **shuttle buses** to the **Central Station** in Milan, and Malpensa has a direct train service, the **Malpensa Express** (https://malpensaexpress.it, one-way €12, round-trip €20), from both terminals to three of Milan's largest train and metro stations: **Central Station, Cadorna,** and **Porta Garibaldi.** Tickets can be purchased directly at the ticket machines at the train station or online in advance. For shuttle buses from all airports, you should purchase tickets directly from the transportation service counter in the arrivals area of the airport, or from the driver upon boarding the bus. For the latter option, they only accept euros in cash, so be sure to have cash on you. Tickets are €5 each way to and from **Linate,** €10 one-way and €16 round-trip to Malpensa.

FROM EUROPE

Traveling internationally in Europe by rail may often be more expensive that taking a budget airline flight or a bus ride between the two countries, so check all of your transportation options for purchasing a ticket. There are pros and cons to each, as a budget airline ticket might be cheaper, but you will not have as much luggage space without paying additional fees, while you will have plenty of luggage space on the train, and you generally have two free pieces of luggage on a bus trip.

By Air

For those coming from the U.K., most major European airlines offer direct service between London and Milan.

You should book at least a couple months in advance. Low cost airlines such as **Ryanair** and **Easyjet** offer direct service to Milan from several major European cities for as low as €50 per round trip, depending on how far in advance you book.

By Train

Milan's Central Station has frequent arriving and departing *freccia* (fast) trains from big cities in Italy as well as in surrounding countries, including Paris and Zurich. Tickets should be reserved online anywhere 3-6 months in advance to ensure best prices and seat reservation. Almost all tickets can be purchased on **Trenitalia** (www.trenitalia.com), while train tickets from France can be purchased at www.sncf.com and tickets from Switzerland at www.sbb.ch.

By Bus

Popular European bus lines such as **Megabus** (www.megabus.com) and **Flixbus** (https://global.flixbus.com) offer bus routes directly from hundreds of European cities, including Paris, Zurich, Munich, Lyon, Basel, Venice, Florence, Rome, and more to various bus stops in Milan. Prices are often as low as €5-20 per trip. Traveling by bus is often the most economical mode of public transportation, although the length of the trip and the times may not be as accommodating as other modes of transportation. Tickets should be purchased online in advance for the best deal.

The most popular bus stations **Milan Lampugnano** and **Milan Sesto San Giovanni,** both of which have a corresponding metro stop on the **M1 (red) line** next to the bus station, and the metro can connect you quickly to the city center.

Milan Central Station high speed train Trenitalia Frecciarossa, which means red arrow

By Car

Milan is easily accessible by car, as the city is served by major highways such as the **A4** between Turin and Trieste and the **A9/2** tollway from Basel, as well as other tollways and highways connecting to all major lakes. Each airport has various car hire services, including **Hertz, Avis, Budget,** and **Europcar,** and there are various locations throughout the city center for car rentals as well. Car rentals start around €35 ($40) per day, with prices increasing from there. Keep in mind that if you want to travel to any of the smaller lakes (Orta, Iseo, Molveno, or Ledro) or around Lake Garda, car hire is your most convenient option, as these lakes are not well served by train directly from Milan.

You will need to obtain an **international driver's license** in order to drive a car in Italy, so be sure to apply for one and obtain it before your arrival. Note that if you reserve a car in advance, you will need to present the same passport and credit card that you used to reserve the car when you pick it up. If you choose not to rent a car in advance, you can do so directly at the airports in each arrivals hall. **Auto Europe** is a highly recommended company, as they show you all costs up front (including insurance) and offer 24-hour assistance in English.

For those that aren't familiar with driving a manual transmission, keep in mind that this is standard in Italy, so most rental cars will have a manual transmission. However, if you want to rent a car with automatic transmission, it's best to book as far in advance as possible due to the limited number of automatic cars available.

Holiday Packages

Whether you're looking for a romantic getaway or a fun family vacation, plenty of websites and travel agencies now offer **all-inclusive holiday packages** that include airfare, hotels, meals, and entrance fees to some attractions ranging from weekends to full weeks. You can search for budget, luxury, family-friendly packages, and more on wesbites like Expedia.com and lastminute.com, but be thorough in your research so you know everything that's included and all upfront costs. Note that weekday packages are usually cheaper than weekend ones.

FROM AUSTRALIA AND NEW ZEALAND

There are several flights from Sydney or Melbourne to Milan, although there are no direct flights, so prepare yourself for a stop or two along the way. Other cities such as Brisbane, Canberra, and Perth also have flight paths with connections to Milan, but Sydney will most likely be your most convenient departure city. Etihad Airways, Finnair, KLM, Emirates, and Singapore Airlines are some of the bigger airlines flying from Sydney, most of which have connections in Abu Dhabi, Dubai, and Qatar. The average price for a round-trip falls between €800-950 (1,280-1,519 AUD), but you can save a few hundred dollars by adding another connection and using multiple airlines, such as Lufthansa and Qantas. Do a quick search on https://skyscanner.net to find your best options.

From New Zealand, you'll need to depart from Auckland and make a connection in cities such as Singapore or Dubai, as there are no direct connections between the country and Milan. The most used airlines are Qatar Airways, Air New Zealand, Singapore Airlines, Emirates, and Cathay Pacific. The average price for a round-trip is between €900-1,200 (1,570-2,092 NZD), but much like trips from Australia, you can always save some money by searching for trips with more connections on https://skyscanner.net. From both countries,

you will need to factor in a full day of travel in either direction when planning your trip.

FROM SOUTH AFRICA

To get to Milan from South Africa, you'll need to fly out of either Cape Town, Durban, or Johannesburg and make a connection in another city such as Zurich, Frankfurt, or Dubai, as there are no direct flights from any South African city and Milan. Airlines such as Swiss, Lufthansa, Ethiopian Airlines, Qatar Airways, and Emirates offer flights to Milan, with a round trip averaging between €550-750 (9,181-12,520 ZAR). The round-trips with one connection are generally both the fastest and cheapest flight schedules, so you aren't likely to save more than €30 or so by adding another connection. The travel is generally around 13-16 hours in each direction, so factor that into your itinerary when planning your trip.

GETTING AROUND

BY TRAIN

Trains from Milan to the lakes are run by two companies: Trenitalia, Italy's main train company, or Trenord, northern Italy's train company. Tickets for both companies can be purchased on www.trenitalia.com or at most (but not all) train stations throughout the city and at the lakes. Trains can be classified into two different categories: regional and *freccia* (fast) trains. When traveling to the lakes, most people opt for regional trains. For example, you can only take a regional train when visiting Lake Como. However, for those traveling to Lake Garda, fast trains are available from Milan's Central Station in the direction of Venice, stopping at Desenzano del Garda or Peschiera del

Garda. While the *freccia* trains are generally cleaner and more modern than regional trains, they stop less frequently than the regional trains, and they are usually double the price (if not more).

First-class tickets are available on all *freccia* trains and on some regional trains. While regional trains have no capacity on the number of tickets that can be purchased per train, fast trains have a cap because they assign seats. In order to ensure that you have a seat, it's best to purchase tickets online in advance whenever possible. For regional trains, you can purchase a ticket that is valid within four hours of the original time of the train for which you bought a ticket. When purchasing tickets online, tickets do not need to be validated using the machines on the train platforms. However, for any ticket bought at a machine at any train station, they ticket must always be validated before you enter the train using the stamping machines found throughout the platform areas. Even if you are traveling on a train for which you have purchased a ticket, but the ticket is not validated, you can still be fined.

BY BUS

While FlixBus (https://global.flixbus.com) offers trips between Milan and several villages on the lakes, often traveling by train is quicker, and train tickets often rival bus prices. If you're traveling to Lakes Como, Maggiore, Lugano, or the southern end of Garda, trains will get you there faster, and regional trains don't sell out of tickets. Various bus services run regional around each lake, such as the ATV Verona bus service that connects a handful of villages around Lake Garda. (Note that, however, from Milan, you will need to catch a train to either Brescia or Verona before hopping on one of these buses.) In general, you can travel by train to the lakes from Milan in most cases, and for the larger lakes, you can hop between most sights by ferry, with the exception of Lake Garda, which is so large that it's best to rent a car in order to village-hop.

BY FERRY

For Lake Como, Maggiore and Garda, the Gestione Navigazione Laghi (www.navigazionelaghi.it) service operates the ferry services to and from a majority of the villages. Official timetables and prices vary depending on the season and the distance to and from each location, so you should always refer to the website for the most up-to-date timetables and fares. Keep in mind that ferries run more frequently during high season April-September. Traveling via ferry is the best option for village-hopping on Lake Como and between the islands on Lake Maggiore, but may not be the quickest option on Lake Garda, as ferries don't run between each village, nor do they run frequently. Tickets should be purchased directly at the ferry stations in each village, and while most will accept credit cards, have cash on hand just in case.

On Lake Lugano, the ferry connects you to other towns such as Paradiso, Gandria, Porlezzo, Mortcote, Porto Ceresio, and Ponte Tresa. The ferry runs roughly every hour during daylight hours during high season, but official timetables and fares can be found at www.lakelugano.ch. One of the most important aspects to consider when taking the ferry in Lugano is that it crosses international borders between Italy and Switzerland, so you need to have your passport handy because you may be asked to present it before boarding the boat. Additionally, when purchasing ferry tickets, have the local currency on hand (Swiss francs in Lugano and other Swiss villages or euros in Italian villages).

On Lake Orta, the ferries running between the other villages as well as the beautiful island in the center is operated by **Navigation Lago D'Orta** (www.navigazionelagodorta.it), with regular ferries running April-early October. As with all ferry companies, you should refer to the official timetables and fares on the website. Lake Ledro and Lake Molveno are small, with no motorized boats running on the lake.

BY CAR

If you're traveling around the Milan area by car, remember that **traffic** in the city can get hectic, and Italians tend to be much more offensive drivers rather than defensive drivers, switching lanes without warning and often trying to get ahead rather than waiting patiently in traffic. Lanes are often narrow and one-way, so study road signs before getting behind the wheel. When driving in the city or in the smaller villages, pay close attention to the **Zona Traffico Limitato** (ZTL) signs, which means a special permit is needed to drive in this area. You'll usually find this in the historic center *(centro storico)* of cities. Similarly, **Area Pendonale** signs mean that motorized vehicles are prohibited from that area, and that it's a pedestrian area only. If your hotel is located within one of these areas, ask them to email you a permit before your arrival or directly upon your arrival in order to avoid hefty fines.

If you're staying in Milan and renting a car, your cheapest option is finding a hotel that offers guest parking. Parking in the center of Milan is limited and often expensive, but there are large **covered parking lots** ran by the city's public transportation services, **ATM** (www-atm-mi.it) in the suburbs next to metro stops, such as Biscieglie, Lampugnano, Cascina Gobba, and Lodi. An official list of parking lots, addresses, and prices can be found on the ATM website. Prices run from €1.50 per hour and up to €7.50 per day per car. While these lots tend to be relatively safe, it's safer to take all of your belongings with you and leave them locked in your hotel.

Within the city, you'll find several privately operated parking garages with hourly (€2+) and daily (€19+) prices. Near Milan's Central Station, the Garage 2000 SrL (Via Achille Zezon 2) is an option that also provides discounted daily prices when you present your train ticket. If you're parking curbside, the process is pay-and-display, so purchase the total number of hours that you want to leave your car in the spot in the nearby meter machine, then display your receipt on your dashboard. Don't park in spaces outlined with yellow paint, as it means the spot is reserved for local residents.

You'll notice that there aren't policemen on the highways and throughout the city pulling cars over for speeding, and that's because **traffic cameras** are responsible for catching you going beyond the speed limit or driving in areas of the city in which you're prohibited from entering with your car. Cameras take a picture of your license plate and send you the fine via mail (or to the rental car agency with your credit card deposit). Speed limits are indicated by a white and red circle with a number in the middle, and are displayed in kilometers per hour, not miles per hour.

Toll roads are marked with an A in front of them and by green road signs, such as the **A4** highway connecting Milan to the southern end of Lake Garda. Tolls range from €2-20, depending on the distance traveled. Not all tollways accept U.S. credit cards, so have cash on hand.

Much like in the United States, use the right lane to cruise and the left lane only to pass. However, unlike in the United States, remember that you cannot turn right at a red light. If you see an inverted red and white triangle on a sign, it means that you do not have the right of way at an intersection.

Visas and Officialdom

UNITED STATES, AUSTRALIA, AND NEW ZEALAND

For American, Australian, or New Zealand citizens, no visa or special documentation is needed other than your valid government-issued passport that does not expire for six months from the date that you leave the Schengen zone (of which Italy is a part). The passport must have been issued no longer than 10 years ago. A tourist visa or any other kind of visa is not necessary for entering and leaving the Schengen zone for a cumulative 90 days within a 180-day period. This does not necessarily mean 90 consecutive days, but rather 90 total days within a 180-day timeframe. Note that this includes any country in the Schengen zone, not only Italy. If you plan on exceeding the 90-day limit, you will need to obtain a tourist visa or another kind of visa to legally stay in the country. Note that your passport will need at least two blank pages for the stamp, and there is an entrance and exit restriction of €10,000 or equivalent (if you're traveling with cash or valuables beyond this limit, you'll need to declare it).

Note that in some cases, you may be required to show proof of a return ticket if your stay is less than one year, or proof of sufficient funds to support yourself during your stay in Italy as well as enough funds to pay for a ticket back to your home country. When checking in online using certain airlines for your flight to Italy, they may block the check-in online if there is no return ticket in the same booking.

EU/SCHENGEN

For citizens in countries that are members of the European Union, you only need a valid passport or government-issued national identity card that is valid during the length of your stay in Italy in order to enter the country. If you plan on staying for more than three months, you will need to go to the local *questura* (police station) and the *anagrafe* office to report your stay along with your passport, national ID card, and documents attesting to your reason of staying longer than three months. However, when entering Italy, you should not be required to show proof of a return ticket or sufficient funds during your stay in the country.

SOUTH AFRICA

For South African citizens, you will need a valid government-issued passport that does not expire for six months from the date that you leave the Schengen zone (of which Italy is a part). The passport must have been issued no longer than 10 years ago. Additionally, you will need to apply for a Schengen visa for the duration of your stay in Italy. If you are only visiting Italy during your trip, then you need to apply for the visa at your nearest Italian consulate in South Africa. If you are visiting more than one Schengen country, you need to apply at the embassy in the country where you will be staying the longest. For example, if you are spending four days in Italy but six days in France, you need to apply for the visa through your nearest French consulate.

You will need to visit your local consulate's website to gather an official list of documentation that you will need to present to the consulate, then pay for the application form, book your appointment at the consulate, and complete the application form. From there, you'll go to the consulate for your appointment to present your documents, then collect your documents and visa when ready. Applications should take place anywhere from three months to two weeks prior to your trip. The Schengen visa will permit you to enter the Schengen zone multiple times a cumulative 90 days within a 180-day period. This does not necessarily mean 90 consecutive days, but rather 90 total days within a 180-day timeframe.

Festivals and Events

FASHION

Fashion is one of the most significant characteristics of the city, so there are naturally various events around Milan throughout the year related to fashion, the most important ones being the spring and fall fashion weeks. **Vogue's Fashion's Night Out,** which kicks off fall fashion week, is a huge event for Milan, with the entire city center completely packed with event-goers hopping in and out of bars and designs stores, which usually stay open all night offering free drinks and finger foods to shoppers.

Fall fashion week generally falls in **mid- to late September;** so does *Vogue*'s event. **Spring fashion week** is held in **late February or early March** each year. However, the collections being displayed are always for the upcoming seasons, so spring clothes are shown at the fall event and viceversa. While the city holds small street events and shops often host various sales and promotions throughout these weeks, getting tickets to runway shows is extremely difficult without connections in the fashion industry, and cost hundreds of dollars a piece when sold.

DESIGN

Design is yet another important and vital part of Milan's makeup, and the annual **Design Week** each **April** draws in some of the world's best designers year after year. The event is globally renowned as one of the most significant and influential weeks for the industry. Unlike Milan's fashion weeks, Design Week tends to be less exclusive, incorporating the residential community through parades, projects, promotions, and sales throughout the city to celebrate local, national, and international design. The Salone del Mobile, which is one of the most famous design fairs in the world, is made up of thousands of designers, architects, and critics, and shoppers and admirers have free access to wander around many of the events.

SPORTS

Football is the king sport in Italy. The regular season, an important part of Italian culture, lasts generally October-May. With two Serie A teams in the city, A.C. Milan and Inter Milan, football fans have plenty of opportunity to catch a match at the famous San Siro stadium. Tickets are generally available for purchase directly at the stadium or online in advance from each team's official website, with the stadium filling up roughly halfway for each match.

For racing fans, the Formula One Italian Grand Prix takes place in the Milanese suburb of Monza in the beautiful Monza Park on the first weekend of September every year. The small villages north of Milan come to life with street parades and festivals, live music, and thousands of race enthusiasts coming to watch the race and take in the vibrant atmosphere. Tickets for the event should be purchased online months in advance.

MUSIC

The most important season for music in Milan is the opera season, which lasts for most of the year and opens on December 7th, the day of Milan's patron saint, St. Ambrogio. If you want to see an opera in Milan, you have to see it at the internationally renowned and historic La Scala opera house, which hosts a number of opera titles, ballets, symphonies, and choral concerts each year. While the entire season is announced a few months prior to December, tickets for each individual show are usually on sale a month or two in advance and should be purchased directly through La Scala's website, www.teatroallascala.org.

Teatro Arcimboldi in Milan also has a similar lineup of performances and concerts throughout the year. Milan is one of the most popular European cities for concerts of a number of popular bands and singers, from rock to pop to hip-hop. Most large performances take place at San Siro Stadium or the Mediolanum Forum arena in the southern area of Milan. I-Days is another extremely popular music festival taking place over the course of a few days in June every year in the Milan area, with the location changing each year. The festival includes huge concerts such as Green Day, Justin Bieber, The Killers, Pearl Jam, The Offspring, and more. Tickets can be purchased for one or multiple days at www.ticketone.com.

Conduct and Customs

LOCAL HABITS

Northern Italy generally follows the Western cultural norms, with plenty of Latin culture influences on daily life as well. For example, Italians always greet friends and relatives with a kiss on each cheek when saying hello or good-bye, starting usually with the right cheek. It's not uncommon for some families to greet each other with three kisses, depending on tradition. While Catholicism has a stronghold on the country, visitors will find that the younger generation is not nearly as religious.

What may suprise and annoy some visitors coming from the United States, the United Kingdom, or Germany is the lack of strict efficiency and queues. Buses and trains are often at least a few minutes late (although this is not nearly as apparent in Milan as in southern Italy), and meetings with Italians often begin 10-20 minutes later than the scheduled start time. Additionally, in public places, forming lines is a literal foreign concept. Be prepared to take a number when necessary, and somehow fight your way to the front of the crowd in other scenarios.

One interesting note that may surprise visitors is that the Milanese are usually very sanitary when it comes to their homes and their food. They always wear house shoes at home. Going barefoot or only in socks is seen as dirty, so don't be surprised if Italians offer you some sort of slippers or sandals if you visit their homes.

Gloves should be worn when touching any produce at supermarkets. It's considered disrespectful to fellow shoppers to touch fruit and vegetables with your bare hands, so use the plastic gloves available in the produce sections of markets.

LOCAL DRESS

Being such a fashion capital, people dress well to explore the city or complete routine tasks, such as grocery shopping or dropping of their kids at school. Wearing "gym clothes" is not normal and is usually only done when someone is actually going to exercise in some capacity. Milan is fairly liberal when it comes to fashion choices, but it's best for women to have a scarf or something to cover their shoulders when entering churches (although this is not strictly enforced due to the high volume of tourists and often very hot summer temperatures). Your knees should be covered as well, if possible.

In past years, wearing comfortable walking shoes or tennis shoes was seen as a very American or touristy thing to do. However, that has changed in recent years, and you'll see plenty of Italians wearing jeans or dresses while sporting a pair of sneakers with brands such as adidas, Vans, and more. However, you won't see them wearing rain jackets on gloomy days, so if you want to fit in, pack an umbrella.

ALCOHOL AND SMOKING

The minimum age for drinking alcohol and purchasing cigarettes or other smoking devices in Italy is 18. However, you will rarely be asked to prove your age with an identity card when purchasing alcohol or something to smoke from restaurants, bars, tobacco shops, or other locations, and you will often see teenagers smoking and drinking without consequences. Smoking in Italy is very common, so don't be surprised to see plenty of people lighting up. While smoking inside bars, restaurants, and nightclubs is illegal, you'll find plenty of people doing so outside on the patio or terrace area of a restaurant or bar, and some bars have specific rooms for smoking.

Drinking alcohol is also a normal part of everyday life in Italy, as many Italians drink wine with lunch and dinner, both in their homes or when out with family or friends. In recent years, craft beers have become popular in Italy, although wine is still favored. Note that public intoxication is technically illegal in Italy, but you probably won't be fined for it unless you are disobeying law enforcement or causing chaos.

DRUGS

Recreational drugs such as marijuana are illegal to use, purchase, and sell in Italy, although just like in many countries, you often see plenty of people in the general population under its influence. While doing so can result in a fine from law enforcement, it is considered much like public intoxication, where you probably won't be fined unless you are disturbing public peace or disobeying law enforcement. Other illicit drugs such as cocaine are illegal in Italy, and being caught with such drugs can lead to jail time and hefty fines.

Health and Safety

EMERGENCY NUMBERS

In case of emergency during your trip, call the following numbers:

- 112: Carabinieri (Local Military Police), Emergency Police Assistance
- 113: Local Police
- 115: Fire Department
- 116: A.C.I. (Italian Automobile Club) Roadside Assistance
- 118: Medical Emergencies and Ambulance

If you have a smart phone in the region of Lombardy (which Milan is a part of), the Where Are U app can be used to locate you in case of emergency. Most operators are required to speak English, but if you have any medical conditions, study the vocabulary in Italian before your trip and have translated phrases on hand. In case your passport has been stolen, you will need to contact your country's local consulate in order to get a temporary emergency passport.

MEDICAL SERVICES

Regardless of the length of your trip, it's always a good idea to get travel medical insurance or check what your current health insurance covers internationally before your trip. In case you need medical attention while in Italy, you can call 118 for medical emergencies or if an ambulance is needed. Italy has universal healthcare, meaning that the government provides free health care to all Italian citizens and legal residents. This is part of a larger integrated health system of the European Union, so if you are an EU citizen, any medical costs that you incur in Italy can be fully refunded by the medical system in your home country (so keep your receipts!).

Regardless of where you are from, foreign travelers from every country in the world have the same rights as Italian citizens when it comes to health care, meaning that emergency medical treatment is free of charge in the emergency rooms of public hospitals. If you have a non-emergency medical situation, you can try going to a local pharmacy or to a public hospital, where you may be asked to pay a bill of around €25 at the end of the visit. However, if extensive non-emergency medical attention is required, expenses that are incurred for non-EU citizens can often be costly.

PHARMACIES

Pharmacies in Italy, called a *farmacia*, are marked with a green plus sign and can be found every few blocks. Milan's Central Station has a pharmacy, as does every village along the major lakes. Opening hours of pharmacies are regulated by the government to ensure that there is at least one open pharmacy in a given zone at night, on holidays, and on Sundays. A pharmacy's general hours are 8am-1pm and 3pm-7pm, but there are a handful of pharmacies around Milan that are now open 24 hours. Alternatively, many pharmacies now offer 24-hour vending machines with general medications, bandages, condoms, and more directly outside on the streets for quick fixes during closing hours.

In case you find a closed pharmacy, each one is required to display their opening hours, where to go for emergencies or other services in case they are closed, and an emergency telephone number on their door or windows for you to easily view. Most Italian pharmacists speak English in some capacity, and are willing to help you find medications that you need if you are able to describe your conditions or symptoms well. If you know the generic name of your prescribed medications, they sometimes fill them up for you as well. Unlike in America, things like generic headache medications and nasal spray are not readily available on the shelves, so you will need to specifically ask the pharmacist for it at the counter, and be prepared to describe your symptoms and reasons for asking for the medication.

Remember that if you have a serious medical condition, you need to pack your medications in their original containers as well as other documentation that may help you in case of emergency. I also recommend studying some key Italian phrases to describe your conditions and symptoms.

CRIME AND THEFT

While crime in Italy is not outstanding or noteworthy, petty crimes such as pickpocketing are not uncommon, especially at Milan's Central Station and other popular train and metro stations. In general, always keep a hand on your purse, and consider bringing a cross-body or front-facing bag that has multiple zippers or entrances. If you're carrying a backpack with you, don't place items like wallets and passports in outward facing pockets that are easily accessible.

Muggings aren't that common in Milan, but considering that it is a decent-size city, general safety measures should be taken. Instead of walking alone at night after 10pm, opt for a taxi. If buses or metro cars are really packed, consider waiting a few more minutes for the next one so you can keep a better eye on your belongings and surroundings.

Practical Details

PASSES AND DISCOUNTS

Most sights and transportation methods offer some sort of discount for students under the age of 25 or 26, as well as travelers over the age of 65. For students, you'll need to have a school-issued identity card on you for proof, and note that some sights only offer discounts to those studying at schools in the European Union. **Trenitalia** also offers discounts for fast train *(freccia)* tickets that are purchased far enough in advance online, which can save you up to €10 per ticket if booked a couple months in advance.

Some attractions, such as the civic museums at the castle in Milan, also offer free admission on the first Sunday or Tuesday of every month. So if you have a specific place in mind to visit during your trip, check the hours and see if there are any discounted prices or free admission hours.

One of the most popular passes for the city of Milan is the Milan Pass (www.themilanpass.com), which includes entrance to several of Milan's top sights, including the Duomo, La Scala Museum and Theater, Pinacoteca Di Brera, San Siro Stadium, and more, The traditional red hop-on-hop-off buses as well as a public transportation pass can be included, with prices ranging from €69-79. Depending on how many sights you're wanting to see in Milan, it may be worth your money, but probably only if you have at least three days in the city.

MONEY

CURRENCY AND EXCHANGE RATES

Italy uses the euro as official currency. One euro equals roughly \$1.14 or £0.91, but note that this number fluctuates daily, so do a quick search before you go as well as each morning during your trip to keep an eye on your spending, especially if you plan on withdrawing money during your trip.

CURRENCY EXCHANGE

Currency can be exchanged at Milan's Central Station, in most train stations in popular villages on the lake, and at all airports in Milan. However, places like **Forexchange** and other official currency exchange places often charge commission up from 5-15 percent, so you lose quite a bit of money from each exchange. Note that most banks in Italy do not exchange currency if you don't have an account at the bank, nor do they cash traveler's checks. While you'll find plenty of currency exchange places near the Duomo and at Central Station in Milan, your cheapest bet is withdrawing euros at an ATM.

BUDGETING TIPS

Simple measures can be taken to keep your spending in check when traveling around Milan and the lakes:

- Take the regional trains and stick to second-class instead of first-class tickets.
- In Milan, purchase a daily public transportation pass for €4.50 instead of purchasing individual trip tickets for €1.50 a piece.

- Eat dinner at places with robust happy hours, so you pay €7-15 for one drink and endless finger foods (hit Navigli for the best spots).
- Book hotels and train tickets a few months in advance to find the most discounted prices.
- At dinner, order a pizza or just a second course instead of ordering multiple courses.
- Stick to window shopping in the city center, and save your money for shopping local in areas such as Ticinese, Navigli, and Brera.

BARGAINING

Bargaining is not common in Milan, nor on the surrounding lakes, especially in shops, restaurants, and any other place besides street markets. In most cases, you may get funny looks from shop owners if you try to bargain for any items within the shop. At street markets, you may be able to bargain with vendors if items are not clearly marked. If they have a printed price tag on it, often they will not budge. For prices that are written by hand or if there are hand-written signs for prices on certain tables or racks, you may get away with bargaining, even though it is still not a commonly used tactic amongst Italians.

TIPPING

Tips are not a common practice in Italy, and many waiters have a fixed salary. Most restaurants have a small cover charge (anywhere from €1-5, depending on the type of restaurant). Tips are not expected by taxi drivers or most other service sector jobs either. However, they may be accepted by tour guides, as well as local entrepreneurs that try to make money by helping with luggage around train stations and such, although it's suggested

to avoid these people altogether, as it could be a distraction tactic for theft.

ATMS AND BANKS

In Italy, ATMs, not to be confused with the ATM public transportation service in Milan, are called *bancomats*. *Bancomats* can be found on streets, tucked in between shops and restaurants and within banks themselves. For safety purposes, you should always use the machines within the banks, as sometimes machines outside of banks have card readers from those trying to commit theft or fraud.

During bank opening hours (which are generally 9am-6pm), you should be able to enter the bank without needing anything special to get inside. However, once the bank is closed for the day, you will need to enter your credit or debit card into the slot outside of the door in order for the doors to open, giving you access to the *bancomat*.

Banks in Italy, such as **Unicredit,** often have partnerships with other international banks, meaning that you may not be charged a withdrawal fee when taking out euros from one of the bank's ATM machines. Check with your bank ahead of time to see if they have any partnerships with Italian banks. Otherwise, expect to pay a €2-7 fee for each ATM withdrawal.

CREDIT AND DEBIT CARDS

Most, if not all, major credits cards are accepted in Milan and along the shores of the surrounding lakes, such as Visa, MasterCard, and American Express. You shouldn't have trouble using credit or debit cards in grocery stores, restaurants, and most shops and bars in Milan. However, it will be hit or miss when you're in any village on the lakes, as many of the local shops still have a cash-only policy, so have cash on hand.

Many machines for purchasing train or metro tickets also accept credit and debit cards, but not all of them, especially at the machines in smaller villages, so you may want to have coins or cash on hand if you haven't purchased transportation tickets. Also, keep in mind that many places require a €10-20 minimum for card purchases.

OPENING HOURS

Most places in Italy adhere to the typical lunch break that is common in Latin cultures, meaning that they have opening hours in the mornings and in the afternoons. While hours of specific sights, restaurants, bars, and transportation lines should be checked on an individual basis (for example, some do not take a midday break), most places follow these hours:

- General morning hours: 9am-1pm
- General afternoon hours: 3pm-7pm
- Restaurant lunch hours: 12pm-2:30pm
- Restaurant dinner hours: 7pm-10:30pm
- Milan public transportation hours: 6am-12am, metro open until 1am on Fridays and Saturdays
- Train hours: 6am-10pm, but check each train for specific times
- Most restaurants and bars are closed on either Sundays or Mondays, so check before making plans.

PUBLIC HOLIDAYS

- January 1: New Year's Day (national)
- January 6: Epiphany (national)
- Mid-February: Milanese *carnivale*
- End of March-early April: Good Friday, Easter Sunday, Easter Monday

- April 25: Liberation Day (national)
- May 1: Labor Day (national)
- June 2: Republic Day (national)
- August 15: Assumption of Mary/ Ferragosto (national)
- November 1: All Saints' Day (national)
- December 7: The Feast of St. Ambrose (local)
- December 8: Feast of the Immaculate Conception (national)
- December 25: Christmas Day (national)
- December 26: St. Stephen's Day (national)
- December 31: New Year's Eve (national)

COMMUNICATIONS
PHONES AND CELL PHONES

The country code for phones in Italy is +39, and most phone numbers in Italy have the country code, then the city or area code, then the phone number. For example, the city code for Milan is 02, so you'll see that a lot of Milanese numbers begin with +39-02. From there, you'll have to dial the rest of the number for each business or person. When you're in the country, there is no need to dial the +39 when calling on a local phone, but you will dial the area code regardless of whether you're in or out of the country.

If your trip is less than a month long, don't waste money on purchasing a phone with a local number or swapping out your SIM card, as it often requires some sort of documentation needed from your end stating that you're staying in Italy for a certain length of time.

However, if you want to stay connected (which isn't a bad idea, especially if you're driving), sign up for an international plan through your phone provider before your trip, and make sure that it's activated before you land in Italy. Most companies now have a plan that is as simple as paying a flat fee per day to use your phone as you would in your home country, while some require you to guesstimate how many minutes and how much data you'll use per day. If you're needing to contact someone in Italy via messaging, install **WhatsApp,** as SMS text messages are not commonly used in Italy.

INTERNET ACCESS
WiFi is available in most hotels, restaurants, and bars, and is often password protected, so ask the reception or staff for the password to access. At restaurants and bars, you will need to purchase at least a drink in order to gain access. Although, keep in mind that the WiFi is not always reliable or fast, so be patient.

SHIPPING AND POSTAL SERVICE
The official postal service in Italy is **Poste Italiane,** and you can find several post offices around Milan marked with a yellow sign with the letters PT in blue. Post offices are used for a number of things other than mail and shipping, such as paying taxes and as the touch point for many bureaucratic processes, so they stay pretty busy. Business hours are generally 8:30am-12pm and 3pm-6pm every weekday, and some are open in the mornings on Saturdays.

While the official postal service has improved in recent years, it is still notoriously slow and chaotic, with letters and packages taking several weeks to arrive and often being lost. If you're wanting to send a postcard or something similar to an international address, consider waiting until you're home to deliver it in person. If you've bought goods that you want to ship home, ask the shop directly if you can use services such as GLS or DHL.

WEIGHTS AND MEASURES
In Italy, they use the standard metric system. Keep these measurements in mind during your trip:
- 1 kilometer = 1,000 meters; 0.64 miles
- 1 meter = 3.3 feet; 1.1 yards
- 1 liter = 0.22 gallons
- 1 ounce = 28.4 grams
- 1 kilogram = 2.2 pounds

TOURIST INFORMATION
TOURIST OFFICES
Milan has plenty of tourist offices sprinkled throughout the city center, with two popular ones located at Central Station and in the Galleria. They will be open during normal business hours on weekdays, with some also open on Saturdays. Bigger villages on the lakes such as **Desenzano del Garda** and **Riva del Garda** on **Lake Garda,** as well as **Stresa** on **Lake Maggiore** and **Como** on **Lake Como,** will also have tourist offices.

Staff at these offices generally speak English well, and you'll find plenty of maps, pamphlets, books, and other material to help you during your trip. Some of them also offer organized tours and other expeditions, such as day trips to Switzerland or guided tours around the city.

INTERNET RESOURCES AND APPS
If you plan on using the public transportation system in Milan, you can download the **ATM Milano** app on your smartphone to purchase passes,

find metro and bus lines, and enter the destination that you're trying to reach, so the app can tell you the best public transport route to follow. To purchase your train tickets on the go, download the Trenitalia app, which also gives you alerts in case there are delays on any lines.

While Google Translate often gets a bad rap, the Google Translate app is actually quite useful when traveling. You can download the Italian language before your trip directly in the app so you can translate offline. Another useful function of the app is the ability to hold your phone's camera over signs, menus, or other physical text, and your phone will translate the text into English directly on your screen. Similarly, you can now use Google Maps and Apple Maps offline.

MAPS

Apple Maps and Google Maps are fairly reliable sources, especially if you're needing a turn-by-turn GPS when driving around the area. Both are available in offline mode as well. Even in smaller villages on the lakes, both sources fare well at giving directions for walking and driving. If you're wanting directions using public transport, try the ATM Milano app or Google Maps. For fine dining, use the Via Michelin website, then insert your location to find the best local restaurants.

Traveler Advice

OPPORTUNITIES FOR STUDY AND EMPLOYMENT

There are several opportunities to study in and around Milan, with a handful of accredited universities, language and art schools, and more in the city. Universities such as Bocconi and the Università Catholic del Sacro Cuore offer many undergraduate and graduate programs in English. If you're wanting to stay in Italy for a while and learn the language, there are a number of Italian language schools in Milan as well as on the major lakes. Note that if you go this route, be sure to find a school that is able to provide you with a study visa if you plan on staying longer than 90 days.

To work in Italy, your best bet is teaching English in some capacity. Language schools are constantly looking for certified and qualified English teachers, so there is plenty of work opportunity if you have a TESL or TEFL certificate. Working in a classroom or going into various schools and homes for private lessons are common practices. Both business English and English for children are popular ways to get work in Milan and on the lakes, although note that most employers do not provide work visas. In fact, most of them pay you directly in cash or "under the table" in order to avoid the intense bureaucracy and taxes that come with owning and operating a language school.

If you're wanting to find long-term work in Italy without teaching English, keep in mind that it's tough and rare for Italian companies to hire you from outside of Italy, as work visas use a lottery system and there is a quota for how many work visas the government issues each year (the number changes every year). Your best bet is coming to Italy legally on a student visa, then trying to find employment once you're already legally residing in the country.

ACCESS FOR TRAVELERS WITH DISABILITIES

Being as old as it is, Italy has a lot of infrastructure that can make it challenging to access many places for travelers with motor disabilities. While there is no official law in Italy that requires buildings, restaurants, bars, sights, and hotels to be accessible, the rise of non-profit and lobby groups has seen the infrastructure improve within the last decade or so. Thorough research will be your best friend, so you know immediately what is and is not accessible. While some hotels (the more modern ones) have elevators, others do not.

In Milan, metro stops that have elevators or escalators are marked accordingly, so check the metro map. Likewise, each train station has a Sala Blu service, which helps travelers with disabilities of all kinds use the trains and find proper seating. However, not all trains are accessible, and those that are do not always offer accessibility in the same capacity, so book tickets ahead and get to the Sala Blu at the station early for assistance.

TRAVELING WITH CHILDREN

Italy is a very family-friendly place, and while art museums may not be their thing, you'll find plenty of kid-centered activities around Milan and the lakes, from the jumping water fountains in Piazza Gae Aulenti to water sports on Lake Garda or the alpine coaster on Lake Maggiore. Many attractions and sights offer discounts for children under the ages of 12 or 18, as well as family passes.

In general, the Italian culture is very accommodating to children, so you'll see plenty of young children out late at night enjoying piazzas or long meals with their parents. The country is safe for traveling around with kids of all ages. At restaurants, you can ask for a *mezzo piatto,* meaning a half portion of food, or a simple pasta with olive oil and parmesan.

WOMEN TRAVELING ALONE

Women traveling alone should take general traveling safety precautions in Milan and around the lakes, but nothing that is any different than anywhere else in the world. Avoid traveling on trains and public transportation at night, and avoid walking alone after 10pm in certain areas of Milan, notably around Central Station or other train and metro stops.

While Italian men tend to be outspoken in terms of compliments or friendliness, that's the extent of it. No different than any other European men, Italian men are, generally speaking, well-raised and polite. Learn some Italian and the general cost of things before your arrival, and don't over-think about traveling solo. The country has plenty to offer for women of all kinds, so enjoy the trip without over-worrying.

SENIOR TRAVELERS

Milan and the surrounding lakes are also senior-friendly places, with many attractions offering discounts to travelers over the ages of 60 or 65. Keep in mind that Milan, as with Italian cities, requires quite a bit of walking basically everywhere you go, so bring comfortable shoes. If possible, mention that you're a senior when making travel reservations, as some hotels and transportation services, including Trenitalia, offer discounts for seniors.

LGBTQ+ TRAVELERS

As Italy's most international city, Milan is far more advanced in terms of LGBTQ acceptance than in some other parts of the country, as Catholicism is still deeply rooted in Italian culture. However, LGBTQ persons should have no problems in Milan or around the lakes, as Italians tend to keep their personal feelings to themselves when it comes to this subject, and you'll find that most in northern Italy are very welcoming and accepting of the LGBTQ community. In fact, Milan holds the largest Pride Parade in Italy each spring.

You'll find plenty of gay-friendly or gay-focused bars and clubs in Milan, notably in the **Porta Venezia** area. In the smaller villages on the lakes, you'll be hard-pressed to find such bars or clubs, but you'll be welcomed in just the same. For information while traveling, reach out to **Arcigay** (www.arcigay.it) or **Coordinamento Lesbiche Italiano** (www.clrbp.it), two of Italy's leading gay and lesbian organizations.

TRAVELERS OF COLOR

Milan, being as international as it is, tends to be very tolerant to travelers of all races, as with most western European countries, and so travelers of color shouldn't expect any problems. In recent years, major immigration patterns from African and Middle Eastern countries have caused a lot of political tension in Italy; however, this really has not affected tourists at this time.

Phrasebook

ESSENTIAL PHRASES

Hello: Ciao (informal)/ salve (formal)
Goodbye: Ciao (informal)/ arrivederci (formal)
Thank you: Grazie
You're welcome: Prego
Good morning: Buon giorno
Good evening: Buonasera
Good night: Buonanotte
Have a nice day: Buona giornata
Have a nice evening: Buona serata
How much does this cost?: Quanto costa?
Where is the bathroom?: Dov'è il bagno?
What time is it?: Che ore sono?
Yes: Sì
No: No
Excuse me: Scusami (informal)/ mi scusi (formal)
Help: Aiuto

BASICS

left: sinistra
right: destra
day: giorno
evening: sera
night: notte
morning: mattina
yesterday: ieri
today: oggi
tomorrow: domani
money: i soldi
who: chi

what: che
when: quando
where: dove
why: perché

FOOD AND DRINK

breakfast: la colazione
lunch: il pranzo
dinner: la cena
menu: il menu
dessert: il dolce
wine: il vino
beer: la birra
water: l'acqua

still water: acqua naturale
sparkling water: acqua frizzante
cover charge: il coperto
the bill: il conto
I am allergic to: Sono allergico/a a....
eggs: uova
milk: latte
gluten: glutine
vegetables: verdure
meat: carne
chicken: pollo
beef: manzo
pork: maiale
fish: pesce

Index

List of Maps

Photo Credits

Acknowledgments

In case I never get another shot at this sort of thing, I best cover it all in the first round.

First and foremost, thank you to Ada Fung and Grace Fujimoto, who found me, grew me, pushed me, and somehow turned my writing and adventures into something worth sharing with people.

To my family. There are a million kinds of thanks that you deserve, but the biggest one is this: Thank you for just rolling with it—whatever "it" is on any given day. You've all achieved sainthood with your love and patience.

To every person on social media who didn't panic when a stranger slid into their DMs to inquire about photos or research. Thanks for proving that the Internet still has little pockets of helpful, generous people. (Dettina, I'm looking at you first.)

To every j-school editor, professor, boss, mentor, and colleague that invested in me as a writer and a person. For the empathy, drive, encouragement that you drilled into me.

To the entirety of Docebo. For not killing me when I was sleep-deprived in the office for six months while writing this book. I owe you all a million pasticcini.

Alla famiglia Venturi, che ha saputo accogliermi come una figlia senza alcuna esitazione. La mia vita in Italia non sarebbe stata possibile senza di voi.

Al mio amore, affinché questo libro possa essere la prova che la mia vita con te al mio fianco è più bella e ricca di significato. Per sopportarmi sempre, in ogni circostanza. Per farmi capire che l'amore supera ogni difficoltà, lingua e cultura.

And finally, to Betty Jane. Everything that I am and everything that I've done is because of you. This book is no exception.

MOON TRAVEL GUIDES TO EUROPE

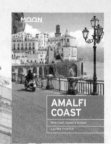

AMALFI COAST
With Capri, Naples & Pompeii
LAURA THAYER

BARCELONA & MADRID
JESSICA JONES

MOON CAMINO DE SANTIAGO
SACRED SITES, HISTORIC VILLAGES, LOCAL FOOD & WINE
BEEBE BAHRAMI

CROATIA & SLOVENIA
SHANN FOUNTAIN ALIPOUR

EDINBURGH, GLASGOW & THE ISLE OF SKYE

ICELAND
JENNA GOTTLIEB

IRELAND
CAMILLE DEANGELIS

NORMANDY & BRITTANY
With Mont-Saint-Michel
CHRIS NEWENS

NORWAY
DAVID NIKEL

PORTUGAL
CARRIE-MARIE BRATLEY

PRAGUE, VIENNA & BUDAPEST
JENNIFER WALKER, AUBURN SCALLON

ROME, FLORENCE & VENICE
ALEXEI J. COHEN

GO BIG AND GO BEYOND!

These savvy city guides include strategies to help you see the top sights and find adventure beyond the tourist crowds.

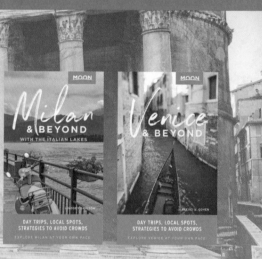

OR TAKE THINGS ONE STEP AT A TIME

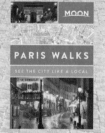

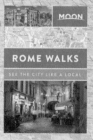

Gear up for a bucket list vacation

MOON · ANGKOR WAT · TRIP OF A LIFETIME

MOON · BARCELONA & MADRID · JESSICA JONES

MOON · ICELAND · JENNA GOTTLIEB

MOON · GALÁPAGOS ISLANDS · TRIP OF A LIFETIME

MOON · MACHU PICCHU · TRIP OF A LIFETIME

MOON · MOROCCO

MOON · NEW ZEALAND · JAMIE CHRISTIAN DESPLACES

MOON · NORWAY

MOON · PATAGONIA · TRIP OF A LIFETIME · WAYNE BERNHARDSON

MOON · VIETNAM · DANA FILEK-GIBSON

MOON · USA NATIONAL PARKS · THE COMPLETE GUIDE TO ALL 59 PARKS · BECKY LOMAX

MOON · CAMINO DE SANTIAGO · SACRED SITES, HISTORIC VILLAGES, LOCAL FOOD & WINE · BEEBE BAHRAMI